NEW COPIES OF THIS TEXTBOOK COME WITH FREE ACCESS TO

CourseBank

To register, follow the directions provided by your instructor

If your instructor has not assigned CourseBank, email support@chicagobusinesspress.com to obtain a URL for self-study

Scratch here for your access code

This code is only valid for a single user.
This code may be invalid if the protective scratch-off coating covering the code has been removed and redeemed by the book's previous owner.

For instructors:

- A turnkey solution for your online sections.
- Auto-graded assignments and quizzes, whether your course is online or lecture-based.
- Integrates with Blackboard, Canvas, and other LMSs for single sign-in and single gradebook.
- Detailed diagnostic tools to assess class and individual student performance.

For students:

- Self-study and practice.
- Immediate feedback from quizzes and assignments, if enabled by your instructor.

Assets:

- Narrated and animated chapter overview
- Lecture PowerPoints
- Confidence-based flash cards
- Quizzes
- Exercises

Contact **support@chicagobusinesspress.com** for registration or technical assistance

MANAGING BUSINESS ETHICS
AND YOUR CAREER

Mel Fugate

Misssissippi State University

CHICAGO
BUSINESS PRESS

MANAGING BUSINESS ETHICS AND YOUR CAREER

Printed in Canada

For product information or assistance visit: www.chicagobusinesspress.com

ISBN-13: 978-1-948426-35-0

Brief Table of Contents

Table of Contents

Preface

I wrote *Managing Business Ethics and Your Career* to achieve multiple objectives, primary among them is to help students develop their ethical compass as well as the knowledge and skills necessary to navigate the countless ethical challenges they will face during their working lives. Many business ethics textbooks emphasize philosophical or legal perspectives, which students often criticize for being too academic or theoretical—in other words, impractical and boring. Although philosophical and legal perspectives are important, this book provides a far greater emphasis on *managing ethics at work*. It is applied and practical and thus prepares students to be conscientious contributors to their employers, communities, and the global society.

This text focuses more on the implications of business ethics for students' careers and the organizations where they will work. Ethical conduct and its evil twin, unethical conduct makes or breaks individuals, departments, organizations, countries and can impact the world. This emphasis on application makes it easier for instructors to engage students by delivering ethics in a context that is real, interesting, and personally valuable for students.

Another objective is to help students avoid the negative impact that unethical individuals and organizations can have on their professional lives. This book provides knowledge and tools, if not also inspiration, for students to lead by example and be more ethical themselves, thereby improving their own lives and the lives of the people they work with and influence.

These objectives stem from my deeply held conviction that business ethics, responsibility, and sustainability are first and last matters of individual choice. Employers have a tremendous influence on the conduct of employees, but organizations are comprised of people, and it is the leaders and other employees who make organizations ethical or unethical. It starts and ends with people—their choices and their behaviors. This book intends to make it easier for students to do the "right thing," even when it is difficult.

Managing Business Ethics and Your Career is built on my profound belief that business ethics can be taught, and thus, the most basic premise for this book is that all of us can and should do better, expect more from our leaders, and thereby meet both small and immense challenges confronting us as individuals, businesses, and global citizens. To realize this potential, this book is designed, written, and delivered to be student-centered.

A Student-Centered Approach

Formulating and following an ethical compass requires reflection, and while this book provides such opportunities, greater attention is given to informed action rather than intellectual or philosophical pondering. This is accomplished in three ways: (1) structure; (2) content selection, writing style, and brevity; and (3) applied chapter features.

Structure

Part 1 provides an overview of what business ethics is and helps to establish a common language and foundation on which to build. This part includes common ethical decision-making perspectives, stakeholders, social responsibility, sustainability, and the implications for these within students' jobs and careers. The intent is to help students organize and apply new knowledge as they learn it. After setting a foundation with the first part, Part 2 delves into topics associated with ethics and the individual. Having cemented the ideas of ethics and the individual, Part 3 explores individual ethics within the context of the organization, as it is organizations and their leaders that enable or influence good people to do bad things. Finally, having established the principles of ethics for the individual and the individual within the organization, Part 4 explores ethics within the global society.

Content Selection and Presentation

Managing Business Ethics and Your Career includes, but is not wedded to, historical and conventional approaches to business ethics. The book prioritizes current, real-world examples and issues relevant to students' careers and the organizations where they will work, along with a global context. Because of this emphasis, the examples and issues are not only recognizable to students but also more meaningful. The chapters are intentionally concise, and each is written in a conversational style with short, easy to digest segments and language. You will not find extended passages of dry text or examples that are pages long.

Applied Chapter Features

A goal of every chapter feature is to encourage students to think critically and consider issues from multiple stakeholder perspectives, thereby helping them develop their own ethical compass to navigate the challenges they will face in their careers. All features are real-world and current, aimed at resonating with students' knowledge and interests.

Where Do You Stand? at the beginning of each chapter gets students *warmed up* and thinking about the chapter content before reading it. Instructors can use this feature to open class discussions and set the stage for subsequent learning and assignments. Instructors can also ask students to answer these questions before class and then discuss them with other students in class or on discussion boards.

Ethics in Action provides illustrations of ethical and unethical behaviors and practices by real world and often recognizable individuals and organizations. For each chapter, students are asked a number of questions intended to bring course material to life, motivate discussion, or put students in the position of a decision maker and explain what they would do and why.

For Discussion use discussion-oriented questions to provoke a conversation about ethical challenges and dilemmas. The intent is to have students reflect on and apply the material immediately after reading about it.

Chapter Case Studies conclude each chapter with a current and real-world case drawn from a variety of sources such as business news, popular press, and academic research. The case studies have been written with four goals: (1) illustrate the content in a particular chapter, (2) facilitate discussion using several questions based on the case, (3) apply the Three-Dimensional Problem-Solving for Ethics (3D PSE) framework presented in Chapter 1, and (4) develop students' ethical reasoning skills.

Three-Dimensional Problem-Solving for Ethics Framework

The practical value of the approach of *Managing Business Ethics and Your Career* is increased further still with a problem-solving framework for ethics. This approach is meant to be complementary to the various historical and ethical decision-making perspectives. The framework is called Three-Dimensional Problem-Solving for Ethics (3D PSE), and the three dimensions are:

Define the ethical challenge

Determine the causes of the challenge

Describe the solutions

The 3D PSE framework is introduced in the first chapter and applied to each subsequent chapter case study. A version of this 3D PSE approach has been used successfully by many students and clients, and it has been adapted here to apply to solving ethical challenges. This approach has benefits beyond business ethics, as employers consistently rate problem-solving as one of the skills most sought in employees. After learning to apply it to business ethics, students will be prepared to apply it to other problems or dilemmas. The 3D PSE framework is a simple, intuitive, and effective tool.

Value-Added Resources for Students and Instructors

Instructor's Manual

A comprehensive instructor's manual has been developed to minimize prep and provide a range of tools and resources, whether teaching face-to-face or online. The instructor's manual contains guidance regarding how to use the numerous features outlined above and additional exercises and examples. Everything in the instructor's manual was created and selected with the goal of effectively engaging students, providing value-added options for teaching, and to enhance student learning and the application of business ethics concepts.

The instructor's manual also includes support for using the comprehensive case study found at the end of the book on the business behemoth Amazon, which is confronted with countless business ethics challenges, making it a great case study to illustrate the breadth, depth, and impact of business ethics on an array of stakeholders. This case can be used in a variety of ways.

1. As a running case to discuss how the concepts from each chapter apply to Amazon.
2. With the book being organized into four parts, the Amazon case can be divided accordingly and used as a review, test, or as a project for individuals or teams to work on for each unit of the course.
3. As a cumulative assignment or capstone discussion for the course.

Test Bank

A test bank has been carefully developed to cover every learning objective and important details from each chapter. The test bank is available in formats compatible with Microsoft Word, Blackboard, Canvas, and D2L. The test bank may also be deployed from CourseBank or an online course management system.

PowerPoints

A comprehensive deck of PowerPoints is available for each chapter, providing robust coverage of the key chapter topics, along with figures and tables from the textbook.

CourseBank for Easy Online Course Creation

This book is available with CourseBank, a ready-made online course that can be easily integrated with Canvas, Blackboard, D2L, or any other LMS. CourseBank includes auto-graded assignments and quizzes, mini-lectures, and flash cards. Use everything or select only the resources that align with your approach. CourseBank also includes an intuitive question-picker, making it easy to create new quizzes and exams.

ACKNOWLEDGMENTS

Academia is my fourth career, and I have directly experienced both the benefits of ethical coworkers, leaders, and the organizations they create, as well as the damage that unethical coworkers, leaders, and organizations can inflict on individuals, departments, schools, businesses, and countries. My personal experience has taught me the importance of business ethics at all levels, and my own experiences have informed a large proportion of this book. These experiences, along with existing research and many years of teaching and consulting, contributed to the motivation, content, and ultimately the creation of this book.

Among the influential people was Rick Scruggs, my regional manager in the pharmaceutical industry, who showed me what it meant to lead with transparency, compassion, and with a commitment to doing the right thing by all stakeholders. He not only took responsibility for his own actions but also those of the people he managed and the larger organization. It is of little wonder that he has since continued on to lead an extraordinarily successful career involving multiple high-level executive positions for numerous companies in the industry. During those same years, John Stevens was my most influential mentor and taught me not only the value of using knowledge to help clinicians solve medical problems, but he also demonstrated, by example, the importance of professionalism, kindness, loyalty, and commitment to staying the course and doing the right thing—even if doing so could be personally costly. As an academic, marketing professor Roger Kerin's advice and conduct were more impactful than he knows. The majority of his advice was informal, during quick chats in the doorway of my office, but he was always more than willing to sit down and have a pointed discussion. He was generous with his wisdom and experience, and his advice was valuable in helping a junior faculty member navigate academia, the tenure process, and organizational politics.

This book would not have been possible without Donna, my sweet wife. I love her even more today than on our wedding day, she makes me a better person, and our life together is a cherished treasure. She is my fiercest advocate, always supportive, my friend, and source of comfort. This book could not and would not have happened without her. She encouraged me to take it on in the first place, and she helped convince me that it was possible in such a short timeline. She said, "How else are you going to spend your time during COVID?" We worked side by side for weeks and months, during which time she was my sounding board, research assistant, proofreader, and cheerleader. She would reenergize me with laughter, prod me to take sorely needed breaks walking our Jack Russell Terrier, Mila, and goofing off. Donna, I am lucky to share my life with you.

I want to thank Paul Ducham; it is because of him this book is happening and happening now. I am especially thankful for his persistence and patience, as eventually the stars, sun, and moon aligned again for us to work together. His direction, commitment, and partnership have been excellent in every way. He has reminded me of what it means to be an effective, committed, kind, and principled publisher and business partner. Thank you, Paul!

The following reviewers provided insightful guidance, ideas, and great advice. *Managing Business Ethics and Your Career* would not be the book it is without their willingness to share their talent and experience. Many of the reviewers were incredibly generous with their time and insights, far exceeding anything I have experienced in my work as a textbook writer. I am deeply grateful.

Jason Anderson, *The University of Kansas*

Carolyn Ashe, *University of Houston Downtown*

Angelo Brown, *Chattahoochee Technical College*

Angelika Buchanan, *Oregon State University*

Robin Byerly, *Appalachian State University*

Monica Eshner, *University of New Mexico*

Chelsea Green, *Miami University*

Marie Halvorsen-Ganepola, *University Arkansas*

Clyde Hull, *Rochester Institute of Technology*

Frank Kellner, *Tarleton State University*

Ksenia Keplinger, *University of Colorado*

Jeff King, *The Ohio State University*

James King Jr., *University of Alabama*

Kevin Lehnert, *Grand Valley State University*

Douglas McElhaney, *Chattahoochee Technical College*

Karen Myers, *Miami University*

Ted Paterson, *Oregon State University*

Gordon Rands, *Western Illinois University*

Brian Ray, *University of Florida*

Sean Valentine, *University of Wyoming*

Arturo Vasquez-Parraga, *University of Texas Rio Grande Valley*

Juan Velasco, *Southwestern College*

Caryl Williams, *Arizona State University*

About the Author

MEL FUGATE is a professor of management in the college of business at Mississippi State University. He has over twenty years of teaching experience and has won seven teaching awards across programs (undergraduate and MBA). His teaching, research, and consulting interests span many topics: ethics and leadership, organizational behavior, leadership, management, strategic human capital, organizational culture, leading and managing change, and performance management. His experience includes various formats of online teaching, crosses all levels and programs (PhD, executive, masters, and undergraduate), and comprises positions in the United States, France, and Australia. Prior to Mississippi State, he served on the faculties of American University, University of South Australia, Southern Methodist University, EM-Lyon School of Management, and Tulane University. His PhD is in management from Arizona State University, and undergraduate degree is in engineering and business from Michigan State University.

Professor Fugate is an active researcher whose interests include employee reactions to organizational change, employability and careers, as well as the effect of leadership and organizational culture on individual, group, and organizational performance. His research has been published in the field's most prestigious journals, and it has been featured in numerous notable media outlets such as *The Wall Street Journal, The New York Times, Financial Times, Fast Company, Dallas Morning News*, CNN, Fox, ABC, and NBC. His work is widely cited and has helped create a strong and growing reputation for him and his work.

Mel continues to actively consult with a large number of organizations across industries and is the author of four highly successful organizational behavior textbooks. Students throughout his career routinely commend his ability to make subjects real, applied, and thus relevant, and these are the same qualities he brings to his textbook writing.

Outside of work, Mel and his wife, Donna, lead active lives. They enjoy traveling, fitness, live music, and spoiling their sweet, savage beast, Mila, the Jack Russell Terrier.

PART 1

Overview of Business Ethics

chapter 1

Understanding Business Ethics

Learning Objectives

AFTER READING THIS CHAPTER, YOU SHOULD BE ABLE TO:

LO1 Differentiate morals, values, and norms and explain how they relate to business ethics.

LO2 Explain why ethics are important to business.

LO3 Summarize how ethics can affect your job, career, and role in society.

LO4 Articulate how to use 3-dimensional problem-solving to improve your ethical performance.

WHERE DO **YOU** STAND?

Cash or Credit?

The airline industry has been one of the most negatively affected by COVID-19. By early April 2020, travel had declined 95 percent—from over 2 million passengers per day to less than 100,000—costing airlines an estimated loss of $1.6 billion per day.[1] One of the most challenging aspects of this is how to handle customer cancellations—refund passenger's money or give them credits for future flights. By late May 2020, airlines had overwhelmingly chosen and issued credits worth $10 billion.[2]

1. As a customer, which do you think is the right thing to do? Justify your position.
2. Assume you are an airline executive, which do you think is the right thing to do? Justify your choice.
3. Now argue the opposite choice.

Introduction

Are you ethical? Of course, your answer is yes, and you can bet that the numerous executives, coaches, university administrators, politicians, celebrities, and the countless others caught up in ethics scandals would answer this question the same way. Yet, you know from both the news and your personal experience that unethical conduct surrounds us. You also know that sometimes *you* do the wrong thing, but what is more common are the situations you face in which right and wrong are less than clear—you are conflicted. Such difficult scenarios occur in all arenas of your life—school, work, and socially. The overarching goal of this book is to help you develop your ethical compass, including the knowledge and skills necessary to navigate the endless ethical challenges in your job and career. Conducting yourself ethically is foundational to your long-term success and the value of your contributions to your employers, communities, and larger global society.

This is accomplished using a practical approach based on the belief that management, of which business ethics is a part, is an applied discipline—it is something you do. This means it is about informed action, and this belief is reflected in the major learning objectives for you. This book was written to *help you:*

1. Understand ethical challenges you will confront in your individual jobs and larger career.
2. Determine the potential causes and solutions, along with the associated consequences, both intended and unintended.
3. Guide your own ethical business conduct.
4. Foster and react to (i.e., manage) the (un)ethical conduct of individuals and organizations.
5. Become a more ethically centered, fulfilled, and productive member of global society.

One way to achieve these objectives is to structure the book in a way to help you organize and apply your knowledge as you learn it. Your journey begins with an overview of business ethics and its importance to business in a general sense, but also for you and your career. The book was written with an emphasis on you, as indicated in the five objectives listed above. This overview introduces some key concepts and creates a common language. The remainder of the book is organized into levels—individual, organizational, and global. As explained later in this chapter, structuring the book and your learning in this way will assist you in organizing your own thinking and understanding the relationships between factors that influence ethical conduct.

Let's begin.

What are Morals, Values, and Norms, and How Do They Relate to Business Ethics?

Just like all of the various disciplines you study in business school—accounting, finance, marketing, human resource management, and others—business ethics has a terminology that enables people to communicate precisely and apply knowledge accurately. Acquiring and using a common language not only facilitates your learning and communication abilities, but it also enables you to apply your knowledge more effectively. To this end, several key terms are related, that is, one is embedded in or in part determined by another. This is another reason why it is especially important to create clarity at the beginning.

Before defining other terms and explaining how they are related, it helps to describe and illustrate what is meant by embedded. Figure 1.1 shows three concentric circles—business ethics norms are embedded in or influenced by business values, and both are embedded in and influenced by societal morals. Configured in this way helps you think of this subject in terms of levels—morals the highest, values next, and ethics last. This mirrors the level of abstraction or precision, such that morals are relatively more abstract beliefs held among people, whereas values are more varied and ethics most variable. With this in mind, let's explore each in more detail.

What Are Morals and Business Values, and How Do They Relate to Business Ethics?

morals
what a society, national culture, religion, or philosophical belief system considers right and wrong

Applying this notion of embeddedness, let's start with the most fundamental element—morals. **Morals** describe what a society, national culture, religion, or philosophical belief

figure 1.1

The Relationship between Morals, Values, and Ethics

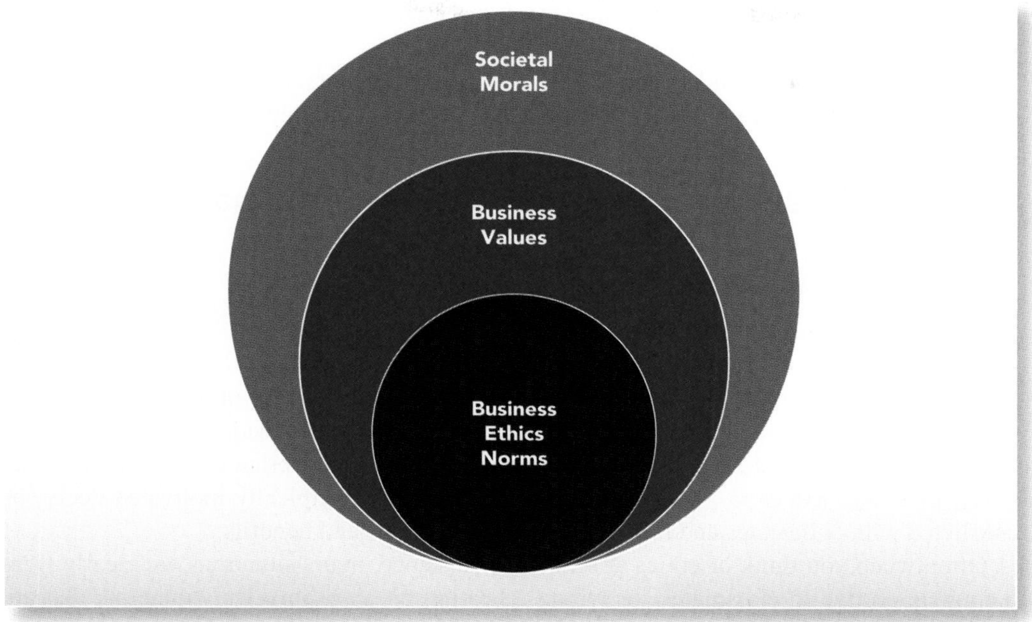

system considers right and wrong.[3] It therefore helps to think of morals as ethics at a higher level, such as the importance of life, liberty, and justice in the United States and other Western cultures. Religion also influences morals, for example, Christianity forbids stealing and Hinduism advocates pleasure and prosperity. Morals operate at a higher level and help shape business values and ethics.

Business values are shared and enduring expectations about what is important, and these in turn guide policies, practices, and behaviors of individuals and organizations.[4] Accordingly, values are brought to life, made real or manifest, in the actual behaviors, policies, and practices of individuals and organizations.

business values
shared and enduring expectations about what is important, and these in turn guide policies, practices, and behaviors of individuals and organizations

Business ethics norms, in turn, are the shared views of what is right and wrong and are reflected in the behaviors, policies, and practices in a given context. They are determined by the morals of society and the values of a particular community or group—employer, industry, and country.[5]

business ethics norms
the shared views of what is right and wrong and are reflected in the behaviors, policies, and practices in a given context

Putting this altogether, **business ethics** is the study of right and wrong behavior between individuals and organizations, and this distinction depends on the morals of society and the values and norms within a specific work context.[6] Although you and everyone else certainly have their individual sense of ethics, these are the result of the shared views of groups about what is appropriate. As such, your ethics may indeed differ from those of a particular group, such as a project team at school or a group of peers at work, but your ethics may align with some other group. More on this later when we discuss ethical dilemmas in this chapter and conflicts in chapter 5.

You can easily see how values have implications for ethical behavior. For instance, your employer may value competitiveness and reinforce this with providing large bonuses to top performers (performance management and reward practices). However, if you "steal" a customer from one of your peers, and/or sell the customer products they do not need, then your conduct is likely to be considered unethical. You will learn much more about values (chapter 4) and their implications for ethics throughout this book, such as value conflicts (chapter 5) and the fundamental role of values in organizational culture (chapter 8).

business ethics
the study of right and wrong behavior between individuals and organizations, and this distinction depends on the morals of society and the values and norms within a specific work context

Before moving on, it is important to note that a critical attribute common to morals, business values, and ethics norms is the fact that they are shared. It is the shared nature that gives them their power to influence the ethical conduct of individuals, organizations, industries, countries, and larger society. The greater the degree of sharing or agreement, the greater the power to influence ethical conduct.

Now that you have a basic understanding of some fundamental concepts and how they are related to each other, let's move on to the concept of ethical dilemmas.

Black & White, Gray Areas, and Ethical Dilemmas

> *"I thought ethical business was good business . . . My colleagues didn't all agree."*[7]

This quote is from Sallie Krawcheck, the cofounder and CEO of Ellevest, a digital financial adviser for women, on her account of very tough and consequential decisions she made when she was an executive at Citigroup and Bank of America during the financial crisis. In a later Ethics in Action box, you'll learn how her ethically motivated decisions conflicted with colleagues and resulted in substantial costs and benefits.

ethical dilemmas occur when a situation requires a choice in which both options have ethical implications, leaving you with no clear right or wrong decision. Such dilemmas frequently also involve conflicting values.

Often when you think of ethics at school, for instance, many situations are clearly right (being supportive to classmates) or wrong (cheating on an exam). But situations that are more challenging are ethical dilemmas. **Ethical dilemmas** occur when a situation requires a choice in which both options have ethical implications, leaving you with no clear right or wrong decision. Such dilemmas frequently also involve conflicting values.[8] Consider the example of finance manager for a large auto manufacturer. The company has been struggling, along with the entire industry, and leadership has decided to cut costs (cutting costs means cutting employees). Calculations need to be done to determine whom to lay off in order to meet the goals set by senior leadership. The finance manager has the responsibility of conducting these analyses, creating the list of those to be let go, and then giving this list to the regional director to take action.

The dilemma can be described in terms of a conflict between the finance manager's values of loyalty, to his job and employer, and honesty to his coworkers, many of whom are his friends. Most people in the office know that the finance manager is involved in determining the list, and if any of his friends ask, then he has to decide between telling the truth (being honest) and being loyal to his job and employer.

Moreover, this same dilemma could easily be framed only in terms of loyalty, on the one hand to his coworker friends and on the other to his employer.

For Discussion

1. Describe *two* ethical dilemmas you have experienced as a student.
2. If relevant, which conflicting values were involved in each?
3. Looking back, would you have done anything differently given the chance? Explain.

These are tough or gray situations, those with no clear answer, and tend to be more common and often more difficult to deal with. The knowledge and tools in this book are intended to better prepare you to deal with such ethical challenges.

Periodically, in every chapter, Ethics in Action boxes are inserted. These have two purposes. The first is to illustrate particular concepts as you learn them with descriptions of behavior, policies, and practices used by individuals, organizations, and larger society. The second purpose is to provide practical tools to help you develop your understanding and application of business ethics—news you can use. This first box does both and describes a practice used by one of the world's wealthiest and most respected people in business.

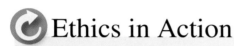

Ethics in Action

The TV Test

Warren Buffett, a legendary investor and one of the world's richest people, explains that ethics, trust, and morals are critical elements of being successful in business. These elements can either make or break your reputation, which he said is something he cannot afford to lose. This is quite a challenge for Buffett who is the face of Berkshire Hathaway which has over 350,000 employees. When confronted with uncertain situations or decisions, he tells his managers to ask and answer the following question: "How would you feel about the details of this situation and your conduct to be written up in the local newspaper for all to see and read?"[9]

Of course, this can include any widely read media outlet online, print, or an interview on the evening news. Scores of students over many years have role-played a modified version of this tool with great success. Specifically, imagine that immediately after you make a decision at school or work that you feel enters the gray zone—not clearly right, not clearly wrong—and a reporter shows up and sticks a microphone and camera in your face, and then asks you to explain yourself.

The stakes are raised further still if you also assume that the interview (or article) will be seen by family, friends, your kids, parents, and your coworkers (current and past).

Bottom line: If the decision passes this test, meaning you'd be willing to do the interview or have the article/post read, then do it. But anything close to the ethical line should not be done. Buffett says, he uses this to guide his own decision making and conduct and encourages managers to do the same.

For Discussion:

1. Think of a tough call you've had to make. If you were required to do the interview—the TV Test—would you have changed your decision or behavior? Explain why or why not.
2. Think of an example or situation where you think someone approached or crossed the line. Imagine you stuck a microphone and camera in their face asking for an explanation. What do you think they would say?

Next, we will begin making the case for the importance of ethics to business, which we will effectively do with every topic in the book.

The Importance of Ethics to Business

Why should you or anyone else bother studying business ethics? The most fundamental answer to this question is because the conduct of businesses can and does dramatically affect employees, departments, entire organizations, and even industries, countries, and the planet. We will explore various effects throughout this book, but let's start with what is legal or not.

Legal Does Not Mean Ethical

The first and last thing to remember about business ethics is that because something is legal does not mean it is ethical! To the contrary, many experts argue that an epidemic of unethical conduct has afflicted business across the globe for decades. The news media regularly reports some enormous business scandal (e.g., see Table 1.1) such that unethical conduct seems commonplace. All of the instances in Table 1.1 share a number of characteristics: executives (and frequently others) broke the law, executives went to jail, and often the companies failed resulting in tens of thousands of employees losing their jobs

table **1.1**

Examples of Well-Known Business Ethics Scandals

Scandal and Year	Industry	Unethical Conduct	Key Players	Consequences
Drexel Burnham Lambert (1990)	Finance	Insider trading	Michael Milken (junk bond king)	Jail time and $500 million fine for Milken; the firm failed
Purdue Pharma, ongoing since the mid-1990s	Pharma	False and misleading marketing and dozens of others	Sackler family	Multibillion-dollar settlement, bankruptcy, and restructuring
Enron (2001)	Energy	Financial fraud (cooking the books)	Kenneth Lay Jeff Skilling	Legal penalties for Lay, Skilling, and others; the firm failed
Arthur Andersen (2002)	Accounting	Fraud		The firm failed; consulting arm spun off as Andersen Consulting
Madoff and Associates (2008)	Finance	Fraud; Ponzi scheme	Bernie Madoff	Jail time; the firm failed
Penn State (2012)	Higher education	Sexual abuse	Jerry Sandusky Penn State	Jail time, settlement, firing of university president and head of football coach
Volkswagen Diesel Emissions (beginning in 2015)	Auto	Deceptive business practices/fraud Stock price manipulation	Martin Winterkorn, CEO	Fines, CEO resignation, damage to brand reputation
Fox News (beginning in 2016)	News	Sexual harassment and discrimination, retaliation	Roger Ailes Bill O'Reilly Jamie Horowitz	Settlement payments, ouster of copresident Bill Shine and very senior managers, resignations and firings, damaged image/brand, hired and elevated women into executive positions

Continued

Wells Fargo (2016)	Banking	Falsifying banking records, harm to customer credit ratings, fraud, lied to investors		Firing and disciplining of employees, billion-dollar settlement, damaged image/brand
USA Gymnastics Sex (2018)	Higher education (sports and medicine)	Sexual abuse	Dr. Larry Nassar Michigan State University Coach Kathie Klages	Jail time, fines, organizational bankruptcy, university officials resign or fired, loss of corporate sponsorship
College Admissions (2019)	Higher education	Bribery and fraudulent admissions materials	William Singer (mastermind) thirty-three parents, athletics coaches, admissions counselors, college administrators	Jail time, fines, job loss, suspensions

and retirement savings. Put simply, unethical conduct in business can and often does have negative consequences.

Nevertheless, we as a society generally assume that if an action is illegal, it is unethical, and individuals and organizations should pay the consequences. The lesson for you—don't break the law—is simple enough.

However, unethical conduct that qualifies as illegal is the exception. Only a puny percentage of all unethical business conduct is actually illegal, and an even smaller percentage results in formal legal complaints. The vast majority of unethical conduct is not illegal. One of the most devastating examples is the great financial crisis beginning in 2008 that caused unemployment to rise above 9 percent, housing prices to fall nearly 32 percent, and the US economy to lose nearly $1.4 trillion—with a T.[10]

Underlying this ethical calamity was unchecked risk-taking and greed by leaders of financial institutions and their activities in the mortgage market. Beyond ravaging the world economy and causing unemployment and financial ruin for millions of homeowners in the United States, hundreds of millions of people across the globe were also affected due to the true global nature of our financial system and economy.

Despite the enormity of the consequences, few to no high-level executives of American financial institutions were charged and convicted of breaking the law.[11] Eric Holder, the Attorney General of the United States at the time, described the situation by saying that the conduct of many executives was unethical and irresponsible but not necessarily criminal.[12] This view was reinforced by Ben Bernanke, the chairman of the Federal Reserve during the same period: ". . . corporate executives should have gone to jail . . . everything that went wrong or was illegal was done by some individual, not by an abstract firm."[13]

This begs the question: If unethical business conduct that is also illegal is the exception, then who decides what is right and wrong if not the courts? One answer is stakeholders.

stakeholders
any entity (e.g., individual, group, or organization) that can affect or is affected by your personal conduct or that of your organization

Stakeholders

Stakeholders are any entity (e.g., individual, group, or organization) that can affect or is affected by your personal conduct or that of your organization.[14] Table 1.2 shows a number

table 1.2

Common Stakeholders, Their Interests, and Means of Influence

Stakeholder	Stakeholder's Interest	Means of Influence
Shareholders	Financial returns	Support with money invested (or not)
Employees	Income; development opportunities; and personal reputation	Loyalty; enhance or erode reputation in the eyes of others
Customers	Reliable products and competent service; safety	Loyalty; enhance or erode reputation in the eyes of others
Suppliers	Integrity; prompt payment; continuing business	Responsiveness; flexibility; repeat business
Creditors	Financial returns	Terms for lending; flexibility
Regulators (e.g., financial and environmental)	Compliance with rules and regulations	Penalties (financial, jail time, licensing)
Governments (city, state, and federal)	Tax revenue and employment of citizens	Favorable tax treatment
Community	Employment of citizens Economic growth Protection of environment	Favorable tax treatment Supportive policies

primary stakeholders those who are critical to an organization's survival, such as employees, customers, shareholders, governments, and communities

secondary stakeholders most often do not have direct relationships with an organization and thus are not critical to its survival, such as trade groups, special interest groups, and the media (old school and social)

stakeholder approach determining how and which stakeholders will likely be impacted by or react to your or your employer's action

of common stakeholder groups, along with their interests and means for influencing the ethical conduct, policies, and practices of organizations.

It is often helpful to categorize stakeholders as either primary or secondary. **Primary stakeholders** are those who are critical to an organization's survival, such as employees, customers, shareholders, governments, and communities.[15] It is likely easy for you to understand how employees, customers, and shareholders (for public companies and the owners of private companies) are essential for most organizations, but governments are also necessary as they regulate and tax most industries. Communities are another stakeholder, and they provide infrastructure (e.g., buildings, roads, and water), even for virtual organizations they are responsible for electricity and Internet service.

Secondary stakeholders most often do not have direct relationships with an organization and thus are not critical to its survival, such as trade groups, special interest groups, and the media (old school and social).[16] The key learning point is to understand that you, and your employers, are well served to identify and consider the values and business ethics expectations of both primary and secondary stakeholders. The following Ethics in Action box illustrates how the focus and importance of stakeholders often changes over time as a company grows.

The Stakeholder Approach

The **stakeholder approach** involves determining how and which stakeholders will likely be impacted by or react to your or your employer's action.[19] Stakeholders therefore are fundamental to business ethics, sustainability (chapters 2 and 12),

Ethics in Action

Primary *and* Secondary Are Powerful at Facebook

For the longest time, Mark Zuckerberg, the cofounder and CEO of Facebook, was able to focus his energy and efforts on building the product with supreme tech talent, attracting users and advertisers, and other activities to make the company and stock price grow. He, and other Facebook leaders, had tremendous success serving all of these primary stakeholders.

However, as Facebook grew so did its challenges with secondary stakeholders, which in the past years have consumed much of Zuckerberg's and other leader's attention. Allegations have been made that the company's advertising for financial services illegally discriminates against particular groups (e.g., older and female users).[17]

The company has also attracted unwanted attention regarding its influence of the 2016 presidential election and not sufficiently acting on hate speech and misinformation. The latter issue resulted in more than 1,000 companies boycotting the social media giant, by pulling their advertising on the platform.[18]

For Discussion:

1. Which stakeholders are more powerful—primary or secondary—for Facebook today? Explain.
2. Which three stakeholders do you think consumed the majority of Zuckerberg's attention now? Why?

corporate social responsibility (chapter 2), and other concepts you will learn about in this book. We will learn much more about the stakeholder approach in chapter 2 and apply it throughout the book. But because it is fundamental to business ethics, it is introduced in chapter 1 as it is necessary to many of the other concepts and discussions throughout the book.

It is worth emphasizing the part of the stakeholder approach definition that states that stakeholders "are affected by or can affect" you and/or your company. Your actions, or inactions, affect stakeholders and vice versa. This means that stakeholders have expectations regarding ethical conduct, and not meeting their expectations can cause problems for you. Making this more difficult still is that different stakeholders may have different expectations about what *they* consider ethical. **Bribery**—offering, giving, or receiving anything of value to influence the actions of another—is a common and good example.[20] For instance, in some countries (e.g., Cambodia, Yemen, Ukraine, and Iraq),[21] bribes are a common part of acquiring a customer's business or support.

bribery offering, giving, or receiving anything of value to influence the actions of another

It is also important to realize that the focus or relative importance of any given stakeholder often changes over time, just as described in the Ethics in Action box regarding Mark Zuckerberg and Facebook. During the early years of the company, he paid little attention to regulators in the United States, let alone in other countries. He likely gave little thought to the role the platform, and social media more broadly, would play in elections. Therefore, understanding who the relevant stakeholders are in a given situation, learning their expectations and the effect of your mutual actions, is critical to your ethical business success and an overarching focus to this book.

table 1.3

Benefits and Costs of (Un)Ethical Conduct

Benefits of Ethical Conduct	Costs of Unethical Conduct
Performance	Legal costs
Employee commitment	Employee theft
High-quality talent	Talent
Investor money	Reputation
Supportive regulators	Greater oversight by regulators

Benefits of Ethical Conduct to Organizations

If you take the stakeholder approach, then you see that a wide range of people and groups may potentially benefit (or be harmed) by your conduct, and vice versa. Table 1.3 outlines some notable benefits of ethical conduct and costs associated with unethical conduct.

And remember that different stakeholders may have different expectations and considerations of what is ethical and what is not. But the bottom line is being ethical increases an organization's competitiveness! Now let's explore how and why ethics are important for you.

The Importance of Ethics to You and Your Career

moral humility
recognizing that you (and all people) make mistakes and can cross the ethical line

Most people are good and have genuinely positive intentions, but being a good person isn't enough when it comes to business ethics. First, you need to have **moral humility** which is recognizing that you (and all people) make mistakes and can cross the ethical line.[22] You therefore need knowledge, skill, and practical tools to effectively navigate the numerous and inevitable ethical challenges you'll be confronted with during your working life.

Second, it also is helpful if you not only avoid unethical conduct but also think of ethical business conduct as something positive and worthy of your efforts. To this end, a fundamental theme to this book is to help you understand and manage ethical challenges more successfully and improve your job performance and career opportunities as a result. We begin with a basic and crucial consequence of ethical conduct—trust.

Competence + Integrity = Trust = Success

competence-based trust
the expectation that the person or organization has the skills, ability, experience, and reliability to deliver on its obligations

integrity-based trust
the perceptions of a person's or organization's (i.e., employees) intentions, honesty, and character

You already know how fragile trust can be, as people violate your trust from time to time, and sometimes these relationships are completely repaired. However, when trust is violated by someone in your professional life, things rarely return to "normal," and unethical conduct is one of the quickest and consequential ways of violating trust. All of this means that the importance of the relationship between business ethics and trust cannot be overstated, for you, other individuals, and organizations.

But as a practical matter, what does this mean? Don't violate another's trust? Sure, but that is a bit simplistic. Volumes of research shed light on the topic and help us understand and thus use knowledge of trust more effectively. To this end, it is helpful to consider two forms of trust—competence- and integrity-based. **Competence-based trust** is the expectation that the person or organization has the skills, ability, experience, and reliability to deliver on its obligations. **Integrity-based trust** involves the perceptions of a person's or organization's (i.e., employees) intentions, honesty, and character.[23] Competence is skill, integrity is ethics.

Both forms of trust reduce the effort or costs of interactions between individuals and organizations, such as more efficient negotiations, smoother dispute resolutions, and greater cooperation and flexibility when dealing with uncertainty and changes.[24] All of these are important for you, your relationship with your employers, and relationships between your employers and other stakeholders. These are the benefits these forms of trust share, but they do differ.

For Discussion

1. Describe a personal experience in which someone violated competence-based trust.
2. How did you feel when someone violated competence-based trust and what effect did it have on your relationship going forward?
3. Describe a personal experience in which someone violated integrity-based trust.
4. How did you feel when someone violated integrity-based trust and what effect did it have on your relationship going forward?

All Breaches of Trust Are Not Equal. If you or your employer fails to meet the competence expectations of another party, only once, they are likely to see it as a simple transgression, an error in one particular aspect of the relationship or business. They may give you and/or your employer another chance—not always, but more often than not. However, people are more likely to perceive a single breach of integrity trust as a general lack of character and dishonesty, and they are likely to apply it to you and your employer across the board. People tend to assume that you and/or your employer are bad actors in every dealing.[25]

The Benefits of Employee–Employer Trust. When employees who trust their employers are compared to those who don't, those who trust are:

- 39% more likely to promote or advocate for their employer to customers and potential employees;
- 38% more loyal;
- 33% more engaged; and
- 31% more committed.[26]

It also is helpful to emphasize that trust works both ways, employees trusting their employers and employers trusting their employees. The ethical conduct of employees can serve to build a sense of trust among their managers, who in turn do not have to spend as much time, energy, and thus money supervising trusted employees. This is exactly what was found in research investigating the benefits of partners at accounting firms and the level of trust generated by the ethical conduct of their subordinate auditors.[27]

fran_kie/Shutterstock

These are very important outcomes and speak volumes to the value of trust in the employer–employee relationship. Employer–employee relationships, however, play out on a larger landscape of trust people have for institutions and those doing particular jobs.

Trust in Institutions and Jobs. More generally, the status of trust in our society is ailing. According to the 2020 version of the annual Edelman Trust Barometer, which surveyed over 34,000 people in twenty-eight countries, it appears that organizations continue to do a poor job of meeting employees' expectations related to trust. Results from the survey revealed that none of the four major institutions is trusted (government, media, business, and nongovernmental organizations), which means no industry received 60 percent or more on the trust measure (see Figure 1.2).

Results were similarly bleak for particular groups of people and particular jobs (see Figure 1.3).[28]

This ugly picture is a warning to you and your employers. Many people already have a less than trusting view, which means special attention needs to be given to potential violations of trust.

Now we turn to what happens to trust in crisis situations.

Trust and Crisis. When a crisis hits, do you think trust in leaders and government goes up or down? What about during the COVID-19 pandemic? If you said "up" for both, then you are correct. Generally, trust increases in both because people expect leaders and the key institutions in their lives to take care of them. But, and importantly, the increase is in the beginning of a crisis, and depending on how it is handled, trust levels can end up much lower than before the crisis. This pattern was supported by an update of the Edelman Trust Barometer. The company conducted a supplemental survey in May 2020 and the results showed a jump in those that trust government from 54 to 65 percent since the original report in January 2020. For perspective, this is the largest increase in the twenty years the Edelman organization has been monitoring trust around the world.[29]

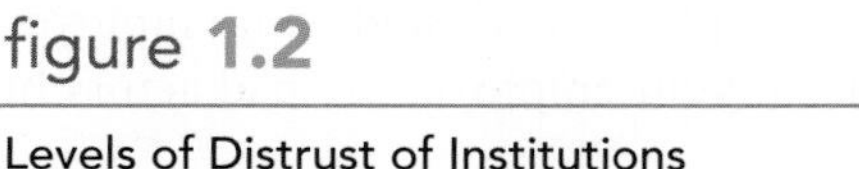

figure 1.2

Levels of Distrust of Institutions

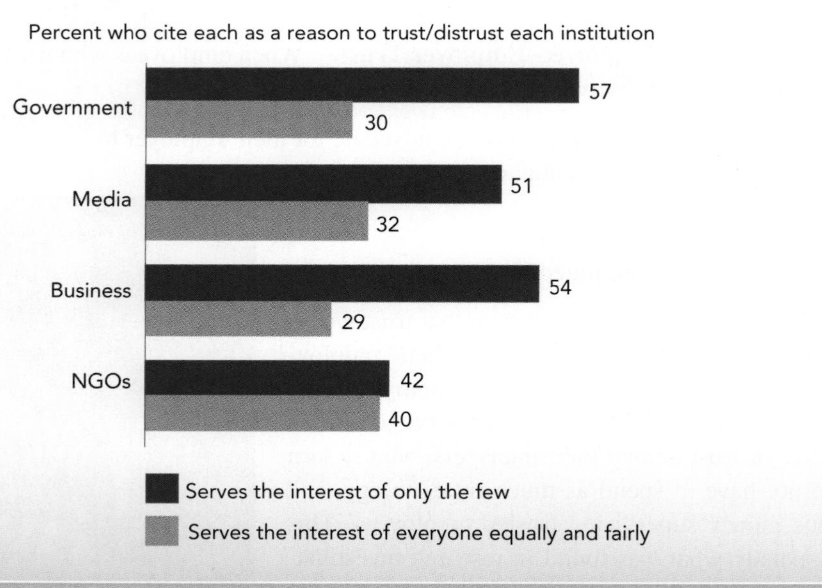

Source figure 1.2 and 1.3: adapted from Edelman Trust Barometer 2020. https://www.edelman.com/sites/g/files/aatuss191/files/2020-01/2020%20Edelman%20Trust%20Barometer%20Executive%20Summary_Single%20Spread%20without%20Crops.pdf

figure 1.3

Percentage of Trust in People Doing These Jobs

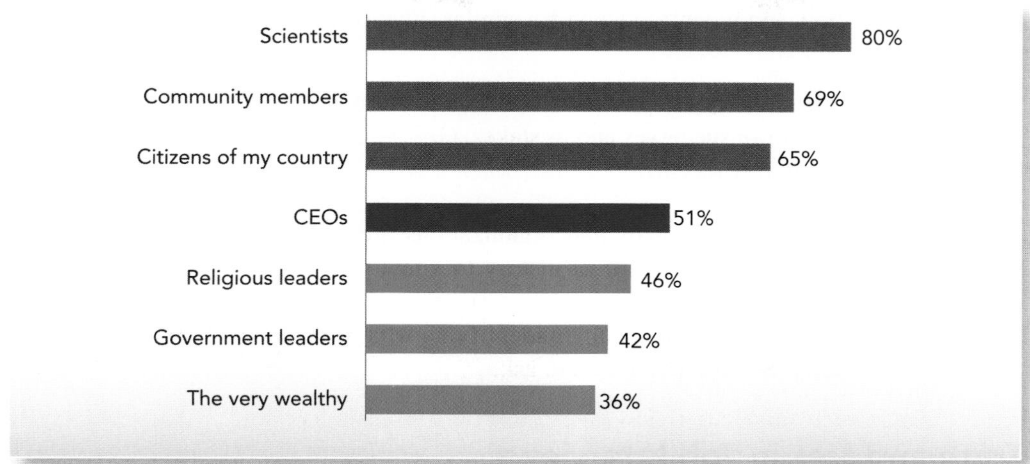

So, what can be done to foster trust during this particular crisis? First, it helps to know the most trusted sources of information related to COVID-19:

1. doctors
2. scientists
3. national health officials[30]

What separates these groups and the individuals within are their competence- and integrity-based trust. Compared to other individuals involved in the pandemic response, people think that doctors, scientists, and national health officials have more relevant knowledge (competence) and thus are more qualified to communicate related information and guide responses. These same professionals also are perceived as relatively more ethical (integrity) than others involved in the response (e.g., politicians and other government officials). This suggests that business leaders and politicians, despite their roles and responsibilities, may be well served to involve experts and let them do the talking. This assertion is reinforced by the fact that in the same survey people reported that only 38 percent of employers are doing well or very well at considering employees before profits.[31]

You hopefully now have an even more compelling sense of the importance of trust. Let's explore ethics and your career next.

Ethics and Your Career

This entire book provides you with knowledge and skills to help you understand business ethics and increase your job and career success. Three overarching actions can be especially helpful—anticipate challenges, reflect and learn, and celebrate successes.[32]

Anticipate Challenges. What are the most likely ethical challenges you'll confront? Generate a list and make a plan for how you will respond. If X happens, then I will do or say Y. Mentors can help in both identifying the ethical issues and planning your responses, and they can be helpful to consult with when such experiences transpire. Being prepared makes it easier to deal with, as ethical challenges often occur very suddenly and without notice.

Reflect and Learn. Relatively simple missteps or even colossal ethical debacles happen, and when they happen to you, it is important to learn from them. A one-time lapse is difficult enough, as it can cost you relationships and/or a job, but you don't want to make the same mistake twice. Rather than being defensive and trying to justify or rationalize what happened, think of your role, how your (in)actions contributed to the situation, and if confronted with a similar situation in the future how will you handle it.

Celebrate Successes. Also be sure to reflect on your business ethics victories. All of us can learn from successes and mistakes. Give yourself credit for doing the right thing, especially if it was difficult.

More generally, both individuals and organizations are encouraged to do all three of these. Organizations have the benefit of history to know what types of ethical challenges are likely and what approaches work best. As for you, until you have years of experience, you will benefit from seeking some help in identifying what is most common in a given job, company, or industry. So, don't be afraid to ask.

Truth and Lies in Job Interviews

Research shows that 81 percent of people lie during job interviews.[33] Strive to be in the minority and don't lie! Use the TV Test presented earlier in Ethics in Action box and imagine your interview is posted online, or the interview is live on the evening news for everyone you know or have worked with to see. Would the answers you provide during the interview hold up to the scrutiny of these people? Not only could you but would you want to defend your interview answers to these people? If you can answer "yes" to both questions, then you're off to a good start. Finally, assume you are the interviewer instead of the interviewee—turn the tables. Also assume you own the company. How would you feel if the person you're interviewing gave the same responses as you?

The next Ethics in Action box offers advice for interviewers who are frequently confronted with the challenge of assessing the ethical nature of job candidates. When reading the questions, think of how you would respond. If you're currently working or have worked, assume you are the hiring manager, then think of how you might modify these questions to make them more relevant for that job and company.

For your jobs and career, remember that trust is fragile, and once lost in the business arena, it can be hard to recover. Therefore:

1. Carefully consider who might be affected by your conduct (stakeholder approach).
2. Effectively deal with ethical dilemmas using the knowledge and many tools in this book, including the problem-solving approach explained next.
3. During interviews and even after accepting a job, ask "What types of ethical dilemmas am I likely to confront in this job?" "How does this company advocate ethical conduct? Please describe policies, practices, or examples related to ethics."

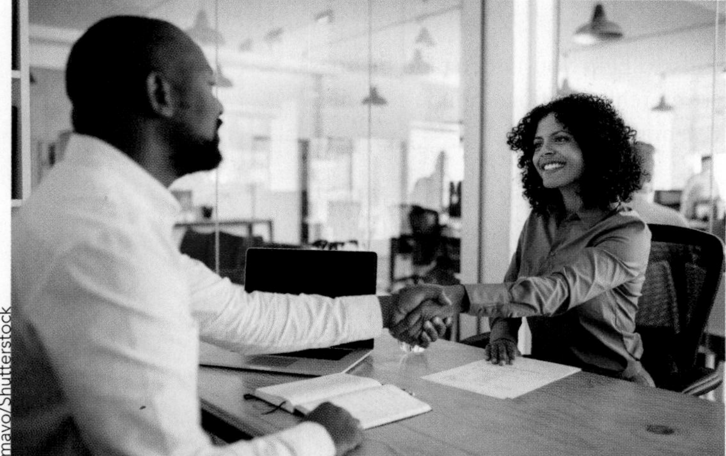
mavo/Shutterstock

Bottom line: Trust is fragile for both individuals and organizations, and people have consistently felt fairly low levels of trust for people in particular jobs and institutions. Also, people are more forgiving for a lack of skill than ethics. If given a choice between ethics and skill, choose ethics.

Next, you'll learn about a widely applicable tool for addressing ethical challenges at work. Versions

Ethics in Action

Ethics-focused Interview Questions

As explained earlier in this chapter, there is no value in asking someone if they are ethical. Even lifelong scoundrels and the most despicable people you'll ever work with would say "yes." Therefore, the challenge in interviews is to get candidates to discuss actual situations and how they have handled or would handle them, and the intent of this is to reveal their ethical compass and character. The following are a few helpful questions to ask if you're the interviewer and to be prepared to answer if you're the candidate.

1. How would you describe an ethical workplace?
2. How do you define honesty and accountability at work?
3. Tell me about an ethical challenge you have faced?
4. Assuming you looked at our web page, what element(s) made an impression on you and why?
5. I assume you've worked with people from different cultures, even if only in college classes. What values and ethics did you find similar and different?
6. When/if you have ethical concerns at work, whom did you consult? Describe.
7. What is the difference between an ethical employee and an ethical employer?[34]

For Discussion:

1. As a job candidate, pick two questions that would make you most uncomfortable?
2. As an interviewer, what are two additional questions you think would accurately assess a candidate's ethicality?

of this approach have been taught to and used by thousands of students over many years. The hope is that you too will benefit.

Using the Three-Dimensional Problem-solving for Ethics (3D PSE) Tool to Improve Your Ethical Performance

Throughout this book, you are provided with practical tools to understand and apply your knowledge about business ethics. The 3-D PSE is one such tool and is used in each chapter. A similar version (3-D Problem-solving—Define the problem, Determine the causes, and Describe the solutions) was used by students and clients for many years, and it was adapted to better fit problem-solving for ethics. This approach has benefits beyond business ethics, as employers consistently rate problem-solving as one of the skills most sought in employees. You can apply it to many business ethics challenges (e.g., dilemmas), and it is especially useful for end-of-chapter cases. In fact, you'll notice the 3D approach in the case discussion questions. It is simple, intuitive, and effective. Let's learn about the approach by applying it to this simple scenario.

Scenario: It is the end of the quarter and you are working extremely hard to meet your sales target. Not only is it what your boss expects, you will also earn a large bonus. The key to making your goal is to close a potential sale with a longtime and significant customer, and the customer told you she will go with your product instead of the competitor's if you provide tickets to the soccer game this weekend. What would you do?

You, like many people, may simply provide the tickets or find something else the customer wants and be done with it. However, you may have a different view if your company forbids gifts of any sort. Now what do you do? Let's increase your chances of success by implementing the 3-D PSE.

Dimension 1: *Define* the Ethical Challenge

problems
gaps between what you have and what you want—current state versus desired state

This scenario, like most other ethical challenges, represents particular types of problems at work, and if approached as a problem to be solved you are likely to be more successful in resolving them. It therefore can be helpful to define ethical challenges as problems, and **problems** are gaps between what you have and what you want—current state versus desired state.[35] Ethics are the same. The critical first dimension in effective problem-solving is defining the problem correctly. The widely used example of this is a visit to the doctor when you are sick. Sound medical practice involves determining the underlying cause rather than simply treating the symptoms. For instance, assume you have a fever and without gathering any additional information, the doctor recommends taking Tylenol every eight hours. Sure, this may reduce your fever, for some period of time. But what if the underlying cause of the fever was a lung infection? You would likely get even sicker, miss school and work, need to return to the doctor, and maybe even need to be hospitalized if you develop pneumonia. It obviously would have been more effective had the doctor defined the problem as an infection, rather than a fever, and prescribed an antibiotic instead of Tylenol.

You need to do the same to address ethical challenges more effectively. Using only information contained in the case, what is the gap in this scenario? What do you have and what do you want? Applying the stakeholder approach, you also need to consider the scenario from the customer's perspective. What does she have versus what does she want?

- Is it simply that you want the sale and don't have it? From your perspective, this makes sense.
- Or, is it that the customer really likes your product better, and actually intends to purchase it instead of the competitor's, but wants to test your ethical boundaries? This makes it more challenging.

You can see that how you define the problem can make a significant difference.

Finally, define your problem in one or at most two sentences and structure it in terms of what is current versus what is desired.

figure 1.4

Three-Dimensional Problem-Solving for Ethics (3D PSE)

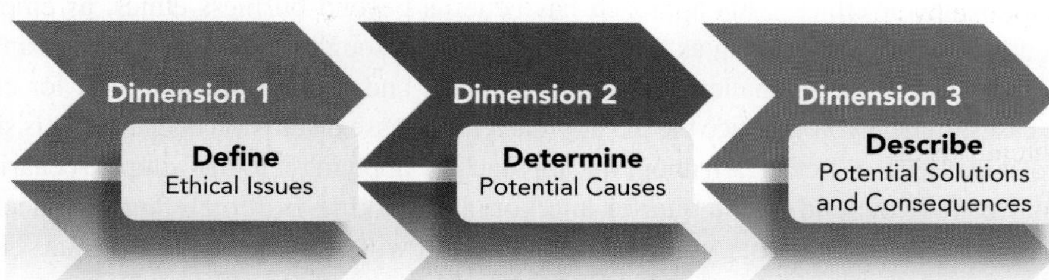

Dimension 2: *Determine* the Causes

For any given problem there may be numerous causes, but you also can see how critical it is to define the problem appropriately. To assist, it can be helpful to think of multiple categories or sources of causes—those that reside with individuals and those that are in the context.

Individuals. Many causes of unethical conduct are due to the traits and behaviors of individuals. For instance, as you'll learn in chapter 7, unethical leaders often possess narcissistic, psychopathic, and/or Machiavellian traits. People with these traits are likely to use people to achieve their own interests, show little or no empathy, and only fake concern for others.

Greed is another trait that causes or motivates unethical conduct. Inserting yourself in the scenario above, are you greedy and willing to close the sale at any cost? Or, is it the case that without the bonus you will be unable to pay your tuition or rent? Part of the cause for the problem in the scenario may be with the customer. Perhaps she is truly testing you to see if you will compromise ethical standards to get the sale. She may be impressed if you do; however, she may also choose not to do any business with you or your employer in the future. She also may simply be trying to get something for nothing and have questionable character (chapter 7).

We will explore and learn about many different personal characteristics that cause (un) ethical conduct at work.

Contextual. These can be policies and practices in particular organizations or industries. One powerful cause in the scenario may be your performance management system (chapters 6 and 8). What if your sales goal is unrealistic, or the economy is in the toilet, and it therefore is unlikely you will achieve the sales goal? This could be made even more difficult if the bonus is large and/or meeting the goal is necessary for a promotion. It is entirely possible such gifts or sweeteners are industry norms, meaning they are common with no formal policies forbidding them.

Given the way you defined the problem, what are the potential causes in the scenario using only information contained in the case? For each cause, it is helpful to refine and clarify by asking "How does this cause the problem I defined?" If you ask this question repeatedly for each cause, you may redefine your problem and be more confident you determined the appropriate causes.

Dimension 3: *Describe* Your Solutions and the Intended and Potential Unintended Consequences for Stakeholders

If you have been diligent in defining the problem and determining the causes (Dimensions 1 and 2), then generating potential solutions will be easier (maybe not easy but easier). Just as doctors do, it is best to "treat" the causes, as addressing these effectively most often improves or remedies the problem. Consider each cause and create a solution, then develop your response by answering the following questions regarding your proposed solution?

1. ***What*** you will do and ***how***? This is your action plan.
2. ***Why*** you will do it? Answering this question can help you gain clarity about your intentions and help resolve dilemmas.

If your responses to these questions are unsatisfactory, then go back to Dimension 1 and repeat the process. If, however, you are comfortable and confident in your problem-solving efforts thus far, then ensure you achieve the desired outcomes and avoid any unintended consequences by considering the following questions.

3. What is the ***desired and likely effect in the short- and long-term*** for you and the key stakeholders involved in the problem and causes (Dimensions 1 and 2)? This question forces you to check your goal and get clear on the desired outcome. Moreover, considering the potential effects in both the short- and long-term gets you to think about the sustainability of your proposed solutions. The negative consequences of some actions only occur over time.
4. What ***potential unintended consequences*** may occur with each proposed solution? In the scenario, for example, if you decide to provide the tickets or some other enticement to the customer, then she may expect it from you again in the future (it becomes a norm) or decide you are unethical and not give you or anyone else from your firm business in the future.
5. What are the **implications for *other* stakeholders** (e.g., individuals, organizations, and communities) besides those noted in Dimensions 1 and 2? The next thing you need to do is to consider the likely or potential consequences for additional key stakeholders. Again, if you provide the tickets, then the customer may expect such exchanges not only from you and your colleagues in the future but also from your competitors. You then earn the (bad) reputation in the market as the one who "bought business," didn't play fair, and caused grief for everyone.
6. Will your solution work in an ethical manner? Make a final assessment of whether your chosen solution will reduce or eliminate the causes determined in Dimension 2, and if yes then it will remedy the ethical problem defined in Dimension 1. If not, then repeat and refine the dimensions.

To conclude the chapter, reflect on what you learned. The intent was to get you off to a fast start by introducing some key concepts in your study and practice of business ethics, along with making the case for why ethical conduct is critical for businesses and you and your career.

As a reminder, the remainder of the book is organized into four sections. Section 1 is intended to help you build a business ethics foundation, introducing key concepts (e.g., social responsibility and sustainability) and developing a common language. Sections 2, 3, and 4 correspond to the individual-, organizational-, and societal-, or global-level influences on business ethics. Arranging the book according to levels assists you in organizing and applying your knowledge as you learn it. The rationale is that individuals work in organizations, and organizations operate in a larger global society, as such your business ethics learning can be thought of as a building process. First, a foundation (section 1), next the individual is added, then the organization, and finally society. These interdependent elements must be considered collectively to understand and effectively navigate the many business ethics challenges you will encounter in your career.

Chapter Summary

1. Morals, values, and norms are fundamental elements of business ethics. Understanding the differences between these concepts is foundational to your understanding and successful application of business ethics knowledge and tools.
2. Many situations are clearly right or wrong with clear, but not always easy, decisions. But ethical dilemmas have multiple difficult or unclear alternatives, which make dilemmas one of the most challenging ethical situations you will be confronted with in your career. The TV Test is a widely applicable and helpful tool for addressing not only dilemmas but challenging decisions more generally.

3. The vast majority of unethical conduct is not illegal, which means throughout your career rarely will the legal system be a remedy to unethical conduct at work.
4. Stakeholders are any entity (individual, group, or organization) that is affected by or can affect your business, and stakeholders' expectations are critically important to determining what is considered ethical conduct.
5. Your ethical conduct is invaluable to your job and career success for many reasons, and one of the most critical is that it influences your trustworthiness. Ethical conduct is essential for building trust, and unethical conduct is one of the surest ways of damaging trust, your reputation, and opportunities.
6. Both domestically and internationally, business is suffering a crisis of trust, as people's reported levels of trust in people doing various jobs and many institutions continue to be low. This means that individuals (e.g., you) may need to overcome low levels of trust customers and others may have for your employer and companies in your industry.
7. The 3-D PSE is a valuable and practical tool to use when solving ethical challenges in the workplace. The dimensions are Dimension 1—Define the ethical problem, Dimension 2—Determine the potential causes of the ethical problem, and Dimension 3—Describe potential solutions and consequences.

Key Terms

CASE STUDY: When Business, Safety, and the Government Collide, Ethics Get Complicated

The COVID-19 pandemic hit the meatpacking industry especially hard. Employees in those facilities have historically worked shoulder to shoulder in conditions that enabled the virus to spread easily, quickly, and widely. The health impact has been real, and nobody denies it. However, it seems that health officials and politicians at various levels (city, county, and state), along with company leaders, have been less than effective in their efforts and responsibilities to employees and the larger public.[36] Put differently, employers, politicians, and public health officials all play central roles in ensuring the safety of workers and the surrounding communities during pandemics. Critics, however, claim that their actions and inactions have endangered employees, their families, and members of the communities in which they work and live.

Close Early. Open Early?

Meat processing facilities were some of the first businesses closed in early 2020 due to COVID, but they were also some of the first to go back to work. Part of the impetus for the early return was President Trump declaring the industry as "essential," meaning they could not close. This decision was in part spurred by the ripple effects of closed meat processors.[37] Grocery stores were reporting shortages, which strained availability

Continued

and increased prices for consumers, and upstream, animals were accumulating on ranches and farms.

Of course, it is appropriate to assume that all of the stakeholders were interested in employee and community safety and health. But it also quickly became evident that this genuine concern was not enough. For instance, extensive testing, tracing, and reporting of infections among employees were essential elements to ensuring the safety of any facility as well as the surrounding community.

Who Is Responsible?

Health departments could have played a role in this, and they did to some degree, but they could only test employees if their employers allowed it. Health officials were also limited by politicians and pressured by company leaders in terms of reporting test results. Politicians didn't want their communities to be stigmatized as hot zones, and company leaders did not want any of their facilities to be labeled hotbeds of infection. Health officials, whatever their intentions, have no authority to force testing or force facilities to close.[38]

This scenario resulted in a lack of data, and that which were released were unreliable or viewed with great suspicion. For instance, in late April and early May, the Centers for Disease Control and Prevention reported that approximately 5,000 meatpacking employees tested positive across the industry. Yet, another report in the same space of time by the nonprofit Food & Environment Reporting Network estimated the number to be 17,000 with 66 deaths. Employees' anxiety and concerns were intensified by the occasional reports from individual facilities, such as a Tyson plant in Waterloo, Iowa, wherein 58 percent of its 730-person workforce tested positive. All of this was further exacerbated by the fact that employers are not required by law to test or report.[39]

Certainly, someone or some organization can compel or otherwise require testing and data sharing, after all, worker safety is a right—isn't it? The short answer is "yes." Among those with such authority and formal responsibility is the Occupational Health and Safety Administration (OSHA), and although the organization disseminated recommendations, OSHA leadership said they would not enforce them out of concern of being overly burdensome for companies during the pandemic.[40]

Consequences

A lack of transparency and unreliability in data is consequential for all parties, as accurate, timely, and appropriate data are needed to make all related decisions. Notably, all stakeholders seemingly need to know who is sick, who should work and not work, which facilities can be opened, which should be closed, as well as the potential health implications for employee's families and the communities in which they live. This seems obvious, but the actions and lack thereof of many of those involved seem to contradict this claim.

Discuss the business ethics implications using the "For Discussion" questions and instructions, then analyze the case using the 3-D PSE that follows.

For Discussion:

1. What morals do you think are evident in the case?
2. What ethical norms are being violated and by whom?
3. Describe the dilemmas confronting each of the following: meatpacking executives, health officials, local government officials (politicians), and employees.

4. From the perspective of executives at the meatpackers, which stakeholder(s) do they appear to view as primary? Secondary?
5. Which stakeholder(s) does it seem health officials treat as primary?
6. The TV Test. Assume you are the plant manager for a meatpacking facility, and you have been told to order your employees back to work. Now, assume you are on the evening news and asked to justify this action. What would you say?

Apply Three-Dimensional Problem-Solving for Ethics

You can apply the 3D PSE from multiple perspectives in this case—meatpacking executives and managers, health officials, politicians, employees, and other members of the communities. Just be sure to specify from whose perspective you are analyzing the case. For our purposes, let's analyze the case as if you were an executive and decision-maker at one of the major meatpackers, as any actions that are taken (or not) involve them. Of course, it would also be appropriate and interesting to analyze the case from the perspective of an employee, especially given that their workplaces were rivaled only by aged care homes as hotbeds for the coronavirus.

figure 1.5

Three-Dimensional Problem-Solving for Ethics (3D PSE)

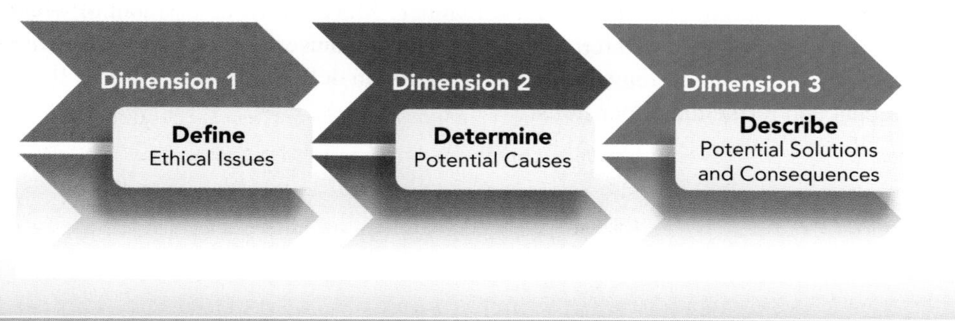

Dimension 1: *Define* the Ethical Challenge

What is the gap in the case?

a. What do executives have and what do they want? (Remember, use only details included within the case for your analysis.)
b. Why is the current situation a problem? What difficulties or undesirable behaviors and outcomes happen as a result of the problem you defined? From an executive's perspective, why would they care about the problem you defined in 1a?
c. Define your problem in one or at most two sentences and structure it in terms of what is current versus what is desired.
d. Who are the key stakeholders who affect or are affected by the problem you defined?

Dimension 2: *Determine* the Causes

a. **Individuals.** Given the problem you defined in Dimension 1, describe how individuals caused the problem. Individuals may not be causes, but you should consider whether there are any or not. If yes, then describe how they contributed to the problem.

b. **Contextual.** What behaviors, policies, and practices caused the problem defined in Dimension 1? These elements may be within the meatpackers or they may reside with other organizations or stakeholder groups.

Dimension 3: *Describe* Your Potential Solutions and the Intended and Unintended Consequences for Stakeholders

For each cause you identified in Dimension 2, answer the following questions:

a. From the perspective of a meatpacking executive, and then other stakeholders, ***what*** do you recommend they do, and ***how*** would you make it happen?
b. ***Why?*** Explain your motives.

If your responses to these questions are unsatisfactory, then go back to Dimension 1 and repeat the process. If, however, you are comfortable and confident in your problem-solving efforts thus far, then ensure you achieve the desired outcomes and avoid any unintended consequences.

c. Describe the ***desired and likely effects in the short- and long-term*** for the key stakeholders involved in the problem and causes (Dimensions 1 and 2)
d. What ***potential unintended consequences*** may occur with your proposed solution for each of the relevant stakeholders?
e. If any, what are the **implications for *other* stakeholders** (e.g., individuals, organizations, and communities) besides those noted in Dimensions 1 and 2?
f. Will your solution work in an ethical manner? Make a final assessment of whether your chosen solution will reduce or eliminate the causes determined in Dimension 2, and if yes then it will remedy the ethical problem defined in Dimension 1. If not, then repeat and refine the dimensions.

Part Opener Photo Source: ultramansk/Shutterstock

Chapter Opener Photo Source: EB Adventure Photography/Shutterstock

chapter 2

Laying a Foundation

Ethical Decision Making, Social Responsibility, Corporate Governance, Stakeholders and Activism, and Sustainability

Learning Objectives

AFTER READING THIS CHAPTER, YOU SHOULD BE ABLE TO

LO1 Articulate common ethical decision-making perspectives.

LO2 Explain what it means to be a socially responsible organization and individual.

LO3 Summarize how corporate governance and stakeholder activism influence business ethics.

LO4 Describe what it means to be sustainable.

WHERE DO **YOU** STAND?

What Are the Limits to Performance Enhancement?

Performing well makes us feel good about ourselves, causes others to view us more positively, and commonly results in more opportunities in various arenas of our lives. For instance, students who earn good grades in high school and score well on standardized tests (where required) typically have more options of colleges to attend. Students who perform well in college often have more rewarding and higher paying job opportunities, and once in the workforce, high performance generates still more attractive opportunities within the same organization or with other employers over time.

Since performance is so important, what are the limits to what you, as a student, will go to improve your performance? The obvious answer is to study, but others may cheat. Perhaps not you, but many surveys have shown that a large percentage of college students cheat to some extent or with some frequency.

But what about performance-enhancing drugs (PEDs)? Whether it is the Tour de France, the Olympic games, or a season of football, some amateur and professional competitors test positive for a banned substance. The primary reason such substances are banned is that those who use them gain an unfair advantage.

This scenario parallels the use of "study drugs" by college students. Ritalin, Concerta, Focalin, Vyvanse, and Adderall are brand names of some of the most common study drugs, which are forms of stimulants that affect neurotransmitters in the brain. They improve memory, concentration, alertness, attention, and motivation, and presumably performance.[1]

Many college students are prescribed these drugs by physicians for legitimate medical reasons—typically attention deficit hyperactivity disorder (ADHD) and less commonly for narcolepsy.[2] However, most students would benefit from increased memory, concentration, and alertness, and it therefore is no surprise that next to alcohol and pot, such stimulants are the most widely available and commonly used drugs among college students.[3]

Some studies show that less than a quarter of the students who take such drugs have a personal prescription. Although the use of these drugs is illegal, their widespread use and acceptance suggest that the perceptions of the users are not influenced by legality. Some argue that the casual attitudes—abundant and willing buyers and sellers—reflect that such forms of performance enhancement are accepted norms.

1. Assume you use study drugs without a legitimate medical reason; explain why you do this.
2. Assume that you and a number of your classmates were caught purchasing Adderall from a fellow student and that you need to explain this to your professors. Dean. Provost. Parents. What would you say (the TV Test)?
3. Assume you do not use and never have used study drugs. Explain why.
4. What is the difference between performance-enhancing drugs (PEDs) in sports and those used to boost academic performance? Don't PEDs provide an unfair advantage in both arenas? Explain.

Introduction

Chapter 2 is intended to complement chapter 1 and introduce additional key concepts related to the ethical conduct of individuals and organizations. The purpose is to equip you with some common language and foundational knowledge, as well as to give you a sense of how individuals and organizations (employees and employers) influence each other's ethical conduct.

We begin with an overview of how people make ethical decisions. This material originates in philosophy and has been applied more broadly to business. It is presented in a simple and applied fashion to give you enough detail to understand these approaches, which you can then use to describe and guide ethical decision making for yourself and others, including your employers. Then, we will answer the question: "What does it mean to be socially responsible?" Historically, academics and practitioners think and talk about social responsibility (SR) related to only organizations, but we can also apply SR to individuals.

Two other important influences on business ethics are corporate governance and stakeholder activism. As you'll learn, boards of directors typically have ultimate responsibility for the conduct of organizations and their leaders and thus have considerable importance and influence. Similarly, stakeholders help determine or even pressure ethical conduct in a host of ways.

Common Ethical Decision-Making Perspectives

Ethical issues surround us, and as we already established, it is tough to simply say, "Be a good person," as life is more complex and challenging, especially at work. However, volumes of research and practical experience can help you understand and guide your ethical conduct throughout your career. In this section, we highlight several fundamental ways to describe ethical conduct and decision making, specifically focusing on the ends, the means, and personal traits. We then conclude the section with a discussion of ethical relativism.

consequentialism (teleological) ethics uses the outcomes or results of an individual's, group's, or organization's actions to determine the ethicality (right vs. wrong)

It's All about the Consequences (Teleological Ethics)

Teleos, a Greek word, means "ends," therefore **consequentialism (teleological) ethics** uses the outcomes or results of an individual's, group's, or organization's actions to determine the ethicality (right vs. wrong). Put differently, whether a decision is right or wrong depends entirely on the outcome of that decision.[4] There are multiple approaches within consequentialism.

Utilitarianism. A common version of this form of consequentialism (teleology) ethics is **utilitarianism**, and it applies when the motive is the greatest good for the greatest number. Philosophers Jeremy Bentham and John Stuart Mill (in the 1700s and 1800s) are often credited with this approach to ethics; they argued that the benefits of the many should be served, not just benefits to the ruling or powerful few.[5] For business ethics and our purposes, this means that consideration of a greater number of stakeholders and the effects of actions over time are more likely when individuals and organizations use a utilitarian approach to business ethics. This is illustrated by Dan Price, CEO of credit card payment processing company Gravity Payments in the following Ethics in Action box.

utilitarianism applies when the motive is the greatest good for the greatest number

More generally, utilitarianism occurs when individuals and organizations emphasize benefits to others or the team over personal gain or benefits to the powerful. This also occurs when cost–benefit analyses and the resulting decisions favor the many rather than the few.

However, a utilitarian approach can present truly challenging ethical dilemmas for managers, for instance, when they need to reduce head count. During a pandemic and most other economic downturns, revenues and profits decline and job cuts are made. But it is little comfort for a manager or owner to say, "We need to terminate 50 percent of you to save the other 50 percent." Or, when your employer, the one you selected instead of another due to the perceived opportunities for professional development, says, "Times are tough, and we therefore are cutting tuition reimbursement and our leadership development program."

It is important to point out, however, that sometimes decisions with undesirable outcomes for some prevent undesirable outcomes for the many or for everyone. Cutting some jobs can save all jobs if not eliminating some would cause the entire company to fold. Moreover, many government policy decisions are indeed focused on providing some benefits to the greatest number.

Ethics in Action

A Rising Tide…

Gravity Payments CEO, Dan Price, famously cut his own compensation to ensure all employees at his company made at least $70,000 per year. Instead of earning $1.1 million, he also makes $70,000. His action resulted in 70 of his 120 employees getting a raise. For 30 employees, their pay doubled! He was motivated by a desire to do his part to reduce income inequality and the belief, gained from some research he read, that $70,000 is a living wage and improves people's quality of life.[6]

Price's actions were not without criticism. He was told by a competitor that if he followed the compensation practices of most other tech companies, he would soon be a billionaire. And as a billionaire, Price could do even more good. Price reflected on this in an interview and said, "He's telling me that the world needs another billionaire philanthropist, and I just don't know if that's the case. Because we've been relying on billionaire philanthropists for so long, and I don't really think that's working out very well for us."[7]

egoists
make ethical decisions based on their personal preferences and what serves their self-interests

Egoism. **Egoists** make ethical decisions based on their personal preferences and what serves their self-interests.[8] As such, egoism is an extreme and individualistic form of consequentialism or teleological ethics. Put another way, you are an egoist if you reason that whatever course of action benefits you is right, and any course of action that conflicts with your interests is wrong, or at least worse. This approach may seem a little black and white or overly simplistic to you, but it has been the basis of economic and behavioral theory and reasoning for nearly one hundred years.

More bluntly, we are self-interested because we are human, and all else equal, you would choose the job with the higher pay over the one that pays less. And when confronted with an ethical dilemma, when push comes to shove, people will often choose what they think benefits them the most.

Adam Smith, the famous Scottish philosopher and capitalist of the 1700s, argued that the pursuit of self-interest is not only satisfying for the individual but that it ultimately benefits the larger society. The rationale is that if an individual or an organization does not strive for their self-interests, they will not generate resources and opportunities for others, such as growth, jobs, and higher wages.[9]

As an example, a large proportion of CEO compensation is commonly tied to company stock. Therefore, many of their goals and actions aim to boost the stock price and thus their compensation. Many argue that the Great Recession, for instance, was in large part a consequence of how people from the top to the bottom of financial organizations were rewarded.

Mortgage brokers and providers sold more mortgages to home buyers, and investment firms on Wall Street packaged these mortgages into investment products that were in turn sold to investors. They all got paid and were often paid well. The rewards were so extreme that the cycle became self-reinforcing. Mortgage brokers did what was necessary to finance more homes (e.g., loosened buyer qualifications), and Wall Street firms created new and more sophisticated packages of mortgages to attract more investors, not just in the United States but around the world. This was rational. This was egoism on a grand scale.

But then it all stopped. Housing prices fell, homeowners defaulted, and all those who had invested in the mortgage-backed products saw the values plummet. This affected homeowners, banks, mortgage companies, and Wall Street firms and their many investors.

Let's be clear. You need to advocate for your personal interests in every job you'll ever have; this is necessary to create and realize opportunities. This is smart and expected, but ethical challenges arise when you pursue your own interests always, without appropriate regard for others. For instance, if you use your power as the boss to tear down another to advance yourself, then you're likely taking egoism too far. Egoistic people often become highly political and will scheme and betray others to serve their own interests.

photo.ua/Shutterstock

Often the more ethical and sustainable approach is to carefully consider the relevant stakeholders and the possible courses of actions and associated consequences and then pursue a reasonable course and outcome. This is exactly one of the intended applications for the Three-Dimensional Problem-Solving for Ethics (3D PSE) introduced in chapter 1.

A couple of phrases you need to beware of are:

"So what, we got a good outcome!"
"It doesn't matter so long as I get paid."

Bottom line: You are well served to be mindful of the consequences of your actions for a wide array of stakeholders, for better and for worse.

Another foundational approach to ethics focuses on the means to the ends (e.g., rules and duties) rather than the ends or outcomes.

Your Motives and Deontological Ethics

Deontologists make ethical decisions based on moral principles of what is right and wrong, and they give primary attention to the intentions or motives of their actions rather than the consequences.[10] "Deon" means duty in Greek, and deontological ethics is closely associated with Immanuel Kant, an eighteenth-century German philosopher. Deontologists believe that some basic principles should be followed in all situations, regardless of the outcome.[11]

deontologists make ethical decisions based on moral principles of what is right and wrong, and they give primary attention to the intentions or motives of their actions rather than the consequences

Universalism. Central to deontological ethics is the concept of **universalism**, which occurs when you follow particular ethical codes or rules in all situations and with all stakeholders, regardless of the consequences. Notable examples are:

universalism occurs when you follow particular ethical codes or rules in all situations and with all stakeholders, regardless of the consequences

- Don't lie
- Don't cheat
- Don't steal
- Don't say anything about someone you wouldn't say to their face.

Applying these codes to business ethics, you might think it is essential to treat everyone with respect and dignity. These ethical codes or rules are reflected in basic human rights, arguments related to equality, as well as many of the world's religions.

Such universal standards are easy to admire, but they are difficult to implement as they are absolute, unwavering, and inflexible. Don't lie. But what if it would save a life? In crisis situations, pilots, medical professionals, and soldiers literally make life-or-death decisions. Do they need to be completely honest without exception? Can individuals in these roles always be compassionate? Could they save or spare every life?

In practice, both individuals and organizations have difficulties following universalism and thus deontological ethics in the work context. Doing so would result in everyone following their own employer's or own country's values and norms everywhere, with everyone, without exception.

At first glance, following deontological ethics seems to be a good idea, but when you get into the implications of implementation it is difficult. Let's make this more applicable by exploring a test, which will help you determine the circumstances where you can reasonably follow universalism and where you cannot. This is done by considering categorical imperatives, a test that can be applied to all situations.

Categorical Imperative and the Golden Rule. **Categorical imperative (CI)** is a rule that applies in all situations regardless of consequence.[12] CIs are ways to test if a particular principle is universal or not. Let's consider "honesty." Most people would agree that honesty is something we should practice—it is universal, a categorical imperative. However, you likely can quickly think of exceptions. Would you tell someone the truth if it would hurt their feelings? Would you tell your friend you think they are unqualified just before they go to a job interview? Would you tell your coworker they are ugly and everyone thinks so? Although this may sound trite or even ridiculous, the point is that there are exceptions. If there are reasonable and real exceptions, then it is not a categorical imperative, and thus not truly universal.

categorical imperative (CI) a rule that applies in all situations regardless of consequence

A quick way to determine if a particular value or principle can be universally applied at work is to ask yourself, "If everyone did X in this situation, would the company be a better off?" If the answer is yes, then it is right according to deontologic ethics, and if the answer is no, then X is wrong.

More generally, despite the potential practical challenges, you, your manager, and the corporate policies and practices or your employers can all uphold some basic standards or categorical imperatives of fairness, kindness, and respect. Put differently, it is difficult to think of situations at work in which individuals and stakeholder groups should not be treated with fairness, kindness, and respect. Can you think of any situation in which you didn't deserve all three?

And if you personally are ever in a tough spot or are confronted with an uncomfortable ethical situation involving another individual, remember the **Golden Rule**—assume the roles are reversed and treat that person as you would like to be treated by them. This won't solve every challenging situation, but it will solve many.

Golden Rule assume the roles are reversed and treat that person as you would like to be treated by them

Virtue Ethics

virtues qualities of an individual that define one's moral character, or "goodness," and are positive contributors to society

virtue ethics focuses on the personal qualities of the individual, rather than the rules followed or resulting outcomes

Virtues are qualities of an individual that define one's moral character, or "goodness," and are positively impact society. **Virtue ethics** focuses on the personal qualities of the individual, rather than the rules followed or resulting outcomes. For instance, a virtuous person is honest and fair (two virtues that are common across cultures), because she or he believes this is what makes a person good. Not because it is expected by others, or because it will generate personal advantage or benefit. The origin of this approach is often attributed to Aristotle, who was interested in understanding the intentions and motivations of good people.[13] He claimed that adopting, embracing, and habitually enacting virtues is what causes people to achieve the ultimate level of happiness and goodness.[14]

So what are common business virtues? Researchers have explored this since the 1990s, and one influential early study identified 45 virtues! More recent work refined the original large number into three broad categories comprising a number of virtues, which are illustrated in table 2.1.

table **2.1**

Business Virtues

Business Virtue	Brief Definition
1. Justice	Deal with people fairly
2. Integrity	Be true to yourself
3. Honor	Be true and hold your head high
4. Articulate	Express yourself clearly
5. Cooperative	Effectively work with others
6. Tolerant	Endure difficulties and differences
7. Autonomy	Make decisions for one's self and establish an identity
8. Cool-headed	Maintain composure
9. Determined	Persist through challenges
10. Entrepreneurial	Take initiative and risk
11. Passion	Evident enthusiasm for something
12. Style	Correctness and clarity of speech
13. Saintliness	Seek excellence of personal character

Source: Created from D. Dawson, "Measuring Individual's Virtues in Business," *Journal of Business Ethics* 2018, 147: 793–805.

On the surface, this may sound quite abstract or at least different, but a virtuous approach to ethics is common and can indeed be quite practical.

A person who takes a virtuous approach to business ethics asks, "What type of person do I want to be?" rather than "What should I do?" (deontological ethics) or "What will produce the most desirable outcome?" (teleological ethics). This approach to business ethics thus focuses on the individual, who by living their positive traits (virtues) consistently and habitually influences others to do the same. (You'll learn more about influencing others through virtuous leadership in chapter 7.)

Real-world examples abound. Religions and professional or trade organizations often have codes of conduct (chapter 9) and values (chapter 8) that guide the behavior of their members. Both of these often represent the virtues of the organization, which are the collection of virtues of the employees. For instance, the Reiter Affiliated Companies, based in Oxnard, California, have existed since 1968 and are known for growing some of the finest berries in the world (strawberries, blueberries, raspberries, and blackberries). They have a long and strong history of sustainable and organic farming, along with a deep-seated commitment to treating their stakeholders according to three virtues—honesty, fairness, and respect.[15] The founding family created and continues to pursue the mission:

> *"Relentless pursuit to delight our consumers and enrich our employees and communities."*

The company's giving is intended to improve the health and well-being of its farmers, their families, and the communities in which they live. They have and continue to base their success on the well-being of multigenerational employees and partners, not just the founding family.[16]

Virtuous people are motivated by the desire and commitment to being a good person, rather than conforming to the expectations of a particular situation or organization, or the rewards and recognition received in return.

Now that you have a sense of the three pillars of classical approaches to ethics, and their application to business, we turn our attention to something completely different—relativism. This approach, rather than applying the same ethical standards in all situations, or pursuing good for the sake of goodness, describes how the appropriate conduct can and should change, depending on the situation. In other words, ethics are relative.

Relativism

Relativism means that ethical conduct is dependent on the norms of the context; thus changing contexts may change what is considered ethical too.[17] If a behavior matches what is considered normal or typical in that particular group, company, or country, then it is ethical. Part of the issue with the relativistic approach is that there are no universals. If, for instance, your job requires you to work in a country where it is the norm to oppress women or other members of the population, then from a relativistic perspective, it would be appropriate for you to do the same. If confronted with such a situation, you might say, "I object, and I'm not going." Okay, and you might even keep your job. But, you would still be working for a company that does business in places and with people that do oppress women. Is this better? Such conflicts or dilemmas are common with a relativistic approach to business ethics.

relativistic approach ethical conduct dependent on the norms of the context; thus changing contexts may change what is considered ethical

More generally, unethical, or at least questionable, behavior can become a norm and cause otherwise well-intentioned and ethical employees to do the wrong thing. You'll learn much more about this in chapter 8 on ethical business cultures, but relativism is one way to explain the downfall of Enron and its accounting firm Arthur Andersen.

Koy_Hipster/Shutterstock

Arthur Andersen was one of the world's premier accounting and consulting firms. Its clients included a laundry list of the largest companies in the United States and around the world, one of which was Enron, an innovative and fast-growing energy supplier and trader in the 1990s. Along with its impressive innovations, Enron was guilty of inflating revenues, hiding expenses, and misleading numerous stakeholders. For its part, Arthur Andersen helped the company make these activities appear above board—legitimate. Once the truth was unveiled about Enron, so too was the scope of Arthur Andersen's role. Making matters worse, it was ultimately discovered that Arthur Andersen systematically destroyed documents in an attempt to hide their misconduct.[18]

In terms of relativism, Enron and Arthur Andersen showed how unethical conduct can appear appropriate if the norms of the context support it. Put differently, between them, the two companies employed nearly 100,000 employees, and although there were some bad apples in the bunch who knowingly did the wrong thing, nearly all of these people were upstanding professionals, devoted to their careers and their employers. It was the conduct of their previously highly regarded employers that legitimized the conduct that ultimately caused their demise.

Relativism also occurs across national borders. The classic expression "When in Rome, do as the Romans do" captures cultural relativism. But this idea is a double-edged ethical sword. If your country's ethical standards are more inclusive and considerate, and you uphold those in a host country, then most will think you are taking the higher ground and more ethical path. However, it can cost you business if the ethical norms in a host country include side payments in the form of cash or other favors, like jobs for those involved in the decision.

Another example is the differing views in preferential hiring of relatives or friends, called nepotism,[19] in Spain and the United States. Although preference for family and friends definitely influences many hiring decisions, laws prohibit many such hires in the U.S. And even when not illegal, it is often frowned upon as the family member is perceived as unfairly favored (e.g., less qualified). In contrast, the Spanish routinely hire family, and are expected to take care of family, including securing them employment even when they may not necessarily be the more qualified candidate. This practice is supported not only by tradition (norms) but also with the belief that hiring family builds employee loyalty. Generations will

For Discussion

1. Why do you think that thousands of employees at large companies (e.g., Enron and Arthur Andersen) engage in unethical conduct on a daily basis, yet they don't think it is unethical?
2. What would you be inclined to do if you found yourself in such a situation?
3. Assume you worked for Arthur Andersen as a consultant on the Enron account during this period, and now you are interviewing for a job. The interviewer notices this part of your history and asks you, "I see you worked at Arthur Andersen, did you work on the Enron account?" How would you respond?

look out for each other, be committed to the employer while being committed to each other, and be less likely to leave for another employer.[20]

Moreover, relativistic organizations most often simply comply with legal standards, and as you learned, being legal doesn't mean it is ethical. This is one reason why many companies have been criticized for outsourcing manufacturing and services to other countries with lower standards in terms of environmental regulations, employee rights, and working conditions—the infamous sweatshops and low-wage work many US-based companies have taken advantage of when sourcing work to China, Southeast Asia, Africa, and Latin America.

Combining the material in chapter 1 with this first portion of chapter 2, you have a good start at understanding and applying some fundamental business ethics concepts. We'll continue building this foundation with SR next.

The Socially Responsible Organization and Individual

The previous sections explained some fundamental and different approaches to the business ethics of individuals. But as we explained in chapter 1, the ethical conduct of individuals is influenced by the organizations in which they work. We therefore explore a fundamental and popular business ethics concept commonly associated with organizations—SR. However, in this book, we expand this notion to also include individuals. **Social responsibility (SR)** is an individual's or organization's obligation to maximize the positive impact and minimize the negative impact on stakeholders. Notice that we also define this concept in terms of both individuals and organizations, as in today's world, we expect both to be socially responsible. Frankly, you expect the same from individuals and organizations with whom you interact and have relationships, and when viewed this way, SR makes perfect sense.

social responsibility (SR)
individual's or organization's obligation to maximize the positive impact and minimize the negative impact on stakeholders

Corporate Social Responsibility

Corporate social responsibility (CSR) is social responsibility at the organizational level and is commonly described in terms of the multiple levels of responsibilities shown in Figure 2.1.

figure **2.1**

Levels of Social Responsibility

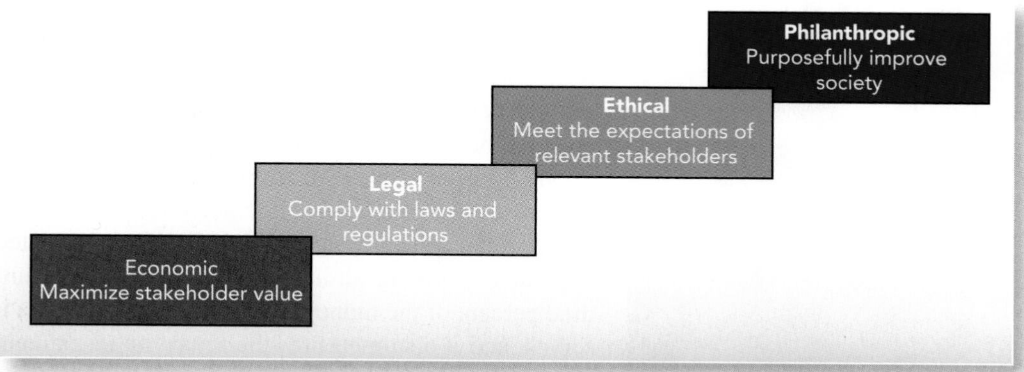

Source: Adapted from A. Carroll, "The Pyramid of Corporate Social Responsibility: Toward the Moral Management of Organizational Stakeholders," Business Horizons, July-August, 1991: 41.

Most organizations need to make money to survive; therefore, making a sufficient profit from its products and services is the most basic economic responsibility. Quite simply, if a business doesn't achieve sufficient profit, then it ceases to exist and business ethics are no longer relevant. Issues of business ethics, therefore, concern how profits are made, the impact of making profit, and perhaps how much profit is made. Economic responsibility needs to be achieved *legally*, enough said. *Ethical* responsibilities we have already defined and will address throughout the book. *Philanthropic* responsibilities are those that are not required for the survival of the business but contribute to the well-being and betterment of individuals, organizations, and society. Environmental and social justice issues are common examples of philanthropic responsibility and are studied in chapters 12 and 13.

Individual Social Responsibility

Although business ethics books do not typically apply SR to individuals, it is necessary to show students and clients how to fulfill these same responsibilities as individuals. Here's how.

Economic responsibility is your need to earn enough income to support your lifestyle—money for your rent or mortgage, car payment, food, student loans, other basic needs, and, of course, for clothes, entertainment, and perhaps health insurance. Many people like you, of course, want to do more than meet their basic needs, and some even want a luxurious lifestyle and cool toys. This is fine, but the issue is how you pursue your own economic interests, beginning with the legality of your actions. Plainly and simply, earn your money legally! To meet *legal responsibility*, don't break the law or violate rules and regulations when doing your job. The next Ethics in Action box provides an interesting dilemma that tested the SR of many people.

Ethical responsibility often concerns how you meet your economic responsibilities. Do you cheat, steal, or undermine others? Are you a bully? These are problematic issues and easy to understand, but what is more challenging is identifying all the relevant stakeholders, both primary and secondary, for a given situation. Understand, consider, and attempt to meet their expectations related to ethical conduct.

impact philanthropy requires strategic partnerships involving action planning, measurable outcomes, and accountability

Finally, do you volunteer your time or donate money to a particular cause or organization? These are obvious and common forms of *philanthropy*. For some people, these actions generate more satisfaction and passion than their jobs. Although individual-level giving is indeed valuable, many organizations have this program as their mission; the Gates Foundation, the world's largest philanthropy (greater than $40 billion in resources), was launched in 2000 with the mission to improve healthcare and reduce poverty around the globe. It is now the full-time focus of both Melinda and Bill, who stepped down from the Microsoft board of directors in 2020.[23] It also has an open access policy, wherein any data collected by the organization is shared with others who may benefit. It has helped revolutionize philanthropy into a more contemporary form—**impact philanthropy**, which requires strategic partnerships involving action planning, measurable outcomes, and accountability.[24] This differs from giving for giving's sake or simply writing a check.

Hung Chung Chih/Shutterstock

Pencils of Promise is a "for purpose" (rather than a nonprofit) charity that adopted a business-oriented approach to giving similar to the Gates'. One hundred percent of the money donated is spent on those it serves, and it also measures the return on investment (ROI) of every dollar spent and ensures appropriate allocation and execution. The mission has helped to

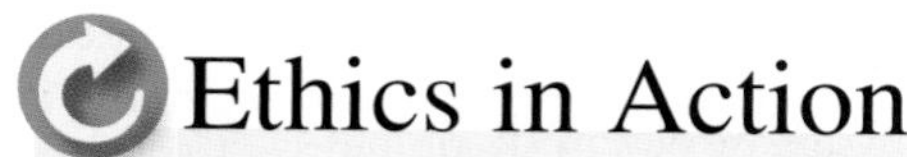

Ethics in Action

A Pay Raise for Not Working? I'll Take It!

What if you were given a choice: be laid off and actually earn the same or more money than when you worked, or change the shift you work and make the same as before? The answer may be obvious or easy. But before you answer, read the following real-world scenario.

The government took many steps to lessen the effects for many employees laid off due to COVID-19. One such action was the paycheck protection program (PPP). In addition to the weekly unemployment insurance check, this program gave unemployed workers an extra $600 per week for several months. This is not the issue. The issue is that some percentage of these same employees had a choice of whether they wanted to be laid off or not, as they worked for companies that only reduced the number of shifts and didn't shut down completely. This subset of employees had a choice: switch to another shift or be laid off.

Many (i.e., likely thousands) employees in this situation actually earned the same or more by not working. Here's how that worked. Assume you earned $600 per week in your job. PPP pays $600, which means regardless of the amount of your unemployment insurance check, you can make the same amount of money by not working. But all of these people were also getting unemployment insurance (average of $378 per week in the spring of 2020[21]). If you do the math, then from a purely economic perspective, if you made $978 or less per week (the median in the United States in 2019 was $936[22]), then you would make the same or more money taking the layoff.

For Discussion:

1. If given the choice and the scenario above, then what would you do? Justify.
2. Now assume you are married, and your spouse remained employed through all of this. This means your bills would still be paid. How does this affect your decision? Explain.

educate children in developing countries, and to this end, it not only helps build schools, but it also helps operate them afterward. As for pencils and pens, the organization has distributed thousands to children in over fifty countries.[25]

The key to meaningful philanthropy, for you as an individual, is to give serious consideration as to where and how to invest your resources of time, money, and expertise—who will benefit. Start with an individual's or organization's needs. Then, assess them to see if who they are and what they do is consistent with your own values, and ensure that they also follow the law and conduct themselves in ethical ways. Perhaps they too are philanthropic and worthy of your donation.

With the various forms or levels of social responsibility in mind, it is time to learn about important influences on the operation of an organization.

The Influence of Corporate Governance and Stakeholder Activism on Business Ethics

So far in this chapter, you've learned there are multiple approaches to making ethical business decisions. You also now know something about what it means to be a socially responsible individual and organization. To further develop your knowledge of business ethics and skills, we next explore boards of directors and their role in overseeing these responsibilities and conduct of organizations.

Corporate Governance

corporate governance the system of rules, practices, and processes by which organizations are managed

boards of directors collections of individuals who have ultimate responsibility for an organization's policies, practices, and performance

Corporate governance describes the system of rules, practices, and processes by which organizations are managed.[26] These responsibilities are typically shared by the top management team and the board of directors. **Boards of directors** are collections of individuals who have ultimate responsibility for an organization's policies, practices, and performance. They are required to act in the interests of the organization and oversee its resources (e.g., human, intellectual, physical, and financial) and many important elements of organizational functions, such as

- Executive compensation
- Executive succession
- Compliance with regulations
- Strategy
- Financial performance (profitability, share price, market share)

shareholder model of governance directors and their governance actions are primarily intended to ensure that top management's actions boost the stock price for shareholders

For many years, businesses, in general, have been criticized for an excessively narrow focus on shareholders, referred to as the **shareholder model of governance**, and this blame is appropriately shared by directors. Directors and their governance actions are primarily intended to ensure that the top management team's actions boost the stock price for shareholders (or value to the owners of private companies). Many scandals in the past decades are, at least in part, attributed to a shareholder model of governance. Laws are a common way society has responded to some of the major scandals, and they often attempt to hold board members personally accountable for the misconduct of the organizations they oversee and the executives who manage them. Some of these laws and regulations are covered in chapter 9.

stakeholder model of governance considers the interests of a broad range of stakeholders both inside and outside the company

In contrast, boards of directors who apply a **stakeholder model of governance** consider the interests of a broad range of stakeholders both inside and outside the company. A fundamental challenge for directors using this model is to determine which stakeholders are primary at a given point in time and thus receive the major focus of the organization's

Ethics in Action

Business Is More than Just Shareholders, Customers, and Employees

The "buy one, give one" business model provides an excellent example of how a growing number of companies are embracing the stakeholder model. Made popular by Blake Mycoskie, founder of TOMS Shoes, companies applying this approach donate one product to people in need for every unit purchased by a customer. For instance, TOMS has donated over 86 million pairs of shoes since its inception and has expanded its offerings to eyeglasses and safe drinking water.[27]

David Heath and Randy Goldberg, cofounders of Bombas, have taken the same approach with socks. They learned that socks were the most sought-after item by the homeless, and what started as a charitable endeavor is now a thriving enterprise—profitable every year since it began. Bombas leadership is also keenly focused on the customer, and the company is intensely dedicated to producing a high-quality, comfortable product. Employees seemingly also love the company, given that only seven people have quit in the first 6.5 years.[28]

resources. The previous Ethics in Action box about the "buy one, give one" business model illustrates the stakeholder approach to governance selected by the founders and leaders of TOMS and Bombas.

Table 2.2 lists numerous companies recognized for giving back and utilizing a broad stakeholder approach. Besides learning about how the companies make their impact, consider if you might like to work for any of them. They could be potential job targets for you, or at least they may give you some practices to look for in companies with whom you interview.

table 2.2

Companies that Care about Stakeholders[29]

Organization	Line of Business	Why named to list/qualifications
Salesforce	Software, customer relationship management	Matches employee charitable giving up to $5,000 and its' Vetforce program offers new skills training, career coaching, and mentoring.
Ultimate Software	HR and Payroll Technology	UltiVETS program helps renovate military veterans' homes and three paid volunteer days annually for employees. Values diversity through various employee "communities of interest." For example, PRIDEUS group formed for LGBTQIA staffers and allies.
Adobe	Software	Create Change Program encourages charitable giving by donating $250 to charity for every 10 employee volunteer hours. Girls Who Code Teaches underserved girls coding and pairs them with a mentor.
Pricewater-houseCoopers	Audit, tax, and consulting	"Check Your Blind Spots" video leadership series by CEO Tim Ryan. Access Your Potential partners' employees and partner organizations with underserved students to teach tech and money skills (128,000 hours helping kids with STEM).
Patagonia	Clothing	Environmental Internship Program provides full pay and benefits for up to two months to an employee who is interning full-time with a nonprofit environmental group of his or her choice. For more than thirty years has donated 1 percent of its sales to grants that preserve and restore the environment, with employees playing a huge role in deciding where the money is given.
USAA	Insurance, banking, investments	Prioritizes giving jobs to vets and family members (over 13,000 hired since 2006). Created the Military Spouse Economic Empowerment Zones (MSSEEZ) program to provide military spouses with employment and career help.
Workday	Information technology	Aspires to create an inclusive and diverse workplace. "Employee Belonging Councils," created by staffers, include Women@Workday to support women, Workday Pride to promote respect for LGBTQ communities, and The Talented Tenth to inspire African Americans about software technology careers.
NuStar Energy	Independent liquids terminal and pipeline operator	Gives each employee 50 hours off a year to volunteer (98,000 hours in 2017 alone) and 100 percent employees donated to United Way (average contribution, $2,148. Hosts Four-Legged Friends Fairs for employees to adopt rescue animals.
SAP America, Inc.	Software	Autism at Work program, in twelve countries, assists people with autism spectrum disorder to enter its workforce (employs over 140 people with the condition). Raises money for autism research.

Stakeholder activism is another way in which the ethical policies, practices, and conduct of organizations are shaped. This is discussed next.

Stakeholder Activism

stakeholder activism (in)actions to influence the leaders of an organization to change its strategies, policies, and practices

Stakeholder activism describes (in)actions to influence the leaders of an organization to change its strategies, policies, and practices. The most common and well-known form is shareholder activism, wherein investors attempt to influence a company's leadership by actually buying or selling its stock or threatening to do so. Activist investors commonly own a significant percentage of the total stock of a company, and this gives them particular rights, such as seats on the board of directors who oversee and help determine an organization's actions. Shareholder activists commonly seek to do one or more of the following:[30]

1. Corporate governance. Influence the organization's strategies, such as where to grow and how to grow.
2. Company mergers, acquisitions, and sales. Influence whether underperforming divisions are spun-off (sold), as doing this gives the activist an improved stock price in the original company, as well as stock in the new or spun-off company. They may also attempt to persuade the company to acquire a competitor.
3. Boost efficiency and profitability. Shareholder activists first, if not foremost or only, are interested in making more money. They, therefore, will typically encourage cost cutting and focus on products and services with higher margins.
4. Spend the company's money. Some companies generate and hold piles of cash. Apple, for instance, had approximately $200 billion on its balance sheet in the first half of 2020![31] Activist investors often seek to get companies to spend this money on acquisitions to boost future performance, or to pay it to shareholders in the form of dividends.

You may have heard of Carl Icahn or Bill Ackman, two legendary shareholder activists. Among Icahn's investment activities are Trans World Airlines (TWA), Take-Two Interactive (video games), Motorola, BEA Systems, and, more recently, Lyft, Xerox, Pep Boys, and Hertz.[32] Bill Ackman has established himself as someone company leaders, boards, and investors should listen to. He made billions betting against financial institutions in the financial crisis, but he also lost more than $1 billion in his campaign to tear down Herbalife, claiming it to be a pyramid scheme. Herbalife's stock recovered, and Ackman has since made piles of other money as an activist investor in Chipotle Mexican Grill and Starbucks, among others.[33]

Numerous other stakeholders act to influence other individuals and organizations. Consumer activism, for instance, occurs when customers either actively purchase or actively withhold purchases of an organization's products or services. To illustrate, in 2018, Nike selected Colin Kaepernick, former NFL quarterback, as a brand ambassador to signal support for his protest against police brutality of African Americans. Consumers did both, increased purchases in support and boycotted purchases in disapproval.

Boycotts also are a part of American history, as they were one impetus for the Revolutionary War. Colonists boycotted British tea in efforts to change what they perceived as unfair taxation (without representation). The colonists' efforts escalated when they dumped tea into the Boston Harbor.[34]

Employees have also become considerably more assertive in their efforts to influence their employers in recent years. A survey by public relations firm Weber Shandwick revealed that nearly 40 percent of the employees who responded spoke either for or against "their employers' actions over a controversial issue that affects society."[35] Table 2.3 outlines the activism of other stakeholders.

In the next section, you'll learn about the importance of considering the implications of conduct, policies, and practices over time, and how the element of time is foundational

table 2.3

Examples of Stakeholder Activism

Stakeholder	Targets of Activism	Motivation for Activism	Description
Customers[36]	SoulCycle, Equinox, Home Depot, and L. L. Bean	Corporate ties to government figures who support policies affecting migration, the environment, and other issues	Boycotted products
Students in Hong Kong[37]	Chinese government	Extradition policies that would send citizens to Mainland China for prosecution	Boycotted first day of school
Employees[38]	Google's senior leadership	Contract with the Department of Defense to use the company's technology in war drones	Employee petition, protests on social media, and resignations
Nongovernmental organizations (e.g., National Center for Public Policy Research—think tank who promotes conservative political policies)[39]	Levi Strauss' senior leadership	Company's anti-gun policies	Research presented at shareholder meeting showing that the anti-gun position could hurt sales

to sustainable business ethics at all levels—individual, group and organizational, country, and societal.

What It Means to Be Sustainable

Sustainability is meeting current needs without compromising the ability of individuals and organizations to meet their future needs.[40] Again, sustainability is purposefully defined in terms of both individuals and organizations to reinforce the importance of personal and organizational responsibility. The other critical aspect of the definition is time, ensuring that actions today do not foreclose or limit opportunities tomorrow.

sustainability
meeting current needs without compromising the ability of individuals and organizations to meet their future needs

The Relationship between Sustainability, Social Responsibility, and Business Ethics

The terms sustainability, social responsibility (SR), and ethics are not synonymous. Consider ethics as an example. Ethics are contextual, meaning they depend on the norms or expectations of the people in a given situation, place, or organization. US auto manufacturers moved a significant portion of their production to Mexico, motivated by lower labor costs (allowing for more hours worked and less pay) and softer environmental regulations (pollution). The trend is a long and strong one, as evidenced by a nearly 10 percent increase between 2018 and 2019 alone, and nearly a 100 percent increase since 2011. One could argue that the auto companies were ethical or even socially responsible because they complied with Mexican labor and environmental standards. However, it would be difficult to make the case that this conduct was sustainable, as it likely compromised the environment if not also worker well-being (long hours, little time off, and poor wages). This story is not just about the US auto companies. Since 2011, Toyota and Honda have increased their Mexico production by 263 and 611 percent, respectively![41] The motives are the same, and so too are the implications for sustainability.

An additional way to help you differentiate sustainability, business ethics, and SR is to consider the effects of decisions, policies, and practices over time.

Ethics in Action

The (Un)Sustainability of Private Equity

Companies need money to compete, survive, and grow. One way to get money is to go public and sell small pieces or shares of ownership in the form of stock traded on public exchanges (e.g., the New York Stock Exchange—NYSE). Think of this as public equity. Another way is to sell the company to a private equity (PE) owner who effectively buys all of the stock.

In this scenario, it is common for the PE firm to put in a relatively small amount of its own money, borrow the rest, and then use it to purchase the target company; but there is a catch. The PE firm borrows the money, but the acquired company must pay it back—it is responsible for the debt used to purchase it. Among additional benefits, the PE firm gets seats on the board of directors and thus can influence strategy and operations, and it can also collect dividend-type fees from the acquired company. Then, the ultimate goal for most PE acquisitions is to take the company public and make a profit on its investment. All of this means that PE firms make a great deal of money in acquiring companies, and they do so with relatively little risk. But in the process, the companies they acquire can be financially handicapped.

J. Crew and Neiman Marcus are two retailers who were acquired by PE firms. They needed the funds to make the changes necessary to compete in today's fast-changing, intensely competitive retail sector. However, those large sums of borrowed money and the fees paid to the PE firms were very expensive and difficult to cover. And, like individuals, if a company can't pay its bills, then it often declares bankruptcy. This is what happened to J. Crew and Neiman Marcus. They owed $1.7 billion and $5 billion, respectively, and when sales went to near zero due to the COVID-19 pandemic, they had no means to make payments on their debt and filed for bankruptcy.

Many experts blame PE firms for these failures, and not just the retailers themselves. One expert said, "Much of the difficulty that the retail sector is experiencing has been aggravated by private equity involvement." The companies borrowed piles of money that would have been difficult to pay back even if they executed their business plans effectively. As further evidence, "10 out of the (largest) 14 retail bankruptcies since 2012 involved companies that private equity firms had acquired." Moreover, opponents argue that the amount of debt and the associated fees charged by PE firms makes it highly unlikely that companies can succeed.

For Discussion:

1. Describe the PE–retail relationship in terms of sustainability.
2. Where do you place the blame for these bankruptcies, considering again how many are also linked to PE investors?
3. What would you do as a PE investor if approached by a retail company? There is a lot of money to be made, but many of the companies ultimately fail.

Sustainability Is About Time

For a moment, put aside our discussion of business ethics, the environment, and SR. If you think of sustainability apart from these, then it makes perfect sense to conclude if something is sustainable, then it is successful or effective over time. That is how you should think about sustainability. You can ask yourself the following questions when confronted with a decision or problem:

- If I do *this*, will it enable me to do the same thing as well or better in the future?
- Will my decision allow others (i.e., relevant stakeholders) to do the same or better in the future?

This same thinking applies to socially responsible individuals (you) and organizations (your employers, other businesses, governments, and their leaders). For instance, assume a food bank in your community received donations only one time—that is, each donor gave money only once. Most people would agree that each donation is indeed socially responsible and philanthropic as shown in Figure 2.1, but it certainly is not sustainable. The food bank either needs to find an endless number of unique donors (impossible) or get some number of donors to contribute regularly.

At an individual level, this same example applies. Assume you donated to a charity one time. Your donation is responsible but not a sustainable effort on your part if it is given only once.

Sustainability and Your Career

Let's conclude the chapter by helping you apply sustainability to your career. But first, remember that applying the Three-Dimensional Problem-Solving for Ethics (3D PSE) has sustainability and SR built in, which means it is a valuable tool to assist you in your career. Be sure to apply it to the end of chapter cases, and other exercises throughout the course, to build this critical skill.

Take Your Jobs Two at a Time. One extremely useful way to build sustainability into your career is to consider your approach to selecting jobs.

First, think of yourself as a share of stock whose value changes over time. Your goal is to approach your job choices in terms of how they will boost your value in the job market. In other

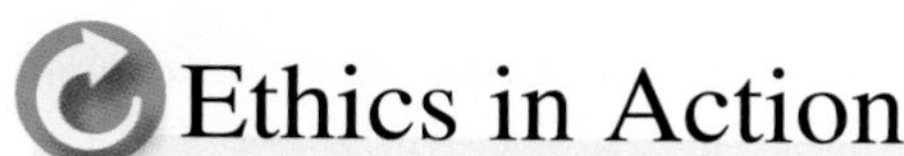

You Can Count on Our Support—Today, Tomorrow, Always

At the organizational level, Home Depot and Lowes provide excellent examples of SR and sustainability. They are well known for providing extensive support for both employees and communities affected by hurricanes. They commonly provide continued paychecks for displaced workers whose stores are closed. They not only stock functioning stores with necessary supplies in advance of storms to help citizens guard against the destruction, but they also establish command centers to help coordinate relief and recovery afterward. Moreover, these companies also send employees from other regions to help in the effort. These practices are clearly socially responsible on many levels, and they are sustainable too because both employees and citizens know that these companies will be there supporting them in their time of need.[42]

For Discussion:

1. Which forms of social responsibility are practiced by Home Depot and Lowes?
2. What is it that makes these practices sustainable?
3. Assume that Home Depot helped only one store, in one city, for one hurricane. Discuss the likely implications for the perceptions of social responsibility, and then the sustainability of its hurricane protection and relief efforts.

words, for any job you consider, think of how it will increase (or not) your value from the perspective of the hiring manager for your next job. This is what is meant by taking jobs two at a time.

To elaborate, most often, you are simply looking for a job. You want or need a job, and you do the "best" you can with the available opportunities. Of course, there is nothing wrong with this approach; after all, you have to eat. Instead, the recommendation is to be more strategic in your job search and selection to increase the number and attractiveness of your opportunities over time (i.e., your career).

Many if not most times throughout your career you see a given job as a stepping-stone to another opportunity within the same company, such as a promotion. Other times a given job is attractive because you believe it will provide you with skills and experience other employers will find attractive (opportunities in another company), or those needed to start your own business. Whatever is the case, in your mind, you often already think of two jobs at once—the one you're interviewing for and the opportunities that job will help create. Taking such an approach consciously will help you to be more successful over time, and thus more sustainable.

Follow Your Passion or Start with Sustainability. Fewer than half of all college graduates have a clear sense of what they will do after graduation, and research shows that only 27 percent take first jobs related to their majors.[43] But, if you are one of these fortunate individuals with a clear path, great, take it! For the rest, you are encouraged to follow the checklist and steps in Table 2.4 to assist your job search efforts, all to help your career to be sustainable—fulfilling and successful over time. There is no magic in this, but this advice has benefited numerous students for over twenty years, and many have found it immensely helpful.

table **2.4**

Job Search and Sustainable Careers Checklist

Completed Y/N	Steps	Objective	Description
	Step 1	Determine Your Geographic Preferences	Where do you most want to live, followed by a list of places you would live, and those you would not. Great job, undesirable location, less than ideal. Great location, less than desirable job might be more tolerable.
	Step 2	Identify Best Places to Work lists	You of course can use *Fortune Magazine's* annual list, as those companies nearly always have offices in multiple cities (and countries). Large metro area newspapers and other periodicals often generate a similar list for companies in the area.
	Step 3	Learn which Industries are Growing	Growth usually means future opportunities. I'm from southeast Michigan where the auto industry was the major employer for generations, but during my entire life, those companies and industry have been shrinking. This does not mean you should not pursue a job or career in the automotive industry. However, if you do not have an industry-specific passion or interest, then you are well-served to look at industries that are growing.
	Step 4	Look for Jobs in these Growing Industries	The intention here is sustainability, finding a job, another job, and a career in a growing versus shrinking industry is more likely to present you with (attractive) opportunities over time.
	Step 5	Healthcare?	If none of the above generates desirable options, consider the healthcare industry. Besides being one of the three largest in the US (government and education are the other two), it contains jobs representing almost every major and interest—marketing, operations, talent management, strategy, finance, and accounting. Moreover, until COVID-19, it was quite rare for the industry to shrink, which meant that historically it was more resistant to downturns in the economy than many others.

Hopefully, you now have a clearer sense of what is involved in business ethics, such as benefits not only to organizations but also to you and your career. You should also appreciate the importance of considering a broad array of stakeholders and how they can be influenced by and, in turn, how they can influence ethical conduct. Finally, you should now have a clearer and more precise understanding of what it means to be socially responsible, and how considering the implications of behavior, policies, and practices over time is what it means to be sustainable.

Chapter Summary

1. Ethical decision making has a long history based in philosophy and includes the following common perspectives—teleology, utilitarianism, egoism, deontology, universalism, and virtue. These perspectives focus on outcomes, rules or norms, and traits of the individual independent of the context, respectively.
2. All of these perspectives contrast with ethical relativism, which is based on the premise that matters of right and wrong are dependent on the given situation.
3. Social responsibility is fundamentally about maximizing positive outcomes while minimizing negative outcomes for stakeholders. Both individuals and organizations can be socially responsible.
4. Corporate social responsibility has four levels—economic, legal, ethical, and philanthropic. Knowledge of these levels can help you identify potential employers who fit with your values, as well as companies with whom you want to do business.
5. Boards of directors are the central means for corporate governance, and they determine which stakeholders' interests are prioritized (e.g., shareholders or customers).
6. Stakeholder activism occurs when a particular stakeholder group asserts influence over an organization to change its strategies, policies, and practices. Activism has increased from shareholders, employees, and customers in the past several years, resulting in numerous changes in both large and small companies.
7. Sustainability is complex and has many applications. Fundamentally, it is about ensuring your or an organization's conduct today does not impede the opportunities of others in the future. Sustainability can also be applied to your career.

Key Terms

boards of directors 38
categorical imperative 31
corporate governance 38
deontologists 31
egoists 30
Golden Rule 31
impact philanthropy 36
relativistic approach 33
shareholder model of governance 38
social responsibility 35
stakeholder activism 40
stakeholder model of governance 38
sustainability 41
teleological ethics 28
universalism 31
utilitarianism 29
virtue ethics 32
virtues 32

CASE STUDY: Dick's Sporting Goods Stops Carrying Guns

More than 180—that is the number of school shootings since 2009, and more than 356 people have died as a result. The tragedy at Stoneman Douglas High School in Parkland, Florida, motivated Ed Stack to act. Mr. Stack is the CEO of Dick's Sporting

Continued

Goods (it also owns Field & Stream and Golf Galaxy), a business founded by his father from whom he bought it in 1984. Since then, Stack took the company public in 2002, and over the years he's cultivated Dick's into a thriving business and the largest sporting goods company in America.[44] Like the students of Stoneman, Stack also felt "enough is enough," and two weeks later the company stopped selling guns to people under 21, along with removing assault rifles and high-capacity magazines from its stores, but not all guns and ammo.[45] This, however, is just part of the history. The company briefly stopped selling assault rifles back in 2012, reacting to the Sandy Hook shooting, but customer complaints caused the company to relent and eventually sell them again.[46]

The Proverbial Straw

This time was indeed different. After pulling guns from the shelves, Dick's destroyed them, over $5 million worth, stating the company did not want their inventory to end up being sold by someone else. Dick's did not immediately remove all guns from all stores, but instead they rolled the initiative out over time as an ongoing strategic initiative.

When asked to explain his actions, Mr. Stack said, "If you see a problem and you have expertise on the problem, and you have a sense of the solution, you should stand up and say something and that's what we did."[47]

Costs and Resistance

These actions have had costs. After one year with the limits in place, store sales declined 3.1 percent ($250 million), approximately the amount of lost gun sales in 2018–2019. After Mr. Stack aligned himself with gun-control activists, others lashed back, such as other gun sellers, gun buyers, and employees of gun manufacturers.[48]

Some of Dick's employees objected too—sixty-two resigned explicitly for this reason (it employs nearly 45,000). And Mr. Stack received personal threats.

Not surprisingly, the National Rifle Association (NRA) objected, along with some (non) customers based on perceived infringements on the Second Amendment right to bear arms. This was expected by Stack, and others, and the impact is difficult to assess.

Responsibility Is Contagious

Numerous other companies changed practices and took actions, similar to those of Dick's. Delta Airlines and MetLife stopped providing discounts to NRA members, and Citigroup and Bank of America implemented new compliance policies for their clients in the gun industry. Several pension funds also requested greater transparency and safety measures from the gun companies in which they invest.[49]

Walmart was and is the largest seller of guns in America. Its initial response to Parkland was similar to that of Dick's; they stopped selling to people under 21. Employees took up the issue again when twenty-two people were killed in a shooting at an El Paso, Texas, store. They publicly protested and threatened to walk off the job, all in the effort to influence executives to change company policies and to stop selling guns and participate in buy-back programs (cash for guns). Walmart leaders did not yield, and the company continues to sell guns as it did before. However, it stopped selling handguns long ago, and discontinued selling some sporting rifles in 2015.[50]

Skeptics

Some say Dick's is really just following industry trends and market realities, rather than rallying for social change. For instance, interest in hunting and thus sales of guns and related products have been on the decline for many years.[51]

Stack, however, is undaunted. In March 2020, he announced plans to accelerate the removal of guns from over 400 additional stores. The company's stock surged 13 percent on the news.[52]

For Discussion: (Note: Although this case happens within the context of a much larger gun control debate in America, our focus here is on business ethics and thus the behaviors, policies, and practices of people engaged in business. Put differently, this is not intended to spur discussion on the Second Amendment, but instead on the concepts presented in this chapter as they relate to the decisions by the CEO of Dick's Sporting Goods, and the resulting impact and reactions of various stakeholders.)

1. What ethical decision-making perspective did Ed Stack seem to use (recall from chapter 2)?
2. Describe the level of social responsibility demonstrated by Ed Stack.
3. Which stakeholders were primary in this case? Which were secondary?
4. Which of the common decision-making perspectives is illustrated by Ed Stack in this case? Explain.
5. Describe the implications of Stack's actions on employees of Dick's.
6. Assume you are the CEO of Dick's, how would your actions differ from those of Ed Stack? Describe and justify.
7. Again, assume you are the CEO, what type of stakeholder activism could influence you to change policies and begin selling guns again? Explain and justify.

Apply Three-Dimensional Problem-Solving for Ethics (3D PSE)

You can apply the Three-Dimensional Problem-Solving for Ethics (3D PSE) from multiple perspectives—Ed Stack the CEO, a shareholder, an employee, family member of a shooting victim, or an average citizen. Just be sure to specify whose perspective you have applied. That said, try analyzing it as if you were Ed Stack, as he has and will continue to determine the gun-related practices of the Dick's Sporting Goods.

figure **2.2**

Three-Dimensional Problem-Solving for Ethics (3D PSE)

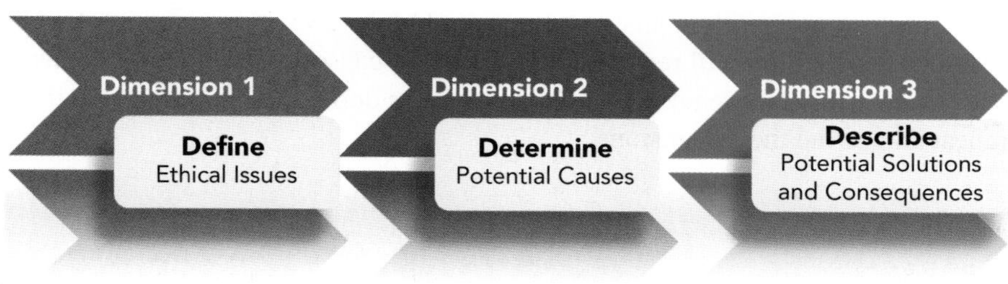

Dimension 1: *Define* the Ethical Challenge

What is the gap in the case? What does Stack have and what does he want? (Remember, use only details included within the case for your analysis.)

a. From Stack's view as CEO, describe what he had versus how he wanted it to be.
b. Why is the current situation a problem? What difficulties or undesirable behaviors and outcomes happen as a result of the problem you defined? From Stack's perspective, why would he care about the problem you defined in Dimension 1?
c. Define your problem in one or at most two sentences, and structure it in terms of what is current versus what is desired.
d. Who are the key stakeholders, those that affect or are affected by the problem you defined?

Dimension 2: *Determine* the Causes

a. **Individuals.** Given the problem you defined in Dimension 1, describe how any individuals caused the problem as you defined it in Dimension 1. Individuals may not be causes, but you should consider whether there are any or not. If yes, then describe how their personal behaviors or characteristics contributed to the problem.
b. **Contextual.** What behaviors, policies, and practices caused the problem defined in Dimension 1? These elements may be within Dick's, the retail industry, government, or they may reside with other organizations or stakeholder groups.

Dimension 3: *Describe* Your Potential Solutions and the Intended and Unintended Consequences for Stakeholders

For each cause you identified in Dimension 2, answer the following question:

a. From the perspective of Ed Stack, and then other stakeholders, ***what*** do you recommend he should do, and ***how*** would you make it happen?
b. ***Why?*** Explain your motives, along with considering if it reflects a particular ethical decision-making perspective (e.g., utilitarian or universal).

If your responses to these questions are unsatisfactory, then go back to Dimension 1 and repeat the process. If, however, you are comfortable and confident in your problem-solving efforts thus far, then ensure you achieve the desired outcomes and avoid any unintended consequences.

c. Describe the ***desired and likely effects in the short and long-term*** for the key stakeholders involved in the problem and causes (Dimensions 1 and 2).
d. What ***potential unintended consequences*** may occur with your proposed solution for each of the relevant stakeholders?
e. If any, what are the **implications for *other* stakeholders** (e.g., individuals, organizations, and communities) besides those noted in Dimensions 1 and 2?
f. Will your solution work in an ethical manner? Make a final assessment of whether your chosen solution will reduce or eliminate the causes determined in Dimension 2, and whether this will remedy the ethical problem defined in Dimension 1. If not, then repeat and refine the dimensions.

Chapter Opener Photo Source: Anatoli Styf/Shutterstock

PART 2

Individual Influences on Business Ethics

chapter 3

Why Good People do Bad Things

Learning Objectives

AFTER READING THIS CHAPTER, YOU SHOULD BE ABLE TO:

LO1 Identify personal factors that influence your ethical decision making.

LO2 Understand the frequency and dangers of moral disengagement.

LO3 Recognize how moral intensity affects your perceptions of ethically challenging situations.

LO4 Describe your ethical blind spots and explain how to remedy them.

WHERE DO **YOU** STAND?

Speak Up and It Will Cost You, Stay Quiet and It May Still Cost You or Someone Else

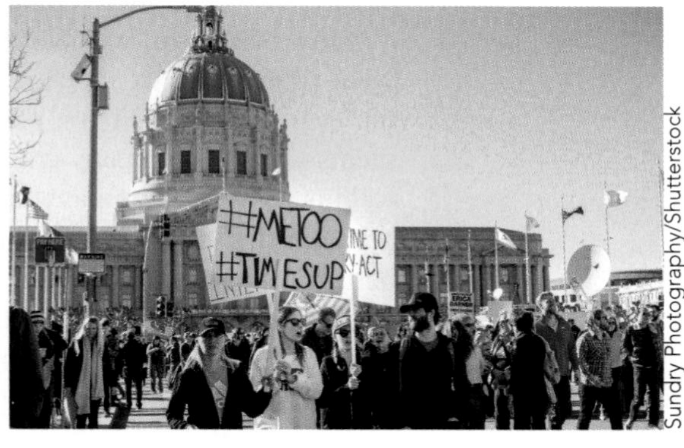

Sundry Photography/Shutterstock

The #MeToo movement brought to light long-tolerated, unethical, and often illegal conduct, resulting in a day of reckoning for hundreds of powerful men,[1] and that is just the number reported in the media. It is safe to assume that hundreds, if not thousands, were confronted and many times more than that were nervous that they might be exposed. Many nightmares and atrocities have been unveiled, and a larger social movement has been put in motion. However, the dilemma remains much the same: Does the victim speak up and potentially suffer undesirable consequences, or does the victim stay quiet and do their best to avoid the offender and future incidents? This may seem like a false choice, meaning that there may actually be additional options. But it nevertheless seems that anyone in such a predicament fundamentally speaks up or stays quiet. Both options have potentially negative implications for the individual.

1. Assume you've been sexually assaulted by a coworker. Explain why you would speak up and tell someone. Who would you tell and why?
2. As with #1, assume you've been sexually assaulted by a coworker. Explain why you would not speak up.
3. Now assume you own a company—your name is on it. Describe how and why you would encourage employees to speak up about sexual assault.

Introduction

Your ethical conduct, and that of other individuals, is strongly influenced by your peers, leaders, and organizational and societal pressures. We consider these in other chapters of the book; this chapter, however, begins our exploration of individual characteristics that affect how people (you) perceive and react to ethical challenges they encounter. In a practical sense, you bring your constellation of characteristics with you to every situation, so looking in the mirror is a good place to start your quest to understand and manage business ethics more effectively.

The Personal Factors that Influence Your Ethical Decision Making

You and every other individual possess an infinite number of characteristics that make you who you are, and many of these affect your ethical conduct. This section focuses on three characteristics that research and practice have shown to be especially relevant—your ethical awareness, ethical intuition, and moral development.

Ethical Awareness

ethical awareness the recognition that your decision or actions may impact you or others in ways that conflict with ethical norms of the particular situation

To act ethically you need to realize there are ethical elements in a particular situation. In other words, you need **ethical awareness**, which is the recognition that your decision or actions may impact you or others in ways that conflict with ethical norms of the particular situation.[2] This is more complex than it appears, however.

Most often, you will become aware because of a conflict between your own values and what you witness or are expected to do in a given situation. For instance, you attend a sporting event with your boss, but not a client, and you notice she pays for tickets and refreshments with the company credit card. You, however, recently attended a training that clearly forbids using the company account for personal recreation. Other times the conflicts occur between the way in which you commonly perform a task, and how you see someone else perform the same task. Your colleague, who does the same job as you, booked sales for a client for this month even though they won't be delivered until next month, and the company policy is to book sales only in the month in which they are delivered.

Both of these situations represent dilemmas or conflicts between your values of honesty and trustworthiness, and loyalty to your company. Such dilemmas may be worsened if policies are in place and you're aware of them. But if you were new to the company and did not know these policies, then it is entirely possible you would think this conduct is acceptable. Worse still, you might adopt it as your own and suffer the consequences.

Reporting inappropriate sexual conduct, as described in the Where Do You Stand feature at the beginning of the chapter, epitomizes ethical awareness. For instance, even if you are not the target and simply report what you've witnessed, it can potentially affect numerous people, including the target who quite possibly did not want to speak up.

Bottom line: Ethical awareness is a shared responsibility. Your manager and peers have a responsibility to inform you of the potential ethical implications of a situation. But you also are responsible for considering and learning about the same. As you'll learn later in the book (e.g., chapter 9), claiming ignorance is inadequate and can be illegal in certain situations.

ethical intuition you "just know" what is right and what is wrong without any purposeful reasoning or thought

Ethical Intuition

What about intuition? Like most people, you may think you "just know" what is right and what is wrong without any purposeful reasoning or thought.[3] This is **ethical intuition**, and it is more complex than this description. First, ethical intuition, like other forms of intuition, is based in large part on past experience—things you've done and things you've seen. If your experience, and thus your intuition, exactly matches the current situation, then your intuition or gut may serve you well and produce the appropriate decision and behavior. Your intuition also will help you decide quickly. The same goes for ethical intuition. It is based on your knowledge and experience of the ethical norms (expectations) in that situation. If they match perfectly, you will likely do the right thing.[4]

A common sign that your ethical intuition is at work is when you say to yourself, "This just doesn't seem right." That is your ethical intuition, likely realizing that the demands of the situation conflict with your values and norms. This is another instance in which your ethical intuition can be beneficial—that is, when it acts as a quick, early warning signal.

However, sometimes our intuition leads us to be overly confident in the effectiveness of our past experience. The world of business is becoming more complex all the time, which means situations are changing and what worked or was ethically appropriate in the past may no longer be applicable in the current situation. Or you may be new and lack experience and thus have little or no experience on which to base your judgments.[5]

Bottom line: Intuition has its place, but you need to be careful. You are often best served if you balance intuition with purposeful thought. Many situations require careful and purposeful consideration, especially when consequences may be great for you and/or others. Just think of the regrets you've had about decisions you've made. If given another chance, you and most other people would have taken more time and made a different choice.

Moral Development

Like other forms of development, **moral development** describes a process of change, wherein an individual's moral reasoning and behavior evolves over time from relatively simple to more complex. As such, individuals differ with respect to their degree of moral development. The most popular and influential approach to moral development is that of Lawrence Kohlberg, who originally studied children to learn how they responded to ethical dilemmas. From this research, he created a six-stage model of moral development that coincided with the more general development of children as they aged. Kohlberg's work has since been adapted and widely applied to business ethics and is illustrated and explained in Figure 3.1. But before reviewing the model and associated details, it is helpful to understand the three levels in which the stages fit.

moral development
a process of change, wherein an individual's moral reasoning and behavior evolves over time from relatively simple to more complex

> **Level 1: Pre-Conventional.** Employees in this level are generally only concerned with self-interests related to business ethics. When confronted with an ethical dilemma, for instance, their reasoning and actions are based only on positive or negative consequences for them personally.
>
> **Level 2: Conventional.** Employees in this level perceive right (and wrong) in terms of the norms and expectations of others—that is, an individual (e.g., manager or peer), group (e.g., peers, department, or organization), or larger society.
>
> **Level 3 Post-Conventional.** Employees in this level look beyond potential rewards and punishment, as well as norms set by others, and their actions are based on their personal values and moral reasoning.

Moral development, as illustrated in the table, describes how individuals perceive their relationship with rules and expectations from others and larger society. It therefore can be instructive in understanding not only your own behavior but also that of others in particular situations. For instance, it is likely you've had or will have a manager who has lower moral development than you, and this will be evident in the fact that he or she will say: "Those are the rules," or "I don't make the rules, I just follow them." These phrases reflect little

table 3.1

Kohlberg's Model of Moral Development

Development Stage	Description of Ethical Reasoning and Action
Level 1: Pre-Conventional Stage 1: Obedience and Punishment	Decisions and actions are based on rules as defined by others (manager or company), and rules are used to define right and wrong and to guide behavior. The simple reasoning is that noncompliance should be punished. Rules may be broken however, if the employee believes there is no way they will be caught.
Stage 2: Individualism and Exchange	Decisions and actions are based on what provides the most benefit for the individual. Rules are interpreted and applied to the extent they serve the person's own interests.
Level 2: Conventional Stage 3: Good Interpersonal Relationships	Decisions and actions consider the interests of others and self, and rules are followed in order to please or meet the expectations of others.
Stage 4: Maintain Social Order	Decisions and actions go beyond the interests of self and others and include considerations of duties and obligations to larger society. The motive is that this helps establish and maintain social order.
Level 3: Post-Conventional Stage 5: Social Contract and Individual Rights	Decisions and actions begin with considerations of the values and rights established by society, and these are used to reconcile and guide conflicts with individuals, organization, and self.
Stage 6: Universal Principles	Decisions and actions are guided by universal ethical standards and a belief they should be followed by everyone. These standards are not determined by an organization or country, but instead are applicable to people everywhere.

Source: Adapted from K. B. DeTienne, C. F. Ellerston, M. C. Inerson, and W. R. Dudley, "Moral Development in Business Ethics: An Examination and Critique," *Journal of Business Ethics*, November 18, 2019; and from S. McLeod, "Kohlberg's Stages of Moral Development," Simply Psychology, simplypsychology.org, 2013: https://www.simplypsychology.org/kohlberg.html.

consideration for you, the situation, or higher-level principles. Generally, lower levels of moral development can be particularly problematic when situations are complex or fast-changing, or when working at an international level (chapter 11). Rules are then more likely to be unclear or even nonexistent, which can leave such people ill-prepared.

For Discussion

1. Based you what you just read, and using Table 3.1, at what stage do you place your moral development?
2. What about if we focus on your moral development as a student? If your answer differs from that of the previous question, then explain why.
3. More generally, do you think moral development will matter as you move through your career? Why or why not?

To summarize, the above concepts are dispositions or stable personal characteristics that influence your thinking and behavior related to ethics. Understanding these is very valuable, as you bring your dispositions with you to every situation, which means they influence your reasoning and conduct all the time. In the next section, we turn our attention to moral intensity, which is a quality of ethical challenges that influences how you perceive and respond to such challenges.

How Moral Intensity Affects Perceptions of Ethically Challenging Situations

In addition to personal characteristics, your perceptions of particular situations impact your business ethics, especially how you perceive the potential severity of conflicts with your values and the severity of possible negative outcomes.[6] A fundamental means for understanding such perception is moral intensity.

Moral intensity (MI) describes issue-related dimensions that determine how strongly one approves or disapproves of the ethicality of a situation.[7] The essence of MI is that the ethical severity of a situation is based on your perceptions, rather than on objective facts, which influences how you typically respond. Moreover, MI is a perception, not a personal trait like moral development, and is determined by six dimensions or characteristics of a given situation (see Figure 3.1). Unpacking these characteristics will help you understand and apply this extremely useful concept. Keep in mind that as any single dimension increases, so too does the moral intensity of that particular situation.

moral intensity (MI) issue-related dimensions that determine how strongly one approves or disapproves of the ethicality of a situation

Magnitude of Consequences

Magnitude of consequences is defined as the sum of the harm experienced by victims (or benefits to benefactors) due to an ethical situation.[8] Perhaps the simplest way to think of this is to consider the same unethical behavior for two groups of different sizes. For

magnitude of consequences the sum of the harm experienced by victims (or benefits to benefactors) due to an ethical situation

figure 3.1

Moral Intensity and Its Component Dimensions

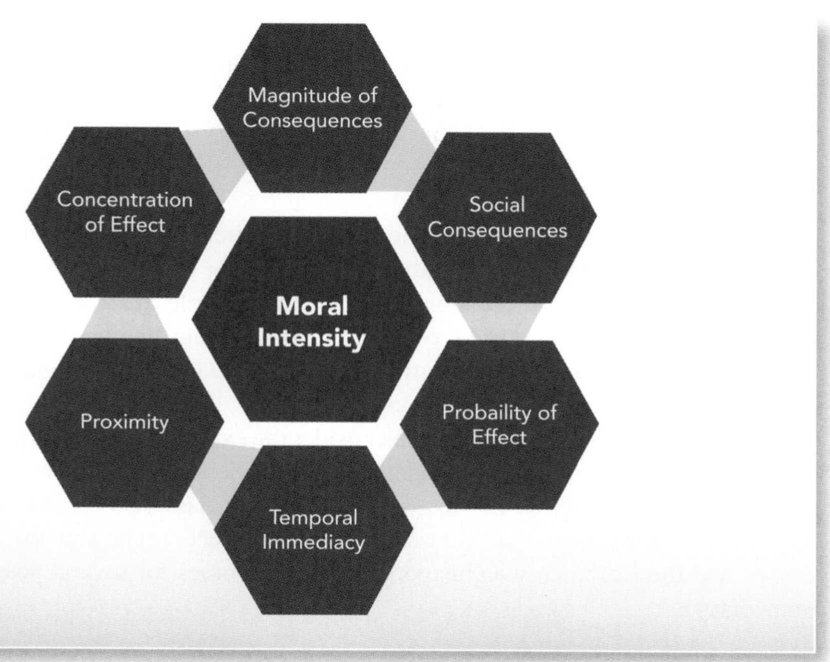

example, the magnitude of consequences for a change to the requirements for graduation that affects 1,000 students is greater than a change that affects only 20 students. Of course, it is serious and has high moral intensity for those 20 students, but the situation itself has a lower magnitude.

Another and fundamental reason magnitude of consequences matters is that some "infractions" are quite minor or trivial, and thus unlikely to cause much of a reaction.[9] For instance, if your coworker is denied her request for vacation time to extend a holiday weekend, it is unlikely to cause you to be outraged. You, that same coworker, and all of your other coworkers, however, may indeed be outraged if the vacation policy is changed from four weeks per year to only two weeks per year.

Social Consensus

social consensus the degree of agreement people have about whether an act is ethical or not

Social consensus pertains to the degree of agreement people have about whether an act is ethical or not.[10] The more the people agree that an act is unethical, the greater the moral intensity. If, for instance, in this course, you are the only student who thinks that any student who cheats should be expelled from the university, whereas the majority of your classmates think cheaters should fail only that particular course, then your position has low social consensus.

Related to social issues (chapter 13), more people likely agree that Hollywood producer Harvey Weinstein's sexual assaults were reprehensible than those who agree with his prison sentence of 23 years.[11] Put differently, the number of people who think that Weinstein's conduct was not unethical is likely very, very small. However, people would have very different views on the type of punishment—some likely think he should have received a life sentence, some the sentence he received, and still others a shorter sentence.

Probability Effect

probability effect a function of the likelihood that an unethical behavior will occur and that negative outcomes will actually result

The **probability effect** is a function of the likelihood that an unethical behavior will occur and that negative outcomes will actually result.[12] In other words, what is the likelihood an individual will act unethically, and the likelihood that action will cause harm? A classic example is selling a handgun to a person with a criminal record of armed robbery versus selling a handgun to a person with no record. Most people would expect that the person with a history of armed robbery is more likely to do it again, whereas the other person would be less likely. The probability is higher in the former than the latter. To better make the point, selling the gun to either person would generate low moral intensity if neither person had previously committed a crime.[13]

Temporal Immediacy

temporal immediacy the amount of time that passes between (mis)conduct and the consequences of that conduct

Temporal immediacy describes the amount of time that passes between (mis)conduct and the consequences of that conduct.[14] The shorter the time, the greater the intensity. This dimension draws on economics, such that people are consistently shown to discount the severity, importance, or value of things that happen in the future. Think of the time value of money. You'd rather receive a $10,000 bonus today than at the end of the year.

To further illustrate the point, again consider the example of changing graduation requirements. If that change affects all students and is made today, then it has greater immediacy (shorter time) and intensity for this year's graduating class than it does for this year's freshman class. The reason is that the seniors will be affected this year (high temporal immediacy), and the freshman won't experience the outcomes for several years (lower temporal immediacy).

Proximity

Proximity describes the closeness or the extent you identify with those that are affected by the (un)ethical conduct.[15] Closeness or identity can be social, cultural, psychological, or physical between the perceiver and those that experience the consequences (e.g., victims). An all-too-common example is layoffs. If people in your office are laid off, this has greater proximity than employees being laid off in another office by your employer.[16]

proximity
the closeness or the extent you identify with those that are affected by the (un)ethical conduct

Proximity is a key driver of moral intensity for many issues, especially those related to the environment and international business. If an American company pollutes the water at a facility in Asia, the moral intensity is lower than if it pollutes the water at a facility in the United States, which is lower than the intensity if it pollutes the water in your neighborhood.

Similarly, paying poor wages and providing unsafe working conditions at operations in other countries has a lesser proximity than the same offenses in your own country.

Concentration Effect

The **concentration effect** concerns the degree to which consequences apply to only a few people.[17] Quite simply, if a change in compensation policy costs one person $50,000 rather than costing fifty people $1,000 each, then the former has a greater concentration effect and thus a greater moral intensity. Again, think of the What's Your Position example at the beginning of the chapter. If you witness sexual misconduct by your boss against many employees, versus just one, the concentration effect is greater as is the moral intensity. This also applies when the misconduct is widespread, perpetrated by many managers or other employees.

concentration effect
the degree to which consequences apply to only a few people

Before moving on, let's first summarize what you learned regarding moral intensity. The premise is that the level of responsibility for ethically challenging situations is dependent on a number of elements, such as the nature or severity of the resulting consequences (magnitude of effect), agreement between people about the ethical offense (social consensus), likelihood (probability of effect) and urgency (temporal immediacy) of those outcomes, the degree to which one identifies with those affected (proximity effect), and the number of people affected (concentration effect) by the decision maker's degree of choice or control. As such, moral intensity is closely linked to punishments in the legal system, wherein consequences are intended to be proportional to the crime.[18] This is not arbitrary or simply created by some "group of experts," but rather, it is based on how people perceive ethical challenges, and these perceptions are based on the dimensions of moral intensity.

Moreover, low moral intensity influences the likelihood that people will both engage in unethical behavior and whether they will take action against another who has—wherein the severity of any punishment may also be influenced. In both cases, low moral intensity enables people to distance themselves in time, familiarity, and the other dimensions.

Next, we explore how people commonly justify their misconduct, at least in their own minds, which enables them to continue down an unethical path without considering themselves as unethical people.

The Frequency and Dangers of Moral Disengagement

A routine question regarding unethical conduct is, "Why does it happen so frequently?" How is it that executives, coaches, leaders, and people not in positions of power get entangled in patterns of unethical conduct that grow into full-blown scandals? Yes, occasionally, these are bad people with bad intentions, but this is relatively rare. But this means that the vast majority of the time other factors are at work that enable otherwise ethical individuals to start and continue down an unethical path. One such contributing factor is moral disengagement.

What Is Moral Disengagement, and How Does It Foster Unethical Behavior?

moral disengagement
a cognitive mechanism that allows individuals to disassociate with their internal moral standards and behave unethically without feeling distressed

Moral disengagement is a cognitive mechanism that allows individuals to disassociate with their internal moral standards and behave unethically without feeling distressed.[19] This means that when people (e.g., business leaders, politicians, and students) morally disengage, they think in ways that enable them to rationalize—explain away or justify—their unethical conduct. In turn, this rationalization enables the same individuals to continue down the unethical path with little or no concern that their conduct is wrong.

There are four stages and eight associated cognitive mechanisms (techniques) people use to disengage morally (see Table 3.2). People progress through the four stages—that is, they begin by rationalizing their behaviors, using the mechanisms of moral justification, euphemistic labeling, and advantageous comparisons. They then move on to agency, disregard the outcome, and then conclude moral disengagement by victimizing others.

The practical value of the information in Table 3.2 cannot be overstated. To help support this claim, complete the following For Discussion box.

table **3.2**

Moral Disengagement Stages and Mechanisms

Stages	Moral Disengagement Mechanisms	Description
Behavioral	**moral justification**	Justify unethical behavior by translating it into a moral or social cause. Their behavior is actually good, well intended, and will benefit others, and as such, it is the "right thing to do."
	euphemistic labeling	Justify unethical behavior by using less damaging or negatively connoted language to describe it, such as "our relationship has fractured" instead of "I stole credit, control, and compensation from my partner."
	advantageous comparison	Justify unethical behavior by comparing one's conduct to another's that is even worse. "Nobody died," or "It could have been worse; the guy in finance embezzled a million dollars."
Agency	**displacement of responsibility**	Obscure the link between their conduct and the consequences by thinking and/or claiming, "I had to do it. My boss told me."
	diffusion of responsibility	Obscure the link between their conduct and the consequences by thinking and/or claiming, "This is how it is done in my department," or "This is the way it is done in this industry; it's the norm."
Outcomes	**disregard or distortion of consequences**	Avoid acknowledging the negative consequences of their conduct, such as by thinking and/or saying, "I wasn't the one that did it; the manager is the bully," when in fact, you were complicit.
Victimization	**dehumanization**	Withdraw empathy, sympathy, or any concern for the victim by distancing one's self (physically, psychologically, or socially).
	attribution of blame	Withdraw empathy, sympathy, or any concern for the victim by considering them responsible or deserving of their circumstance.

Source: Created from A. Newman, H. Le, A. North-Samardzic, and M. Cohen, "Moral Disengagement at Work: A Review and Research Agenda," *Journal of Business Ethics*, May 9, 2019; and M. L. Farnese, C. Tramontano, R. Fida, and M. Paciello, "Cheating Behaviors in Academic Context: Does Academic Moral Disengagement Matter?", *Procedia—Social and Behavioral Sciences*, 29: 356-365.

For Discussion

1. Think of an instance when someone you know from school, work, or your social circle did something wrong. Now think of how they explained what they did.
2. Which of the mechanisms (and then associated stages) were evident?
3. Now, challenge yourself and think of a time when you crossed the line. How did you explain it to others? Which mechanism (and stage) did you use?

Illustrations and Applications to Work and School

Undoubtedly, you've thought that various people in your life have rationalized their bad behavior, and if you give it close thought, then you are likely to see how they were utilizing moral disengagement. Researchers have done just this and applied this concept to executives involved in numerous scandals. Specifically, they have used interviews, court depositions, and other documents to learn how these executives described their thinking—that is, their process of moral disengagement.

Moral Disengagement and Business Scandals. There are reports that Bernie Madoff, the $50 billion Ponzi schemer (taking money from one investor to pay another), blamed his clients rather than himself (attribution of blame). He is alleged to have said that they knew there were risks investing in the stock market. Madoff took it a step further and claimed the government was the biggest Ponzi scheme, as they are taking in money with one hand and giving it away with the other (diffusion of responsibility and advantageous comparison). Top executives at Siemens, the German industrial giant, also shifted blame for a long-lasting and far-reaching bribery crime to a few "bad apples" (i.e., a small number of employees). The company persisted with this claim even though investigations revealed senior management knowledge and lack of action to discourage or stop it (diffusion of responsibility).[20]

Moral Disengagement and School. Moral disengagement has been studied with students and cheating. Not only are they related, but they reinforce each other. This means that the more you cheat, the more you utilize moral disengagement, and vice versa.[21] Researchers have also shown that students will morally disengage from other students and professors. This means that they rationalize cheating in terms of other students: "It is useless to blame a single dishonest student because they all are." It also means they will rationalize cheating behavior by shifting blame to the professor: "If students fall behind, it's because professors overburden them with work." This, in turn, pressures them to cut corners (cheat).[22]

More generally, moral disengagement can be especially dangerous as it seems to be an amplifier of unethical conduct. And the next time you think someone is "rationalizing" their bad behavior, hopefully you will understand that they are likely morally disengaging.

This section addressed how people rationalize their misconduct, and in the next you'll learn about ethical blind spots. These are common ways in which situations become unethical without our intention. It is highly likely you'll realize that you have experienced a blind spot or two.

Syda Productions/Shutterstock

Identifying Ethical Blind Spots and How to Remedy Them

ethical blind spots predictable, systematic, and unintentional ethical lapses.

Most people are good, well intentioned, and ethical. Thankfully. However, even the most virtuous and ethically determined individuals sometimes have unintentional ethical lapses. Researchers Max Bazerman and Ann Tenbrunsel have identified a few common types of such lapses they refer to as **ethical blind spots**, which are predictable, systematic, and unintentional ethical lapses. Five particular blind spots are listed in Table 3.3, along with descriptions, examples, and remedies.[23]

Practically speaking, it is important to note that blind spots are unintentional, but this does not mean they are unavoidable. To help you manage these more effectively, and thus improve your own ethical conduct and that of others, let's explore each in more detail.

ill-conceived goals those that fail to consider likely and problematic unintended consequences.

Guarding Against Ill-Conceived Goals

Ill-conceived goals are those that fail to consider likely and problematic unintended consequences. Volumes of research and practical experience show the benefits of specific, challenging goals with specific timelines. Therefore, doing away with goals is not the solution.

table **3.3**

Common Ethical Blind Spots

	Ill-Conceived Goals	Motivated Blindness	Indirect Blindness	The Slippery Slope	Overvaluing Outcomes
DESCRIPTION	We set goals and incentives to promote a desired behavior, but they encourage a negative one.	We overlook the unethical behavior of another when it's in our interest to remain ignorant.	We hold others less accountable for unethical behavior when it's carried out through third parties.	We are less able to see others' unethical behavior when it develops gradually.	We give a pass to unethical behavior if the outcome is good.
EXAMPLE	The pressure to maximize billable hours in accounting, consulting, and law firms leads to unconscious padding.	Baseball officials failed to notice they'd created conditions that encouraged steroid use.	A drug company deflects attention from a price increase by selling rights to another company, which imposes the increases.	Auditors may be more likely to accept a client firm's questionable financial statements if infractions have occurred over time.	A researcher whose fraudulent clinical trial saves lives is considered more ethical than the one whose fraudulent trial leads to deaths.
REMEDY	Brainstorm unintended consequences when devising goals and incentives. Consider alternative goals that may be more important to reward.	Root out conflicts of interest. Simply being aware of them doesn't necessarily reduce their negative effect on decision making.	When handing off or outsourcing work, ask whether the assignment might invite unethical behavior and take ownership of the implications.	Be alert for even trivial ethical infractions and address them immediately. Investigate whether a change in behavior has occurred.	Examine both "good" and "bad" decisions for their ethical implications. Reward solid decision processes, not just good outcomes.

Source: M. H. Bazerman and A. Tenbrunsel, "Ethical Breakdowns," *Harvard Business Review*, April 2011: 1–9.

Instead, the person responsible for goal setting needs to modify their approach to help guard against the shortcomings described in Table 3.1.[24] Specifically, the following must be considered:

- **View from the Performer's Eyes.** Many goals at work are handed down or dictated from managers to those responsible for achieving them. This approach too often doesn't consider or even understand the unintended consequences that may occur.[25] As an example, consider a pharmaceutical company wherein multiple employees were responsible for sales to a single medical practice with locations that spanned multiple territories. Goals and rewards were not team based, which caused representatives to compete against each other to get sales credited to their own territories. The situation was made worse because the representatives did not share helpful information with each other. This resulted in suboptimal service and sales to that extremely important customer. National-level management, who set the goals, did not "see" these consequences. Had top management consulted those responsible for the large account, they likely would have devised an alternative set of goals and rewards, which in turn could have established a team approach wherein representatives would have cooperated to achieve better outcomes for the customer, themselves, and the company.
- **Ensure Goals Are Not Too Narrow.** This does not mean they should not be specific. It instead means that performance goals need to include the key elements of performance, which are typically broader than defined and measured. The example in Table 3.2 shows that professional service firms expect more than simply hours billed. They also expect quality client service, business development, and client satisfaction and loyalty. Accordingly, "performance" should be defined, measured, and rewarded with more than simply hours billed. It also is helpful to measure progress toward goals, and not only ultimate achievement. Doing this should help guard against employees focusing on a single performance metric and thus cutting corners or doing other undesirable things to boost one performance metric.[26]

You'll learn more about performance management and business ethics in chapter 8.

Seeing through Motivated Blindness

People see what they want to see, and **motivated blindness** occurs when people look for information that confirms their beliefs or desires and discounts or completely disregards contradictory information. (You'll learn more about this and other biases in chapter 4.) This phenomenon is extremely common and problematic in terms of business ethics. You only need to think of one of the many scandals that have emerged in college sports for an example. Infamously, many people from Penn State University failed to believe, and thus did not pursue as they should have, the sexual abuse allegations made against coach Jerry Sandusky. This was in part because of his association with legendary head coach Joe Paterno. This situation escalated, in part, because people perceived Paterno to be an honorable man and one of the longest-serving and best-performing college football coaches of all time. Some, therefore, were likely to discount or disregard information related to Sandusky's conduct, which conflicted with their beliefs and desired views of the program and Paterno.

motivated blindness when people look for information that confirms their beliefs or desires and discounts or completely disregards contradictory information

More generally, this blind spot often occurs when you hear or read someone say, "She is a wonderful colleague, a top performer, everybody likes her … I can't believe she would do such a thing." The allegations are inconsistent with previously held views. Put differently, many scandals occur when the misconduct is a pattern over time, and the related information is discounted or disregarded because it is contradictory to other peoples' beliefs or interests. Motivated blindness helps explain why a significant proportion of unethical business conduct is swept under the rug.

What can be done? One thing is to genuinely consider allegations of serious misconduct, but to do so with evidence, not simply based on rumor or hearsay. And, if you or others feel there is the potential for conflict, meaning you are unable to objectively consider damning information, then involve an independent third party. Another way to combat motivated blindness is to establish codes of conduct (chapter 9) and expectations, or even requirements, that certain alleged behaviors are reported. For instance, most states require teachers and other school employees to report any suspicion of child abuse or neglect to the appropriate authorities.[27] Similar expectations and policies can be set for employees in companies.

Indirect Blindness—Delegating Responsibility

indirect blindness when responsibility for unethical conduct is discounted because it is carried out by another party

Indirect blindness occurs when responsibility for unethical conduct is discounted because it is carried out by another party. The example in Table 3.1 is an excellent and not an uncommon one. Merck once sold two products that generated very little revenue to Ovation. Ovation, in turn, raised the prices by 1,000 percent, making them quite profitable. Merck still benefited as it continued to get paid by manufacturing the products for Ovation. Ovation caught grief for its price hikes, but little negativity was assigned to Merck.[28]

Turing Pharmaceuticals made a business model out of this practice. The company, and its CEO Martin Shkreli, became infamous for acquiring drugs from other companies and then boosting the prices by over 1,000 percent. In one instance, the drug Daraprim, used to treat a life-threatening infection, was acquired from Impax Pharma and then sold at 5,000 percent more than it was by Impax.[29]

A hotly contested example is holding gun manufacturers liable for illegal acts conducted by gun owners. To be clear, our interest here is not in the political or Second Amendment aspects of the gun debate, but instead the scenario in which one party is shielded from the potential consequences as the result of another party's actions.[30]

For Discussion

1. Do you think companies should ever be responsible, in any way, for what someone else does with their product, including raising the price?
2. If you answered yes, then explain under what conditions.
3. If you answered no, then justify your reasoning.
4. What about the leaders of employees whose conduct is unethical?

A more common example of indirect blindness occurs when multiple employees of a company are accused of unethical conduct, but their leader is neither accused nor accepts responsibility. SAC Capital, a hedge fund founded and run by Steven A. Cohen, epitomized indirect blindness. More than eighty employees pleaded guilty or were convicted of financial crimes. Yet, Cohen himself was never found guilty. It seems that the responsibility for unethical conduct was borne directly by his employees.[31]

This also sometimes happens when executives, athletes, and others engage attorneys, agents, or accountants to act on their behalf, such as in the case of salary negotiations and other business deals. They are instructed to get "the best compensation package, best deal, or best price." Responsibility for the conduct is shifted to another party.

Indirect blindness can be mitigated, if not remedied, by requiring the original individual or organization to share in the responsibility. This, of course, is not always possible. But, an ethical individual, like you, may want to ask yourself when you delegate or transfer responsibility to someone else: "What is the potential for unethical conduct, and what can I do to ensure it doesn't happen?" Sometimes conditions can be agreed upon, if not formally (e.g., in a contract), then at least informally.[32]

Slippery Slope

The **slippery slope** occurs when "increasingly major infractions are accepted as long as each violation is only incrementally more serious than the preceding one."[33]

slippery slope when "increasingly major infractions are accepted as long as each violation is only incrementally more serious than the preceding one"

The definition is simple enough and highlights both the pros and cons of a universalism approach to business ethics. Adhering strictly to universal ethical values—don't cheat—avoids the slippery slope problem. But strict, unwavering practices can be rigid and make it very difficult to adapt to complex situations, such as those that are novel, like doing business in another country, with new employees, or a new customer.

The challenge when combatting the slippery slope is to understand when an individual is engaging in appropriate flexibility, versus what is inappropriate and likely to set a bad precedent and multiply. Generally, when you are dealing with other people's money, reputation, or opportunities, it is a good idea to adhere to little-or-no variance in practices.

Overvaluing Outcomes

Overvaluing outcomes occurs when unethical conduct is excused because the outcome is desirable, rather than encouraging appropriate conduct that delivers a less-desirable outcome.[34] This blind spot highlights "the end justifies the means" approach to business ethics. It is similar to motivated blindness, such that many people will conclude that since "things worked out," punishing the misconduct is unnecessary. This is especially problematic when it happens to managers and leaders who oversee (i.e., are responsible for the conduct of) others. By focusing only on the outcome, they effectively reward only the outcome and fail to correct or punish the inappropriate process for generating that outcome. The Ethics in Action box highlights how outcomes are commonly overvalued in sports.

overvaluing outcomes when unethical conduct is excused because the outcome is desirable, rather than encouraging appropriate conduct that delivers a less-desirable outcome

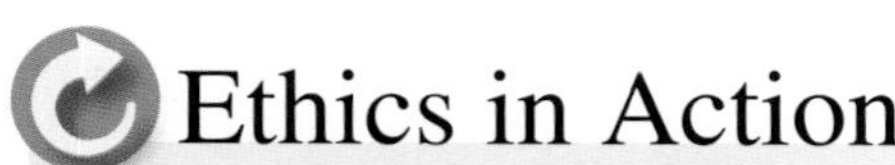

Did You Win? That's All that Matters

Again, college sports scandals are excellent examples. Pete Carroll, now the head coach of the Seattle Seahawks in the National Football League (NFL), is heralded by some as the most successful coach in the history of the University of Southern California (USC). Some experts claim that Carroll left the USC head coach job, what he previously said was his dream job, because he knew that sanctions would soon be levied against the university's football program for misconduct. Among the allegations that were eventually proven, one was that illegal payments were made to Reggie Bush, a running back for USC, who also won the Heiman Trophy (as the top football player). Bush, like Carroll, has since had a successful career in the NFL.

Continued

Investigations showed that Bush was paid hundreds of thousands of dollars as a student, which violated college football rules.[35]

The sanctions were numerous and severe for the USC football team:

- It was banned from post-season play for two seasons.
- Scholarships were cut by 30 for three seasons.
- Previous wins were forfeited, including the national championship game.[36]

The pattern has continued during his time in the NFL. The Seahawks are a top-performing team, yet Carroll's team has been fined nearly $1 million dollars for breaking rules related to excessive contact during offseason workouts during multiple seasons since 2012. They also lost a draft pick and had other sanctions.[37]

For Discussion:

1. Given that Carroll left before the sanctions were handed out, what, if anything, do you think should have been done?
2. Assume you own the Seattle Seahawks, what would you do in such a situation?
3. More generally, when evaluating a top performer for a job, including an executive, coach, or dean, how would you ensure past conduct is considered too?

There are several blind spots, common and predictable ways, wherein people are unintentionally unethical. Besides applying the knowledge and guidance provided above, you are encouraged to ask yourself: "What are the potential ethical implications associated with decision X or action Y?" Doing both should help you identify and avoid your blind spots.

To conclude, this chapter explored some key factors that influence how you and others perceive and respond to ethical challenges. Applying this knowledge will give you power and help you differentiate yourself from others at work. Be sure to review the chapter-ending key terms and summary, and then build your problem-solving skills by applying your knowledge to the chapter-ending case. It's an excellent one pertaining to executive compensation.

Chapter Summary

1. Ethical awareness, ethical intuition, and moral development powerfully influence how you and others perceive and respond to ethically challenging situations.
2. Moral development is comprised of three levels and six embedded stages, and it describes how people view rules and others' expectations related to ethical norms.
3. Moral intensity is a quality of a given ethical challenge, and it describes such challenges using six dimensions or characteristics: magnitude of the consequences, social consequences, probability of effect, temporal immediacy, proximity, and concentration of effect.
4. Moral disengagement is another individual characteristic that influences how people think about and behave regarding business ethics. Moral disengagement is a cognitive process that enables people to disconnect their moral standards from their behavior. It is a common way in which people rationalize their misconduct.

5. Ethical blind spots are predictable, systematic, and unintentional ethical lapses. The common types are ill-conceived goals, motivated blindness, indirect blindness, the slippery slope, and overvaluing outcomes.

Key Terms

CASE STUDY: Hard Times for You, for Them, but Not for Me

The title of this case describes the relative position of various stakeholders in companies that declare bankruptcy. It is a fact of business life that numerous public companies declare bankruptcy each year during normal economic times, the number rises during economic downturns.[38] The great recession and the pandemic each caused many times more cases of bankruptcy. In addition to the large number of companies, and the eye-popping amount of dollars involved, there are tremendous negative and often devastating effects on numerous stakeholders such as employees (job loss and loss of retirement plan savings), investors (investment value goes to zero), suppliers (unpaid bills and lost future business), and surrounding communities (plummeting sales due to customer unemployment).

Pink Slip for You, and a Cash Bonus for the Boss?

Although many large public companies still operate after filing for bankruptcy, many employees lose their jobs, and the other stakeholders suffer the consequences noted. However, some employees actually get cash bonuses, and typically, the only employees in the "some" category are executives. Such decisions are made by company's boards of directors, as one of their key responsibilities is to determine compensation of top executives. Some boards of directors decide before filing to pay the CEO, and occasionally other executives, large cash bonuses. For instance, during the economic devastation due to COVID-19, J. C. Penny paid its CEO $4.5 million; Whiting Petroleum paid $6.4 million to its CEO and nearly $15 million to other executives;[39] Neiman Marcus CEO received $2 million;[40] and Hertz paid $16.2 million to 340 director-level and above executives, and $700,000 to its CEO.[41]

Supporters and Critics

How can this be justified? Again, this type of action is not new, and supporters commonly explain that it helps retain the executives and other senior leaders through the tough times, encouraging them to stay and do the tough work of weathering the recession and improving the company's financial position.[42]

Continued

J. C. Penny's board of directors, for instance, issued the following statement:

> "We are making tough, prudent decisions to protect the future of our company and navigate an uncertain environment, including taking necessary steps to retain our talented management team ... Maintaining continuity of leadership is and will continue to be critical to the future of our company's long-term success. Our compensation program is in line with those of other companies in similar situations and is aligned with milestone-based performance goals to continue incentivizing our team to drive results."[43]

Supporters also appropriately point out that when the entire economy tanks, like it did during the great recession of 2008 or the pandemic, many of the financial difficulties confronting companies were not the fault of any executive or any other employee. And for perspective, the dollar value of bankruptcies in the first half of 2020 due to COVID-19 already surpassed the total in all of 2008.[44]

For their part, some critics argue that instead of paying millions of dollars to one executive, that money would have a much greater impact if paid to frontline workers, the ones that most often suffer the greatest hardships. They also show little concern or sympathy for CEOs who often receive a large proportion of their compensation in company stock, which usually goes to $0 once bankruptcy is filed. This means that bankruptcy filings can and do wipe out millions and millions of dollars in accrued compensation. But again, for employees who have retirement plans composed of company stock, their compensation too goes to $0.

What Does Control Have to Do with It?

Another point to consider is relative control. The vast majority of employees have no responsibility in what happened or what will happen to their company before or after filing for bankruptcy, including not saddling the company with piles of debt. Prior to the pandemic, both Chesapeake and Hertz were struggling to service billions of dollars of debt incurred over the years, and any downturn would make this more difficult.

Finally, it is worth noting that the actual practices are legal and have been common for years. Nearly one-third of large companies filing for bankruptcy due to the coronavirus awarded bonuses to executives within a month of filing for bankruptcy.[45]

For Discussion

1. Assume you're a board member who voted to change policy and award executive bonuses. Justify this action using two different concepts in the chapter.
2. Since this practice is so common, do you think executives even see this as a potential ethical issue? Why or why not?
3. What is the responsibility of an executive receiving such a bonus?
4. Consider a CEO who has accepted a pre-bankruptcy bonus and assume that this same CEO thinks that this practice is appropriate. Now analyze that CEO in terms of Kohlberg's Model of Moral Development.
5. Repeat #3 but assume the CEO thinks the practice is inappropriate. How does your moral development analysis change?
6. Explain how a board member or a CEO in a bankruptcy-bonus-granting firm might rationalize this practice. Work through all eight mechanisms (four stages) of moral disengagement. To clarify, give an example of what this person might think or say for each mechanism to justify this practice.

7. Assume you are the CEO of J. C. Penny, who received a multimillion-dollar bonus, while hundreds of stores were closed, thousands of employees lost their jobs, and the company was saddled with piles of debt. Now, assume you are taking the TV Test and have to justify your bonus on the national evening news. What will you say?

Apply Three-Dimensional Problem Solving for Ethics (3D PSE)

You can apply the 3-Dimensional Problem-Solving for Ethics (3D PSE) from multiple perspectives, such as that of an executive receiving a pre-bankruptcy bonus, board member offering such bonuses, employee at such a company, investor in same company, restaurant owner in the surrounding community, or an executive at a competitor who filed for bankruptcy but did not offer bonuses. Be sure to specify whose perspective you are considering, as your problem-solving is likely to differ considerably. Let's try this in two ways: first with you being an executive who received a bonus, and then you as an employee who was laid off by the same company.

figure 3.2

Three-Dimensional Problem-Solving for Ethics (PSE)

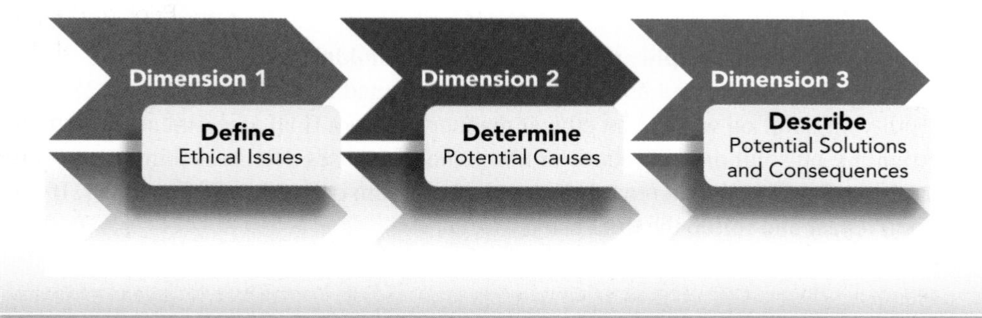

Dimension 1: *Define* the Ethical Challenge

What is the gap in the case? What do you have and what do *you* want?

From your standpoint as the CEO, what is the current situation and how do you want it to be?

a. Why is the current situation a problem? What difficulties or undesirable behaviors and outcomes happen as a result of the problem you defined? Why do you care about the problem you defined in Dimension 1? Why does it matter to you?
b. Define your problem in one or at most two sentences, and structure it in terms of what is current versus what is desired.
c. Who are the key stakeholders, those that affect or those that are affected by the problem you defined?

Dimension 2: *Determine* the Causes

a. **Individuals.** Given the problem you defined in Dimension 1, how do characteristics of individuals (including you, other CEOs like you, board members, employees) cause the problem, such as ethical decision-making approach, moral development, moral disengagement, ethical blind spots, work values, and moral principles?
b. **Contextual.** Are there particular norms (practices) that caused the problem, as defined in Dimension 1? Are there industry or country norms that caused the problem you defined?

Dimension 3: *Describe* Your Potential Solutions and the Intended and Unintended Consequences for Stakeholders

For each cause you identified in Dimension 2, answer the following question:

a. ***What*** do you recommend as a solution(s), and ***how*** would you make it (them) happen?
b. ***Why*** would you do it the way you proposed? Does this reflect a particular ethical decision-making approach (e.g., utilitarian or deontology)? Stage of moral development? Moral disengagement?

If your responses to these questions are unsatisfactory, then go back to Dimension 1 and repeat the process. If, however, you are comfortable and confident in your problem-solving efforts thus far, then ensure you achieve the desired outcomes and avoid any unintended consequences.

c. What is the ***desired and likely effect in the short and long-term*** for the key stakeholders involved in the problem and causes (Dimensions 1 and 2)?
d. What ***potential unintended consequences*** may occur with each proposed solution?
e. If any, what are the **implications for *other* stakeholders** (e.g., individuals, organizations, and communities) besides those noted in Dimensions 1 and 2?
f. Will your solution work in an ethical manner? Make a final assessment of whether your chosen solution will reduce or eliminate the causes determined in Dimension 2, and whether it will then remedy the ethical problem defined in Dimension 1. If not, then repeat and refine the dimensions.

Part Opener Photo Source: Rawpixel.com/Shutterstock
Chapter Opener Photo Source: fizkes/Shutterstock

chapter 4

Individual Factors That Influence Your Ethics-Related Thoughts and Actions

Learning Objectives

AFTER READING THIS CHAPTER, YOU SHOULD BE ABLE TO:

LO1 Describe how values, honesty, integrity, and moral courage influence your sense of what is right and wrong.

LO2 Understand and manage your biases.

LO3 Ensure your conduct is ethical.

WHERE DO **YOU** STAND?

You Cheat, You Pay?

The scenario: You know for a fact that three of your classmates hired a paper writing service to complete their team paper—they cheated. You are simply an acquaintance, neither friend nor stranger with them, and you gained your knowledge by overhearing them talk in a shared study space on campus.

1. What are the potential consequences of their cheating to you? Your career?
2. What would you do? Explain not only what you would do, but also what you would consider or resources you would consult in making your decision to act or not to act.
3. Now assume that this same course is graded on a curve, which means that your grade drops if they get a higher score on the paper than you and your team. Does this change your action? Why or why not?
4. Do your answers change if these same students are your friends? Why or why not?

Introduction

This chapter continues our exploration of individual characteristics that influence business ethics. We begin with learning about your personal values, honesty, integrity, and moral courage and the role they play in how you perceive and respond to ethical challenges at work. Next, you'll learn about common biases to which you and everyone else are susceptible, and that can meaningfully impact your thoughts and behaviors. The chapter concludes with practical guidance on how to ensure your own conduct is ethical.

Key Personal Characteristics That Influence Your Sense of What Is Right and Wrong

As adults, even as children, we all think we have a clear sense of what is right and what is wrong. But you don't have to have a business ethics class in college to know that life is not that simple. So, what explains the differences in what people think is correct and what they do? Many things, of course, but one of the most fundamental are a person's values.

Values

The best place to start is with your personal values. As we covered in chapter 1, values are enduring beliefs about what is important that guide your behavior, and they are relatively stable over time and across situations. Oftentimes, we are confronted with ethical dilemmas, conflicted or less than clear on what is the right thing to do, because the situation conflicts with our values. As such, your values serve as your ethical beacon or alarm that something isn't right. Therefore, it is critically important to identify your key values, as knowing them can help you understand your feelings about situations and ultimately guide your decision making and conduct. The Ethics in Action box walks you through the process.

Ethics in Action

Determining Your Work Values

As you've learned, and will learn throughout this book, values are important guides for ethical behavior at all levels, but it all starts with you.

Step 1—Rank Your Values. The first step is determining what you value *at work*. Use Table 4.1 to rank key work values from 1 (most valuable to you) to 18 (least valuable to you).

table **4.1**

Key Work Values

Work Values	Rank (1–18)
1. Achievement—Regularly feeling a sense of accomplishment	
2. Recognition—Receiving praise or otherwise being acknowledged for your efforts and/or outcomes	
3. Relationships—Rewarding interactions with coworkers	
4. Support—Having supportive managers	
5. Working Conditions—A comfortable and productive work environment	
6. Autonomy—Latitude to do your job according to your own ideas and pace	
7. Helping Others—Assisting individuals and/or groups	
8. Prestige—The respect and admiration of others	
9. Job Security—Stability of employment (remaining employed)	
10. Collaboration—Working with others	

Continued

11. Helping Society—Making an impact on the world
12. High Income—Receiving high compensation
13. Utilizing Your Skills—Opportunity to apply your knowledge, skills, and/or experience to your job
14. Leadership—Opportunity to supervise others
15. Creativity—Opportunity to develop and use your own ideas
16. Variety—Have changing tasks and responsibilities
17. Challenging—Performing tasks that are demanding or new but achievable
18. Influence—Opportunity to affect how other people do their work

Source: List of values adapted from D. Rosenberg McKay, "Clarifying Your Work Values Leads to Job Satisfaction," *thebalancecareer.com*, November 21, 2018, https://www.thebalancecareers.com/identifying-your-work-values-526174.

Step 2—Identify Your Key Values. Focus on values ranked 1–5. These are your priorities or key values. Fulfilling these in particular jobs and over the course of your career is one of the most fundamental and powerful determinants of your satisfaction. It is solely your responsibility to find jobs and create opportunities that match these key values.

Step 3—Conduct the Fulfillment Test. If you have worked or are currently working, then this next step will make the point in Step 2 more real. Think of your current or a past job and ask yourself: "How well does that job fulfill my top five values?" If the answer is "very well," it is likely you are quite satisfied with that job. If, however, your answer is "not well at all," it is a safe bet that you are not satisfied and would gladly accept an offer for a different job.

Your values may change over time. For instance, when doing your undergraduate or MBA degrees is generally the time when you value high pay more than at other times in your lives. However, it is rare for your top five to be replaced by five different values over time. Nevertheless, these values can assist you in your job search, understanding why some jobs are more fulfilling than others, and why you leave certain jobs and are attracted to new ones.

For Discussion:

1. What about your values surprised you?
2. Explain two ways you can use this knowledge about your values.
3. Describe the characteristics of a job that would most likely fulfill your top three ranked values.

As you can see, your personal work values are useful in identifying jobs and employers that are likely to be fulfilling, and they, of course, have implications for business ethics.

Honesty

Are you an **honest** person? If you answered yes, then this means you adhere to the facts and are sincere in dealings with others—you are truthful. The importance of honesty to ethics cannot be overstated. To make the point, think of someone you feel is dishonest. Do you

honest
adhere to the facts and are sincere in dealings with others—you are truthful

trust that person? If you don't trust that person, then can you actually consider them ethical? Not entirely. One of the quickest and most effective ways to undermine your reputation is to lie. Right? Well, not always and not everybody.

(Dis)honesty also has significant financial consequences. Researchers estimate that dishonesty accounts for approximately 30 percent of inventory losses in American business in the form of employee theft and $3.7 trillion in the form of employee fraud each year. Perhaps more shocking are research findings that suggest 75 percent of employees steal from their employers at least once.[2] Even if these numbers are far off, the situation is still quite dire. Combined, the interpersonal and financial costs make a compelling case for the importance of honesty to business. However, not only are people often dishonest, as shown by these statistics, there are many situations in which others argue that dishonesty is *not* unethical in business.

The well-known challenge to this comes from those who argue business is a game, and it thus has its own set of rules that allow for lying.[3] Like poker, for instance, you can bluff or otherwise play your cards and bet in ways to manipulate your opponent. The same happens in negotiations. Even if not explicitly meant to deceive, many tactics do aim at misleading or influencing the other party in ways that benefit you and cost them.[4]

Bottom line: You have a choice, and you are cautioned to choose carefully. You can approach business as a game to win, even if it is by deceiving or otherwise being dishonest. But, recall the concept of sustainability, which can be defined as success over time, and consider what might happen if your "opponent" learns that you were less than honest. How might that influence your future business with that person? How might it affect your reputation? You may even cross paths again in the job market, what will happen then? Would you hire him or her, the one you "beat"? Would they hire you?

Integrity

integrity
your actions align with your values

If you have **integrity,** then your actions align with your values. People with integrity do the right thing even when "nobody is watching," meaning their beliefs prevail despite temptations or the opportunity to take advantage of others.[5] Therefore, people with integrity would confidently step to the microphone and camera if put to the TV Test (stage fright aside). Another way to think of integrity is if your personal espoused values align with your enacted values, who you say and think you are is consistent with what you actually say and do.

Gerain0812/Shutterstock

The old expression "he or she is two-faced" can be illustrative of someone who lacks integrity. They say one thing in one situation to serve their personal interests, and then they contradict this when speaking to others about the same thing. This is what a lack of integrity looks like. Now what does it look like to live *with* integrity?

Imagine the following scenario, which occurs at both school and work. You're the member of a team, and two other team members are complaining back and forth about another member when you enter the room. Instead of sitting quietly and listening, or joining in on the gossip session, you ask your teammates: "Have you discussed these issues with him?" This is acting with integrity.[6]

Can you think of a person who is dishonest or lacks integrity but you still trust? The answer to this simple question helps make the point and show the importance of both honesty and integrity in business ethics. Another common business scenario in 2020 provided more evidence. Due to COVID-19, many business leaders had to make difficult decisions and cut costs in a variety of ways. Some leaders regularly kept their employees informed of the situation, shared details related to the financial strains, and built trust even during trying times. This made it easier, but certainly not easy, for these same leaders when they had to cut employees' pay by 15 percent in order to keep the doors of the business open and avoid layoffs. Employees were not blindsided and were more likely to trust the leader was being honest and would follow through on her or his word in the future.[7]

If honesty and integrity are so important, then how can you build and preserve them? The following Ethics in Action box provides some guidance.

Lastly, if you have honesty and integrity as values, like so many *Fortune* 500 companies, you can use these same behaviors as a test of how true you are to these values in how you live your life.

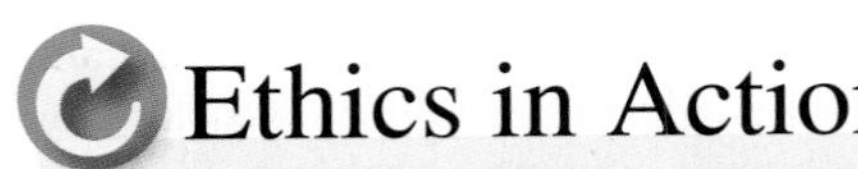

Ethics in Action

How to Develop Honesty and Integrity

1. **Be True to Your Word.** Plainly and simply, do what you say you will. Of course, you want to do this, but the most common obstacle is not bad intentions on your part, rather procrastination. You just don't get around to delivering on your word in a timely fashion, which can lead people to think you don't deliver on what you say.
2. **The Fair Way Is the Only Way.** We'll address this in more detail next. But making decisions in ways that people perceive were appropriate can go a long way to building and preserving your integrity. Think of it this way. Have you ever met anyone who has directly said, "I am unfair"? Not likely. This means that when people are unfair, they are inconsistent with how they think and speak of themselves. This undermines their credibility.
3. **Give Credit to Whom It Is Due.** You don't have to be a suck-up or a brown-noser, and lavish praise or credit excessively, but be sure the person who deserves credit gets it. A common sign of those who lack integrity are people who steal the credit.
4. **You Are a Truth Teller.** Tell people the true story, even when the news is bad. It is easy for everyone to share or present good news, but sometimes the news is less than favorable, or downright horrible. And don't confuse empathy with not telling the complete or true story. They are not mutually exclusive.[8]

For Discussion:

1. Describe how you can apply this knowledge with a project team at school.
2. How could you use the above guidance in a job interview?
3. How could you implement this advice when starting a new job?

Moral Courage—"Integrity Under Fire"[9]

moral courage allows an individual to do what he or she believes is right, despite the fear of social or economic consequences

"**Moral courage** allows an individual to do what he or she believes is right, despite the fear of social or economic consequences."[10] As such, moral courage supports or represents consistency between your intentions to do what is right and actually doing it. Notice, however, that because the definition includes both social and economic consequences, it can be difficult at work. Confronting questionable behaviors and practices has numerous potential costs to you, such as relationships, promotional opportunities, money, or even your job. That is why it is courage.

So why bother? One reason is that saying or doing the difficult but right thing is where positive change comes from. If nobody spoke up or ever took the difficult path, then we as individuals, organizations, and countries would fail to advance and thrive. Moreover, you already know and have learned from this book that one ethical misstep can be very costly to you as an individual, and that patterns of misconduct can destroy employers and negatively impact many stakeholders. Courage, therefore, is an important way to prevent a single misdeed from escalating or turning into a norm.

Like other forms of behavior, moral courage can be contagious, which means the actions of one can influence the actions of others. This can be self-reinforcing. As the courage spreads to others, it, in effect, supports the first person and motivates other people to speak up, speak out, and to act. Countless examples of moral courage and moral champions occurred in the Black Lives Matter and social justice protests in 2020.

Given these benefits, how can moral courage be fostered?[11]

1. **Complain Constructively.** Set expectations so that people support disagreements with reasonable arguments and examples. If something is causing a problem, then also explain why it is a problem and what to do about it. Remember, dissent is a key component of improvement.
2. **Promote Opinion Sharing.** Light is the best disinfectant. Therefore, hotlines, blogs, one-on-one meetings, ethics committees, ombudsmen are all means for enabling employees to speak up and speak out. Also, simply asking if there are issues can be remarkably effective.
3. **Seek to Understand, Not Punish.** A lack of action is bad enough, but retaliation and other negative consequences create a culture of silence. You, your coworkers, and the leaders of organizations need to thoroughly understand and make great efforts to ensure moral courage is not punished.
4. **Explain Versus Attack.** You don't have to agree, of course, but it is important that you explain why you think the issue raised is not a problem.
5. **Patience Is a Virtue.** Whether it is an investigation into misconduct, an analysis of data, or implementing a solution, it takes time. Consistent and genuine progress regarding ethical issues is essential, but do not rush to judgment.

Colin Kaepernick taking a knee during the national anthem in 2016 was a notable act of moral courage. Afterward he explained: "I am not going to stand up to show pride in a flag for a country that oppresses black people and people of color. To me, this is bigger than football and it would be selfish on my part to look the other way . . . if they take football away, my endorsements from me, I know that I stood up for what is right."[12] His actions epitomize moral courage, and the impact is arguably stronger today.

Whistleblowing is often an illustration of moral courage and moral championing, which you'll learn more about in chapter 5.

Understanding and Managing Your Biases

First, because you are human, you have biases—it is a fact of life and inevitable. What is more important is that you understand what biases are, identify the ones you have, and learn how to guard against their undesirable effects. This is our goal, and to achieve this goal, it is necessary to understand the origin and function of biases. It's all in our brains.

Our brains are magnificent and incomprehensibly complex. Because of their own complexity, and the complexity inherent in our lives as humans, our brains do many things to work more efficiently. Despite their computing power, we wouldn't survive a full day if we had to consciously process every stimulus we encounter. Our brains, therefore, use shortcuts to make many things subconscious, quick, or seemingly automatic. The technical term for this is **heuristics**, which are mental shortcuts that allow you to make decisions efficiently and quickly. Most heuristics serve us well most of the time, but there are exceptions, and some of those exceptions are biases.

heuristics mental shortcuts that allow you to make decisions efficiently and quickly

Biases are heuristics that cause systematic errors in judgment and decision making, and several of these can have undesirable consequences for your ethical decision making. Let's explore some that are especially relevant for business ethics.

biases heuristics that cause systematic errors in judgment and decision making

Fundamental Attribution Error

Fundamental attribution errors occur when you consistently ascribe a person's behavior to their internal characteristics and ignore potentially legitimate external influences. Applying this to business ethics, you would assume that any and all unethical conduct is purely the result of bad people doing bad things because they chose to do so. This means that you would ignore or discount the effects of performance management systems that may reward bad behavior, leaders or managers who pressure you to cut corners in order to perform, or organizational cultures that legitimize or make questionable behavior seem acceptable.

fundamental attribution errors occur when you consistently ascribe a person's behavior to their internal characteristics and ignore potentially legitimate external influences

For instance, the executives at Wells Fargo seemed to blame the more than 5,000 employees who participated in and were fired for falsifying accounts as purely their own doing—bad actors doing bad things—while at the same time refusing to acknowledge the role their own attitudes and the company's reward programs played.[13]

Self-Serving Bias

Self-serving bias occurs when you attribute your successes to you, your efforts, and factors you control while assigning all poor performance to factors beyond your control. You likely see the implications for business ethics. If you suffer from this bias, then you are not likely to take any responsibility for your own actions and blame inappropriate conduct on your professor or classmates at school, your boss, or the reward system at work.

self-serving bias when you attribute your successes to you, your efforts, and factors you control while assigning all poor performance to factors beyond your control

Confirmation Bias

Confirmation bias occurs when the only information considered is that which is consistent with one's prior beliefs. This can be especially devastating in terms of business ethics and happens all of the time. Think of most any scandal you hear about in the news, most often at least one person interviewed says: "I've known him for 20 years, I can't believe he actually did that." Or, "she would never do that." "He is a top student. He wouldn't cheat." Confirmation bias is a serious problem when people don't consider, investigate, or act against questionable behavior because they refuse to consider information that is inconsistent with their own views.

confirmation bias when the only information considered is that which is consistent with one's prior beliefs

Halo and Horns Effect

halo and horns effect when your perceptions of a particular characteristic of an individual, group, or organization are applied to them generally

The **halo and horns effect** occurs when your perceptions of a particular characteristic of an individual, group, or organization are applied to them generally. If you think Director

Terri Shyster of Fraud-Hill and Associates is friendly based on your one meeting, and as a result, assume she must be a fair and ethical person, then you have applied the halo effect. This becomes problematic if you allow your halo to influence whether you will consider reports of bullying presented by coworkers and customers against Terri.

Despite the allusion to angels and desirable conduct, you can also have a negative halo or horns effect. For instance, if you learned that Mit Scoundrel was fired from a previous job for "misconduct," and you then assume that he will cross the line in his new job, or if you hear rumors about misconduct in his department and attribute it to him, this is a negative halo or horns effect.

Escalation of Commitment

escalation of commitment when individuals, groups, or organizations continue a given path even though doing so will likely result in negative outcomes

Escalation of commitment happens when individuals, groups, or organizations continue a given path even though doing so will likely result in negative outcomes. Unethical leaders who create unethical organizations are often guilty of this bias. They think that continuing to sweep misconduct under the rug, or not confront it and take appropriate action, that it will go away. Often times it doesn't, and instead, continues. Two examples are the child abuse scandal committed by Jerry Sandusky at Penn State and the sexual assault scandal involving Larry Nassar, the US Olympic gymnastics team doctor. People knew, they notified others, and those notified failed to take appropriate action. The abuse continued, and people did not intervene until it was revealed to the public, but this was many years and over one hundred victims later.

Stereotypes

stereotypes assumptions about individuals based on the characteristics of a group to which they belong

Stereotypes are assumptions about individuals based on the characteristics of a group to which they belong. The problem with stereotypes is not that they are inaccurate, it's that they are assumed to apply to everyone in that group. Stereotypes are part of many unethical behaviors, policies, and practices. Many challenges confronted by women, for instance, as well as those related to age, are stereotypes with common ethical implications. The classes protected by the Equal Employment Opportunity Commission are examples of groups that are stereotyped and often discriminated against in the workplace. You will learn much more about formal controls (laws and regulations) in chapter 9.

The following Ethical in Action box provides a scenario illustrating one or more of these biases, see which you can identify.

Ethics in Action

We're All in This Together

Imagine you are the new provost of your university, hired from another university, and you learn the following about the dean of the business school and one of its departments. The department in question has a history of discrimination and bullying, and leadership in the department (but not the dean) has changed. With this in mind, the senior members of that department are accused of bullying and intimidation of junior faculty. This is brought to the attention of the dean, but the dean chooses to do nothing.

The dean is well known, generally well-liked, and brings in substantial donations. And one of the accused senior people in the department is a little known but well-liked minority hire. One of the other senior offenders is a woman.

Continued

The bullying continues and spreads to other members of the department. One of the targets of the abuse files a complaint with the university because the dean did nothing. The ethics committee does an investigation and finds that the claims are true—bullying and intimidation occurred. The ethics committee makes recommendations for action against the members of the department. But instead of taking action against the offenders, the dean retaliated against the person who filed the complaint—gave an inaccurate and low performance evaluation, lower raise than average and a lower raise than those given to the bullies, and removed the person from a key committee, among other things. When the dean was subsequently confronted by the target about these retaliatory actions, the response was, "So, if you don't like it you can leave."

As the provost, you learned about all of this and did nothing.

For Discussion:

1. Using the biases you just learned, how might they explain the (lack of) action of the provost?
2. What are the potential implications of doing nothing?
3. Again, assuming you are the provost, what might you do instead of nothing? Explain your reasoning.

Now that you've learned about how some individual characteristics influence ethical conduct, what can you do about it? This final section provides some pointed advice, including actual language, to consider when you encounter dilemmas or gray areas, as well as conduct you feel clearly crosses the ethical line.

Ensure Your Conduct Is Ethical

As we've already established, you're confronted with ethical challenges throughout your professional life. These situations are often quite difficult, but this does not necessarily mean you are powerless. You'll learn more about what to do and how to handle these situations throughout this book, including the section on blowing the whistle in chapter 5. But the following are some widely applicable recommendations for dealing with ethical challenges diplomatically. Students and clients have found these especially useful.

"That's How We Do Things Here"

When you witness or are confronted with questionable behavior, a common reaction is to simply stay quiet and see how things play out. In other words, if you feel uncomfortable, maybe someone else will feel uncomfortable too, but they will speak up. This is especially true if you are new to the organization and wonder, despite your own discomfort, if this is how things are done. You don't want to make waves and may use one of the following clichés not to speak up or speak out:

- *The incident isn't all that serious . . . .*
- *Calling out such behaviors is not my responsibility. I'll leave it to the manager or somebody else more senior.*
- *Loyal workers don't make waves.*
- *Go along to get along.*

In reality, these are not simply clichés, but highly consequential excuses, as not speaking up or not speaking out is exactly how unethical conduct continues and the costs mount. These costs can be paid by individuals, groups, organizations, and even you. Understand and accept that confronting unethical conduct is part of your job, and everyone else's too. If an action or policy seems out of line, act immediately. To do your part, consider the following:

Ethical Issues Are Business Issues. Similar to revenues, costs, and profits, ethical conduct is a critical element of business performance. If you're not convinced, recall the examples in Table 1.1 wherein patterns of unethical conduct were the demise of many organizations. This means that all of those employees not only lost their jobs, but they also had to deal with the stigma (or negative halo) when looking for future jobs. Therefore, if you want to make a case against unethical conduct or for ethical conduct, build it like you would do for a new product proposal. Identify and communicate the benefits of behaving ethically and the costs of not doing so. You can even measure it, as you'll learn in chapter 8 about ethical organizational cultures.

Challenge the Justification. When you witness conduct that seems to approach or cross the line, particularly if a rule or policy exists about a given issue, ask that person, "If this is common practice, then why do we have a policy against it?" Of course, you could use the TV Test and ask, "How would you feel about explaining what you did and why to our manager or customers, during an interview on the evening news?

Use Your Junior Status to Your Advantage

Part of the challenge for you is that you are new, you just don't know how things are done, what is okay, what isn't, and what is simply gray. Again, this is not an excuse not to act. Instead, try using your junior status to your advantage. In many ways, your lack of experience is a genuine advantage. People know you don't know and expect questions. Try these:

Help Me Understand. "As you know, I'm new and therefore may have misunderstood something, but it seems that what you've done could cause problems. Will you please explain and help me understand?"

What about the Long Term? "I see how this course of action could be beneficial in the immediate term (e.g., make the sales number for this quarter), but what might be the effects over time—next quarter, year-end, or the next project? It seems there might be some unintended consequences." Unethical conduct is often motivated by short-term pressures, which causes people to cut corners. Therefore, framing your questions in terms of long-term consequences can help. (Recall our discussion of individual sustainability in chapter 2.)

Problem-Solving versus Complaining. As with many challenges, you are often better off presenting an ethical problem along with a solution. Problems alone can be and often are seen only as complaints. But when you pair them with suggested solutions, people, especially managers, are more interested and more likely to act.

Let's now turn our attention to personal ethics during the job search.

Your Job Search and Ethics

Regardless of how many jobs you've interviewed for at this point in your life, you almost certainly will interview for many more. And as you either know or will learn, the motivation to get a job can tempt you to approach or even cross the ethical line. The intent of this section is to provide some insights and guidance on how to put your best ethical foot forward and succeed.

Andry_Popov/Shutterstock

You already know the first thing to remember—don't lie. Astonishingly, lying seems more common than not. For instance, one study of employers found that 85 percent of them have caught candidates lying on their resumes.[14] Thirty-six percent of participants in another study reported they lied, and nearly all (93 percent) of these people said they know someone who lied.[15]

Falsifying resume info isn't just for entry-level employees, executives do it too, and even deans of admissions at Massachusetts Institute of Technology. A now-former dean of admissions was dismissed after it was learned she had not earned the master's or bachelor's degrees she claimed. And when confronted, she explained that she did not have the courage to correct her resume at the time or since.[16]

Mina Chang, formerly deputy assistant secretary in the State Department's Bureau of Conflict and Stability Operations, embellished and then some. Among her now-disputed claims are the following:

- Part of a UN panel on drones and humanitarian relief efforts.
- Harvard alumni (only a seven-week course).
- Overstated the size, activity, and impact of her humanitarian nonprofit organization.
- Selfies on social media with notable politicians with whom she has no relationship (e.g., President Bill Clinton, Gen. David Petraeus, and Secretary of State Madelaine Albright).
- Created a fake *Time Magazine* cover featuring her.

You don't want to add to those statistics.

The potential consequences are numerous. Not getting the job is an obvious one. Another, and less obvious, is that you need to "keep track" of and continue to live your lie. If you said you have experience, skills, or credentials that you actually don't possess, then chances are you'll be discovered. This could result in you getting fired, and in the process, trashing your reputation and foreclosing future opportunities.

The three most common lies during job searches (e.g., on resumes and during interviews) and how to avoid them are outlined in Table 4.2:

table 4.2

Most Common Lies and What to do Instead

Most Common Resume Lies	What to do Instead
Education. Claiming you have a bachelor's when you only have an associates is obviously wrong and easily caught. But saying you have a "graduate degree" and implying it is a master's when you only have a certificate or completed a training course becomes problematic. Or, if one course in a particular topic is presented as deep or expert knowledge, it can also be an issue.	State your formal degrees, certificates, and training directly, as awarded. Instead of exaggerating your education, provide more details about how you've applied what you learned. You can also add awards, special projects, or school-sponsored consulting projects. It's better to show your motivation for continuous learning, what you would like to do in the future, rather than be creative with the past.

Continued

Dates. The career landscape has been volatile for decades, which means many, if not most, people have been out of work for some period(s) of time. Some of these gaps are no fault of their own, and in fact, some are due to the unethical conduct of executives, other leaders, and entire industries (e.g., the great recession). Therefore, resist the urge to connect the dates between one job and another or to create a fake "interim" position.	Gaps are expected and happen. It, therefore, is best not to avoid them, but instead be prepared to explain. Sometimes it's downsizing, sometimes you take time to reflect and reassess your path, sometimes you've been fired. All of these happen and can be addressed. Some experts recommend being proactive during interviews about date gaps in your resume. They suggest bringing them up yourself, rather than waiting for the interviewer to raise questions.
Skills. Skills, skills, skills, and more skills. Many candidates feel that the more skills they list, the better their chances. With AI now screening resumes, this approach has some merit. However, if you advance to later rounds and talk to real people, then your exaggerations will likely be discovered. Language skills are also commonly overstated. Because you had one or two classes of Spanish in your freshman year does not mean you will be able to conduct business in Spanish with native speakers.	Only list the skills you genuinely have and can demonstrate. Your embellished resume may get you an interview, but just imagine if your interviewer suddenly addressed you in a language listed on your resume, asked about your approach to valuing a merger candidate, or requested you to give a high-level outline of new product development.

Source: Adapted from D. Papandrea, "The Biggest Resume Lies to Avoid," *monster.com*, accessed June 18, 2020, https://www.monster.com/career-advice/article/the-truth-about-resume-lies-hot-jobs.

To conclude, in this chapter, you were asked to look in the mirror and consider characteristics about you that may contribute to your (un)ethical conduct. Self-awareness is an essential element of any development or self-improvement plan. With this chapter, you just increased yours. In the next chapter, we'll explore some of the common types of ethical challenges you'll experience at work and how to deal with them, including when and when not to blow the whistle.

Chapter Summary

1. There are many characteristics that influence your sense of what is right and wrong; some well-known ones are your values, honesty, and integrity.
2. Moral courage is another powerful individual characteristic that influences whether people speak up and speak out when they are aware of questionable conduct, even when there may be social and/or economic costs to them personally.
3. Biases, including stereotypes, affect our perceptions of an individual's and group's ethical conduct.
4. You can do many things to ensure your own conduct is ethical and combat existing norms, such as "that's how we do things here."
5. Ethical issues are business issues. You will be well served to treat them this way. Make the business case in terms of benefits and costs for (un)ethical conduct to help illustrate the potential positive and negative consequences.
6. If you are new to a particular job or organization, use your lack of experience to your advantage – question and clarify policies, practices, and acceptable conduct.
7. Be mindful of embellishing your education or skills on your resume or during interviews, as well as falsely filling in gaps in time.

Key Terms

CASE STUDY: Impressive, But Is It Really You?

What if, by any measure, you were considered number one in your industry, so far out in front that nobody even knows who is number two or number three?

What if your success rate was nearly 100 percent, while others in your field are only 50 or 60 percent successful?[17]

What if your bio included: ". . . has written more bestsellers and created more enduring fictional characters than any other novelist today"?[18]

If this is you, then you are James Patterson, who since his first book in 1976 has produced over 158 titles and sold 325 million copies. Roughly one in twenty hardcover books sold in the United States has his name on it. And by the way, these are only estimates, as exact and current figures are difficult to come by. However, *Forbes* estimated his annual earnings to be $80 million, and if that isn't impressive enough, he sold nearly 5 million books in the twelve months between June 2019 and June 2020.[19]

These numbers are all remarkable. He has been described as an industry of his own and his process as a factory, wherein he marshals an army of others to write his books. To be clear, Patterson works incredibly hard and shows no signs of slowing down in his seventies. Many other novelists have adopted this approach, such as Tom Clancy (e.g., *The Hunt for the Red October*), Robert Ludlum (e.g., *Jason Bourne* series), and Michael Crichton (e.g., *Pirate Latitudes*). Many books written by politicians (e.g., Ronald Regan, Hilary Clinton, and Donald Trump) and executives (e.g., Jack Welch of GE and Howard Schultz of Starbucks) are actually written by others too.[20]

Nevertheless, in other industries and to unaware observers, these practices may conflict with laws, rules, and the cultural norms that exist about these very issues. Most notably, college students and professors. It is wrong for students to hire someone else to write a paper for a class and take credit for it, and the same goes for professors. They are not allowed to have someone else write a research paper for publication in an academic journal, and then accept sole credit for it.

This begs the question: How is it acceptable practice for novelists and other writers to do this?

Part of the answer is ghostwriting. Ghostwriters agree to give credit and rights for their work to others for a fee. It's a mutual agreement—the ghostwriter does the work, and the author whose name is on the cover takes all or most of the credit, and the lion's share of the money.[21]

Another part of the answer is whose idea is being written about. Patterson, for instance, is a veritable hurricane of ideas, many of which he cultivates into detailed outlines that are then handed off to others to develop and complete.

Some may see all of this as plagiarism, which occurs when a person (1) steals or passes off another's work as one's own, (2) uses another's work product without giving credit, or (3) presents an idea as new when it is derived from an existing source.[22]

Continued

One slight variation that seems more common in books written about celebrities and politicians is they give some level of credit, such as "Homer Simpson: The Enlightened One with Ms G. Writer." The "with" at least reveals that someone else was involved. One could still wonder, if Homer didn't write the book, and Ms. G. Writer wrote every word, then how can this be acceptable. Again, think of the college student. It would be unacceptable for a student to hand in a paper that someone else entirely wrote yet turn it in assigning credit in such a way—"Susan Student with Hans Helper."

As for a professor, doing this would violate ethics codes of the industry, cause the work to be retracted, and potentially result in other severe sanctions (e.g., termination from a university and expulsion from the academy).

For Discussion:

1. Assume you are a novelist who uses ghostwriters, justify.
2. Assume you are a novelist who does not use ghostwriters, argue why not.
3. Assume you are a publisher, justify the use of ghostwriters.
4. What ethical challenges discussed in the chapter are potentially illustrated in this case? Describe.
5. Create an argument explaining why hiring writers and not giving them (appropriate) credit is acceptable in some industries (e.g., novel writing) but not for students in college.
6. Now extend your thinking to paid speech writers. Do the same arguments and rules apply? Explain.

Apply Three-Dimensional Problem-Solving for Ethics (3D PSE)

You can apply the 3D PSE from multiple perspectives (Figure 4.1), such as that of a novelist who uses ghostwriters, novelist who does not use ghostwriters, or a college student. Be sure to specify whose perspective, as your problem-solving is likely to differ considerably. Let's try it with you assuming you are a novelist who does not use ghostwriters.

figure **4.1**

Three-Dimensional Problem-Solving for Ethics (3D PSE)

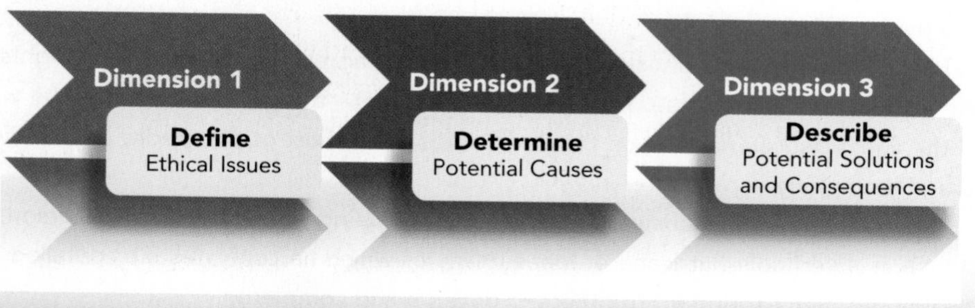

Dimension 1: *Define* the Ethical Challenge

What is the gap in the case? What do you have and what do *you* want?

a. From your view as a novelist, what is the current situation with the industry and how do you want it to be?
b. Why is the current situation a problem? What difficulties or undesirable behaviors and outcomes happen as a result of the problem you defined? Why do you, and novelists like you, care about the problem you defined in Dimension 1?
c. Define your problem in one or at most two sentences and structure it in terms of what is current versus what is desired.
d. Who are the key stakeholders, those that affect or are affected by the problem you defined?

Dimension 2: *Determine* the Causes

a. **Individuals.** Given the problem you defined in Dimension 1, how do characteristics of novelists (including you, others like you, as well as those who use ghostwriters) cause the problem, such as ethical decision-making approach, work values, and moral principles?
b. **Contextual.** Are there particular norms (practices) that caused the problem, as defined in Dimension 1? These norms (practices) may be for the publishing industry or higher education.

Dimension 3: *Describe* Your Potential Solutions and the Intended and Unintended Consequences for Stakeholders

For each cause you identified in Dimension 2, answer the following question:

a. ***What*** do you recommend and ***how*** would you make it happen?
b. ***Why*** you would do it? Does this reflect a particular ethical decision-making approach (e.g., utilitarian or deontology)?

If your responses to these questions are unsatisfactory, then go back to Dimension 1 and repeat the process. If, however, you are comfortable and confident in your problem-solving efforts thus far, then ensure you achieve the desired outcomes and avoid any unintended consequences.

c. What is the ***desired and likely effect in the short and long term*** for the key stakeholders involved in the problem and causes (Dimensions 1 and 2)?
d. What ***potential unintended consequences*** may occur with each proposed solution?
e. If any, what are the **implications for *other* stakeholders** (e.g., individuals, organizations, and communities) besides those noted in Dimensions 1 and 2?
f. Will your solution work in an ethical manner? Make a final assessment of whether your chosen solution will reduce or eliminate the causes determined in Dimension 2, and if this then will remedy the ethical problem defined in Dimension 1. If not, then repeat and refine the dimensions.

Chapter Opener Photo Source: STUDIO GRAND WEB/Shutterstock

chapter 5

Common Ethical Challenges and How to Handle Them

Learning Objectives

AFTER READING THIS CHAPTER, YOU SHOULD BE ABLE TO:

LO1 Manage common ethical issues at work.

LO2 Understand and navigate issues related to employee monitoring.

LO3 Recognize and influence where the line is drawn between your professional and personal lives.

LO4 Appreciate whistleblowing—why, why not, and how.

WHERE DO **YOU** STAND?

Watch This, but Not That

Employers across industries and around the globe are increasingly faced with the dilemma of monitoring their employees working remotely. Technology has made remote working possible, and technology is also being used to monitor what employees do and don't do during their working hours, where they are, and when they do their work. As soon as an employee first logs on, an array of services and apps can be used to track their activities: which websites are visited, precise measurements of keystrokes and mouse movements, relative time spent actively using any app (e.g., email vs. Excel), location throughout the entire day (using your phone's GPS), as well as screenshots in intervals of minutes or seconds, including actual photos of those who participated in video calls.[1]

Much of this monitoring, from the employer's perspective, is in the name of ensuring productivity. For instance, many companies providing employee monitoring services use data collected to generate productivity scores and even employee rankings.[2] Employers then choose how to use these data and whether to share it with their employees.

Some employees who know they are being monitored—not all employers notify employees, and still others don't communicate what is being monitored, when, and how—report that simply knowing they are being monitored has changed their behavior and directed it toward activities labeled as "productive" versus "unproductive."[3]

1. What are your thoughts about monitoring employees working remotely?
2. Assuming you would draw the line somewhere, where would it be (i.e., what would be off-limits and what would be acceptable)? Explain.
3. Assume you own a company, and due to the pandemic, all of your employees work remotely. Now assume you are interviewed for the evening news (the TV test), and you are asked to justify why you monitor your employees.

Introduction

You may face innumerable ethical conflicts during your professional life, the nature of which are likely to change over time along with technology, work arrangements, job responsibilities, and societal norms. We, therefore, focus our attention on some of the most common conflicts you are likely to experience at work. This material will serve as background for our exploration of employee privacy and monitoring, which are two contemporary, quickly evolving, and contentious issues. We then investigate the conflicts related to what is considered a part of your professional versus your personal life. Our always connected world has blurred these lines and created formidable challenges for you and your employers. The chapter concludes with the always difficult issue—whistleblowing.

Managing Common Ethical Issues at Work

At work, some ethical conflicts are obvious but not common, while others are common but perhaps less obvious. For instance, we all know that offering or accepting bribes is wrong, but many people go through their entire careers without being confronted with bribes—at least that's what you might think. What about giving an internship to the daughter of a colleague? Is that bribery? What if that colleague is your boss?[4] Part of the challenge is that many things we know in our minds to be unethical can be difficult to identify in real life. Helping you identify and effectively deal with such situations are main foci of this chapter. We will address a subset of issues that are common, perhaps subtle, but potentially highly consequential—lying, conflicts of interest, and misuse of company time and other resources. Let's begin with perhaps the oldest issue—lying.

Lying

lying
sharing inaccurate or withholding relevant information with the intention of deceiving another

Lying is sharing inaccurate or withholding relevant information with the intention of deceiving another.[5] This definition covers both lying by commission and lying by omission. Both are problematic for business ethics. Examples of lying by commission are as follows:

- Telling your boss you are working remotely when you're actually playing golf.
- Claiming a product is organic when it's not.
- Lying under oath in court (perjury).

Lying by omission also has limitless forms:

- Not informing customers of health risks associated with your product.
- Not sharing relevant information (e.g., a bankruptcy) when applying for a loan.
- Not telling investors that your start-up is being sued for patent infringement.

The problem with lies is that they can cause people to make bad decisions because of a lack of accurate information or presence of inaccurate information. Moreover, the consequences for the liar can also be great. One can go to jail, be fined, or lose their license. For instance, Dr. Jacques Roy hit the trifecta and experienced all three consequences. His Texas medical license was revoked for defrauding (lying) to Medicare and Medicaid as part of a nearly $400 million scam.[6] But arguably, the other penalties were more severe—420 months in prison and a $268 million fine.[7] Besides such punishment, we know that liars cannot be trusted, and the damage to the liar's reputation and perceived integrity may last longer and be more costly than fines or other formal penalties.

For Discussion

Assume you are interviewing for a job, and one of the major reasons why it is attractive is that you think the hiring manager is terrific. The two of you seemingly have good chemistry, and you are convinced she is genuinely committed to your development. If you get the offer, you'll take it. But what you don't know is that the manager has already accepted a job with a different company.

1. If she doesn't reveal this to you, is she lying by omission? Explain.
2. Now, imagine the roles are reversed. Would you reveal this information with candidates you interview? Why or why not?

Conflicts of Interest

conflicts of interest situations when you must choose to either serve your personal interests or those of another individual, group, or organization

Conflicts of interest involve situations when you must choose to either serve your personal interests or those of another individual, group, or organization.[8] For instance, there is a conflict of interest when you hire a customer's friend or relative who is less qualified than other candidates; give business to less qualified or more expensive vendors because you get a kickback or some personal favor (e.g., a gift); or start a company that competes with your current employer, while you still work for them.[9]

One of the more common conflicts occurs when managers and subordinates are romantically involved. Former McDonald's CEO Steve Easterbrook, for instance, violated company policies by having a relationship with a subordinate. Despite being consensual, and Easterbrook being divorced, the relationship still violated company policies and values. Mr. Easterbrook resigned, but it didn't end there. An anonymous tip (whistleblower) caused the company to dig deeper, which revealed multiple such relationships between Easterbrook and company employees. The company then sued Easterbrook claiming, among other things, that he lied during the investigation, destroyed documents, and approved a stock grant to one of the women.[10]

There are many ways to avoid or otherwise discourage conflicts of interest. A common mechanism is a code of conduct that you'll learn about in chapter 9, which outlines likely types of conflicts in a particular organization along with suitable courses of action. Employee handbooks, essentially books of rules you often receive when first hired, also commonly have sections on conflicts of interest. Ethics training frequently involves similar content, and hotlines for reporting are also valuable.

Bottom line: Avoiding and remedying conflicts of interest is a shared responsibility. Sure, some conflicts may be obvious, but many are not. Therefore, it is essential that employers identify the relevant conflicts for their employees, communicate them, and prepare employees proactively. As for you, and other employees, if you're unclear about a potential conflict . . . ask! It is likely someone has the answer, and if they don't, then you might be part of creating one.

Company Time and Other Resources

Perhaps the most widespread or common ethical issues relate to how employees use their work time and employer's other resources (devices and networks). The majority of workers continue to be paid by the hour, nearly 60 percent.[11] But even if you have a salaried job, your employer still expects you to work a "full day." Think of it like this. Assume you went to work tomorrow, spent part of your day in your office, at your desk, diligently fulfilling your job responsibilities. Now imagine that throughout your workday you went to the lobby to meet with your best friend and chat, shopped in a store in the lobby, met your parents who stopped by because they were in the neighborhood, made your fantasy football selections with the others in your league, and rendezvoused with someone you met on an online dating site. These are things people effectively do throughout the day when they communicate with these people online, on social media, and over the phone. Multiply this by days in the week, weeks in the year, and by the number of employees in your company, and it is a huge loss of time, money, and productivity.

March Madness is an excellent example. Some estimate that 75 million American employees actively follow the annual college basketball tournament, and these employees spend approximately six hours of work time, amounting to a loss of over $13 billion in productivity.[12]

For Discussion

The scenario. Assume you own a company and employ 100 people. Personally, you are a moderate fan of the NCAA March Madness college basketball tournament, but you are too busy and focused at work to bother with it then. However, you know that many employees do follow the tournament, and their time is your time, and that time is money.

1. What would you do knowing what commonly happens with employees and the tournament? Explain.
2. More generally, what would you do about employees using company time and equipment for the "time theft" activities noted above?

What can be done about it? Creating policies and communicating them is one part of the solution, but like other policies, you cannot possibly identify and include any and all potential abuses of company time and other resources. Therefore, it is best if you apply a more philosophical approach, such as focusing more on performance than on how time is spent. It rarely is a good idea to micromanage and "nickel-and-dime" employees for every minute of every day. Nevertheless, employers are well served and often do explicitly address the following:[13]

Internet usage. We all know the Internet in general, and social media in particular, can be a black hole and consume all of the time you give it. We'll address monitoring and privacy in more detail later in the chapter.

Socializing with coworkers. To be clear, there are some genuine benefits to socializing with colleagues, as doing so can foster a more positive and productive work environment. The issue, like others, is not zero-sum, all or nothing. Whether online or face-to-face, some people, even departments, seem to spend more time socializing than working. You can build social opportunities into the day, such as lunching together, having "mandated" coffee breaks, and participating in regular social events outside of work.

Personal phone calls and texts. Today, it is unrealistic and counterproductive for most employers to forbid employees from taking or making personal calls, but it is not only reasonable but also advisable to establish some expectations. For instance, limiting both to lunch and other breaks and being strict about not texting during meetings. Ethics aside, it's just rude.

Also, don't forget, modeling the behaviors you want to see from others sends powerful signals regarding what is expected.

Employee Monitoring

Employee monitoring involves observing or otherwise collecting data on employee activities.[14] The most fundamental motives for monitoring employee activities are protecting the organization from theft and legal liability and improving employee performance. Technology now plays an ever-greater role in the forms of data gathered and their applications.

employee monitoring observing or otherwise collecting data on employee activities

From a business ethics perspective, the challenge with monitoring is to balance the needs of the employer to protect the company's resources (e.g., time, money, intellectual property, and data) and the reasonable expectations of privacy by the employees.[15] This means that the issue is how, when, and where employees are monitored rather than if employees should be monitored or not. At the root of this are technology and the blurring of our professional and personal lives. (This last point is addressed in the next section of this chapter.)

This business ethics challenge, like many others, is addressed in part by laws but also company policies and practices. We, therefore, focus our attention on these elements, along with advice for both employers and employees regarding monitoring and privacy.

Monitoring and the Law

In matters of business ethics, the law is the lowest bar to clear for ethical conduct, too narrow, and lags reality. But the laws do matter. The most basic legal requirement is that employees need to be informed that they can and will be monitored and how. This means that whatever an employer does in terms of monitoring needs to be communicated to employees. In so doing, employees become informed, which in turn helps set their expectations regarding privacy. Many of the horror stories we hear in the news are about stealthy monitoring—employees are unaware of being monitored.

Electronic Communications Privacy Act (ECPA). The **Electronic Communications Privacy Act (ECPA)** of 1986 protects wire, oral, and electronic communications when these communications are being made, are in transit, and when they are stored on computers. It applies to e-mail, telephone conversations, and data stored electronically.[16] A major motive for the ECPA is to guard against invading employees' privacy with technology.

Electronic Communications Privacy Act (ECPA) protects wire, oral, and electronic communications when these communications are being made, are in transit, and when they are stored on computers. It applies to e-mail, telephone conversations, and data stored electronically

Critically important is that the Act allows employers to monitor e-mails, texts, phone calls, and other communications if they have a legitimate business purpose. If, for instance, your employer gives you a company phone and tells you it is to be used only for business, then the company can monitor any and all calls, as the phone is given specifically for business. The same goes for a company car. If it is to be used only for business, or during business hours, then it should be used only for that specific purpose, and your employer would have the right to track it using GPS.[17]

In addition to legitimate business purpose is employee consent. If you consent to be monitored, which employees often do when they sign their employment contracts. This applies even, as is often the case, when consent to monitoring is not in the contract itself, but is instead located in the employee handbook.

State Laws and Union Agreements[18]. Many states have their own laws, which are varied and continually change. Some guarantee employee privacy, which does not mean employers

Gorodenkoff/Shutterstock

cannot monitor the employees. This becomes even more important for employers to communicate what, why, and how they plan to monitor employees, as the key is to manage employee expectations. In California, employees cannot be recorded without giving consent, and the same goes for video monitoring. If audio is added to the video, then this needs specific consent.

Unions often include details of what is acceptable in terms of what, how, when, and why employees will be monitored. Any changes typically need to be agreed to by the parties of the agreement.

Common Types of Employee Monitoring

Employers monitor employees' behaviors and communications; this has remained constant over time, but what has changed is the technology used to communicate and monitor.

Phone and Voicemail. The Federal Wiretap Act forbids intercepting live phone calls and stored voice messages. But, if doing so has a legitimate business reason, then employers are permitted. Where businesses offer telemarketing and customer service, employers listen in real time to ensure quality service performance. Even though this is considered reasonable by employees in these jobs, it is still advisable to get employee's consent. Employers, however, must immediately stop listening when they realize a call is personal in nature.[19]

E-mail and Texts. These two forms of communication are intertwined in every area of our lives—we live, we breathe, we drink water, we e-mail, and we text. When employees use business networks for personal use, employers are potentially at risk for being liable for employee behavior and data security. To clarify, if an employee misbehaves while using an employer's network, then the employer can be held liable. Plainly and simply, your employer usually has the advantage if such matters are challenged in court. However, there are instances in which judgments have favored employees when they accessed personal e-mail accounts via web-based apps that are also password protected. The reasoning is that it is difficult for an employer to make the case that they have a legitimate reason to monitor or search such accounts.[20]

Internet. The Internet, in many ways, is a more complicated communication network than others. On the one hand, the ECPA does not clearly cover web surfing, as viewing pages is arguably not "communication." But on the other hand, if employees are viewing material that can be perceived as sexual harassment, then it is a problem. Employers and IT professionals are also often required to report any child pornography found during monitoring. Courts have, in fact, held employers liable for not reporting such matters.[21]

Video. Video is a digital watchdog and deters misconduct and serves as evidence. Body cameras for police are perhaps the prime example during these times. Video footage can be key to making a case for guilt or innocence, not just for police but for employees across industries. Retailers have used video cameras to deter and prosecute theft for many decades. Employers, however, need to consider many details when using video monitoring, such as:

- public space or private space;
- video only or audio too;
- camera in plain view or hidden;
- meeting rooms and offices.[22]

It is also wise to consider the location and whether employees have the expectation of privacy there. Restrooms are the obvious one, but what if your employer has a gym and locker room, provides onsite health care, and has parking garages and lots. Many employees feel their cars are their personal space. Regardless, state laws governing these details vary greatly and require both employers and employees to be informed.

Location. Thanks to GPS, employees can be tracked in the office or anywhere else for that matter. An entire and growing industry now exists that helps clients track employee movements and interactions, and employers can use these data to improve office designs and other employee performance-enhancing practices.[23] Employees are most commonly tracked if their jobs involve deliveries, such as UPS, FedEx, and many others. Employers use these data to increase efficiency, measure performance, and ensure employees are not wasting employer time or other resources (e.g., gas). Company cars can also be tracked, but this is less common.

More troubling can be the tracking of cell phones or cars if they can also be used during "off hours."[24] For example, if your employer learns that you are at the bar every night of the week or have attended a contentious protest event, then there is debate whether they can use this against you. We'll explore the ethical issues related to blurring the line between professional and personal lives in the next section.

Ethics in Action

Your Temperature Please

Among the reactions to COVID-19 are new forms of employee monitoring, such as taking employee's body temperature and COVID testing itself, before entering the office. The idea is to prevent sick people from potentially infecting others. To ensure they do not conflict with legal limitations, employers are advised to take every employee's temperature so as to avoid any discriminatory charges. They also need to treat any findings as confidential medical records, thus sharing information regarding who has a fever or other COVID symptoms only with management who needs to know.[25]

These precautions will help provide safe workplaces, while at the same time prevent violation of existing laws regarding discrimination (EEOC) or the Americans with Disabilities Act. As of the middle of 2020, no government agency had issued specific COVID-related temperature check guidelines. Once again, laws lag behind practice.[26]

Legal experts provide the following guidance[27]:

1. No Surprises. Communicate to employees that their temperatures will be taken, and if theirs is high, they will be sent home.
2. Set a Standard. Select and enforce a specific standard; the Centers for Disease Control and Prevention recommends $\geq$100° Fahrenheit.
3. Touchless. Make measuring as noninvasive as possible to protect all parties and ensure disinfecting protocols are set and followed.
4. Appropriate Skills. Ideally, certified medical professionals will do the measuring.
5. Don't Forget Other Precautions. Maintain social distancing, which may require multiple temperature measuring stations, otherwise employees may crowd in a single line and location.

For Discussion:

1. As an employee, what are your feelings about COVID temperature checks?
2. What if they did other tests before allowing you to enter work, such as a nasal swab, does your position change? Explain.
3. Take the employer's position and provide at least two or three reasons to support COVID testing as a requirement to enter the workplace.
4. Why might an employer resist such testing, even if required by the state in which they operate?

Now that you have a sense of the types of monitoring and the implications for employee privacy, let's outline what employers and employees (you) should do.

Employer and Employee Best Practices

The goal is to balance the employer's need to enhance productivity and protect the organization from various risks, while at the same time respecting employees and their right to privacy. Table 5.1 provides recommendations for employers to effectively monitor employees without violating the law or destroying employee trust and morale.

As for you, the employee, assume everything is monitored all of the time. It is just that simple. Use separate e-mail accounts and separate devices for personal use, if necessary.

table **5.1**

Employee Monitoring Best Practices

Action	Description
Communicate	The first and last best practice is to tell employees they should expect to be monitored.
Specifics	Outline what will be monitored (e.g., phone, e-mails, Internet, and computer) at any time and for any reason "without further notice."
Not Obligated	Legal experts strongly recommend employers explicitly state they are "not obligated to monitor" although they reserve the right to do so. Otherwise, employees can and have held employers liable for not monitoring a situation in which they were harmed (e.g., harassed or assaulted).
"Limited Personal Use"	It is quite difficult and unrealistic, if not counterproductive, to tell employees they cannot ever use company equipment or time for personal use, but that such use needs to be reasonable and limited.
Never	Porn and other offensive material and activities should be banned (zero tolerance), as well as sharing intellectual property, trade secrets, or confidential information.
Implement and Enforce	Consistency is key. Tell them the expectations and hold them to the expectations . . . top to bottom of the organization, keenly minding potential discrimination.
New Hire	Ensure all new hires, including executives, have read, understood, and signed the policy.
Follow Up	Periodically communicate the policies and expectations, reaffirming the policies and actions taken.

Source: Adapted from "Managing Workplace Monitoring and Surveillance," *shrm.org*, March 13, 2019, https://www.shrm.org/resourcesandtools/tools-and-samples/toolkits/pages/workplaceprivacy.aspx.

The hassle and personal expense is worth it to avoid any unwanted grief. For instance, and regardless of the normal practices, when someone comes after you, suddenly everything is mined and scrutinized, even communications and actions many years in the past. Protect yourself, just like your employer.

One last piece of advice for both employers and employees is to apply an adaptation of the Golden Rule: monitor others only in ways you too would agree to be monitored.[28]

Mauricio Graki/Shutterstock

The Line between Professional and Personal

Technology and the changing nature of work continue to blur the boundaries between our professional and personal lives. But that isn't all. Increasingly, employers are monitoring and acting on employee conduct in nonwork hours and arenas. When this happens, it begs the questions: (1) where is the line between professional and personal and (2) who draws it? The answers to these questions have genuine business ethics implications for your employers and you.

Conduct

Conduct outside of work that affects your job performance, increases health insurance costs for your employer, or makes the company look bad is a cause for your employer's concern. Professional athletes, for instance, are often forbidden from playing extreme sports, such as skydiving, or participating in activities that could cause injuries and prevent them from playing. Many organizations increasingly ban tobacco use at work, and some even ban it altogether for their employees. This is often justified when the organization's key values and business is promoting and preserving health, like hospitals and other health-care providers.

The conduct we will focus on relates to social media and nonwork behaviors (both criminal and noncriminal). For perspective, in 2006, only 12 percent of companies used social media to research job candidates. By 2010, it was 25 percent, and now it is over 70 percent. The top three turnoffs for employers were posts of provocative or inappropriate videos or photos, drinking or using drugs, and discriminatory comments (gender, race, or religion).[29]

It is possible that none of these surprises you, and you mind your posts and privacy settings effectively. However, as our digital footprints grow and the lines between our professional and personal lives blur, we are increasingly confronted with **employer trespassing**, which occurs when employers inappropriately intrude into employees' nonwork domains, including considering personal information in professional assessments and decisions.

employer trespassing occurs when employers inappropriately intrude into employees nonwork domains, including considering personal information in professional assessments and decisions

Many employees argue:

- "What I do on my own time is my business."
- "So long as I'm not breaking the law, my employer shouldn't care."
- "My employer doesn't own me. They can't tell me what I can and can't do twenty-four hours a day."
- "Even if I break the law, in America, I'm innocent until proven guilty. My employer can't take action if the court hasn't."

Most of these likely make some sense to you, but employers have routinely taken a different position. Historically, employers routinely included a box on job applications asking candidates, "Have you ever been convicted of a crime? Yes or No." Mark "yes" and you get cut. Now, however, the majority of states, the federal government, and more than 150 cities have created policies to ban the box, which limit if or when in the hiring process employers can ask candidates about their criminal histories.[30] Many companies have chosen to do this voluntarily as well, such as Walmart, Koch Industries, Target, and Home Depot.[31]

And it wasn't until June 2020 that the US Supreme Court ruled that the Civil Rights Act of 1964, prohibiting sex discrimination, also applies to sexual orientation and gender identity. Put simply, it is illegal to fire an employee merely for being gay or transgender.[32] Many states changed their laws on the matter only in the past few years.

In these examples, laws are part of the solution. Other times, employers act on their own. But again, our professional and personal lives can overlap or collide in so many ways that the legal system could not possibly address all of the potential issues. Besides the fact that legality is the lowest bar, from a business ethics perspective, such issues are first and last organizational issues, and they need to be determined by leadership. This means that organizations need to determine what personal social media information and other conduct they will considered while hiring. This, however, leaves the infinitely important question—who decides?

Who Decides?

Assume one of your coworkers is caught on video hitting his girlfriend at a party last weekend. The video went viral on the Internet and he was subsequently charged by the police. Your employer fired him on Monday.

1. Is this justified? Explain.
2. Does it matter if your coworker's contract, like yours, says employees can be fired for activities that damage the company's reputation?
3. Is this sort of contract language ethical in your opinion? Explain.
4. Does your employer have an obligation to wait to learn what the court proceedings find?
5. How does your position change if he is found not guilty?
6. Now assume the video doesn't exist, and the only thing anyone knows is that he has been charged. Does this change any of your answers? Explain.

Let's now assume you agree with the action by your employer. Then doesn't your employer have to investigate whether any other existing employees have ever been involved in the same or similar circumstances? After all, fairness and perhaps a desire to be nondiscriminatory both suggest that all employees should be treated equally and subject to the same consequences (punishment).

Now, with all of this as background, who should decide the answers to these questions? The CEO? A committee of employees? What about if personnel change over time, then should these decisions be reviewed and revised? Explain.

These will be some of the most difficult and consequential business ethics considerations for employers for the coming decades. Employers, employees, and the larger society will continually need to ask and answer the questions—where is the line and who draws it?—and the answers will matter to you throughout your career.

We'll conclude the chapter with whistleblowing, which is something you may be tempted to do, and in some circumstances should do, but in all circumstances should consider very carefully.

Whistleblowing

Whistleblowing is the act of drawing public or an authority's attention to perceived unethical conduct.[33] Whistleblowing is not specific to any industry or job, and the misconduct does not need to be illegal to qualify. Whistleblowing illustrates an ethical dilemma (chapter 1) for the whistleblower and often requires considerable moral courage (chapter 4). The dilemma is that reporting bad behavior may cause the perpetrators to change their behavior and they may be punished, but whether these outcomes occur or not, you might damage your relationships or even lose your job. You thus must have considerable moral courage to speak up and blow the whistle.

whistleblowing the act of drawing public or an authority's attention to perceived unethical conduct.

Let's explore when and why to do it, when and why not to do it, and then how.

When and Why to Be a Whistleblower

Sometimes unethical conduct needs to be called out, or as you have and will read throughout this book, employees must speak up and speak out. You may get to this point because of the following situations:

- sense of morality to speak out regarding right versus wrong
- revenge
- other efforts to stop or remedy the conduct have been unsuccessful
- the offense is so severe (to you and/or others)
- you are required to report misconduct by law

You'll learn in chapter 9, for instance, that the Sarbanes–Oxley Act requires those with knowledge of particular forms of unethical financial conduct to report it. This act, and other laws, tries to incentivize employees to speak up by offering financial rewards linked to the value of the offense.

As an example, Cheryl Eckard, a quality assurance manager, reported contamination issues at a facility operated by pharmaceutical giant, GlaxoSmithKline. Her review of the facility revealed serious issues which she reported. Not only were her reports ignored, but she was fired. The company ultimately settled a suit with the US government for $750 million, and Ms. Eckard was awarded $96 million![34] This, however, is rare. The Securities and Exchange Commission (SEC) that oversees such matters receives more than 5,000 complaints per year, but in the recent past it has only paid out on average eight per year.[35]

Whether financial rewards are available or not, your employer's policies and practices are important factors to encourage or discourage employees from reporting.

1. Clear means of reporting misconduct are essential. Employees need to know that they exist and how to access them.
2. Confident complaints will be acted on.
3. Genuine and effective protections must be in place to guard against retaliation.

Despite the perceived potential damage to individual and organizational reputations, research highlights compelling benefits. Organizations with robust internal reporting practices were found to experience 7 percent fewer lawsuits and 20 percent less in settlement payouts.[36]

Intellectually, whistleblowing makes sense, but reality makes it quite different.

Why NOT to Be a Whistleblower

The reasons for not speaking up are varied, but the most common reported by employees essentially mirror the three things noted above that encourage employees to report, which are also illustrated in Figure 5.1.[37]

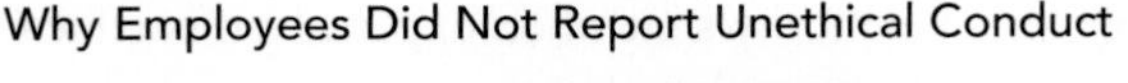

figure 5.1

Why Employees Did Not Report Unethical Conduct

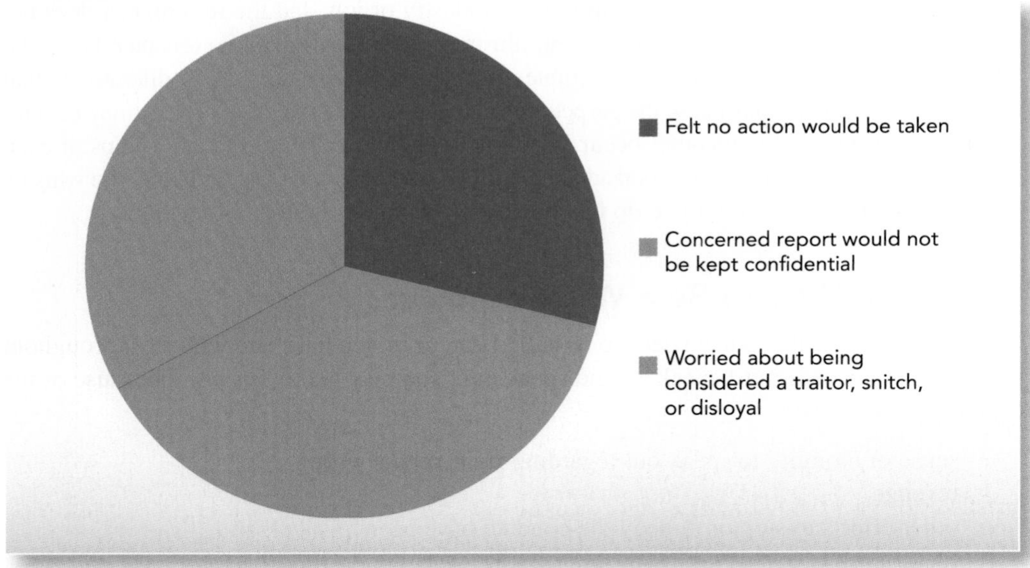

Source: T. Agovino, "Whistleblowers: An Early Detection System," *shrm.org*, February 1, 2020, https://www.shrm.org/hr-today/news/all-things-work/pages/whistleblowers-an-early-detection-system.aspx.

Moreover, blowing the whistle is risky as illustrated in the Ethics in Action box.

Ethics in Action

Are Snowden and Watkins Familiar Names?

Do the names Edward Snowden or Sherron Watkins sound familiar? Maybe not, but they are two of the most notable whistleblowers in the 2000s. Snowden was a former IT contractor who worked for the National Security Agency (NSA), and he revealed that the NSA was secretly (and inappropriately) monitoring phone and e-mail records and Internet search histories of US citizens and hundreds of millions of other people around the world.[38]

Sherron Watkins was the former Vice President of Corporate Development at Enron, who is known for being the central whistleblower in that case. She first alerted then CEO Kenneth Lay of accounting irregularities (fraud), and she was ultimately called to testify before Congress when it investigated misconduct at the company. The results of this investigation factored heavily in the creation of the Sarbanes–Oxley Act mentioned previously and explained in more detail in chapter 9 under laws and regulations aimed at business ethics.

What has happened to them since? Snowden was accused of espionage and theft of government property, and he fled the country in 2013. He lived in exile in Hong Kong for some time, and over the past few years, he has been living in Moscow.[39] Watkins was fired, has not worked in accounting or finance again, and has mostly done public speaking and writing about her experience and whistleblowing more generally.[40]

For Discussion:

1. Why do you think Snowden blew the whistle?
2. Why do you think Watkins blew the whistle?
3. If you were them, would you? Explain

It was a complete shock to to Sherron Watkins when she realized she needed legal help to defend herself. She said the following in an interview:

> *"I naively thought facts were going to rule out. And I gave a lot of facts to Kim Lay, Enron's CEO, and I thought he would investigate. I never thought he was going to shoot the messenger . . . I didn't even think I'd done anything wrong or needed a lawyer. I'm just delivering truth to power. You've got to have a lawyer.'"*

How to Blow the Whistle

Let's assume either despite or because of what you've learned, you're inclined to blow the whistle and report misconduct. The Government Accountability Project protects whistleblowers and suggests you carefully consider the following first[41]:

- **You First.** Think of potential benefits to you, personally, as well as potential costs.
- **Employer Processes.** Don't make your first call or e-mail to the media or an external authority. It generally is best, if not required, to utilize grievance processes or hotlines first.
- **You Will Be a Target**. It may be only one person, or it may be many, but you and your character may be attacked. And sadly, the employer's legal and human resource departments protect the employer more than they protect you. HR and legal departments are there to "protect" the organization, not you.

After considering these points, look at Figure 5.2 that outlines some basic steps to follow if you decide to report. Importantly, although these are presented in sequential steps for execution, you may be well served to educate yourself on all of the steps simultaneously and upfront. You may also want to seek the advice of trusted others first, and depending on the offense, offender, and your relationship with your manager, you may want to seek his or her advice. If the matter involves illegal activity (e.g., discrimination or fraud), then you'll need to identify the appropriate agency and associated process (e.g., the Equal Employment Opportunity Commission—EEOC), and perhaps also personal legal counsel earlier in the process.

Step 1—Manager: Your immediate manager will likely be involved in resolving the majority of issues on which you will report misconduct. This is because you are most likely to witness misconduct in our own department and job. In circumstances when the misconduct is committed by your direct manager, taking the issue up with this person often is still the appropriate first step. Norms of professionalism support approaching the offender before taking it to someone else (Golden Rule?). This, however, is not always the case, and sometimes your first step would be to take the matter to someone else higher in the chain of command—your boss' boss.

Step 2—Trusted Others: Consulting trusted others is an excellent idea for most issues. Someone you genuinely trust within your organization will know the context, be able to identify potential blind spots in your issue, perhaps provide some historical knowledge of other whistleblower examples, and guide you to appropriate others. Trusted others outside the organization can constructively "test" or

figure 5.2

Basic Steps for Blowing the Whistle

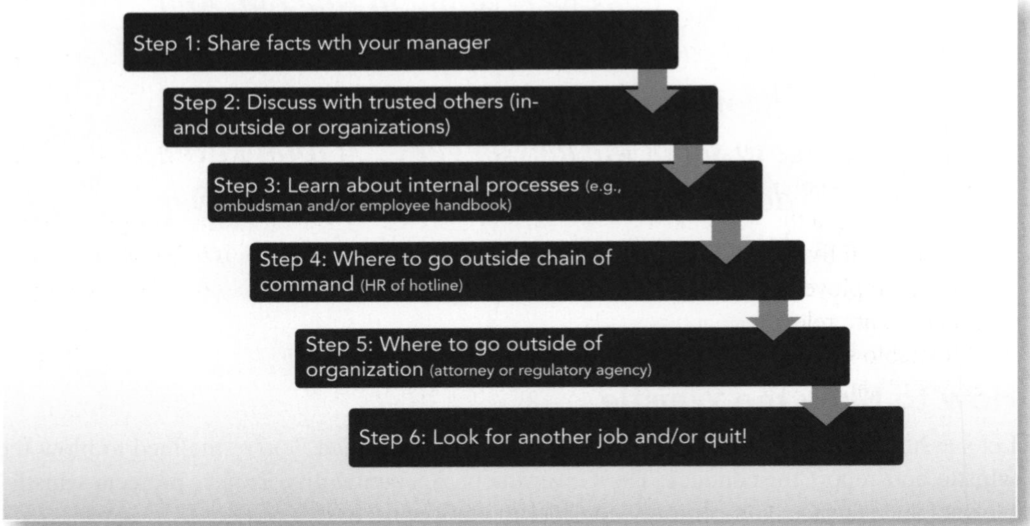

challenge your complaint, as well as your approach. They may also offer you perspective, such as what do you hope to gain? Should you just look for another job? The insider and outsider may provide social support you will likely benefit from.

Step 3—Learn: Educate yourself. Most organizations have processes for grievances; consult the employee handbook for processes and guidance on how to file a written complaint. And, if your issue has clear legal implications, there are particular agencies and processes for filing a claim (e.g., the EEOC and SEC).

Step 4—Outside the Chain of Command: Many whistleblower complaints are the result of patterns of unethical conduct that are the result of corrupt leaders (chapter 7) and corrupt organizational cultures (chapter 8). As such, many individuals in your chain of command may be the perpetrators, which means you may be best served to go outside of that chain to another part of the organization. For instance, your organization may have an ethics committee, or if your issue relates to a particular office, then perhaps you need to go to human resources at the headquarters in another city.

Step 5—Outside the Organization: You may want or even need an attorney. As you have learned, and will continue to learn, many organizations are only concerned about not doing something that is illegal, and this may be their first and only test. You may also become the target of retaliation. In both instances, you may benefit from the advice of legal counsel. This same person is likely to also help direct you to and navigate filing a claim with a regulatory agency if appropriate.

Step 6—Be Prepared to Leave! You may want to start looking for another job. Some leaders and organizations are toxic. You may expect the truth and ethical action to eventually prevail, but sadly this is not always the case. The stress and other personal consequences may not be worth it.

Now that you've completed this chapter, you hopefully are more aware and better equipped to deal with numerous ethical challenges at work. Moreover, if you feel blowing the whistle is what needs to happen, now you should be better prepared to evaluate the pros and cons and what to actually do.

Chapter Summary

1. Some of the most common ethical issues that you personally control are lying, conflicts of interest, and inappropriate use of company time and other resources, many related to information technology and the Internet.
2. Employee monitoring can be a particularly useful tool for improving performance and guarding against theft. But the challenge is to balance protecting the employer's interests and reasonably preserving the employee's expectations of privacy.
3. Laws (federal and state) and union agreements are in place to help govern some of the challenges associated with monitoring.
4. Monitoring and the nature of work are blurring the boundaries between your professional and personal lives, which pose numerous and complicated ethical challenges for employers and employees. One fundamental challenge is who decides what aspects of your personal life are relevant to your professional life?
5. Whistleblowing is an essential element of ensuring ethical conduct at work, but it is not easy and should be considered and implemented carefully.

Key Terms

conflicts of Interest 89
Electronic Communications Privacy Act (ECPA) 91
employee monitoring 91
employer Trespassing 95
lying 88
whistleblowing 97

CASE STUDY: Life or Death, You Decide

During normal times, many clinicians in the developed world simply treat patients on a first-come-first-serve basis, and this works well for both parties because available resources meet patient demand. This, however, is not always the case, and few if any ethical dilemmas are more difficult than those faced by medical professionals who must ration care because patient needs outstrip the resources available to treat them.

Some clinicians are confronted with rationing routinely, such as transplant surgeons who have approximately 8,000 patients die each year in the United States awaiting donor organs that either go to another patient or aren't available in the first place.[42] Crisis situations, either on the battlefield or mass casualties due to accidents or natural disasters, also require doctors to triage patients not only in terms of severity of injuries and needs, but also in terms of the likelihood of survival.

However, the coronavirus pandemic made rationing common and frequent in many places where it was otherwise rare. In Northern Italy, which was hit especially hard and facilities were overwhelmed in every way, physicians often denied treatment based on age. One doctor stated the situation very plainly: "There is no way to find an exception . . . We have to decide who must die and whom we shall keep alive."[43]

This problem for clinicians is further complicated by the fact that no two patients are the same, their conditions can and do deteriorate rapidly, and multiple patients are being treated simultaneously, not to mention the enormous stress experienced by everyone involved. This means that it is difficult for one doctor, for instance, to ensure her own decisions are consistent, which means it is significantly more difficult to ensure consistency for a hospital's entire medical staff.

Continued

Doctors, hospitals, and medical organizations have attempted to help, providing some criteria to help guide such decisions. Among the goals of such guidelines are to facilitate appropriate and consistent care by alleviating the need for doctors to make such difficult decisions on the fly, at the bedside, all day, and day after day.

Some of the criteria suggested are:

1. Who has the greatest chance of survival?
2. If survival chances are more or less equal, then treat the patient with the greatest long-term benefit. Younger people, for instance, have more of their lives ahead of them and potentially more to contribute to society.
3. Another criterion to consider is a given patient's impact on treating others. This means that medical workers and other first responders would be treated if all other factors were equal.[44]

To clarify, these are intended simply as guidelines or factors to consider, rather than a protocol etched in stone. Moreover, true cultural differences exist. Americans, for instance, are not as likely to accept rationing of any sort, especially when a loved one is critically ill, whereas Europeans some say would be more amenable.[45]

Now let's see what you would do.

Consider a scenario involving three gravely ill patients: (1) a fourteen-year-old boy with diabetes, (2) a twenty-seven-year-old mother, and (3) an eighty-year-old grandfather. Also assume you're their treating physician and suspect there is a high probability each will die without a ventilator, but you have only one.[46]

For Discussion:

1. For whom would you give the ventilator? Answer this question before moving to #2.
2. On what basis did you make your decision? First-come-first-serve? The one with the greatest chance of surviving? The one with the most people depending on him or her? If their chances are the same, do you give it to the youngest? Explain.
3. What approaches to ethics are represented in your decision?

Apply Three-Dimensional Problem-Solving for Ethics (3D PSE)

You can apply the 3D PSE from multiple perspectives, such as that of a treating physician, hospital administrator, or a gravely ill patient's spouse. Just be sure to

figure **5.3**

Three-Dimensional Problem-Solving for Ethics (3D PSE)

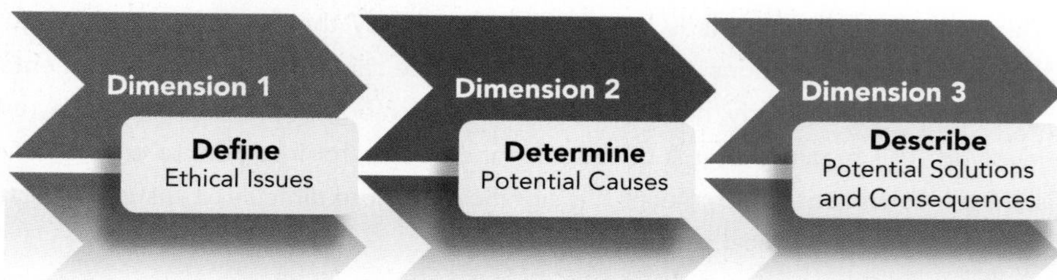

specify whose perspective. Try it from the perspective of a doctor in an overwhelmed hospital.

Dimension 1: *Define* the Ethical Challenge

What is the gap in the case? What do you have and what do *you* want?

a. From the doctor's view, what is the current situation with the patient, and how do you think you would want it to be?
b. Why is the current situation a problem? What difficulties or undesirable behaviors and outcomes happen as a result of the problem you defined? From the doctor's perspective, why do they care about the problem you defined in Dimension 1?
c. Define your problem in one or two sentences, and structure it in terms of what is current versus what is desired.
d. Who are the key stakeholders, those that affect or are affected by the problem you defined?

Dimension 2: *Determine* the Causes

a. **Individuals.** Given the problem you defined in Dimension 1, how do characteristics of the doctor cause the problem, such as ethical decision-making approach, work values, moral principles, and perhaps biases?
b. **Contextual.** Are there particular policies or practices that caused the problem, as defined in Dimension 1? These policies and practices may be for the hospital in which the doctor works, norms of the profession or the country.

Dimension 3: *Describe* Your Potential Solutions and the Intended and Unintended Consequences for Stakeholders

For each cause you identified in Dimension 2, answer the following questions:

a. ***What*** do you recommend and ***how*** will you make it happen?
b. ***Why*** will you do it? Does this reflect a particular ethical decision-making approach (e.g., utilitarian or universal)?

If your responses to these questions are unsatisfactory, then go back to Dimension 1 and repeat the process. If, however, you are comfortable and confident in your problem-solving efforts thus far, then ensure you achieve the desired outcomes and avoid any unintended consequences.

c. What is the ***desired and likely effect in the short and long term*** for the key stakeholders involved in the problem and causes (Dimensions 1 and 2)?
d. What ***potential unintended consequences*** may occur with each proposed solution?
e. If any, what are the **implications for *other* stakeholders** (e.g., individuals, organizations, and communities) besides those noted in Dimensions 1 and 2?
f. Will your solution work in an ethical manner? Make a final assessment of whether your chosen solution will reduce or eliminate the causes determined in Dimension 2, and if this then will remedy the ethical problem defined in Dimension 1. If not, then repeat and refine the dimensions.

Chapter Opener Photo Source: Triff/Shutterstock

chapter 6

Common Organizational Practices with Ethics Implications

Learning Objectives

AFTER READING THIS CHAPTER, YOU SHOULD BE ABLE TO:

LO1 Explain how hiring practices can be wrought with business ethics issues.

LO2 Understand the limits of freedom of expression at work.

LO3 Know how to prevent unfair performance appraisals.

WHERE DO **YOU** STAND?

Sure, Speak Up. But Don't You Dare Say the A-Word.

If you're an employee at Google, perhaps you've joined many of your coworkers and criticized or even actively protested about your employer's decisions to develop artificial intelligence technology for weapons (a contract for the Pentagon), or how senior leaders have handled sexual harassment claims against other executives. Many employees have also spoken out about the company's decision to build a censored search engine for China. Google employees have organized and publicly addressed these and a growing number of other issues. As for the company's leadership, it has taken a more tolerant stance to employee dissent in the recent past. However, the company's leaders have no tolerance for employee comments, discussion, emails, or any other communications about its size, power, and approach to competition, or put more simply—antitrust charges against the company.

Google's dominance in search and online advertising has caused it to be the focus of regulator's attention in many places around the world. European Union regulators have already fined the company billions of dollars, and the Department of Justice and numerous attorneys general in the Unites States have also filed similar charges. Nevertheless, the company has been and continues to monitor, restrict, and rebuke employees for commenting in most any manner about the subject. This happens despite the company having no formal policies against such communications. The topic is monitored and forbidden in emails, for instance, and a former Google executive described coming down on an employee "like a ton of bricks" in response to an off-handed message about antitrust concerns. In short, employees know the issue of antitrust should not be discussed in any venue.[1]

1. Should Google monitor and take action against employee's comments about antitrust concerns? Explain your position.
2. Assume you are Google's CEO, what would be your position about employee's speaking out about the company's conduct?
3. More generally, explain your position about restricting employee's speech about their employer's conduct?

Introduction

Among the many business ethics challenges organizations are confronted with are those involving how they interact with employees. For instance, countless processes are in place during the entire tenure of your employment—beginning with your recruitment, ending with your exit from the organization, and the many interactions in between. In this chapter, we address a few challenges that are often business ethics flash-points, such as hiring employees and performance appraisals. We also address issues related to employees' freedom of expression (e.g., speech) at work, as the limits are often misunderstood, and because employees' expressions can become issues during hiring and during their employment.

Given that this chapter is in the organization section of the book, it is to be viewed primarily from the employer's perspective. However, these topics are only relevant because of how they cause employees to respond. Performance appraisals, for instance, will generate some of the most intense and possibly contentious experiences you will have during your working life, both positive and negative. Therefore, to provide an accurate and complete view, both the employer and employee perspectives will be included.

Ethical Issues When Hiring Employees

The mantra—"employees are our most valuable asset"—is what thriving, sustainable, and responsible organizations both say and do. That is, they "do" by aligning their operations with their stated value for employees. For employers who value employees, everything begins with hiring. Like most other operations, hiring can be done in better and worse ways, and most of these have genuine implications for business ethics. Please note, however, because this is not a human resource management course, we will not cover all the elements involved in hiring employees (attracting, screening, interviewing, and selecting), but instead, we will focus on potential ethical pitfalls in the process.

Factors to Consider

discrimination
negative or unwanted actions taken against a group of employees based on membership in one of nine protected classes

From a legal perspective, labor laws in the United States primarily focus on avoiding **discrimination**, which the Department of Labor (DOL) defines as negative or unwanted actions taken against a group of employees based on membership in one of nine protected classes:

1. Race
2. Color
3. Religion
4. Sex (including gender identity, sexual orientation, and pregnancy)
5. National origin
6. Age (40 or older)
7. Disability
8. Genetic information
9. Parental status[2]

(Note: We will use this same protected class information in chapter 8 when we discuss harassment as an organizational culture issue, as it is also based on legally protected classes.)

This means, quite simply, you need to be a member of a protected class to claim discriminatory hiring practices.[3] Denying you or anyone else an employment opportunity—an interview or ultimately a job—based on a protected class, is both illegal and unethical. Such claims are extremely difficult to make and win, however, and like most other matters of business ethics, the law is too narrow, too slow, too expensive, and too often not an effective remedy.

To make the point, between 2010 and 2018, Americans filed nearly 1 million discrimination claims with the Equal Employment Opportunity Commission (EEOC), the agency responsible for enforcing the antidiscrimination laws. More than 82 percent of the workers who filed claims did not receive any relief, meaning no finding of wrongdoing, and less than 1 percent received money or a change at work. Please note, this is for all forms of discrimination, not simply claims related to discriminatory hiring, which incidentally, was not even in the top five most common forms of discrimination reported.[4]

Not surprisingly, there are exceptions to discrimination law. Small businesses (15 or fewer employees) are exempt from many regulations, including this one, in order to reduce the expense of dealing with too many regulations. Organizations with an explicitly religious purpose are also exempt, as are organizations that can genuinely claim that a particular employee characteristic is crucial to its mission or type of work. For instance, if a retailer sells women's clothes, they could justify hiring women for dressing room attendants, but they may have difficulties limiting hiring for cashiers to women only.

So, what should organizations consider?

1. First, an organization is well-served to ensure the profile of its job candidates (and existing employees) reflects those of the people in the surrounding area that are also qualified. This means that both candidates and employees should resemble the local population in terms of protected class characteristics.
2. Second, and perhaps most constructively, organizations should recruit candidates based on qualifications and ability, as specified in the job description. This means that appropriate attention and detail should be applied to the job description, specifying what is needed and desired for each job. Then, once prospective employees are identified based on these qualifications, it is critically important to screen based on fit for the organizational culture.

Following these two practices should help an organization not only to stay within the law, but also increase the chances of hiring employees that are qualified, fit the values of the organization, and perform well.

Hiring Bias and Artificial Intelligence

Artificial intelligence (AI) is the simulation of human processes by machines,[5] and its increased use in hiring processes has both pros and cons.

artificial intelligence (AI) the simulation of human processes by machines

How AI Helps Hiring Effectiveness. For perspective, how effectively do you think you would review 10 resumes? 100? 10,000? Computers and other machines do repetitive tasks more efficiently and effectively, which is how and why AI is employed in the hiring process.

Given the fundamental goal of hiring processes is to identify and select the best candidates, AI has the potential to efficiently and reliably analyze (e.g., screen, compare, and calculate) massive amounts of data related to candidates and jobs. The reasoning is that removing humans from the process makes hiring more reliable and cheaper, and thus more cost-effective. Human bias is also supposed to be removed, but as you have likely heard this does not always happen.[6]

How AI Hampers Hiring Effectiveness. AI runs on algorithms and data. And who creates them? Humans. This means that if code writers are biased, and those who collect the data are biased (data based on past hires is biased), then the AI hiring process is likely to produce biased results.[7] That's a problem. The source of this problem lies in large part on biased conventional hiring practices, such as the following:

implicit biases attitudes, or stereotypes toward some people or associate stereotypes with them without our conscious knowledge

1. **Many Human Biases Are Unconscious**. Volumes of data show that we have **implicit biases**, attitudes, or stereotypes toward some people or associate stereotypes with them without our conscious knowledge.[8] This means quite simply that if the

coders and others involved in creating the AI have implicit biases, then these biases are likely to show up in the AI algorithms, related processes, and outcomes.

2. **Paring Mountains of Data**. Thanks again to technology—the Internet and social media services like LinkedIn—companies now routinely get hundreds of applications for each role. This means that some very fundamental culling criteria need to be used, regardless of whether it is done by humans or machine. For instance, it is common to recruit only from a particular set of universities to screen applicants based on education, or to recruit from a specific set of competitors for unique and valuable work experience. Such criteria may reduce the pool by 80 percent or more, but these same criteria make the pool more similar than different, in other words, biased.[9]
3. **Self-Reinforcing.** Federal law allows companies to discriminate based on the characteristics that are "job-related," or otherwise claimed to be necessary to do the job effectively. This means that whatever diversity (or lack of) an organization's current group of high performers possesses is exactly what the AI will select. This can be advantageous as AI will process data to select candidates based on winning qualities. However, it can be problematic as AI excludes others who also may be high performers if their characteristics do not match those of current high performers whose data is used to make the decisions.[10]

The Ethics in Action box describes some of these issues in the real world, along with examples of what is being done to combat biased AI hiring processes.

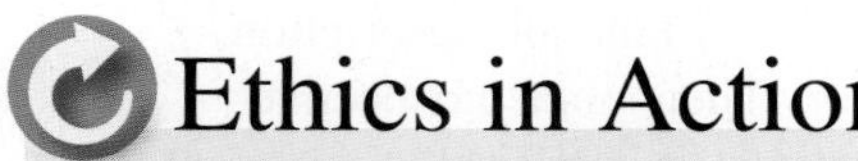

Rethinking and Revising AI

Amazon made headlines when it was found that its AI hiring tool was biased against women. One of the company's core capabilities is using data to predict shopping behaviors. So, why not use the same capabilities to predict top performers (i.e., the best job candidates)? This made perfect sense but was not a perfect practice. Given that it used past applicant histories, which were biased toward men, the resulting algorithms produced biased results. Despite efforts to eliminate particular forms of bias, it still repeatedly produced biased recommendations.[11]

Other companies employ other techniques to guard against such shortcomings. For instance, Blendoor, a recruiting platform, hides applicant names and photos and purposefully populates its candidate pool with individuals from underrepresented groups, such as people of color, women, and people with disabilities. They, of course, need to meet the qualifications for the posted jobs, but the idea is to start with data that include diverse candidates and hide that which can and does lead to various forms of bias.[12]

Yet another company, ORCAA, provides a service to test AIs for bias. The intent is to offer a form of certification and give users—companies and candidates—confidence about the technologically mediated hiring process.[13]

For Discussion:

1. As a job candidate, what are your thoughts about AI being used in hiring?
2. Assume you are a manager, who on average hires 20 people per year, which means you would likely receive more than 20 × 250 resumes. Would you be inclined to use AI in your hiring process? Justify your answer.
3. Again, as the manager, assume you use AI in hiring. What would you do to ensure it doesn't introduce bias?

The benefits of AI in hiring are immense, which means that many efforts are being made to increase its effectiveness. AI has tremendous promise because it can process such vast amounts of data simultaneously and quickly. As one example, AI can evaluate performance data and candidate characteristics of employees by hire date and job type simultaneously. For instance, AI can concurrently analyze the performance for employees hired in the past three months and over the past year, and do these types of assessments by specific jobs, employee and candidate characteristics, and bring all of these insights to bear on hiring decisions today. This means AI can be updated in real time, not just once a year, but potentially every time a person is hired. It will also never tire and or ever feel pressured to take bias-inducing short-cuts in order to reduce a candidate pool from 400 to 10 by tomorrow morning![14]

Next, let's explore the use of social media in hiring employees and the potential ethical challenges.

The Use of Social Media in Employee Screening

Google, Facebook, LinkedIn, Twitter, and other platforms have forever changed the job search for employees and hiring for employers. Research, for instance, shows that over 80 percent of organizations use social media to find candidates, and nearly 50 percent use it to screen those they find.[15] And due to the success of these major companies, others are entering the business of employee–employer matchmaking, but our interest is the business ethics implications for using search engines and social media to screen job candidates.

Depending on what a company decides to use, and the details of a candidate's life that are accessible to the public, the Internet can provide volumes of potentially useful information, such as:

- Education
- Experience
- Memberships in professional organizations
- Volunteer activities
- Political views
- Hobbies
- People and organizations friended or followed[16]

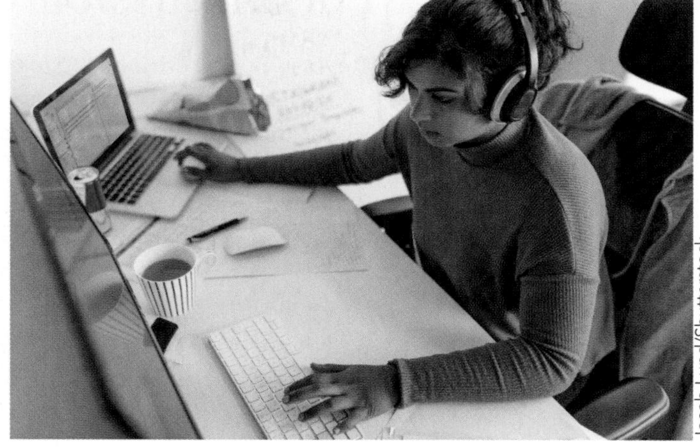
Jacob Lund/Shutterstock

Some candidates may have no concerns about a prospective employer discovering any of these details, while others may be fine with a potential employer discovering some, but not all of these details. Still other candidates may not be comfortable with a potential employer knowing any of these personal details. But

table 6.1

Potential Ethical Issues When Using Social Media in Hiring

Potential Issue	Description	Appropriate Action
What Is considered?	Relevance and consistency	Ensure that only job relevant information is considered. Guard against discrimination.
		Be consistent; search for and use the same information for every candidate.
When in the process?	Beginning, middle, or end	Decide when—initial screening, after phone interview, or at offer stage—and only use it then for every candidate.

Continued

Who does the digging?	HR person, hiring manager, multiple people	If the hiring manager does the social media review, then that should be the only person, and she/he should review each candidate the same way at that stage. Need to avoid someone using social media to remove only certain candidates (risqué posts used against one candidate but not another).
Where and how deep do they dig?	Sites and how many steps	Determine the sites in advance and then limit the search to only those sites. Resist following a cyber-path beyond to other places.
Is the candidate notified?	Are candidates told	Some companies choose to notify all candidates that social media searches are used. Be consistent.

Source: Inspired by Society of Human Resource Management, "Screening and Evaluating Candidates," shrm.org, accessed July 21, 2020, https://www.shrm.org/resourcesandtools/tools-and-samples/toolkits/pages/screeningandevaluatingcandidates.aspx.

the power really lies with the organization, and it is what it considers in screening employees that matters most. Many issues can emerge, some of which are outlined in Table 6.1.

To summarize, regardless of how and when social media is used in hiring, it is critically important from an ethical standpoint to be fair and avoid discrimination; treating all candidates the same way, and treating everyone the same, is key to avoiding discrimination. But it is also necessary to pay attention to the treatment of the protected classes. This means that organizations are wise to test or evaluate their practices in terms of protected classes.

For Discussion

1. Assume you are a hiring manager and are seeking to fill a position that is critical to the success of your department, and thus your own success. What do you think are the boundaries of appropriate search and social media use when screening and hiring a candidate? Explain.
2. Now, assume you are soon to graduate. You have excellent grades, impressive internship experience, and have engaged in valuable extracurricular activities. What social media content do you think is appropriate for a prospective employer to consider? Explain.
3. Now assume that your prospective employer requested your passwords and wanted to view the content *behind* your privacy settings. How would you respond?

Reference Checks

Throughout your career, your next employer will likely ask for references and may check with your past employer(s). Most of the time, most people don't give this any thought. At least for the candidate, you, it is simply information you need to dig up and enter in a field in the online application. However, given that it is common for employees to have held more than 12 jobs,[17] and that conflicts happen, comments from a past employer can make or break your chances with your next employer. As with many other business ethics issues, the law provides limited guidance and protection, and state laws are numerous and varied. We, therefore, focus our discussion on what is commonly done and best practices.

As we cannot actually know what someone will say about us, it leaves us wondering: What can a past employer say? Because the consequences are potentially so great, it's worth exploring the answer, especially given that someone can inappropriately undermine you and kill an opportunity.

What Can Be Shared? Anything Truthful. Some things a past employer can say about you:

- Were fired
- Always late
- Did poor work
- Were disliked by everyone.[18]

Although, this type of information is not shared, it can be. No federal laws forbid employers from telling the truth, but some state laws are a bit more restrictive. And while some individuals are determined to see you fail, most are not. Others that do share less-than-flattering details must do so truthfully, and in some situations, this is the responsible and ethical course of action. If, for example, an employee was fired for selling drugs at work, or doing something else illegal, then sharing this information would likely be understandable.

Nevertheless, from the organization's perspective, it is generally best to say little, beyond verifying employment dates and job title. One reason that less is better is simply because so many lawsuits have been filed against past employers claiming they shared inaccurate information. Saying less is especially wise, given that most communications with past employers are with somebody in the human resources department rather than your direct supervisor, and the information available to the HR staff will be secondhand at best.

Best Practices for You. Don't assume. This means don't assume that your past employer won't share information about you. To be fair, many large companies have policies and robotically execute them—sharing the same details the same way for every former employee. Some don't have such policies or are unaware of potential legal consequences, especially small companies.[19]

Therefore, you are well-served to ask the boss or HR what will be shared, and you are better off asking the question long before you actually plan to leave. If you don't learn early, don't be afraid to ask when you leave. It is helpful to know what their policy or practice is so you know how to handle this issue in your search for future jobs. Some specific words of advice:

1. If you were terminated, then learn what the company will or will not say. If they will share this information, then try to negotiate what they will and will not say before you leave. If they will not negotiate these terms, then you may want to consider being proactive or at least having your story clear in your head. Put differently, if you get to the interview stage with another employer and you are asked about your previous position, you want to explain not only what happened, but why your story may differ from theirs. Be honest and upfront. You don't want the interviewer to fill in the blanks or try to reconcile your story with what was said by your former employer. You want to fill in the blanks for them.[20]
2. If you expect a negative reference, then use references either from other employers or perhaps from someone other than the manager with whom there was the issue. The idea is to have the negative comment be an outlier among otherwise positive references.[21]

3. Some individuals use ghost reference checkers, which means they have a trusted friend contact their references as if they are a prospective employer. Like everything else, such services are also advertised on the Internet. If a concerning reference is identified, then you may want to reach out to that person and ask, "I know I didn't leave on the best of terms, but I'm curious, and hopeful, that you'll let that be water under the bridge and simply confirm that I worked here and wish me well in my future endeavors."[22]

For Discussion

1. What ethical issues might arise with references?
2. If you were contacted by a former employee's prospective new employer, what do you think is the ethical way of handling a negative reference?
3. As a former employee, what do you think is the ethical thing to do when confronted in an interview about being terminated by a past employer?

Before moving on, a bit of advice you likely already know. Research shows that the three most common social media content reasons for dropping a candidate from consideration are posts with

1. Provocative or inappropriate videos or photos
2. Drinking or drugs
3. Discriminatory comments[23]

Freedom of Expression at Work

Citizens in the United States, and elsewhere, feel that they have an inalienable right, not only their opinions, but also to express them freely. Many of these same people also believe they have this right in the workplace and every other arena of their lives. And now, because our lives are so tightly intertwined with technology and social media, many people just assume the same for what they post and share online. In this section, we take a closer look at these assumptions regarding freedom of expression at work, and how they intersect with business ethics.

First Things First, the First Amendment

In the United States, the First Amendment to the Constitution states the following pertaining to freedom of speech: "Congress shall make no law… prohibiting the freedom of speech." Very importantly, legal experts point out that it simply prohibits the government from making laws restricting speech or government employees taking actions that restrict your speech. Therefore, unless you are employed by the government, your protections are far more limited than you, and most others, may think.[24] Employers, however, cannot shut down all speech.

Employees do have the right to assemble or engage in what is called "concerted activity," such as to form unions, and they can discuss or complain about their work conditions, safety, and compensation. They also can speak out about unlawful conduct including, but not limited to, discrimination, harassment, and racism.[25] This is the essence of whistleblowing and is discussed in detail in chapter 4. Whistleblowing or not, speaking out against your employer can have undesirable consequences for employers and employees.

Employers don't want bad press and often claim, or hide behind the allegation that an employee's comments hurt the business. Employees often get fired or have concerns that their future employment opportunities may be limited. For instance, Amazon fired four employees who spoke out about coronavirus health concerns in its warehouses. This caught the attention of a number of US senators who requested that the company explain how the terminations were justified rather than retaliation. The company responded by saying that the employees were fired for repeatedly violating policies related to physical distancing, intimidation, and others.[26]

The above addresses what federal laws protect. Individual states have their own laws that may provide additional protections. For instance, employers generally can forbid employees from expressing political speech at work, but some states (e.g., California) explicitly protects workers from any action taken by their employers for "off duty" political activity. Similarly, Oregon prevents employers from requiring employees to participate in political meetings or distribute politically oriented materials.

Political Views

To begin with, a police officer (a government employee) cannot arrest you for expressing your support for a particular political candidate, party, or philosophy.[27] The fact that we are in the most politically polarized environment in generations makes the expression of political views at work a hot business ethics topic. Mounting research shows that well over 50 percent of employees either feel excluded or have experienced overt conflict at work based on differing political views. If you think these numbers seem high, then remember that many workers are connected on social media; and if you're on social media, then you are exposed to political commentary, and some of that will be from your coworkers.[28] If you think this number seems low, then keep an eye out for the next study, because research often lags reality.

It's Not All about You. You, your boss, and other coworkers are not the only ones who learn about and are affected by divisive political posts; current and potential customers too may be affected. Of course, any particular position or comment can attract support, but it can hurt business too. Notably, charged and/or controversial political expressions can and do result in the following:

- **Cause Conflicts in the Ranks.** Posts can cause conflicts between employees and interfere with their performance and create a negative work environment for others.
- **Confusion and Concern.** A fundamental issue with employees' social media activity occurs when those that read it are unclear whether the views are simply those of the person, or do they represent those of the company. The Ethics in Action box provides an excellent example. Although this argument is more relevant for founders and senior executives, it is still sometimes given as the reason for taking action against lower-level employees.

Where Is the Political Line, and Who Draws It? Considering the federal law doesn't offer much protection, and state laws vary, employers have considerable latitude for limiting and otherwise acting against what employees say. This doesn't mean that your boss can simply sit back and fire people for comments or posts he or she doesn't like, because even

Ethics in Action

Tweet This!

Owner, CEO, influencer, and problem? Yes. All of these describe Elon Musk and his relationship with social media. The iconic entrepreneur, founder of SpaceX and Tesla, among others, is known for charting his own path, as well as creating and taking on critics along the way. His reputation and 35 million Twitter followers give his words weight and reach, but this has caused trouble for him and investors in his companies.[29] The following is a short list of tweets that have caused some problems:

1. He once suggested he was seeking private funding to take Tesla private, which dramatically moved the stock price. The Securities and Exchange Commission (SEC) fined him $20 million and required future tweets about Tesla to be screened by an attorney.[30]
2. In one exchange, he called a rescue diver a pedophile, which caused a defamation lawsuit.[31]
3. He declared he is selling all of his possessions, including his home, and called for the government to free citizens from the coronavirus lockdowns; he even stated that Tesla's stock price is too high. All of this in one tweet. Guess what? Tesla's stock price dropped 10 percent.[32]

When asked about his social media issues, he told one reporter that although some of his tweets were dumb, and he wishes he could take them back, he appreciates being able to communicate directly and immediately.

For Discussion:

1. Do you think Musk and other owners and/or CEOs have different responsibilities related to social media than the average employee of their companies? Explain.
2. If you were an owner, how would you perceive your freedom of expression?
3. What is your position on discussing politics at school? At work? With your friends at dinner? If your answers differ between any of these contexts, then explain why.

if not illegal, this sort of conduct would destroy morale, productivity, and potentially the reputation of the company.

This means that companies should not look to the law for guidance on how to handle employees' political expressions, inside or outside of work, or on social media. In fact, many concepts explained in this book are your best tools:

1. Leader Conduct (chapter 7). Leader role-modeling is very powerful and can set the tone for the employees. If leaders are one-sided, disrespectful, and steamroll others, then this sets an example for others. If the owner, manager, or other leader engages in political discussions at work, or posts online where employees can see them, then this signals that this is acceptable.
2. Codes of Conduct (chapter 9). Most codes specify how employees are expected to treat each other and customers, and this often explicitly indicates the expectation of respect. As such, if employees engage in heated exchanges that devolve into name-calling and insults, they would be violating the code of conduct, rather than anything related to politics.[33]
3. Company Values (chapter 8). If a company's values suggest or explicitly indicate freedom of expression, employee individuality, employee initiative, community

involvement, or social justice and change, then it may be inconsistent to attempt to limit politically oriented discussions, posts, and activities by employees.

4. Consistency. Don't discriminate. If your employer has allowed employees to wear T-shirts for Make America Great Again, then your employer would be hard-pressed and likely crossing the ethical line to forbid Black Lives Matter clothing.[34] Starbucks had just this experience in 2020. It banned employees from wearing Black Lives Matter clothing, but in response to massive pushback from employees and customers, it reversed its decision and then some. It had 250,000 BLM shirts made and distributed them to employees. The tension had two elements. First, the company's existing policy bans clothing (and accessories) that promote a personal, religious, or political issue. However, the company has allowed employees to wear items related to marriage equality, LGBTQ rights, and gay pride.[35]
5. Expect and Protect. Effective and comprehensive social media policies both encourage employees to report inappropriate social media activity, including specifying how to report, and protect the reporters from retaliation via any channel (online or in the workplace).[36]

Bottom line: Once again, laws lag behind reality. But realize that most people interpret freedom of speech more broadly than what the law actually protects. Employers are wise to have specific and effective policies, describing what is acceptable and what is not, and what to do when someone crosses the line. Employees are similarly wise to exercise caution. It is unrealistic to suggest people do not express themselves at work or online, but many need to exercise a bit more caution than they do. For instance, it is important to keep your professional and personal accounts separate, including the emails used to sign-up. As an individual, you may want to also explicitly state, "These views are mine, solely mine, and are in no way intended to represent those of my employer or anyone else."[37]

Performance Appraisals, Rewards, Punishment, and Business Ethics

performance appraisals processes by which employers review and rate employees' achievement of performance expectations and goals

distributive fairness how an individual perceives the balance between outcomes received for the associated work and other inputs

Performance appraisals are processes by which employers review and rate employees' achievement of performance expectations and goals.[38] Despite the fact that many companies have moved away from formal conventional reviews, such as GE, Deloitte, and Adobe,[39] more than 90 percent of companies still do them.[40] And regardless of their form, many of the issues related to ethics and performance appraisals pertain to perceptions of fairness. Fairness often comes into play during performance appraisals, associated rewards, and disciplinary actions.

Quite simply, a performance appraisal that is perceived as unfair is almost certainly perceived as ineffective. To make the point, have you ever thanked someone for treating you unfairly, ever? It is important to emphasize the word "perceived"—as it is employees' perceptions that matter. So, what influences employees' perceptions of fairness during performance appraisals? There are three fundamental attributes—distributive, procedural, and interaction fairness.

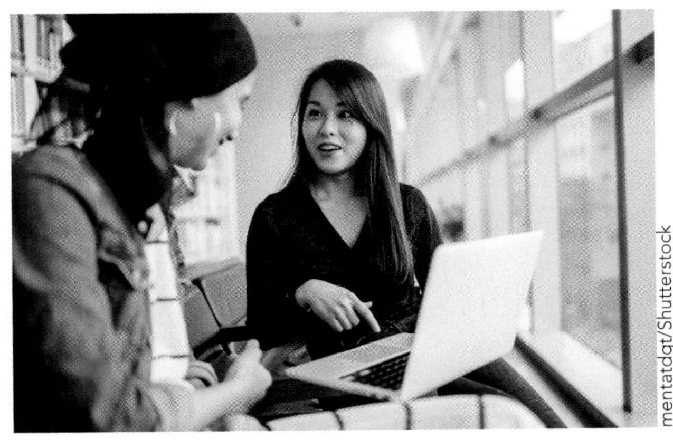
mentatdgt/Shutterstock

Distributive Fairness and Rewards

Distributive fairness describes how an individual perceives the balance between outcomes received for the associated work and other inputs.[41] Most often, distributive fairness comes down to your perception of whether you think the performance ratings and rewards (pay raise, bonus, or promotion) linked to those ratings are fair.

Your judgments related to distributive fairness are based on comparisons in your mind about the outcomes related to your inputs, and if the ratings and rewards align with your expectations, then you're typically satisfied. If the rewards exceed your expectations, then you're likely delighted, even ecstatic! But ethical issues, at least from your point of view, occur when the rewards don't align with your expectations. Research shows that these situations lead to many undesirable reactions, notably, retaliation in the form of

- Withdrawing from work—not putting in effort and showing up late.
- Ignoring instructions.
- Not going above and beyond to help others.
- Using company property inappropriately (time, technology, company cars).
- Theft.[42]

Interactional Fairness and Your Manager

interactional fairness how an individual perceives the extent to which they are treated with consideration, politeness, and respect, as well as provided with appropriate explanations

Interactional fairness describes how an individual perceives the extent to which they are treated with consideration, politeness, and respect, as well as provided with appropriate explanations.[43] This is just as it sounds—how well are you treated by the person responsible for your performance appraisal. When done effectively, managers have the opportunity not only to review the outcomes of your efforts but also the means by which you achieved them. It also is an excellent opportunity to be developmental by providing guidance regarding future goals and how to pursue them. Put more simply, performance appraisal meetings are opportunities to provide employees with feedback.[44]

Consider, for instance, a scenario in which your manager provides you with a good review outcome, meaning that you were rated the top performer in your department and received the largest raise and bonus. You feel these outcomes are appropriate and you are delighted. However, consider how this "news was delivered." One possibility is your manager not only tells you of the ratings, raise, and bonus, but also gives you praise, explains the impact of your performance on the department and organization, and expresses gratitude. The interactional justice multiplies the effects of the distributive justice or positive effects of the rewards.

Now, consider the same scenario, except this time, your manager simply reports the ratings, raise, and bonus with little emotion or explanation. It is likely you are still delighted, after all, you are the top performer and received the greatest rewards, but it is highly unlikely that the same boost or multiplying effect occurs. As such, low or weak interactional fairness can diminish an otherwise positive outcome.

Appraisals and Procedural Fairness

procedural fairness your perception of the process by which outcomes were determined

Procedural fairness describes your perception of the process by which outcomes were determined. Outcomes of performance appraisals matter, of course. If the outcomes exceed your expectations, then you are surprised in a positive way. If the outcomes only meet your expectations, then your reactions are likely to be quite calm or muted. However, when your expectations are not met, you may react with blinding outrage. But regardless of the outcome—positive or negative—the process always matters. Moreover, it is the process part of the appraisal process that is often the most difficult for you and for your manager conducting the appraisal.

Why? This is the part of the appraisal process where biases (conscious and otherwise), blatant favoritism, politics, relationships, and countless other factors can influence the outcome. As the employee, you expect the process to be fair and consistent, if not objective, but this is rarely the case. And to be clear, being objective does not ensure accuracy and fairness, no more than subjectivity equals arbitrary and inaccurate. A detailed explanation of this is beyond the scope of this book, but let's make the point with a simple illustration.

Assume you have a sales job, and your compensation is 100 percent commission-based, and you earn a 50 percent commission on everything you sell in the year. If you sell $100,000 of your product, then you earn $50,000. Your sole performance measure is sales dollars. Now, consider the scenario wherein your largest customer relocates its headquarters in November, and with it, all credit for sales goes to another employee's territory. You no longer get credit for the sales you made, the relationships you built, and the pipeline of business you developed that will continue to pay into the future. All of that work, and credit ($$$$), goes to the other employee. Is this a fair outcome? Probably not. Is this a fair process? Definitely not. By using a single objective measure and calculating performance only

Ethics in Action

Inflation and Deflation Are Unfair and Problematic

Appraising employee performance is a frequent, difficult, and consequential responsibility for managers. How well or poorly performance evaluations are done can undermine, boost, or have no effect on employees' performance, and thus the appraisal process has important implications for individual employees, teams and departments, and the larger organization. A fundamental and ubiquitous challenge is intentionally inflating or deflating employees' ratings. Some of the most common are outlined in Table 6.3.

table **6.3**

Common Motives for Inflating and Deflating Employees' Performance Ratings

Common Motives for Inflating Ratings	Common Motives for Deflating Ratings
1. Accurate ratings would decrease motivation	1. Motivate more effort
2. Accurate ratings would decrease the likelihood of raises and bonuses	2. Punish a difficult or disliked employee
3. Avoid "punishing" a top performer who is distracted due to issues outside of work	3. Motivate an employee to quit
4. Avoid confrontation and hurt feelings	4. Justify actions to terminate an employee
5. Reward impressive effort that did not produce desired results	5. Comply with organizational policies to force rank or distribute performance ratings and rewards

Source: C. Longenecker and D. Ludwig, "Ethical Dilemmas in Performance Appraisal Revisited," *Journal of Business Ethics*, 1990, 9: 961–969.

Continued

For Discussion:

1. From the manager's perspective, select two motives in the left column and justify inappropriately inflating a subordinate's ratings.
2. Now assume you are the owner of the business. Would you support having any of your managers inflate performance ratings of employees using the motives in the left column? Explain.
3. From the manager's perspective, select two motives in the right column and justify inappropriately deflating a subordinate's ratings.
4. Now assume you are the owner of the business. Would you support having any of your managers deflate performance ratings of employees using the motives in the left column? Explain.
5. Assume you're an employee. Explain your position on your manager inflating your performance ratings.
6. Assume you're an employee. Explain your position on your manager deflating your performance ratings.
7. Reconcile the differences in the views described in 1–6.

at the end of the year, which are both elements of the performance appraisal process, you just got cheated out of multiple rewards.

The Ethics in Action box outlines some of the most common reasons managers intentionally inflate and deflate employees' performance appraisal ratings, which can and do result in perceptions of unfair procedures.

Generally, even the value of positive outcomes is diminished by faulty or unfair processes. Returning to our previous scenario, you're the top performer, earned the top rating and largest raise and bonus, and your manager delivers all of this news with great enthusiasm and gratitude. However, also assume that you didn't expect these outcomes. You instead thought that at least two of your colleagues clearly outperformed you.

Sure, you received impressive rewards, but given that you feel you didn't deserve them, you may feel guilty rather than proud or happy. It would be more difficult to celebrate and accept the credit. This scenario describes an unpredictable and also unfair procedure, and despite it delivering positive outcomes to you this year, it is highly likely that you and all of your colleagues will have little confidence in the outcomes next year.

Bottom line: Always pay attention to the process. As illustrated, if the process is perceived as unfair, even the best outcomes are undermined. Moreover, unfair outcomes paired with unfair processes are likely to generate employee outrage and a storm of undesirable behaviors—lack of information sharing, active disengagement, sabotage, turnover, and destruction of the manager's and organization's reputations.

Making Appraisals Fair and More Effective

Now that you have a sense of what causes appraisals to be perceived as unfair, let's conclude the section and chapter with some simple and widely applicable ways to help make them better for all stakeholders.

1. **Begin with Existing Goals**. This may be hard to believe, but the majority of managers surveyed say they simply start writing an employee's appraisal without first

looking at the goals they were responsible for achieving. Start with the standard—the goals—they are supposed to meet.

2. **Create a Rubric or Guide**. Many appraisals include open boxes wherein managers are supposed to enter comments. These are well-intentioned, as they provide flexibility, and managers can make comments that are relevant for a given employee. However, too often the reality is that this wide-open space is too vague, and managers don't exactly know what to write. They, therefore, include comments that are not especially focused on the goals or actions. A rubric outlines the specific relevant criteria, including examples or evidence that corresponds to different ratings. Rubrics can assist in building relevance, consistency, and actual evidence into the appraisal process.
3. **Specific Evidence**. On the appraisal form completed by the manager, prompt or ask the rater for three specific examples of how the employee met, exceeded, or missed expectations. This provides more compelling, specific, and legitimate evidence on which to base (and defend) appraisals and link rewards.[45]

This chapter highlighted some of the most common and potentially problematic business ethics issues that arise between employees and their employers. Now that you have a better understanding of the many potential ethical pitfalls of hiring, you should be better prepared to avoid them altogether, or at least mitigate the potential undesirable consequences. It also is important for you to know that freedom of expression has limits at work, for better and for worse. Most people inaccurately think freedom of speech means say anything anywhere, but now you know to be more cautious as an employee, but also how to be more purposeful when setting policies pertaining to employee expression.

And finally, few if any organizational practices create as much widespread stress and conflict as performance appraisals. You, whether in the role of an employee or manager, now have a better sense of how to make them better, or less bad, and that process always matters; fair processes can make undesirable outcomes a bit easier to take.

Chapter Summary

1. Hiring employees is one of the most important activities for any organization, but it can also generate numerous ethical issues when the processes are discriminatory.
2. Artificial intelligence and social media are essential tools in the hiring process, but it is important to guard against bias and ensure consistency.
3. The First Amendment, commonly referred to as the "freedom of speech" act, is far more limited than most people think.
4. Employers in fact have considerable latitude to limit or act against employees' expressions, such as those made online and those related to politics.
5. Performance appraisals are one of the most important, and emotionally charged, management processes in organizations. Critical business ethics issues often relate to fairness in its various forms.

Key Terms

artificial intelligence 107
discrimination 106
distributive fairness 115
implicit biases 107
interactional fairness 116
performance appraisals 115
procedural fairness 116

CASE STUDY: What Good Does Testing Do?

Why do employers test candidates for drugs? Among the more common reasons are that managers assume that sober, nonchemically altered, and nonaddicted employees are more productive and safer. Employers, of course, want productive workers and have a responsibility to provide a safe environment for all employees. Most people would agree that this is reasonable for jobs where any form of intoxication could potentially impede safety, such as surgeons, bus drivers, and pilots.[46] This is reflected in the most common situations in which employees are tested—pre-employment, after an accident, randomly, and when there is reasonable suspicion.[47] In other jobs, particularly those with no apparent safety issues, fewer people agree that testing is appropriate or achieves the stated goal of increasing productivity.[48]

When Did It Start and Why?

Employee drug testing began in the early 1970s when many soldiers returning from Vietnam were either actually addicted or continued recreational drug use that began when they were deployed. Testing really took off in 1988 when the then President Ronald Regan initiated the war on drugs and required all federal employees to be tested. This spawned an entire drug-testing industry—test manufacturers, consultants and attorneys to write policies, and companies to administer and process tests—to support the hundreds of thousands of required tests. Corporate America, although not legally required, jumped on the testing train and rode it to its highest point in the mid-1990s, when over 80 percent of companies reported they tested employees.[49]

Changing Times and Changing Practices

Then, as now, marijuana was far and away the drug most commonly detected during testing, and this may not be a surprise today, given the significant growth in legal medicinal and recreational use. As of mid-2019, pot is legal for some purpose in 33 states, and approximately 12 percent of American adults reported they smoke it. This percentage has been basically at the same level since 2016 but up from 7 percent in 2013.[50] These statistics reflect changing public, and thus political views on pot, as over 66 percent of Americans say they support legalization, which is more than 30 percentage points greater than in 2005.[51]

Increased Change Brings Increased Challenges

However, these changes have brought tremendous challenges for companies. For starters, pot is still illegal at the federal level, which means it is currently governed by a patchwork of state and local laws. Yes, some cities have their own, which means the complexity can be immense. If a company does business in only the roughly three dozen states in which pot has some legal status, then it could still be confronted with many different regulations. It is not binary—legal vs. illegal.

This means that a company may need multiple practices just for hiring. For instance, in some states, you can only test after an offer is made, but in others you cannot conduct pre-employment testing unless mandated by the federal government. Still other states may require testing for certain jobs but not others (e.g., truck drivers). Certain states require candidates to be notified and others don't. That is just hiring. The complexity increases greatly when a company also wants to test after accidents or randomly, as some states and cities prohibit these forms of testing separately from the laws governing pre-employment testing.[52]

These then need to be established in accordance with each state. As with most parts of the hiring process, nearly all these responsibilities fall to human resource departments, and in even the largest companies they can be underresourced and understaffed.

A Positive Test Is More Complex Too

The current situation means that employees are confronted with policies on quicksand, ever shifting and never stable. Distinctions also need to be made between medicinal and recreational use of drugs, and it can be confidently assumed that employers don't want to confront employees any more than employees want to be confronted. Furthermore, if pot is legal recreationally in your state, does that mean that your employer needs to allow its employees to use it? No, they don't. What about it being illegal in the state in which you are located, but then you visit an office for a meeting in another state in which it is legal, and your colleagues are smoking?

Talent or Just Warm Bodies

Marijuana specifically, and drug testing more generally, can present a serious staffing challenge for many companies in diverse industries across the country. If a given organization does drug testing and eliminates all candidates who test positive from consideration, then that limits their talent pool and makes hiring more difficult. Exacerbating this situation is the fact that many potential employees will avoid applying to companies they know test for drug use, thereby reducing the talent pool further still.

Some managers and business owners also think, "I don't want potheads working for me anyway," only to find that in a tight labor market, they are unable to attract needed talent. This situation may also occur in small towns where the absolute number of workers is already small, and anything that shrinks the candidate pool means positions cannot be filled. Finally, and as a word of caution, some of these same managers and owners harbor stereotypes and think that their employees are "not the kind of people that smoke pot." But they might be just one law or one happy hour away from realizing how wrong they are.

For Discussion:

1. Assume you are the executive vice president of human resources at your employer, and you thus are in charge of making all employee-related policies. Regarding hiring, what would you do in terms of drug testing? Explain.
2. Would your practices differ for marijuana? Explain.
3. Does your answer change if your name is on the company? Explain.
4. Would you handle drug testing differently for prospective employees versus existing employees? Why or why not?
5. Again, assume you are EVP of HR and are making monitoring policies for your employer. Nearly all of your employees work remotely; describe and justify how you would monitor these employees.
6. Would your monitoring policies change if half of the employees worked in the office and half remotely? Explain.
7. You own the company. Would you limit your employees' freedom of expression (e.g., speech and attire)? If yes, then explain how and why. If no, then explain why not.
8. Assume you are about to have your first performance appraisal for your first job after graduation.

Apply Three-Dimensional Problem-Solving for Ethics (3D PSE)

You can apply the Three-Dimensional Problem-Solving for Ethics (3D PSE) from multiple perspectives (see Figure 6.1), such as that of the executive vice president of human resources (EVP of HR), the owner of a company with your name on it, a manager, or an employee (prospective or current). Be sure to specify whose perspective you are applying, as your problem-solving is likely to differ considerably. Let's try it with you being the EVP of HR and thus in charge of all employee-related policies. Also, assume that your company has historically conducted drug testing for new candidates and random tests of current employees, as well as after accidents, when it is suspected an employee is under the influence. Although your company has offices in nearly all the states in the country, you have no jobs that have federally mandated drug testing (i.e., all testing your company does is voluntary).

figure 6.1

Three-Dimensional Problem-Solving for Ethics (3D PSE)

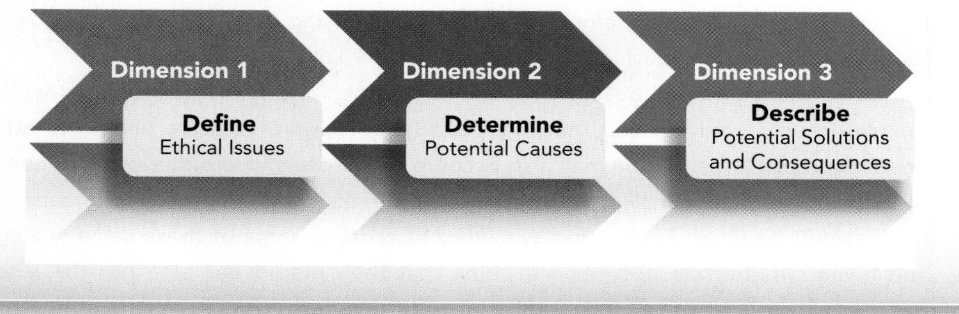

Dimension 1: *Define* the Ethical Issue

What is the gap in the case? What do you have and what do *you* want?

a. From your view as the EVP of HR, what is the current situation and how do you want it to be?
b. Why is the current situation a problem? What difficulties or undesirable behaviors and outcomes happen as a result of the problem you defined? Why do you and other executives in your company care about the problem you defined in Dimension 1?
c. Define your problem in one or at most two sentences and structure it in terms of what is current versus what is desired.
d. Who are the key stakeholders, those that affect or those that are affected by the problem you defined?

Dimension 2: *Determine* the Causes

a. **Individuals.** Given the problem you defined in Dimension 1, how do characteristics of individuals (including you, other executives like you, and employees) cause the problem, such as ethical decision-making approach, work values, and moral principles?

b. **Contextual.** Are there particular norms (practices) that caused the problem, as defined in Dimension 1? Are there industry or country values, norms, or regulations that caused the problem you defined?

Dimension 3: *Describe* Your Potential Solutions and the Intended and Unintended Consequences for Stakeholders

For each cause identified in Dimension 2, answer the following questions:

a. *What* do you recommend as a solution(s), and ***how*** would you make it (them) happen?
b. *Why* would you do it the way you proposed? Does this reflect a particular ethical decision-making approach (e.g., utilitarian or deontology)?

If your responses to these questions are unsatisfactory, then go back to Dimension 1 and repeat the process. If, however, you are comfortable and confident in your problem-solving efforts thus far, then ensure you achieve the desired outcomes and avoid any unintended consequences.

c. What is the desired and likely effect in the short- and long-term for the key stakeholders involved in the problem and causes (Dimensions 1 and 2)?
d. What potential unintended consequences may occur with each proposed solution?
e. If any, what are the implications for other stakeholders (e.g., individuals, organizations, and communities) besides those noted in Dimensions 1 and 2?
f. Will your solution work in an ethical manner? Make a final assessment of whether your chosen solution will reduce or eliminate the causes determined in Dimension 2, and whether it will then remedy the ethical problem defined in Dimension 1. If not, then repeat and refine the dimensions.

Chapter Opener Photo Source: Tor Kreutzer/Shutterstock

chapter 7

The Double-Edged Sword of Leadership and Business Ethics

Learning Objectives

AFTER READING THIS CHAPTER, YOU SHOULD BE ABLE TO:

LO1 Articulate what it means to be an ethical leader.

LO2 Identify the characteristics of unethical leaders.

LO3 Explain what it means to lead with ethical versus legal liability, character, and empathy.

LO4 Apply your knowledge to ensure ethical leadership in yourself and others.

WHERE DO **YOU** STAND?

Disclose or Not to Disclose?

Nondisclosure agreements (NDAs) are legal contracts regarding confidentiality between two parties, and they have been used extensively between employers and employees. For instance, employers want to protect themselves from employees (or contractors) leaking or taking valuable information to others, notably to competitors.[1] NDAs are also commonly used to help conceal the details of misconduct, often the misconduct of a senior leader or other employee.

Although common, the use of NDAs to contain the details of misconduct has come under intense scrutiny in recent years, in part, spurred by the MeToo movement. It was revealed that many of the powerful men exposed in the movement had patterns of misconduct and multiple NDAs with the victims. For instance, talk show host Bill O'Reilly supposedly paid more than $30 million to settle claims with multiple women.[2]

On the one side, NDAs prevent the circulation of embarrassing details about the horrible sexual assault experiences of victims. Although the victims desire justice genuinely, many of them do not want their friends, family, coworkers, and future employers to know about their experiences. Victims often are concerned about retaliation, being treated differently, or simply do not want this type of attention. NDAs can also generate larger payments for victims, as the accused are likely to pay more to keep the matter quiet.[3]

On the other side, critics of NDAs for sexual offenses at work argue that confidentiality prevents victims from getting justice, as the accused pay nothing more than money, whereas some victims will lose their jobs and suffer from the psychological effects for the rest of their lives. Critics also argue that if misconduct is kept silent, then there is no deterrence, meaning that even if the accused is held accountable, others do not see the costs and thus are not discouraged from similar conduct.

However, as some cases in the media suggest, NDAs may also remove deterrence for offenders who will continue misconduct, such as O'Reilly and Hollywood producer Harvey Weinstein, who was found guilty of assaulting many women over time.[4]

These views have motivated state governments (e.g., California, New York, and New Jersey) to pursue legislation banning employers from utilizing NDAs in cases related to sexual misconduct.[5] Some companies are following suit. Sundar Pichai, Google's CEO, said he doesn't want employees, especially women, to remain silent about workplace issues including sexual harassment. Susan Wojcicki, YouTube CEO, echoed his views.[6]

1. Assume you are the CEO of a company. What position would you take on the use of NDAs related to employee's sexual misconduct? Explain.
2. If you were an employee accused of misconduct, then provide at least two reasons why you would want to use an NDA and two reasons why you would not want to use an NDA?
3. Assume you were a victim. Would you want your employer to use an NDA in a settlement with you? Why? Why not?

Introduction

The importance of leaders for business ethics cannot be overstated. They can either make or break the ethical conduct and thus the success of individuals, teams, organizations, and even countries. Their power to influence the conduct of others can set a positive, but not always easy, ethical path, or they can undermine the best intentions of others. The potential vastness and impactful consequences are why understanding and applying knowledge related to leadership are foundational to your own success. As you read this chapter, look for ways to relate leadership to the concepts you studied in the previous chapters. After reading this chapter, you will see how leaders and leadership (the act of leading) influence the vast majority of ethical challenges in business. To better equip you to meet the leadership challenges ethically, and avoid the undesirable outcomes associated with unethical leadership, we explore numerous valuable and applicable concepts. Let's start with what it means to lead.

The Role of Leadership in Business Ethics

Most people make simple, quick judgments about what constitutes ethical leadership, and most often, this judgment is made in terms of legal versus illegal activity. This is especially true when the leader in question is one we don't know personally, such as the CEOs involved in scandals we see on TV or read about in the news.

nondisclosure agreements (NDAs)
legal contracts regarding confidentiality between two parties

However, when it is your direct supervisor or a leader within your company, you quickly realize that your view of ethical leadership goes far beyond what is legal. To understand this, it is helpful to clarify what leadership actually is and then we can explore what ethical versus unethical leadership looks like.

leadership
the ability of an individual to influence, motivate, and enable others to contribute toward the effectiveness and success of the organization

Leadership and Ethical Leadership

For starters, **leadership** is the "ability of an individual to influence, motivate, and enable others to contribute toward the effectiveness and success of the organization."[7] Being a leader is all about influencing others and thus does not require formal authority and a title such as the role and title of manager, director, or executive. Although being a formal leader has particular forms of influence (e.g., the authority to give you raises, promotions, and hire and fire), the essence of **ethical leadership** is using appropriate means to influence others toward an appropriate goal.[8] The word appropriate is used to remind you that business ethics are a function of expected behaviors, practices, and processes in particular contexts (organizations, industry, country, and cultures—organizational and national).

ethical leadership
using appropriate means to influence others toward an appropriate goal

An example is your boss giving you a poor performance evaluation because you openly disagreed with the plan that she presented at a meeting with your team. The plan was her goal, and the poor review score was retaliation (unethical influence). Another common example is a coworker who has the same title as you, and thus no authority over you, but he can undermine your reputation and opportunities by telling members of your team things that are untrue about you, simply to make you look bad and himself better (also inappropriate influence). In both cases, your manager and coworker may be wonderful people in other spheres of their lives—kind supportive friends, partners, and parents. This disconnect between personal and professional lives can, in part, be explained using the moral person–moral manager distinction.

Moral Person and the Moral Manager—Two Worlds, One Person

Extensive research has been conducted on ethical leadership, and a common and helpful way to understand and apply it is in terms of the moral person and the moral manager, which distinguish ethical conduct in one's personal and working lives.

moral person
one who lives (i.e., believes and practices) the morals and ethical standards of his or her culture and society in their personal lives

The **moral person** is the one who lives (i.e., believes and practices) the morals and ethical standards of his or her culture and society in their personal lives.[9] In Western society, and others, this includes integrity, honesty, fairness, trustworthiness, and respect. Such attributes and expectations are captured in the Declaration of Independence (e.g., all people are equal) and the fundamental beliefs of religions (e.g., Ten Commandments for Judeo-Christians).

moral managers
live the morals and ethical standards of his or her culture and society in their professional lives, and they hold others accountable for doing the same

Moral managers live the morals and ethical standards of his or her culture and society in their professional lives, and they hold others accountable for doing the same.[10] This means they treat employees and others at work according to the same standards, and they ensure that others also do the same. Therefore, moral managers are consistent across the different areas of their lives, and often, they have expectations that others also do the same.

For Discussion

1. Can you think of someone who is a moral person but not a moral manager? If yes, then describe the different or inconsistent behaviors.
2. Describe an example of someone you know or have heard of in the news who appears to be a moral manager.

More generally, employees and society at large are increasingly expecting leaders to align conduct in both their personal and professional lives. To make a point, something that you are highly unlikely to hear from a moral manager, and an ethical individual more generally, is the statement—"business is business." This phrase is often used by a person who takes

table **7.1**

When Personal Conduct Conflicts with Professional Expectations

Alleged Incident	Professional Consequence
Juli Brinksman, Virginia bicyclist, flipped off the presidential motorcade in 2017.	Fired for violating her company's social media policy, even though she was not the one who posted the video. (Side note, in 2019, she won a seat on the county board of supervisors that oversees his golf club in Sterling, VA.)[11]
In May 2020, Amy Cooper called police to report that a black man (bird-watcher) threatened her and her dog in Central Park.	The video went viral, revealing the racially driven and unsubstantiated nature of her claim. Her employer, Franklin Templeton Investments, initially placed her on administrative leave and then terminated her after a brief investigation.[12]
Michael Vick, a star quarterback in the National football league (NFL), pled guilty to involvement in a dogfighting ring.	The NFL placed Vick on an indefinite suspension; he served twenty-one months in prison, two months in house arrest, and was fined nearly $1,000,000. He was rehired and returned to football in 2009 (he retired in 2016).[13]
Travis Kalanick, cofounder and the then CEO of Uber, was caught on a video berating an Uber driver.	One of the several questionable incidents that investors used to force Mr. Kalanick to resign as CEO in 2017.[14]
Ray Rice, an NFL player, was caught on a video assaulting his fiancée.	He was suspended for two games by his team (Baltimore Ravens) and then released at the end of the season. He has not returned to the NFL and works as a high school coach.[15]
Dr. Patrick Hugh Conway, CEO of North Carolina Blue Cross Blue Shield, was arrested for DWI.	The CEO resigned at the company's request.[16]
Pennsylvania's "Porngate" in 2016 involved the exchange of sexually explicit images and racially and religiously offensive materials among judges, prosecutors, and other top government officials.	Two State Supreme Court Justices were either suspended or resigned, several top aides to the former State Attorney General were terminated, and numerous others were reprimanded.[17]

advantage of another person, or knowingly does something that would be questionable to most people in another context. Examples of conflicts between conduct in these two realms are growing, some of which are outlined in Table 7.1.

Another way to identify such conflicts between personal and professional lives is when leaders don't walk the talk, do what they say, or make their actions consistent with their words. They encourage or even demand their employees to be honest, yet they lie. They would never admit to being unfair, yet they are. Turn others in for cheating but "cut corners" themselves. They criticize others for unethical conduct without acknowledging their own.

Table 7.2 provides you with a tool to help you assess the ethical leadership of others. Take a minute now to assess your current direct supervisor, if you're currently working, or a supervisor from a past job.

Another helpful way to understand ethical leaders is to view them in terms of virtues. Recall from chapter 2 that virtues are qualities that define an individual's moral character and positive contributions to society.[18] Virtuous leaders, like other individuals, have positive

table **7.2**

How to Assess Ethical Leadership?

My Manager...	Strongly Disagree	Disagree	Neutral	Agree	Strongly Agree
1. Conducts personal life in an ethical manner.	1	2	3	4	5
2. Defines success by BOTH results and the way they are achieved.	1	2	3	4	5
3. Disciplines employees who violate ethical standards.	1	2	3	4	5
4. Listens to employees.	1	2	3	4	5
5. Is fair and balanced in decision making.	1	2	3	4	5
6. Is trustworthy.	1	2	3	4	5
7. Discusses own views of business ethics or values with employees.	1	2	3	4	5
8. Role models ethical conduct.	1	2	3	4	5
9. Has the best interests of employees in mind.	1	2	3	4	5
10. Considers the "right thing to do" in decision making.	1	2	3	4	5

Source: Adapted from M. E. Brown, L. Trevino, and D. Harrison, "Ethical leadership pulling a social learning theory perspective for construct development and testing," *Organizational Behavior and Human Decision Processes* (July 2005): 117–34.

intentions, are genuinely motivated to contribute to individuals and larger society by drawing on a number of qualities we unpack next.

Virtuous Leadership

As we covered in chapter 2, virtues are qualities that define an individual's goodness, moral character, and genuine desire to contribute to individuals and society. Accordingly, **virtuous leadership** is characterized by a focus on doing good for the sake of doing good, regardless of the situation. Efforts are directed toward flourishing and positive outcomes, not avoiding the undesirable.[19] Virtuous leaders value and display six common virtues illustrated in Figure 7.1.

virtuous leadership
A leader who focuses on doing good for the sake of doing good, regardless of the situation

If you don't recall the meaning of these virtues from chapter 2 (see also Table 2.2), then the character traits are briefly described again here:

Courage = Enables one to pursue which is right without fear.

Temperance = Enables one to control emotions and desires.

Justice = Motivates respect for the rights of others, fairness, and adherence to positive norms.

Prudence = Enables one to select the "right" ends and the "right" means (i.e., goals and paths).

Friendliness = Genuine love, care, and respect for others.

Truthfulness = Reflected in telling the truth and keeping promises.[20]

figure 7.1

Virtuous leadership character traits

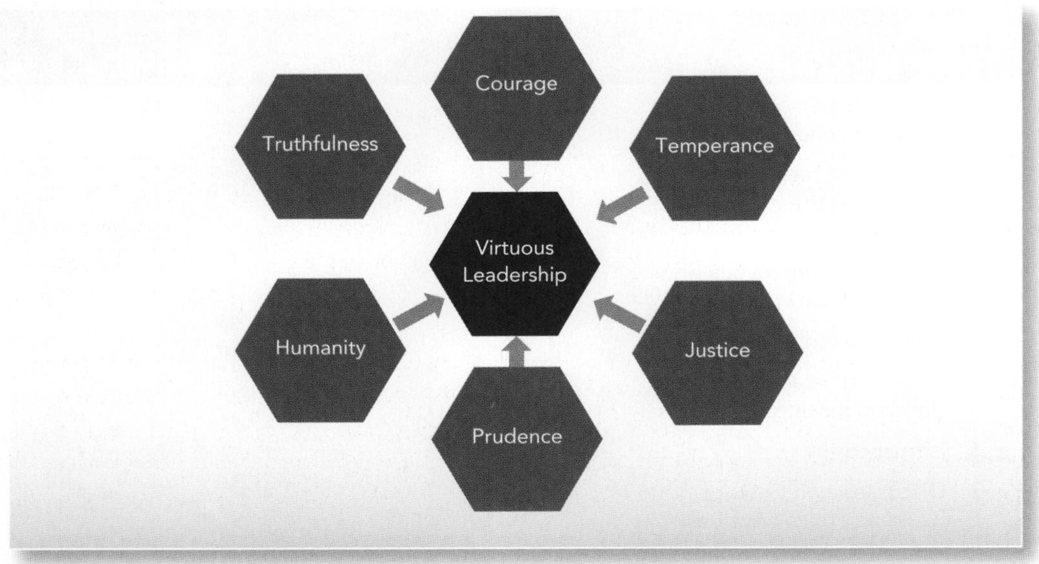

Pertaining to virtuous leadership, it is important to emphasize that virtuous leadership does not require a title or authority and it is not something granted by an individual, group, or organization. It is something that individuals (and organizations via their employees) choose to do. As a well-known expert in positive management and organizations describes it:

> Virtuous leadership is less a means to another more desirable outcome than an ultimate good itself.[21]

Virtuous leadership is built on three pillars or assumptions:[22]

1. Human beings, by nature, are good and want to be good.
2. Doing good is a sufficient end in and of itself. Good acts have no motivation or intent beyond being good (e.g., nothing is expected as an outcome or in return).
3. Virtuous behavior amplifies the positivity in the actor and in others. As such, it fosters an environment of reinforcing positivity.

Based on what we've covered thus far, you likely have the sense that virtuous leadership not only differs from many other forms of leadership and management, but it is also a different approach to ethics. Virtuosity has an inherently positive bias and is narrowly focused on doing good. Thus, it can be very beneficial to individuals, groups, and organizations. To explain, even in the most hectic and uncertain times, virtues can act as a beacon and help in decision making.

Research involving numerous companies across sixteen industries that downsized a significant portion of their workforces showed impressive benefits for virtuous leadership. The companies with higher virtuousness scores (compassion, integrity, forgiveness, trust, and optimism) also reported higher productivity, quality, customer retention, and lower employee turnover. In addition, these companies were more profitable than their less virtuous competitors during this time. For instance, when confronted with a dilemma, the choice can be made to do what is consistent with a virtue rather than which choice will generate the greatest profit.[23]

Put differently, virtuous leaders pursue the good rather than avoid the bad.

Before moving on, it is important to note a common underlying theme—other-oriented. Ethical leaders consistently (always) and genuinely consider others in terms of both outcomes and the means by which outcomes are achieved. Next, we will explore the dark side of leadership and ethics.

Characteristics of Unethical Leaders

Research and your own experiences reveal that many unethical leaders possess the **dark triad**—a collection of three interrelated traits—narcissism, Machiavellianism, and psychopathy. Can you think of a leader known to possess these traits? After reading this section, you'll have a clearer idea. More importantly, however, one doesn't have to lead a department, company, or country to qualify; such a person can be your team member, coworker, business partner, parent, significant other, or you.

dark triad
a collection of three interrelated traits—narcissism, Machiavellianism, and psychopathy

Whether in business, politics, education, or elsewhere, when people in power possess the dark triad, bad things often happen to individuals, groups, organizations, countries, and beyond. Put more simply, the dark triad is the antithesis of ethical leadership, as people who possess these traits are more prone to behaviors that are callous, selfish, and unethical.[24] Learning what it looks like can be invaluable to your satisfaction, success, and overall well-being in any job and over the course of your career.

Narcissism

Narcissists are characterized by an inflated sense of self-importance, need for excessive attention and admiration, entitlement, and a lack of empathy for others.[25] Don't be fooled; many narcissists appear extroverted or charismatic, and they may express considerable, but fake, concern for others. If **empathy** is the ability to understand and share the feelings of others, then narcissists can be highly effective at showing false empathy. In fact, they can be perceived initially as charming, especially when the relationship with the individual (e.g., you) or the group is new, members of the group don't know each other well, and the relationships are more like that of acquaintances than close partners.[26]

narcissists
characterized by an inflated sense of self-importance, need for excessive attention and admiration, entitlement, and a lack of empathy for others

empathy
the ability to understand and share the feelings of others

For Discussion

1. Think of a narcissist you either know personally or have heard about in the news. Describe what you think demonstrates that a person is a narcissist.
2. Describe an empathetic leader you know or have personally experienced. What were the benefits to you and to others?

Larry Ellison, the founder and executive chairman of Oracle, has built the company into a bellwether tech company and amassed an enormous personal fortune of $59 billion, making him the fourth richest American in 2020.[27] Some attribute his success, in part, to his narcissism. A former executive at Oracle described Ellison this way:

> *"The difference between God and Larry is that God does not believe he is Larry."*[28]

Wedding and Lifestyle/Shutterstock

The truth is, and research confirms, that narcissists can climb the ladder at work by being top performers, earning promotions, and gaining power. When push comes to shove, narcissists think, say, and behave in ways that serve their own interests, running over or otherwise undermining others if necessary. One implication is that the true negative costs of narcissism are not revealed early in relationships or in the early days of a specific job. Instead, their true nature and damage are revealed over time.[29] Therefore, you can see how it is difficult for such people, when in leadership roles, to truly commit to other-oriented social responsibility and sustainability, pillars of business ethics.

To help you spot a narcissist, look for these traits:[30]

1. Inflated sense of self-importance. When working with others, they not only often exaggerate their achievements and talents, but they also frequently insist that their own contributions were inaccurately greater than those of others. They feel entitled.
2. Dreams of greatness. Although they may not share such grand dreams with you, they may possess an extraordinary desire for power, recognition, and success in various areas of their lives.
3. "I am special." Yes, we are all special and deserve respect. But narcissists help fill this need by associating with people they want to be perceived as similar to—the rich and powerful, for example.
4. Demand or at least require the admiration of others. They think they are great and expect you to think and say the same.
5. Expectation of special treatment. Even though others may be governed by rules and other ethical norms, they feel they are the exception.
6. Others are exploited and disposed to achieve goals. People are the means for achieving the narcissist's goals. To the extent you are serving those goals, you may receive relatively favorable treatment (although not truly genuine), but if you are perceived to interfere with those goals, then you should expect intensely negative treatment.
7. Lacks empathy, which is the ability to understand and consider another's feelings from his or her point of view.

You may be thinking, what happened to arrogance and conceit? Narcissists also often exhibit these, but not always. So, don't be fooled and dismiss someone as not being narcissistic simply because they do not appear arrogant. To reiterate, narcissists can be especially dangerous exactly because they can appear charming, caring, and humble, but when they don't get what they want, few people are more cruel or vindictive.[31]

Psychologists believe that narcissism is significantly influenced by parenting—a combination of overly indulgent parents (especially mothers) or those who are overly harsh or critical.[32] Part of the reasoning is that this develops an inflated sense of importance, while at the same time, making the individual feel his or her value to be contingent on "looking good" (performance and admiration). Narcissists likely received conditional love, and the love or favor they share can also be conditional.

Whatever the cause, narcissism at work grows in strength and leads to destructiveness if not checked. Just like bullies, if you don't stop them, narcissists persist and create even more damage.

Machiavellianism

Machiavellian leaders are those who are strategic and skilled at manipulating others to create and preserve their own power. Like narcissists, **Machiavellians** see people as either tools to use for their own purposes or obstacles to be eliminated. Such people think that manipulation is acceptable and that others would do the same if the roles were reversed. Research consistently shows that this trait is associated with a

Machiavellians see people as either tools to use for their own purposes or obstacles to be eliminated

1. Lack of morality
2. Desire for control
3. Desire for status
4. Distrust of others[33]

These characteristics can emerge as entitlement, similar to narcissists, in that Machiavellians feel they deserve credit and control. The emphasis is on control, as Machiavellians observe few limits to achieve and maintain it, including violating ethical standards. Machiavellians epitomize *the ends justify the means* approach and egoist decision making.

If you did not read the *Prince*, and you are still having difficulties imagining what a Machiavellian looks like, then popular culture's fascination provides many examples on TV (see Table 7.3).

How do you spot one at work and elsewhere? Look for these characteristics.

1. They are often likable and friendly initially in order to hide their true intentions.
2. They prefer using subtle tactics (charm, friendliness, self-disclosure) and are masters of the sneak attack.
3. They want to be able to deny allegations, blame others (gaslighting), or use guilt if their self-serving motives are discovered. However, they have no problem in using aggressive tactics if necessary.
4. They tend to succeed best in jobs and social situations with ambiguous rules and boundaries.
5. Emotional detachment enables them to be patient and cunning in manipulating others. Similar to narcissists, the danger and damage may not be evident until it's too late.
6. They are more competitive than average.[34]

Psychopathy

Psychopathy is evidenced by a lack of empathy, impulsive behavior, selfishness, and absence of conscience. Some experts claim that this is the most problematic of the three. Psychopaths tend to have little concern for the emotions of others, especially in one-on-one dealings with no witnesses, and often bully others to get their way.[35] If this isn't bad enough, psychopaths lack empathy, guilt, or regret when their actions harm others. Similar to narcissists and Machiavellians, they are willing to be dishonest to get their way.[36]

psychopathy a lack of empathy, impulsive behavior, selfishness, and absence of conscience

People, probably you too, often use the terms psychopath and sociopath interchangeably. Let's clear this up. First, they are similar. Both lack empathy, but psychopaths may genuinely believe that their misconduct is not inappropriate or unethical (even though it is) and deceive you as a result. Sociopaths will likely realize they are out of bounds but won't let that stop them from crossing the line.

Psychopaths are "skilled actors whose sole mission is to manipulate people for personal gain," says psychologist L. Michael Tompkins. The danger of their acting abilities is amplified by their charm and intelligence, making them even more difficult to spot. Sociopaths are far less interested in acting or pretending that they care and that you're important. It's all

table 7.3

Dark Characters on TV[37]

Character and Show	Dark Trait and Behaviors
Tony Soprano in *the Sopranos*	Fear was a common tool for Tony, and the body count was high. Cross him at your peril. Besides, it's generally accepted that if you kill people as part of your business, you have questionable ethics.
Lords Varys and Baelish in the *Game of Thrones*	Very different characters with very similar issues, deceit, egoism, ends justify the means, master manipulators, and plenty of human carnage in their wakes. Trust either one at your peril.
Gustavo Fring from *Breaking Bad*	Upstanding citizen and motivated contributor by day, but behind the scenes, he was a ruthless crystal meth distributor.
Francis Underwood in *House of Cards*	Amoral, manipulative, self-interested, charismatic, and most every other characteristic associated with devastating and powerful people. His bad behavior got him all the way to the White House.

about them. Sociopaths tend to be more hotheaded, impulsive, and less composed, whereas psychopaths are the "cold-hearted killers" and are calculative. For instance, psychopaths will make well-thought-out plans to remove obstacles between them and their goals, even when one of those obstacles is you, your job, or reputation.[38]

How do you spot a psychopath?[39] Look for these characteristics:

1. Superficial charm
2. Grandiose sense of self-worth
3. Lies with ease
4. Cunning and manipulative
5. Lack of remorse or guilt
6. Reduced emotional response
7. Callous and lacking empathy
8. Parasitic lifestyle (take from others)
9. Promiscuous sexual behavior
10. Lack of realistic long-term goals
11. Impulsive
12. Irresponsible
13. Failure to accept responsibility for one's actions (deflect and blame others—gaslighting)

Psychopaths are among us at work. Some estimates suggest that between 4 and 20 percent of CEOs possess psychopathic traits, which, when compared to 1 percent for the overall U.S. population, is quite troubling.[40] This suggests they too climb the corporate ladder. Perhaps one of the most astounding examples is someone you likely haven't heard of, David Colby. He is the former CFO of WellPoint, now a part of Anthem Health Insurance. Colby received many professional accolades for his professional work, but it was his off-the-job conduct that qualifies him as a first-rate psychopath. Legal proceedings revealed that he had affairs with more than two dozen women, proposed to at least twelve, and even texted one of them—"ABORT" when he learned she was pregnant.[41]

Why Do They "Succeed?"

Being charming, competitive, decisive, along with their often-extroverted personalities, help dark leaders get ahead. Such leaders can, at the same time, be seductive, luring people to support them, and intimidating or frightening away potential competitors. This can make them savvy "actors" at work and in society.

Steve Jobs was widely viewed as a leader with low empathy who seemingly made few close friends along the way, but many enemies. He routinely violated rules and social norms such as parking in the handicap spot and bullying employees. Elon Musk is also an entrepreneurial icon well known for confrontations with Wall St. analysts, the media, and employees. Elizabeth Holmes, the founder and destroyer of Theranos, lost her fame, fortune, and potentially her freedom by lying, faking, and defrauding her way to personal wealth with a fantasy blood-testing technology.[42]

All this success and recognition often come with significant costs to others who are used in the service of dark leader's desires. If organizations do not provide consequences for their antisocial behaviors, then the darkness grows and the carnage mounts.

One expert described the dark triad and its problems as overplayed strengths. They can serve you, individually, in the short run but can cost you in the long term if you are unaware. The traits are toxic elements of your personality, and you need to be careful about using them as weapons—"the group will generally lose the more you win." This, of course, is increasingly problematic as one's position and responsibilities grow, the costs grow too.[43]

What to do about this?

Avoiding the Perils of the Darkness

Quite simply, apply the knowledge and measures presented in the previous sections. You now have knowledge and tools to help you identify such bad actors, and there are additional methods.

No Close Friends (NCF) Test. Although we did not discuss the triad in terms of clinical psychology, all three are what are termed as antisocial personality disorders. Quite simply, this means they have difficulties with establishing and especially maintaining long-term, mutually beneficial social relationships.

Therefore, one way to spot people at work who have one or more of the dark triad traits is that they rarely have true, close relationships at work or in their other life spaces. Over the course of your career, you will undoubtedly interact with individuals who possess one or more of these characteristics in problematic levels. When this occurs, such people rarely have true friends at work, are likely to have actual enemies, although they may have worked in the same position and organization for decades. In the author's experiences working in multiple industries, including numerous universities as a professor, he's worked with leaders who would not get so much as a "hello" in the elevator and never had lunch with anyone in his or her large department. Seventy percent of the people reporting to another would have quit within the hour if they had another job opportunity. When yet another retired after thirty years, nobody thought to give the otherwise common retirement celebration. Then, one kind soul felt bad and organized such an event. However, sadly, he or she had to diligently beat the bushes to get people to show up.

To be fair, not everyone wants to or does make close friends at work, and this does not mean he or she possesses one or all of the dark triad traits. However, if these people have ascended to higher positions of power, have worked in the same organization for years or multiple organizations over many years, and have accumulated numerous enemies and few or no true close friends, then there are chances that they are "dark."

Funeral No-Shows (FNS) Test. Eulogies can be quite touching and provide rich and wonderful insights about the person who has passed away. Friends, family, colleagues, and other loved ones share their fondest memories. Besides a measure of comfort, eulogies offer a glimpse into who the person was, the life they lead, and the people they touched.

However, for business ethics purposes, it can be insightful to consider who will *not* be at someone's funeral. Absences can be as much or more telling than that of attendees. Specifically, while reading and learning about unethical and dark triad leaders, you likely thought a particular person, now think of who won't be at that person's funeral. Think of a dark leader who is still living, then assume they died today. Who would not show up at their funeral? Which people in their lives would not shed a tear?

Persons of great power, such as executives, politicians, and celebrities, often have large numbers of people attend their funerals, and this can be for a host of reasons. One such reason is that attendance is expected or even a part of your job responsibilities. Many presidents and prime ministers, as a matter of duty, attend funerals of other leaders, even if they were sworn enemies. However, given a choice, many people would not and do not attend the funerals of narcissistic, Machiavellian, and psychopathic leaders who left them in their wake.

The next time you suspect someone might be a narcissist, Machiavellian, or psychopath, think about the outcomes of the NCF and FNS tests.

To conclude our discussion about unethical leadership, it is worth noting that none of the dark triad or other characteristics in and of itself makes someone unethical or dangerous; neither does having unfavorable answers to the NCF and FNS tests. Instead, you should collect this sort of information as evidence, and the more evidence you collect for an individual, the more likely they are to be dark and dangerous, and you should proceed with caution. It also greatly increases the chances such people will be **corrupt leaders**, those associated with patterns of personal and follower misconduct over time.[44]

corrupt leaders those associated with patterns of personal and follower misconduct over time

Now, let's move on to the key characteristics that help distinguish ethical leaders from the dark ones.

Leading with Ethical Liability versus Legal Liability, Character, and Empathy

As noted in chapter 1, only the smallest percentage of unethical behavior is illegal, which means to address the vast majority of what constitutes unethical conduct cannot be remedied via legal processes (courts). To be clear, it is important to abide by the laws, obviously, as it is difficult to argue that any illegal conduct is actually ethical. But ethical leaders have higher standards and embrace higher levels of social responsibility. As Figure 7.2 illustrates, the standards for ethical liability are often higher than those for legal liability.

figure **7.2**

Legal vs. Ethical Liability

Ethics in Action

President Donald J. Trump has been accused of many misdeeds since his election in 2016, and he was impeached for some of his conduct (abuse of power and obstruction of Congress). He, his supporters, and the majority of the media (both for and against) have focused almost exclusively on whether any of his conduct was illegal and even the legality of investigations, firings, hires, and numerous other actions he has taken.

The legality of a president's actions of course matters, but as we've clearly established in this course, all employees, and especially leaders, need to meet a higher standard. They need to be ethical, not just legal.

For Discussion:

1. What is your reaction to the argument that being legal is not enough?
2. What examples can you think of where a leader (or any individual) only did what they had to based on the law, rules, or a contract? What were your reactions?
3. Assume you expect both legal and ethical conduct of the managers of a company you own, then what are the two things you would do to ensure that they act ethically?

Legal Liability—Necessary but Insufficient

Legal liability refers to the compulsory and adverse legal consequences assumed by people who commit illegal acts.[45] Complying with legal standards is not only expected but is also part of being socially responsible (as you learned in chapter 2). However, the larger point is that employees, employers, and the general public have placed entirely too much emphasis on doing what is legal, suggesting that ensuring your conduct is legal is sufficient. Many people have, and many still do, conduct business as if behavior, policies, and practices that are legal are ethical. In other words, being within the law or following only the contract is sufficient. This view is entirely too narrow to qualify as ethical leadership.

legal liability the compulsory and adverse legal consequences assumed by people who commit illegal acts

What is legal and expected is essentially the content and purpose of contracts. However, it is neither possible nor desirable to include every possibility in a contract. Nobody can see the future and know every potential situation, which means ethics are not the letter of the law but instead they capture the spirit! Ethical leaders do both! Ethical leaders don't rely simply on contracts, and they certainly do not hide behind contracts. For you, every time you hear someone say, "I'm only doing what I have to based on the contract," the risk is high for unethical leadership, especially if one party has more money and resources to navigate the legal system than the other, which is almost always the case between employees and employers and individuals and large companies.

Let's raise the bar.

Ethical Liability—The Higher Standard for Leaders Everywhere

We expect more from our leaders. Simply conducting one's self in a legal manner is not enough, nor is it enough to only expect those for whom you are responsible to act within the law. As employees and members of society, we expect much more and hold leaders **ethically liable**, accountable for their own ethical conduct and that of those they manage, work with, influence, or witness.[46] Leaders who uphold ethical liability conduct themselves according to the highest ethical standards in a given situation, not the least, and they also hold others accountable for similar standards of ethics. As such, holding ourselves and our

ethically liable accountable for their own ethical conduct and that of those they manage, work with, influence, or witness

leaders ethically liable promotes social responsibility, respect and dignity for themselves and others, and sustainable business behaviors, policies, and practices.

You can compare and differentiate these leader liabilities further by thinking about legal liability as a test of smarts and ethical liability as a test of character. Many legal lapses by leaders, and people more generally, are just plain stupid. Getting drunk at work, stealing money from your employer, cheating on an exam, and paying a bribe to get into college are illegal and punishable. However, character is something more complex and important for ethical leadership and is explored next.

Character—The Foundation of Ethical Leadership

What does it mean to say, "She has a strong character?" You know it is important, and you assume it matters. If you cannot describe it, then how do you recognize it? What does it mean to lead with character? If you can't answer these questions with precision, you really can't know if someone has it, if you have it, or you have the potential of developing it. Fortunately, there's help.

character comprised of four morals that one applies universally: forgiveness, integrity, responsibility, and compassion

leading with character living with morals (fortiveness, integrity, responsibility, and compassion) in your personal and professional lives and doing your part to ensure those you influence to do the same

Character is comprised of four morals that one applies universally: forgiveness, integrity, responsibility, and compassion.[47]

Therefore, **leading with character** is living with morals (fortiveness, integrity, responsibility, and compassion) in your personal and professional lives and doing your part to ensure those you influence to do the same.

Morals, and thus character, matter when they are translated into behaviors, policies, and practices. So, what does leading with character look like? An intensive study showed that the character of a CEO and top management team is demonstrated by

- Standing up for what is right
- Expressing concern for the common good
- Forgiving mistakes
- Showing empathy.[48]

Character also is profitable. The same study showed that companies led by executives and top management teams that exhibited strong character had a 9.3 percent return on assets, while those with weak character delivered only 1.93 percent (more than four times better financial performance). Employees of these same exemplary organizations also reported higher CEO ratings for vision, strategy, focus, accountability, and executive team character.[49] It's safe to say you would prefer to work for such a company.

Another way to clarify and emphasize what it means to lead with character is to contrast it with the common characteristics of those with dubious or weak characters.

Monkey Business Images/Shutterstock

- **Truth**. Their relationship with the truth is weak and sporadic.
- **Trust**. False trust. Like those with the dark triad, those with weak character develop your trust to take advantage of you.
- **Blame**. It's a hot potato, they pass it on to others quickly, readily, and often skillfully.
- **Ruthless**. Punish others for their mistakes and lack of loyalty.[50]

Like those who possess the dark triad traits, leaders with weak character are commonly blind to it. In fact, they gave themselves much higher scores on character qualities than the scores given by their employees. Meanwhile, leaders with strong character scored themselves a bit lower than their employees scored them.[51] It seems that strong character is also associated with humility.

Those with strong character have deeply engrained (habits) thoughts, emotions, and behaviors intended to promote human excellence and social betterment.[52] Ask yourself, aren't these the qualities you would want in your supervisor, coworkers, and the person you see in the mirror?

The Ethics in Action box shines a light on another common and critical characteristic of ethical leaders—empathy.

Ethics in Action

Leading with Empathy during COVID

Employees report feeling their employers are better prepared to deal with the pandemic than either the government or the media, and not surprisingly, employees put more trust in the leaders at work to consider their well-being than those of other organizations (e.g., government).

The same research shows that effective leaders are not only honest in communications and share factual information, but they also address the emotional well-being of employees. An effective way of doing this is leading with empathy.

Empathetic leaders exhibit the following:

- **Vulnerability**. Many leaders try to act tough or even invincible, but this is not realistic and can be counterproductive during a time of crisis, like COVID. Show others you're just like them, concerned, affected, and emotional. This makes you real and builds trust.
- **Sacrifice First, If Not Most**. If employees are laid off or asked to make sacrifices, then be sure you make your own. Some CEOs, such as Oscar Munoz at United Airlines, did not take a salary. Microsoft committed to paying its 4,500 hourly service providers full pay regardless of the time actually worked.
- **Safety Before Performance**. Surveys show that, by a wide margin, employees prefer to hear about efforts to keep COVID out of the workplace, and about infected employees, before news about business impact.
- **Not Just Your Own**. A large percentage of employees surveyed (78 percent) reported they expect their employer's leaders to protect the larger community and not just their own employees.
- **Express Gratitude!** Recognize employees for not just their successes but their efforts too. Better still, recognize the many others outside of the organization for the same (e.g., first responders).[53]

For Discussion:

1. What is common to all of these elements?
2. Describe an example of someone you know and the empathy they showed related to the pandemic.
3. If these characteristics make a leader effective, describe how you can implement two of those listed above to increase your effectiveness at school, work, home, or other aspects of your life.

Part of empathy, and thus character, as noted in the box, is vulnerability. One convincing sign of vulnerability is tears. Many more people in power are showing tears, which historically has violated deeply-seated norms for leaders. Leaders are supposed to be composed, strong, and able to withstand more than those who follow them. These norms have been difficult for women and men leaders. Women who showed emotion were labeled stereotypically as women—emotional and unable to perform under pressure. When men cried, they violated their gender stereotype. This view was even reinforced by a president, who said, "When I see a man cry, I view it as a weakness . . . The last time I cried was when I was a baby."[54]

Norms, however, are changing, and it is possible that the widespread and intense grief associated with the pandemic will accelerate the acceptance of and even power of expressing emotion. Put more simply, vulnerability is real, persuasive, and a part of being human. Why not make it part of your leadership?

Now that you have learned much more about ethical leadership and the personal traits and behaviors that make it and break it in a given individual, we next turn our attention to the organizational factors that foster (un)ethical leadership. We will explore some warning signs and enablers of unethical conduct in leaders, and other employees, which will help you identify and avoid these qualities in others. These also can be particularly useful in helping you identify mentors, teammates, business partners, and employers who could bring you tremendous joy (or grief).

Why Aren't All Leaders Ethical, and What Can Be Done About It?

In this chapter, you've learned part of the answer: the moral person and the moral manager, dark triad, and character. These are largely stable traits that follow people throughout their lives, from job to job. But you also know that business ethics happen in the context of organizations, which assert powerful influences on the conduct of leaders and all employees. It is appropriate to interpret much of what is shared next as two sides of a leadership coin—ethical leader on one side and unethical leader on the other.

Warning Signs

To reiterate a point made previously, everyone makes mistakes, including our leaders. Ethical leaders are aware of moral humility, learn, and do not repeat the same ethical errors. The real issue with unethical leaders is that their misconduct, and the employees and cultures of the organizations they run, becomes a pattern. Patterns are critical problems, and some common causes of what enables patterns to develop and continue are outlined in Table 7.4.

Conflict Is a Red Flag

Conflict is another warning sign, especially escalating conflict. As you'll learn in chapter 9, unethical leadership leads to unethical cultures, which perpetuate bad behaviors. The next Ethics in Action box describes how unchecked unethical conduct persists and escalates.

Ethical leaders do not delegate ethics or "sweep issues under the rug." They make knowing a priority, hold themselves accountable for knowing and acting, and do the same for those they lead. This approach cascades and embeds ethics throughout the organization.

table **7.4**

Common Causes of Unethical Conduct and Antidotes

Cause	Description	Potential Antidotes
Sweep it under the rug.	Unethical leaders commonly cover up, defend (in words and in court), or act as if nothing happened.	Anonymous tip lines, ethics audits, enforcement with authority, 360-degree feedback
Delegate ethics	Many organizations, because leaders allow it, make ethics a policing function of HR or legal. This effectively shifts responsibility to others.	Include leaders in the ethics reporting and response process and hold them accountable for issues start to finish.
"I didn't know."	Plausible deniability has been a tactic used by leaders throughout time, despite occasional regulations intended to hold them accountable. The essence is, "If I don't know about it, then I'm not responsible."	Ethics is a shared, not a delegated, responsibility. Hold all managers responsible for the conduct of those who report to them. If you are a manager and didn't know, oftentimes you should have.

Why Some Unethical Leaders Get Away with It

You have already learned many answers to this question, but there are a few others worthy of note. These occur in every industry and at many levels of organizations. See how many of these apply to bad actors who work currently, worked in the past, and related to scandals you hear about in the news.

Ethics in Action

When Unethical Conduct Is Baked In

At one firm, the most senior people served themselves very well, and often at the expense of the more junior people in the department. The same group had a long history of intimidation, harassment, and bullying. Most people did not dare speak up for fear of the consequences.

In one instance, when an employee did speak up about misconduct, the person was bullied and retaliated against. When this happened, a complaint was made to management within the division who did nothing. The complaint then went to the ethics committee who investigated and recommended people be removed and sanctioned. Sadly, the committee had no authority to implement the recommendations, and the managers chose not to implement them. The managers instead retaliated against the individual filing the complaint with a low score on a performance review and the smallest pay raise in the department.

The misconduct continued, and the matter escalated to the highest levels of the organization, wherein the most senior leader delegated it to the general counsel (head attorney of the organization). The general counsel purposefully dragged the matter out for months and ultimately dropped the matter when the employee quit.

Subsequently, two of the offenders were promoted and given pay raises.

Halo of Reputations. "Everybody likes him," "She's a top performer," and "I would never believe he would do that," are among the phrases you hear from people who are interviewed about a colleague, leader, neighbor, or someone they "think they know" is accused of unethical conduct. Recall our discussion from chapter 4. Yes, and thankfully, some claims are inaccurate, and sometimes, individuals are exonerated. However, and importantly, people tend to dismiss information that is inconsistent with their impressions of a person. The halo of reputation occurs when your generally positive impression of a person causes you to dismiss negative information (they can do no wrong).[55]

This commonly occurs when misconduct is alleged, proven, or otherwise verified related to successful CEOs, university coaches, presidents, deans, and celebrities. Colleagues, students, fans, and the general public find it hard to believe that someone achieving such success could possibly do something terrible. But keep in mind that many narcissists can appear charming, even charismatic, and those possessing high levels of the dark triad often climb to high positions.

Performance Measures. The way performance is measured is another reason that unethical leaders often get away with patterns of unethical conduct. A record of strong performance on these key metrics earns leaders recognition, rewards, and additional opportunities. The key metric for CEO performance is stock price. For coaches, it is wins and championships. For university presidents and deans, it is endowments, enrollments, buildings, presidential libraries, and institutes. Ethical conduct is not measured, and a combination of the elements in Table 7.4 causes misconduct to be hidden.

hubristic leaders characterized by an inflated sense of self-confidence and abilities, the tendency to attribute successes to themselves, and failure to appropriately consider external forces, and perceive risks to be favorable to them

Hubris. **Hubristic** leaders are characterized by an inflated sense of self-confidence and abilities, the tendency to attribute successes to themselves, and failure to appropriately consider external forces, and perceive risks to be favorable to them.[56] The implications for business ethics are that such leaders will overestimate their ability to get away with questionable behavior. Nearly every perpetrator of financial fraud you hear about in the news thought they were too smart and clever to get caught.

Bernie Madoff is an excellent and infamous example. He was a long-time and highly regarded investor, former chairman of the Nasdaq stock exchange, and pioneer of electronic trading. Another part of Bernie's reputation was that he delivered positive returns for his investors even when the market was down. It was ultimately revealed that this was indeed too good to be true, as he was operating a $50 billion Ponzi scheme, taking new investors' money to pay existing investors' returns. The scheme included little actual investing but instead a complex charade of false statements and deceit. He did this for decades and was ultimately caught, sentenced to 150 years, and ordered to pay $170 billion.[57]

Those with high levels of hubris think that they can do things that others can't . . . that rules and other norms do not apply to them. They are better and above other people and feel they are exempt from rules that apply to others. Such leaders also tend to think that the downside risk of getting caught or called out for their behavior is small . . . they can minimize or escape it.

Been the Boss Too Long Syndrome. Syndromes are groups of symptoms that occur together, and most often, for no fault of their own, senior leaders have been in senior positions for a long time.[58] This is especially true of business owners, many senior administrators, and managers with considerable seniority in a particular organization. The issue here in terms of business ethics is not so much what they do but instead what they don't experience.

Because such individuals have been the boss for a long time, they have not been the target of bad behavior and unethical conduct. To be clear, this doesn't mean they don't have to deal with it. After all, it is their responsibility to monitor, prevent, and address misconduct when it occurs. However, managing or dealing with unethical conduct of others is quite different from being the target and suffering the direct consequences. Think about it, when was the last time the CEO of your company was likely bullied? What about the university president, provost, deans, and head coach of your university's football team? President of the United States? As a result, it is something that happens to someone else. They are not the target, and this makes it fundamentally different, even if that person is genuinely concerned.

For Discussion

1. Why do you think leaders often sweep unethical conduct under the rug, as described in Table 7.4?
2. What is worse—not knowing or knowingly not acting? Contemplate and explain your answer.

The Most Powerful Tool for Ethical Leadership—Modeling

In terms of business ethics, modeling does not involve fashion, runways, or photographs, but instead behavior. The most powerful tool for influencing others is your own behavior. This applies to any position you will every occupy, including the president, prime minister, CEO, business partner, teammate, parent, and student. Model what behaviors? Those consistent with what you've learned in this chapter, for starters, and then the others you have and will learn in this book.

Modeling behavior has special meaning in the context of business ethics. If you demonstrate moral courage (see chapter 4) and resist the temptation to cut corners or take advantage of others, or if you speak out when someone else is approaching or actually crosses the ethical line, then this shows others you are a person of strong character. You walk the talk, including doing the tough thing when other choices are easier. Among other benefits, demonstrating integrity translates into trust, which is essential to building productive relationships and the ability to positively influence others. Therefore, your own actions are your most powerful business ethics tool.

Once again, the Golden Rule can be an excellent guide for which behaviors to model, along with the TV test.

To conclude, we covered a great deal of useful material in this chapter. Now you have a better understanding of how critical leadership is to business ethics, and how leadership is truly a double-edged sword. Ethical leaders can cause individuals, groups, organizations, and countries to flourish, whereas unethical leaders can cause stress and misery at all the same levels. You were introduced to several easily applicable and valuable tools to identify both dark and positive leaders. Use this knowledge for your personal development as well as to help navigate relationships and employers throughout your life. Perhaps you will choose to be a virtuous leader and do good because it is the right thing to do. Even if you don't, then you are now equipped to hold yourself and others to higher, more positive, and ethical standards.

Chapter Summary

1. Leadership is about influencing others, and this influence can be via both positive and negative means and ends. Ethical leaders use appropriate means toward appropriate ends.
2. Moral people's ethical standards are consistent across the various arenas of their lives (personal and professional), and moral managers model these behaviors and standards in their professional lives and hold others accountable for doing the same.
3. Virtuous leadership is comprised of six virtues and focuses on doing good for goodness sake, rather than as a means to an end.
4. Unethical leaders can harm individuals, teams, organizations, countries, and larger society.
5. Many unethical leaders possess some combination of narcissism, Machiavellianism, and psychopathy, also known as the dark triad.
6. Unethical leaders, including those who possess the dark triad, can achieve success, but they often use, abuse, and manipulate others to reach their goals. The damage they do often takes time to be noticed.
7. Society is coming to expect leaders to do more than simply avoid doing harm or breaking the law, but also to pursue what is good and right and beneficial to society. Legal versus ethical liability is a way to describe this phenomenon.
8. Beware of unethical leaders using a number of warning signs such as conflict, hubris, and the halo of reputations.

Key Terms

character 138
corrupt leaders 136
dark triad 131
empathy 131
ethical leadership 127
ethical liability 137
hubristic leaders 142
leadership 126
leading with character 138
legal liability 137
Machiavellians 133
moral manager 127
moral person 127
narcissists 131
nondisclosure agreements (NDAs) 126
psychopaths 133
virtuous leadership 129

CASE STUDY: When a Vision Goes Dark

Imagine a resume that reads: high school National Merit Scholar who learned Mandarin, studied engineering at Stanford, spent the summer of freshman year working in Singapore at the Genome Institute, acquired a patent, and became an entrepreneur who created a company once worth $9 billion and made the covers of Fortune, Forbes, and numerous others.

Behind these achievements is an intensely determined and competitive individual who at a very young age (twenties) was able to persuade internationally known politicians (former President Bill Clinton and former Chief of Staff and Secretary of State James Baker), and Silicon Valley titans, Larry Ellison (founder of Oracle), and Tim Draper (venture capital investor), to invest in and otherwise support the company. The association with and support from such notable others gave the founder and the company credibility.[59] This was leveraged to attract over $700 million from investors. The vision of the company was to change the world of medicine, which in the process would help achieve the founder's childhood goal of becoming a billionaire.[60]

It "Worked" Until It Didn't

This same person ran the company like a despotic dictator. Investors were not allowed to learn how the technology worked or to have any influence regarding how the company was run. Departments were isolated from each other, and absolute loyalty was demanded from employees. Employees were monitored, such as when they arrived and left each day, which eventually morphed into the expectation that they would work incredibly long hours and take no vacations—just like the boss. Employees were intimidated from disagreeing and retaliated against or fired if they did. The president, and also the romantic partner of the founder, was eventually forced out of the company.[61]

The Reveal

If you haven't guessed, this now infamous individual is Elizabeth Holmes, the founder and ex-CEO of defunct Theranos, the revolutionary blood-testing company that was revealed to be a massive fraud. Holmes, once personally worth over $4 billion, has been charged by the alphabet soup of federal agencies—Food and Drug Administration, Securities and Exchange Commission, and Centers for Medicare and Medicaid Services—for a range of illegal activities with potential penalties including millions of dollars in fines and twenty years in jail. She has already been banned from leading a public company for ten years.[62]

The idea behind Theranos was impressive, even intoxicating to investors, the public, and large partners such as Walgreens, Cleveland Clinic, and Capital Blue Cross Blue Shield. She was a celebrity. However, it turned out that Theranos's equipment could not perform 240 tests on just drops of blood as hoped.[63] Worse still, prototypes of the Theranos testing machine did not work, and demonstrations for various partners were shams. The results reported were generated using conventional testing equipment already on the market and then presented as if they came from the Theranos machine.

Who Knew Who Was Responsible?

Holmes insisted on such privacy and total control that it seems only she and her romantic partner and President, Sunny Balwani, knew the whole truth.[64] In fact, reporting (books, news articles, and an HBO documentary) shows that Holmes intensely resisted and even refused to reveal the operational and financial "truth" to the company's board of directors, some of whom challenged her optimistic views and messages. All accounts indicate that Holmes would not allow oversight by anyone, not even the most determined and well-qualified individuals on the board, such as Avie Tevanian who was Apple's former head of software engineering, and Don Lucas, venture capital investor and chair of the board.[65]

For Discussion:

1. What ethical decision-making perspective did Elizabeth Holmes seem to possess (recall from chapter 2?)
2. How would you describe the ethical decision-making perspectives of the investors?
3. Describe the level of social responsibility demonstrated by Holmes.
4. Describe Elizabeth Holmes in terms of the dark triad?
5. Imagine you worked at Theranos. Describe your ethical dilemma and what you would do.
6. What was Don Lucas's responsibility as chairman of the board?
7. What was his responsibility, given his venture capital firm invested other people's money in Theranos?

Apply Three-Dimensional Problem-Solving for Ethics (3D PSE)

You can apply the 3D PSE from multiple perspectives (Figure 7.4)—a major investor, an employee, board member, or even Holmes herself. Just be sure to specify whose perspective. However, let's analyze the case as if you were Don Lucas, chairman of the Theranos board of directors and significant investor. Remember, the board of directors are ultimately responsible for how an organization utilizes resources, its reputation, and the interests of a range of stakeholders.

figure **7.3**

Three-dimensional problem solving for ethics (3D PSE).

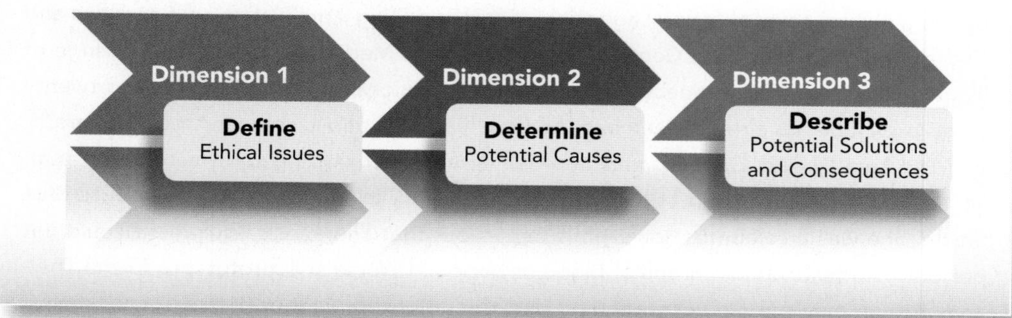

Dimension 1: *Define* the Ethical Challenge

What is the gap in the case? What do you have and what do *you* want?

a. From Lucas's view as chairman of the Theranos board (not as an investor), describe what he had versus how you wanted it to be?
b. Why is the current situation a problem? What difficulties or undesirable behaviors and outcomes happen as a result of the problem you defined? From Lucas's perspective, why would he care about the problem you defined in Dimension 1?
c. Define your problem in one or two sentences and structure it in terms of what is current versus what is desired.
d. Who are the key stakeholders those who affect or are affected by the problem you defined?

Dimension 2: *Determine* the Causes

a. **Individuals.** Given the problem you defined in Dimension 1, describe how Holmes caused the problem as you defined it in Dimension 1. Describe who else and how they contributed to the problem.
b. **Contextual.** Are there particular policies or practices that caused the problem defined in Dimension 1? These policies and practices may be within Theranos, or they may reside with regulators, investors, board members, or others.

Dimension 3: *Describe* Your Potential Solutions and the Intended and Unintended Consequences for Stakeholders

For each cause you identified in Dimension 2, answer the following questions:

a. From the perspective of Lucas, and then other stakeholders, ***what*** do you recommend and ***how*** would you make it happen?
b. Why? Explain your motives, along with considering if it reflects a particular ethical decision-making perspective (e.g., utilitarian or universal)?

If your responses to these questions are unsatisfactory, then go back to Dimension 1 and repeat the process. If, however, you are comfortable and confident in your problem-solving efforts thus far, then ensure you achieve the desired outcomes and avoid any unintended consequences.

c. Assuming you could have gone back in time and intervened, then what were the ***desired and likely effects in the short and long term*** for the key stakeholders involved in the problem and causes (Dimensions 1 and 2)?
d. What ***potential unintended consequences*** may occur with each proposed solution?
e. If any, what are the **implications for *other* stakeholders** (e.g., individuals, organizations, and communities) besides those noted in Dimensions 1 and 2?
f. Will your solution work in an ethical manner? Make a final assessment of whether your chosen solution will reduce or eliminate the causes determined in Dimension 2, and whether it will then remedy the ethical problem defined in Dimension 1. If not, then repeat and refine the dimensions.

PART 3

Organizational Influences on Business Ethics

chapter 8

Organizational Culture and Business Ethics

Learning Objectives

AFTER READING THIS CHAPTER, YOU SHOULD BE ABLE TO:

LO1 Articulate the elements of organizational culture and their effect on business ethics.

LO2 Identify various forms of incivility and explain how organizations both perpetuate and stop them.

LO3 Describe how to create and foster ethical cultures.

WHERE DO **YOU** STAND?

Unethical? Yes. Pay a Severance?

If an employee quits or is terminated because of unethical conduct, should they receive severance pay? In the university context, athletic directors, coaches, and senior administrators (presidents, provosts, and deans) often receive severance packages when they depart, even when it is because of unethical conduct—for example, when teams are caught paying recruits to attend a particular school.

1. Assume you are a member of a university's board of trustees, and thus you, along with other board members, are responsible for the university and all of its employees. Would you pay the remainder of a coach's contract who left or was dismissed for paying recruits to attend the university? Explain your position.
2. What about a professor who plagiarized other's work?
3. Does your position change, knowing that professors don't have contracts like coaches, which are specified as five years at $2 million per year? This means there is no pay remaining. They will just be unemployed and receive nothing from the university. Explain your position.

Introduction

In any organization in any industry, if there is a pattern of bad behavior, slight to severe, then there is an organizational culture problem. This applies to workgroups, departments, entire organizations, and governments at all levels. Organizational culture is the stage on which all employee behavior is played. As it shapes employee behaviors, it is essential to know the culture of an organization in order to understand

and manage business ethics. Understanding organizational culture will enable you to better understand and explain the conduct of your coworkers, managers, and employers throughout your career.

If a group persists for some period of time, then that group will establish a culture. And an organization's culture is a fundamental determinant of how individuals, departments, and the organization approaches business ethics.

Organizational Culture and How It Affects Business Ethics

organizational culture a system of shared values (defining what is important), norms (policies, practices, and behaviors), and artifacts (elements you see, hear, and touch) among members of a group or organization

Organizational culture is a system of shared values (defining what is important), norms (policies, practices, and behaviors), and artifacts (elements you see, hear, and touch) among members of a group or organization.[1] It is helpful to think of these elements in layers (see Figure 8.1).

The Layers of Organizational Culture

If you recall morals, values, and norms from chapter 1 (Figure 1.1), then that will help you understand organizational culture. Organizational culture builds on a similar framework. The foundation is morals—the high-level ideals or assumptions on which societal order is maintained, such as don't cheat, don't steal, and be fair. All businesses function in this environment and (are expected to) build their particular organizational cultures on this moral base. For clarity, however, morals are excluded from our model as it is understood that they are always there operating in the background.

organizational values beliefs shared by members about what an organization deems important, and they thus serve to guide behaviors, policies, and practices

Organizational Values. As you learned in chapter 1, **organizational values** are beliefs shared by members about what an organization deems important, and they thus serve to

figure **8.1**

Model of Organizational Culture for Ethics

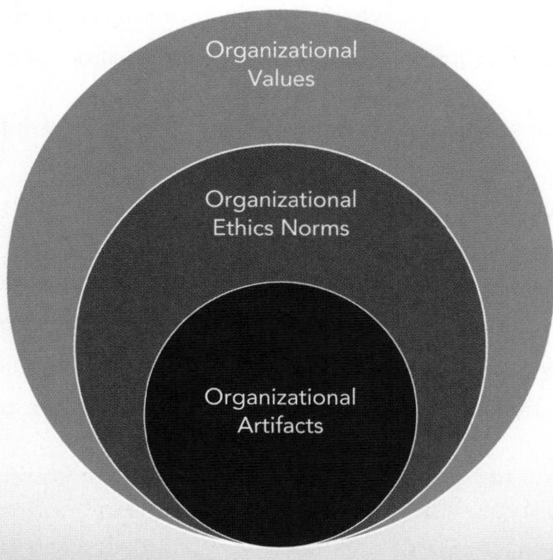

guide behaviors, policies, and practices. Generally, people like to align their conduct with their personal values and to what their employers expect of them. This is why organizational values are so fundamentally important to the behaviors of employees.[2] It also is important to understand the distinction between two types of values—espoused and enacted. **Espoused values** are those that organizations and their members state in discussions and on websites, and otherwise actively promote. These may differ from **enacted values**—those that manifest in behaviors, policies, and practices. For instance, 55 percent of *Fortune* 500 companies have integrity as an espoused value.[3] Yet, many of these companies undoubtedly have double standards for frontline employees and executives, punishing unethical behavior for the former and sweeping it under the rug for the latter.

espoused values
those that organizations and their members state in discussions and on websites, and otherwise actively promote

enacted values
those that manifest in behaviors, policies, and practices

Nearly all unethical business conduct illustrates a conflict or inconsistency between espoused and enacted values. Think of it this way. If espoused and enacted values were aligned for the Sackler family (family charged in oxycontin and opioid crisis), then their company, Purdue Pharmaceuticals would have stated, "We value money and will do anything to get it, including misleading doctors, regulators, and patients." None of the family members who ran the company actually said this, but they did it. Enron provides a similar example. Enron had integrity as an espoused value, yet the company committed systemic financial fraud that ended in disaster for all stakeholders.

To counter these negative examples with a couple positive ones, The Honest Company, in addition to its purposeful name, promotes nontoxic, eco-friendly consumer goods, such as diapers, cleaning products, and vitamins. Its espoused values are

- Honesty
- Make beauty
- Outperform
- Service matters
- Sustain life
- Be accessible
- Pay it forward
- Fun![4]

Warby Parker, the eyeglass company, also has a compelling and ethics-focused set of values:

- Treat customers the way we'd like to be treated
- Create an environment where employees can think big, have fun, and do good
- Get out there
- Green is good

The company punctuates its values by stating, "Our customers, employees, community, and environment are our stakeholders. We consider them in every decision we make."[5]

Business Norms. Values are brought to life—made real or manifest—in the norms or actual behaviors, policies, and practices of individuals within the organization. More precisely, **organizational ethics norms** are the shared views of what is right and wrong in terms of behavior, policies, and practices. Values differ from norms in that values are just empty words on a website or a poster on the office wall, but it is norms that give meaning to values by putting them into action via policies, practices, and behaviors. Therefore, enacted values are those that are embodied or reflected in the norms. The next Ethics in Action box provides examples of values and norms from Accenture.

organizational ethics norms
the shared views of what is right and wrong in terms of behavior, policies, and practices

Ethics Artifacts. **Organizational artifacts** are things you can see, hear, and touch. Examples of organizational artifacts are uniforms, offices, stories, logos, and countless others that you will physically find in an archeological dig, or experience during a visit to the headquarters, during training as an employee, or during a service encounter as a customer.

organizational artifacts
things you can see, hear, and touch

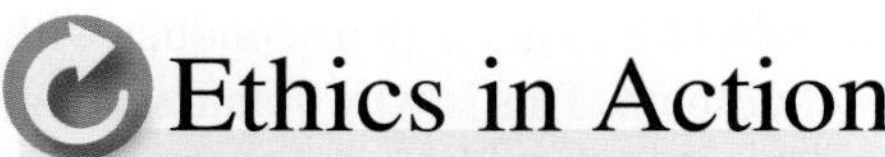

Accenture Espouses Strong Ethical Values

Accenture, one of the world's largest consulting companies, espouses a very strong ethical culture. This is especially interesting, given that Accenture was originally the consulting component of Arthur Andersen, the major accounting firm that served Enron. Arthur Andersen ultimately failed because of its unethical and illegal conduct associated with Enron, but its consulting business was split off and resurrected as its own, and since then it has grown into a highly successful business.

table 8.1

The Key Values for Accenture[6]

Value	Norms
Integrity	The organization is committed to ethics, human rights, and corporate governance, which are parts of its strategy and key to growth and financial performance.
Supporting and respecting the rights of all people	Fair and safe employment conditions and working practices Diversity and equal opportunity in employment Protecting the privacy and security of personal data
Adhere to best practices and policies	Corporate citizenship starts at the top with the board, executive team, and is cascaded throughout the organization. Committed to increasing nonfinancial performance

Another important way to differentiate values, norms, and artifacts is in terms of their relative flexibility. Like our personal values, organizational values tend to be quite consistent over time. Many organizations have espoused the same values for decades. Apple, for instance, espoused the following set of values in its earliest day of the 1980's:

- One person, one computer.
- We are going for it and we will set aggressive goals.
- We are all on the adventure together.
- We build products we believe in.
- We are here to make a positive difference in society, as well as make a profit.
- Each person is important; each has the opportunity and the obligation to make a difference.
- We are all in it together, win or lose.
- We are enthusiastic!
- We are creative; we set the pace.
- We want everyone to enjoy the adventure we are on together.
- We care about what we do.
- We want to create an environment in which Apple values flourish.[7]

Do you feel the company lives these same values today? Chances are you do which lends more support for the claim that values endure over time, even as technology, customers, industries, and the world change. Organizational norms, however, are much easier to change than values. Apple has changed its product design processes, how it utilizes suppliers, how it involves and serves customers, and countless other policies, practices, and behaviors (i.e., norms) since the 1980's.

More generally, if you are the owner of a company, you have the authority and ability to change performance review policies and practices (norms) now, today. More commonly, committees and management teams have such authority and can change the norms of how things are done, such as how customers are greeted or which reports are required. Artifacts are often the most easily changed. How you dress, for instance, can change day to day, or your employer can implement casual Fridays (a norm reflected in the attire of employees, an artifact). As another example, your employer's logo can be changed quite easily.

The implications of values, norms, and artifacts for business ethics are consequential.

- Values. Because values are difficult to change, it is important to implement values that support ethical conduct.
- Norms. Because norms are how values are actually lived by employees—behaviors, policies, and practices— it is essential to ensure they support the underlying values in ethical ways.
- Artifacts. Stories, in particular, can go a long way in supporting an ethical organizational culture. If those shared stories describe how an employee turned down business due to the perceived unethical conduct of a customer, then this is far more constructive than stories about how someone in your role took advantage of the sick leave policy or fudged expense reports.

Collectively, values, norms, and artifacts are the fundamental elements of organizational culture, which exist on the backdrop of the morals of society. Next, you'll learn how these layers relate to each other and what gives organizational culture the power to influence ethical conduct by organizations and their members.

Why Culture Is a Critical Influence on Business Ethics

Organizational culture is one of the most powerful and fundamental determinants of behaviors of employees and their employers. For you (as an employee), organizational cultures of your employers will play a significant role in your job successes, frustrations, and ethics. If it is so powerful, then why are values and norms so influential? (Note: Artifacts can be interesting but often relatively less consequential than values and norms, and thus they will receive less/little detail in our coverage.)

Flamingo Images/Shutterstock

Formal and Informal Controls. The power of culture comes from the fact that it is shared among members. The more intensely the values and norms are shared, the stronger the culture. Sharing results in pressure to conform with the expectations of the group, and pressure can be applied through both *formal and informal controls*. When you comply with or meet expectations, you receive formal and/or informal rewards. Formal rewards come in the form of greater pay, performance ratings, promotions, interesting work, and development opportunities; and informal rewards are illustrated in being invited to lunch or happy hour, sharing important or interesting information with you, and coworkers/supervisors advocating for you and your interests. Both formal and informal rewards represent organizational culture norms.

In contrast, when you *do not meet or you violate* the shared values and norms, you are generally sanctioned or penalized formally or informally. Simply think of the opposite of the previous examples—small or no raise and exclusion from "being in the loop." You can easily see how organizational culture asserts its power via both formal and informal control, and the many ways this control is enacted are considered as norms. In turn, an organization's values and norms can be reflected in and reinforced in its artifacts (e.g., stories, attire, and offices). If, for instance, the best offices are occupied by the most senior employees, then this artifact may be construed as inconsistent with an organization that espouses equality.

Alignment Yields Trust and Success. The most important aspect of organizational culture and business ethics is alignment of values and norms. If your organization espouses honesty, like many *Fortune* 500 companies,[7] then it is critical that its norms clearly and strongly account for honesty from top to bottom of the organization, including how it deals with all other stakeholders. No lying, no hiding, no deceit.

A common example of how values–norms alignment is violated is with the value of teamwork and performance management norms (defined and unpacked later). Assume, for instance, your employer not only lists teamwork as an espoused value on its website, but executives and your manager say at every meeting, "We're one big family. We're in this together. We will win or lose as a team!" But, when it's time for evaluations and bonuses, the focus is on evaluating individuals. This approach is made even worse if evaluations are force-ranked (top performer, second best, next, etc.), and a giant bonus check is given to the top performer. This scenario is common and illustrates a disconnect between values and norms.

The same thing happens with ethics. Many organizations list "having respect for others" as an espoused value, which is also a moral in many places in the world. However, many of these same organizations do not have clear procedures in place for preventing or punishing managers and other employees who are bullies and thus disrespectful. Another example is, when times are tough and the company needs to cut jobs, it delegates this to HR, an outside consultant, or terminates employees via email. None of these actions would be consistent with valuing respect.

Finally, if employees from the top to the bottom of an organization are not held similarly accountable, then this reveals the trust-destroying potential due to a lack of alignment.

Leadership. Leaders and leadership (the act of leading) are intimately linked to organizational culture. The purest example of this are founders and the cultures of the organizations they create. The values and preferences (norms) of the founding and early leaders are reflected in how the organization functions.

This situation is similar for existing groups, departments, organizations, and countries. Leaders create or otherwise shape the culture of the groups that follow them. Therefore, the importance of ensuring ethical leadership to ensure ethical cultures cannot be overstated.

As stated previously (chapter 7), the most powerful tool of influence leaders at any level have is their own behavior. The behavior and preferences of leaders become norms for their followers, and these norms reflect their underlying values. If your boss is open, fair, caring, and vulnerable, then this likely reflects an underlying value for respect and equality. The leader's followers are likely to behave the same way. If, however, your boss is intimidating and self-important, then besides possessing one or more of the dark triad traits from chapter 7, the leader may value his or her own success above that of the others (even at others' expense). As such, leaders can make or break the experience and success of employees and entire organizations.

Organizational Culture and Your Career. The culture of the organization can influence many aspects of your working life. Positive cultures with which you fit (see the next Ethics in Action box) can foster very satisfying and fulfilling experiences for you. Therefore, you want to get it right. Consider the following advice.

- As an entrepreneur, be purposeful and clear about the values and norms you want. If you just let the culture evolve, you may end up with one that you don't like, and that doesn't embody the type of organization you envisioned.
- As an employee, be sure to assess each prospective employer in terms of values–norms fit. Many organizations value competitiveness and high performance of the employees, but the way in which they compete matters and is evident in the norms. For instance, is it a "winner-take-all" culture, cutthroat competition, do anything to get ahead? Or, is it a collaborative environment wherein people genuinely succeed together? The following Ethics in Action box provides additional insights regarding organizational ethics, selecting jobs, and your career.
- Quit! If you don't fit in an organization, or if it has an unethical culture and it is run by a "dark" leader(s), then you have little chance of succeeding there. Move on. They don't deserve you.

Bottom line: Organizational culture is fundamentally and critically important to business ethics. Along with the behavior of leaders that help shape and embed it, organizational culture sets the tone and direction of the good and bad conduct of employees. And, because of its complexity, it can be difficult to change. It will either help you or hurt you. Choose wisely.

The next sections of the chapter outline some of the most common and destructive characteristics of unethical cultures. These warning signs can help you avoid taking jobs in such organizations, or help you realize that the culture in your present organization is toxic and it's time to leave. We'll conclude the chapter on a high note and describe how to foster ethical organizational cultures.

Incivility—Reflecting and Reinforcing an Unethical Organizational Culture

No individual or organization will ever say they value disrespect, harassment, and the general mistreatment of others. Even the people in our professional lives we are personally convinced are the devil incarnate will not espouse such awfulness. However, individual employees, groups of employees, and seemingly entire organizations of employees are mistreated.

This can be very consequential, as research shows that 58 percent of employees who quit their jobs did so because of a toxic culture, and their managers played the leading roles in their workplace horror show. Besides the emotional, career, and financial costs to the unfortunate employees, one estimate shows such mistreatment cost employers $223 billion in lost productivity over a five year period.[8]

Let's learn more, so you can avoid such situations or manage these situations more effectively.

Ethics in Action

Select for Values Fit

Research and popular press show that you are likely to be more satisfied and successful, even with less pay, with employers whose values more closely match your own. This makes sense. If you value fairness, collaboration, and personal development, then you will be attracted to and be more likely to stay with an organization that appears to share these values.

So how can you ensure values fit? Check a company's website where many list their values. But these are just words. You need to learn how a company's values are lived—that is, how are the values translated into behaviors, policies, and practices. During an interview, you could ask the following:

- I notice from the company's website that you value employees; they are your greatest asset. Please give me some examples of policies and practices that reflect this.
- The company web page also describes how important it is to give back to the community. Please describe for me how people in the position I'm interviewing for have such opportunities.

Ideally, sometime in the interview process, you'll have the opportunity to communicate with people who are currently doing the job for which you are interviewing. You will be able to ask them for their actual experience of the organization's values. Does it walk the talk?

fizkes/Shutterstock

Unethical Cultures Breed Incivility

Incivility is any harmful behavior of an individual or group toward another that violates norms of respect. If you feel you've been treated disrespectfully, then chances are you've experienced incivility. Some of the more common forms at work are intimidation, aggression, harassment, bullying, social undermining, and abusive supervision.[9] It is important to note that such behaviors are often subtle or in the background, which can make the experience even worse, as many coworkers may not notice the incivility. Generally, uncivil behavior is overt and clear for everyone to see, but it is not always an obvious public event.

incivility
any harmful behavior of an individual or group toward another that violates norms of respect.

Mistreatment often comes from someone in power, your boss usually, but this isn't always the case. Moreover, since respect is a moral, thus a widely held expectation in society, incivility is a deep and fundamental manifestation of unethical behavior, and given its many forms there are numerous undesirable outcomes, such as the following:

- Lower creativity[10]
- Lower employee engagement
- Lower job satisfaction

- Lower commitment
- Increased stress
- Increased turnover of employees[11]

Let's explore some of the more common and problematic forms of incivility—bullying and harassment.

Bullying

We will begin this section a bit differently with a very simple "For Discussion" scenario to provide context for the concepts, and then finish the section by revisiting the same dilemma.

For Discussion

1. If you were bullied by your boss, what would you do?
2. If you witnessed one of your close coworkers being bullied by your boss what would you do?

Bullying is repeated mistreatment of an employee by one or more employees in a manner that is threatening, humiliating, or intimidating; involves sabotage or verbal abuse; or inappropriately withholding from or excluding the target.[12] Because bullying is a pattern, it is an organizational culture issue. Statistics show (see Figure 8.2) that there is an epidemic of bullying. Also, it is worth noting that no laws currently exist forbidding workplace bullying in the United States.

bullying
repeated mistreatment of an employee by one or more employees in a manner that is threatening, humiliating, or intimidating; involves sabotage or verbal abuse; or inappropriately withholding from or excluding the target

figure **8.2**

Experience of Bullying at Work

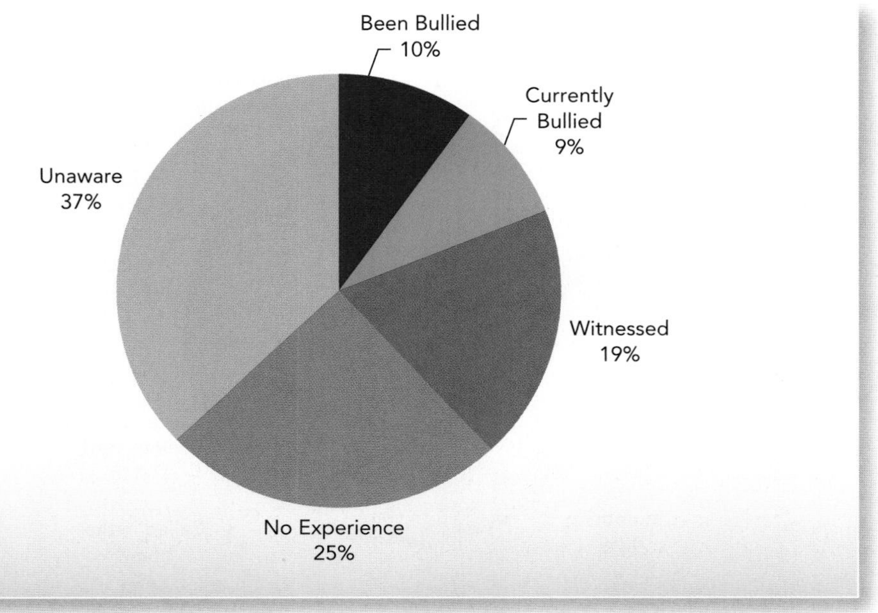

Source fig 8.2 and 8.3: adapted from https://www.workplacebullying.org/multi/pdf/2017/Prevalence.pdf

Who does it? According to the Workplace Bullying Institute, 63 percent of the time bullying is done by one person, and 61 percent of bullies are at a higher rank. This means that often

- bullying involves more than one perpetrator
- the bully is not always a senior coworker[13]

Perhaps the most damning statistics on bullying concern the actions taken by the witnesses and the employers (see Figures 8.3 and 8.4). More than half of witnesses did nothing or actually acted against the target, and less than one in four actions by employers resulted in positive outcomes for the target.

A recent survey about employers' responses to bullying suggests that the matter is not often handled in a way that is satisfactory to the target of the bullying. Specifically, employees who participated in the survey reported these outcomes:

- 26 percent said despite a complaint, nothing was done
- 46 percent said the investigation was inadequate and nothing changed
- 23 percent said the investigation resulted in positive outcomes for target of the bullying
- 6 percent said the investigation resulted in negative outcomes for the perpetrator[14]

You, your colleagues, and your employer, more generally, can either facilitate or eliminate bullying and other forms of incivility at work. But these statistics show that too often it is facilitated—both witnesses and employers do little or nothing, and what they do is ineffective. After all, more than 50 percent of the time the target quit or lost his or her job.[15]

Now let's see if your responses change, given what you just learned.

Another reminder, bullying is not illegal. Remedies, therefore, lie with you, the bully, and your employer.

figure **8.3**

Bullying Witness Actions

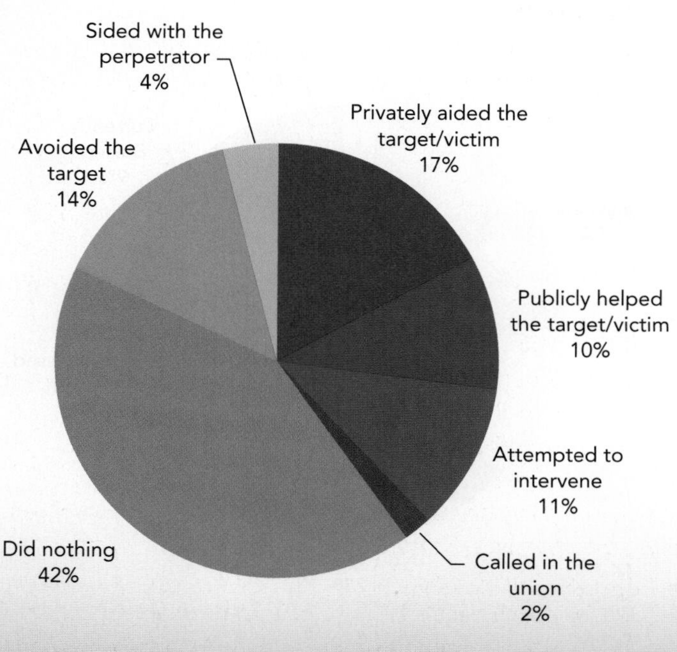

Harassment

Business ethics issues often, but not always, have legal implications. In addition to discrimination, which we covered in chapter 6, harassment is another common form of incivility, and thus unethical conduct, that is often the result of organizational culture.

Harassment is any negative or unwanted act *against an individual* based on their protected class. Harassment is similar to discrimination (chapter 6), in that according to the law you need to be a member of a protected class (listed again in Table 8.2 for your convenience). The difference between the two is that is discrimination is against a group and harassment against an individual.[16] Both are illegal and unethical.

harassment
any negative or unwanted act *against an individual* based on their protected class

Sexual harassment has two common forms: quid pro quo and hostile work environments. **Quid pro quo sexual harassment** is when one action is exchanged for another—you do this (a sexual favor) for someone in order to get this (the job, promotion, a raise, not get terminated, etc.) in return.

quid pro quo sexual harassment
when one action is exchanged for another—you do this (a sexual favor) for me in order to get this (the job, promotion, a raise, not get terminated, etc.) in return

What is important to realize, however, is that unless the harassment against you is based on your membership of a protected class, the conduct is not considered as harassment under the law.

This means that unwanted, negative, and undesirable conduct, whether legal or not, is often a matter of organizational culture. Culture either discourages or enables such conduct. This point was echoed by the CEO of the Society of Human Resource Management, Johnny C. Taylor, when he noted that nearly all US companies have a sexual harassment policy, and this alone shows the magnitude of the problem. He succinctly captured it with this statement: "… clearly the problem is bigger than policy; it's a matter of culture."[18]

Hostile work environments are those that negatively affect one's job performance, the cause of which is tied to one of the ten protected classes. Unwelcomed touching, jokes, comments, emails, texts, or other communications of a sexual nature, as well as repeated flirting or requests for dates are examples of a hostile work environment.[19]

hostile work environments
those that negatively affect one's job performance, the cause of which is tied to one of the ten protected classes

For Discussion

1. What types of harassment have you witnessed? To which protected class was it linked?
2. Do you think the scope of harassment should be expanded beyond protected classes? If yes, how? If no, why not?
3. Assume someone you manage was accused of sexual harassment. What would you do?

In terms of business ethics, harassment is an ongoing challenge. Employers don't want to be regulated, employees don't want to be mistreated, and neither wants to go to court. As always, the law evolves more slowly than our workplace realities.

Unquestionably, employees beyond the defined protected classes also feel harassed. This means the challenges for you are to find employers that establish cultures with values and norms that are consistent with respecting all employees, regardless of identifying characteristics (protected class or not). You don't want to be taken advantage of because your employer can get away with legal misconduct.

Moreover, if you're a manager, then you don't want your employees to mistreat each other and file grievances and potentially pursue legal action. You instead would appreciate a

table 8.2

Protected Classes for Harassment (and Discrimination)

1. Race
2. Color
3. Religion
4. Sex (including gender identity and pregnancy)
5. National origin
6. Age
7. Disability
8. Genetic information
9. Sexual orientation
10. Parental status[18]

culture wherein informal social controls clearly and strongly discourage anything that could be construed as discrimination or harassment, as if all employees were indeed treated appropriately, respectfully, and thus ethically.

The following Ethics in Action box provides some guidance on how organizations can combat these and other forms of incivility.

Discouraging Incivility

Some expert recommendations to discourage incivility are outlined below. The key is to practice them consistently—from the top to the bottom of the organization, with top performers and low performers, and with all stakeholders. The top bosses should send the message that respectful behavior is not a choice, it is a requirement.

1. Clarify who can and should file complaints. Leadership at all levels should make it clear that the expectation is that both targets and witnesses have a duty to report misconduct. Remember, the strength of a culture is based on agreement. Therefore, all employees need to discourage and report incivility to ensure a respectful culture for all employees and other stakeholders.
2. Define and illustrate. Define what discrimination and harassment mean in your organization, and what they look like in the jobs people do in your company. Apart from the legal definition, the higher standards that ethical cultures live and breathe should be defined. Provide examples of what constitutes inappropriate conduct.
3. Multiple contact points. A common problem with the existing complaint processes in many organizations is that the first step is to only inform one's direct supervisor. However, given the statistics, it is likely the manager is involved. He or she may not be the perpetrator, but the manager likely knows about the misconduct but did not intervene or do so effectively. Having a contact person in HR is one option. Another is having a manager in another area of the company, or perhaps a committee, devoted to such matters.

4. Hotlines and third parties. Anonymous hotlines and other reporting avenues can encourage people to speak out, and if these parties are independent of the organization, it can help free the employees of organizational politics and other undesirable forms of influence.
5. Prevent and punish retaliation. The number one reason targets and witnesses don't report (bullying) is the fear of retaliation. The steps noted above will help, but they are insufficient. Specific policies and practices need to be put in place to guard against retaliation, such as zero tolerance policy and severe penalties (termination). Without such formal controls well-intended efforts are likely to fail. This should include any social undermining, such as speaking poorly about someone involved or ostracizing (excluding) them.
6. Legal or not, it is unethical with consequences. Communicate clearly and strongly that legal standards are a minimum, but insufficient. Describe and implement consequences for violations of ethical conduct expected in the organization. To clarify, potential disciplinary actions should include demotion and termination.[20]

One more thing to note about incivility is that it is contagious. Bad behavior begets more bad behavior. Research across disciplines (e.g., marketing and management) consistently shows that the targets of uncivil behavior are more likely to treat others poorly. Making matters worse, when managers at work treat subordinates with disrespect, this not only affects the target but others too. It sends the message that such conduct is acceptable. If the vice president, dean, product manager, CEO, or director behave in an uncivil manner, and he or she is promoted, then some employees may assume that similar behavior is a way to get ahead. Thus, norms of incivility are established, and the organizational culture becomes toxic, which then likely affects multiple stakeholders (e.g., customers and suppliers).[21]

Bottom line: **Corrupt organizations** are those whose cultures facilitate or otherwise allow unethical conduct over time, and such cultures are created and/or perpetuated by corrupt leaders. As noted in the previous chapter, corrupt leaders are those who are personally unethical or allow the same from those they influence (e.g., followers, subordinates, and mentees) over time. Given the intimate relationship between leaders and culture, corrupt organizations are the result of corrupt leaders.

corrupt organizations those whose cultures facilitate or otherwise allow unethical conduct over time, and such cultures are created and/or perpetuated by corrupt leaders

"Just go along to get along" is a mantra of unethical organizational cultures. Don't be a silent witness. Do your part to stop incivility at school, work, and elsewhere! We conclude the chapter by learning how to create ethical organizational cultures.

Create and Foster Ethical Organizational Cultures

Organizational culture is a critical and powerful determinant of business ethics. However, cultures are resistant to change. Fortunately, if an organization already has a culture that fosters and reinforces ethical behavior, it is likely to persist. Unfortunately, this also means that changing a culture that does not support ethical conduct is challenging. To be simple, direct, and clear, if you happen to work for this type of organization, you may want to start looking for another job. Even with substantial influence possessed by senior leaders, such organizational culture is difficult to change.

More constructively, if you are starting your own company and thus have the opportunity to create the culture of your organization, or if you have the capacity and the will to implement change in your current position, then the following insights on how to create and foster ethical organizational cultures can help. Please recognize, however, that covering even the most important elements involved in culture change are beyond the scope of this book. So, we'll focus, instead, on some notable elements of business ethics specifically, beginning with an ethics audit.

Ethics Audit

ethics audit
an examination of an organization's business ethics performance, assessing how well the organization lives its ethical standards

An **ethics audit** is an examination of an organization's business ethics performance, assessing how well the organization lives its ethical standards.[22] In other words, an ethics audit is a comparison between what an organization expects and what it actually does in terms of ethics (columns 1 and 2 in Table 8.3). An ethics audit may include both formal and informal aspects of culture. The 3D Problem-Solving Approach for Ethics (3D PSAe) may also be useful for ethics audits. In short, there are many ways to perform an ethics audit.

Ethics audits are best used as a form of feedback to help leaders and other employees develop individual and organizational ethics muscle. Ethics audits should not be used to measure an individual's job performance and determine rewards or punishment.

Table 8.3 provides a high-level description of some common elements to consider. But please note, appropriate audits must be tailored to a given organization as no two organizational cultures are the same. Data for each of these elements are collected in various ways, like accounting measures (profit, sales, market share) or surveys and interviews of employees, customers, and other stakeholders.

For our purpose here, do not get hung up on how to actually score performance. What matters most is the process of identifying relevant functions and stakeholders, setting expectations, and then reviewing how well those expectations were met.

That said, a good place to start with performance measures is to assess them as (column 3 in Table 8.3):

- Does not meet expectations
- Meets expectations
- Exceeds expectations

Also include specific examples of each (column 4 in Table 8.3)—when the organization (individuals doing their jobs) does not meet expectations, meets expectations, and exceeds expectations for each element in the first column in Table 8.3. After all, business ethics is all about behavior and actions, not numbers. Employee actions generate numbers (e.g., sales, market share, prices, quality, and profits); numbers don't just happen.

Ethics audits can force the organization's leaders and employees to engage each other, along with key stakeholders, regarding ethical behaviors, policies, and practices (formal and informal).

Leaders' Role in Fostering Ethical Cultures

You may have noticed or wondered why leadership is missing from the ethics audit. Of course it is essential to include leadership ethical performance in your audit. But, given the critically important role of leadership in shaping ethics and organizational culture, it is discussed separately.

Beyond what you learned in chapter 7 regarding ethical leadership, there are a number of other leader responsibilities and actions that impact their organization's culture:

1. Ethics Audit
2. Alignment with Values
3. Reinforce the Values

table **8.3**

Components of an Ethics Audit

Key Stakeholders and Cultural Elements	Expectations	Performance 1 = Does not meet 2 = Meets 3 = Exceeds	Specific Examples to Support Scores
Business Functions			
Financial	Numbers are legitimate and not engineered (no cooking the books)		
Marketing (products and services)	Presented with integrity (do what you claim) and priced responsibly (no gouging or other unfair practices)		
Operations	Safe, efficient, quality, and environmentally and ethically sound.		
Community service	What activities do employees engage in, and what activities does the organization sponsor? Then, what is the positive impact on the community, rather than the organization?		
Social justice	Which issues are addressed and how has the organization and its employees engaged these issues? What impact was made?		
Stakeholders			
Suppliers	How well do they meet the standards of the organization (labor, environmental, employee rights)?		
Customers	Treated with respect		
Community	Treated with respect		
Environment	Explicit consideration given to environmental impact of all organizational actions.		
Employees	Respectful treatment in terms of formal culture norms, such as hiring, firing, evaluating, rewarding, developing, assignments, and decision making. Respectful treatment in terms of informal culture norms, such as communications, meetings, involvement, opportunities, informal decision making, and social interactions.		

Leader Responsibilities and the Audit. Leaders are responsible for the elements included in the ethics audit. More specifically, leaders need to engage those performing the various business functions and the relevant stakeholders to determine the expectations in terms of business ethics. They then need to be involved in the audit itself. Data gathered in the audit are then used to create action plans aimed at both refining ethics expectations and improving performance. Leaders then need to be held accountable for implementing the resulting action plans.

Alignment with Values. Another responsibility of leaders is to ensure that the organization's policies and practices, formal and informal cultural norms, align with its values. For example, leaders need to ensure the values of the organization are aligned in practice with how employees are treated in interactions with managers and other employees, how customers are treated in all communications, and how the organization interacts with the surrounding community. Table 8.4 provides examples of small things leaders can do to align behaviors with and reinforce the organization's values.

You Get What You Tolerate. One way to describe a leader's role in fostering ethical cultures, or not, is the statement: "You get what you tolerate." If leaders tolerate employees cutting corners in their work, taking advantage of company resources, or mistreating each other, then these behaviors continue. Therefore, leaders need to be engaged and take action. The leader's role and responsibilities related to culture is one of action—in his or her own behaviors (modeling) and intervening when needed in the behaviors of others.

To conclude the chapter, organizational culture is an ever-present and powerful influence on the ethical conduct of individuals, departments, and entire organizations. Organizational culture is what sustains (un)ethical conduct over time and is intimately linked to leadership. Ethical leaders foster ethical cultures, and together, they can make or break your own ethical conduct. Choose both, leaders and cultures, wisely.

table **8.4**

Actions that Align and Reinforce Organizational Values[23]

Organizational Value	Perspective and Action
Customer satisfaction	Inviting customers to product/service development meetings. Including them in awards ceremonies. Random calls thanking them for their business and asking how the organization can improve.
Innovation	Mix it up. Have junior members set and present agendas for meetings instead of managers. Identify one thing you can do in a different way one day a week (your personal innovation day). Tell people you're doing this, have them hold you accountable, and ask them to do the same.
Teamwork	Make a point of recognizing members that work remotely. Call individual members periodically and see how they are doing. Create names for project teams. Play games or sports.
Respect	Have others hold you accountable in small but consistent ways. Call it the "disrespect jar," like the swear jar, in which you have to contribute cash each time you approach the line, just like people put money in a jar when they swear.
Integrity	Mean what you say and say what you mean. People are good lie detectors and notice insincerity.

Chapter Summary

1. Organizational culture comprises values, norms, and artifacts, and it is a powerful determinant of the ethical conduct of employees and the larger organization.
2. Aligning organizational artifacts and norms—policies, practices, and behaviors—with values is critically important in building trust within an organization and success with its stakeholders.
3. Leaders arguably have the greatest influence on organizational culture and thus on the ethical conduct of the organizations' employees. Their personal conduct impacts them personally and many other stakeholders.
4. Incivility comes in many forms (e.g., bullying and harassment), and it is organizational culture that enables such misconduct to occur in the first place and persist over time. Again, leaders' personal conduct and response to incivility either discourages or reinforces unethical conduct in their teams, departments, and organizations.
5. Ethical organizational cultures can be fostered using ethics audits, which measure ethical performance against agreed-upon standards related to business functions (e.g., finance, marketing, and operations) and particular stakeholder groups.
6. Leaders again are essential to fostering ethical cultures, such as their attitudes, roles, and actions related to ethics audits. Leaders are also fundamentally responsible for ensuring alignment of organizational policies, practices, and employee behaviors (i.e., norms) with its values.

Key Terms

bullying 159
corrupt organizations 163
enacted values 153
espoused values 153
ethics audit 164
harassment 161
hostile work environment 161
incivility 158
organizational artifacts 153
organizational culture 152
organizational ethics norms 153
organizational values 152
quid pro quo sexual harassment 161

CASE STUDY: It's Just Part of the Game

Baseball players and teams at all levels throughout the history of the game have attempted to steal the signs used between catchers and pitchers. The rationale is simple; if a batter knows the type of pitch (e.g., fastball or curveball) before it is thrown, then the can prepare and have an advantage. This is against the rules—both formal and informal—but the norm was blatantly ignored by the Houston Astros in the 2017 season when it won the World Series, and part of the 2018 season.[24]

Tactics

The tactics were quite extensive and involved the entire team, led of course by the managers. Cameras were used, as part of the process, to view the signs shown by the catcher, and this information was then relayed to the dugout, where it was then communicated with the batter in various and often low-tech ways. Managers or other personnel would

Continued

bang on a garbage can, whistle, or clap to communicate to the batter which pitch was going to be thrown. Other techniques involved runners on second base, who have a clear view of the catcher's signs, and using electronics to communicate with the batter.

Players know such things happen, which is one of the reasons why pitchers and catchers conference on the mound between pitches frequently (more than they used to). They speak to each other with their mouths covered so nobody can steal their signs. Among other things, this stretches the game out, making it longer and less exciting for fans.

Formal Punishment

Not only are their written rules against such conduct, which were communicated again to all teams in 2017 and 2018, but many stakeholders—players and fans—also think this is inappropriate. Major League Baseball's new commissioner, Rob Manfred, doled out the following punishments:

- Suspended Astros's general manager, Jeff Luhnow, assistant general manager, Brandon Taubman, and manager, A. J. Hinch, for one season.
- Astros had to forfeit first- and second-round draft picks in the next two seasons.
- Fined the team $5 million, which is the maximum allowed in the league's contract with the team.

The Astros subsequently fired Luhnow and Taubman.

Notable Nonactions

Among the notable additional details is that no players were prosecuted. Manfred said that disciplining players would be difficult because of the challenges of assigning blame, and managers should instead be held accountable. Moreover, players were given immunity for cooperating in the investigation, which incidentally, they are required to do based on league rules.

Other Consequences

Fans are angry! Sports are supposed to be fair, and fans expect professionals to keep a higher standard. Players also are angry and speaking out, saying they've been cheated and the Astros have damaged the game. Such vocal disapproval from players is rare, as baseball has a strong norm of keeping quiet and not speaking out against teammates, other teams, or the league more generally.

The lack of punishment for players has also attracted heat. They are the offenders, yet have no consequences. Rather than admit to wrongdoing and receive reduced punishment, as often happens in courts of law, these players were instead excused. Some suggest Commissioner Manfred went easy on them because he did not want to start any trouble, given that contract negotiations between the league and the players' union was to happen soon.

Regardless, some argue the league rewarded bad behavior and hasn't done enough to prevent this from happening again. It doesn't help that the Boston Red Sox are under investigation for similar conduct. Although the season has been postponed as of June 2020, many players and fans were concerned that Astros's players will be targets for retaliation, such as pitchers throwing at them and other potentially dangerous actions.

For Discussion

1. In general, what types of espoused values do you think Major League Baseball teams have?
2. Describe two enacted values evident for the Houston Astros?
3. What norms do you think would be necessary to enable the widespread sign stealing to happen with the Astros?
4. Explain how the Astro's team leaders—general manager, coaches, and senior players—influenced the sign stealing scandal. In other words, what was their role and how did each of these leaders influence the conduct of other players?
5. Using concepts from the chapter, give three reasons why you think players do not commonly blow the whistle on the misconduct of their competitors and their own teams.
6. Assume you are the Commissioner of MLB. Outline at least three actions you would take to mitigate sign stealing in baseball.
7. Assume you were the new head coach of the Astros. Outline at least three actions you would take to stop sign stealing and restore the credibility and trust within the team and with other teams.
8. As new head coach, what would you do to rebuild trust with the fans?
9. Assume you were a player on the Astros during the sign stealing scandal, which means you likely participated, and must do an interview with a reporter (the TV Test). What would you say when questioned about your conduct and that of your teammates?

Apply Three-Dimensional Problem-Solving for Ethics (3D PSE)

You can apply the 3D PSE from multiple perspectives, such as that of Rob Manfred, the commissioner of Major League Baseball; MLB baseball fans; or players not on the Astros. Just be sure to specify whose perspective you have considered. Let's analyze the case from Commissioner Manfred's perspective.

figure 8.4

Three-Dimensional Problem Solving for Ethics (3D PSE)

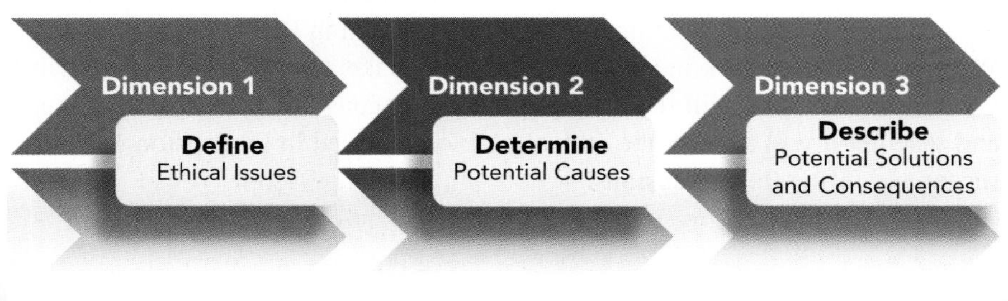

Dimension 1: *Define* the Ethical Challenge

What is the gap in the case? What do you have and what do *you* want?

a. From the commissioner's view, what is the current situation in the league, and how do you think you would want it to be?
b. Why is the current situation a problem? What difficulties or undesirable behaviors and outcomes happen as a result of the problem you defined? From the person's perspective, you chose to analyze this case, why do they care about the problem you defined in Dimension 1?
c. Define your problem in one or at most two sentences, and structure it in terms of what is current versus what is desired.
d. Who are the key stakeholders, those that affect or those that are affected by the problem you defined?

Dimension 2: *Determine* the Causes

a. **Individuals.** Given the problem you defined in Dimension 1, are particular individuals the cause, such as leadership at the league level (e.g., Rob Manfred), Astros players, other players in the league, team managers, or others?
b. **Contextual.** Are there particular policies or practices that caused the problem, as defined in Dimension 1? These policies and practices may be for a particular team, the league, or even the culture of sports or America more broadly.

Dimension 3: *Describe* Your Potential Solutions and the Intended and Unintended Consequences for Stakeholders

For each cause you identified in Dimension 2, answer the following question:

a. ***What*** do you recommend and ***how*** will you make it happen?
b. ***Why*** will you do it? Does this reflect a particular ethical decision-making perspective (e.g., utilitarian or universal)?

If your responses to these questions are unsatisfactory, then go back to Dimension 1 and repeat the process. If, however, you are comfortable and confident in your problem-solving efforts thus far, then ensure you achieve the desired outcomes and avoid any unintended consequences.

c. What is the ***desired and likely effect in the short term and long term*** for the key stakeholders involved in the problem and causes (Dimensions 1 and 2)?
d. What ***potential unintended consequences*** may occur with each proposed solution?
e. If any, what are the **implications for *other* stakeholders** (e.g., individuals, organizations, and communities) besides those noted in Dimensions 1 and 2?
f. Will your solution work in an ethical manner? Make a final assessment of whether your chosen solution will reduce or eliminate the causes determined in Dimension 2, and whether it will remedy the ethical problem defined in Dimension 1. If not, then repeat and refine the dimensions.

Part Opener Photo Source: fizkes/Shutterstock

Chapter Opener Photo Source: G-Stock Studio/Shutterstock

chapter 9

The Role of Laws, Codes, and Training in Business Ethics

Learning Objectives

AFTER READING THIS CHAPTER, YOU SHOULD BE ABLE TO

LO1 Explain how laws and regulations influence business ethics.

LO2 Describe codes of ethics and conduct and their functions and benefits.

LO3 Create relevant and effective codes of ethics.

LO4 Outline and describe the elements of a high-quality ethics program.

WHERE DO **YOU** STAND?

When Random Isn't Random

Assume the company you work for conducts random drug testing. It is random in that a computer algorithm selects a list of employees to be tested, and you are in charge of implementing the testing program. Also, assume that after learning about the names of selected employees, the CEO approaches you and wants you to substitute some people on the list with others suspected to have substance abuse problems or use drugs recreationally.

1. What are some of the potential issues with the executive's request? Describe both legal and ethical issues.
2. What are some potential consequences you are likely to face if you comply with the request?
3. What are some potential consequences if you do not comply with the request?
4. Describe what you would do and justify your decision.
5. Would you recommend any changes to the program to prevent this from happening again? Explain.

Introduction

This chapter focuses on laws, regulations, and codes of ethics. These build on what you have learned regarding organizational culture, and all can be classified as formal cultural norms or policies that guide the behavior of employees, groups, and departments and the larger company. You have also learned, however, that formal rules (norms) are insufficient in and of themselves—legal does not mean ethical. We will also explore the role of leadership in ensuring the alignment between such norms and organizational values. However, laws, regulations, and codes can send strong signals to employees about what is expected, and they can reinforce desired conduct by rewarding what is desirable and punishing what is not. We will read on and learn how.

The Role of Laws and Regulations in Influencing Business Ethics

Most basically, laws, regulations, and rules are tools to guide the behaviors, policies, and practices of individuals and organizations and provide consequences of misconduct. In this section, we will explore four highly notable examples of laws that were enacted in reaction to unethical conduct that had enormous and extremely negative consequences. Before doing this, we will first define and distinguish these related yet different concepts.

laws
describe which conduct is appropriate as determined by the legislative process of the federal, state, or local government

regulations
describe expected conduct typically created by government agencies to enforce laws

rules
organizational guidelines or instructions for doing something correctly that do not necessarily have a legal foundation, although often do have consequences of noncompliance

Laws and Regulations—Formal Cultural Norms

Laws describe which conduct is appropriate as determined by the legislative process of the federal, state, or local government, and **regulations** describe expected conduct typically created by government agencies to enforce laws. For example, the United States Congress passed the Securities and Exchange Act of 1934 to guard against securities fraud and insider trading, both of which contributed to the market crash of 1929 and the resulting depression. The Securities and Exchange Commission (SEC), a government agency, was created to produce regulations and enforce the Securities and Exchange Act. For instance, the SEC established guidelines for investigating and punishing the illegal insider trading.[1] **Rules** are organizational guidelines or instructions for doing something correctly and do not necessarily have a legal foundation, although they often have consequences for noncompliance.[2] Your employer may have rules about dress code such as not wearing torn jeans to work. If you did wear torn jeans to work, you would likely "get in trouble," maybe even fired if you continued to do so after being told not to, but it is highly unlikely you would be breaking any laws passed by Congress or the regulations of any government agency.

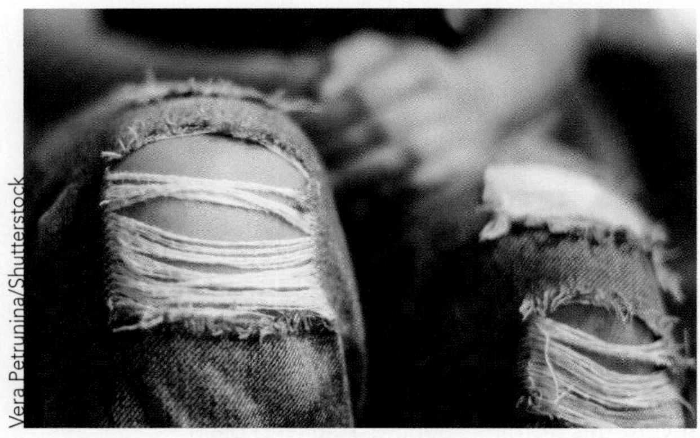
Vera Petrunina/Shutterstock

It is important to put these tools in perspective for business ethics purposes. All three simply outline the minimum acceptable expectations along with the consequences of noncompliance. They are the last resort, as they typically apply only when people behave unethically. That said, they have had a substantial impact on how businesses, other organizations, and countries have conducted themselves since the 1970s, beginning with the Foreign Corrupt Practices Act (FCPA).

Foreign Corrupt Practices Act (FCPA)

Foreign Corrupt Practices Act (FCPA)
forbids using bribes to obtain or retain business when doing business internationally

The **Foreign Corrupt Practices Act (FCPA)** of 1977 and other laws that followed were intended to both deter and punish organizations for exploiting local norms in countries, as well as attempt to establish consistency across organizations and the planet. The FCPA forbids using bribes to obtain or retain business when doing business internationally. It has three primary functions:

1. Deter unethical conduct everywhere. A primary motive is to forbid bribes everywhere in the world that an organization does business, regardless of local norms.
2. Make punishment consistent. Prior to the FCPA, there were no standards to judge conduct, which resulted in inconsistent if not also unfair and ineffective enforcement.
3. Require accounting controls. Companies must track their assets and financial transactions to comply with the Act.[3]

Ethics in Action

Corruption Is Rampant

The federal government passed the FCPA, the Department of Justice (DOJ) and SEC enforce it, and they did a lot of enforcing in 2019.[4] The value of fines the DOJ levied was $2.9 billion, and 95 percent of those were for infractions in China and India but also in South Korea, Thailand, and Vietnam.

The agencies' actions included the largest fine to date—$1 billion against Ericsson (a Swedish telecom company). The essence is that the company made illegal payments (bribes) in the form of gifts, travel, and entertainment to win Chinese telecommunications business.

But that's not all. The case covered misconduct that spanned sixteen countries and occurred for more than seventeen years! One way the scheme was implemented was through a sham consulting company that Ericsson established, and through it, fake accounts and transactions were created, and real money was paid.

For Discussion:

1. Do you think that senior leaders in Ericsson did not know about the scheme?
2. If you answered yes, then why do you think they did this? What could be done to ensure it doesn't happen again?
3. If you answered no, then explain how this could be possible.
4. Assume you started working for Ericsson in 2015, many years into the illegal practices, and you learned this is the way they do business in Asia, and you are expected to do the same. What would you do?

The FCPA is an example of a universal approach to ethics that you learned in chapter 1, as it applies to all employees and anyone else acting on behalf of the organization (e.g., consultants and contractors) doing any type of business anywhere in the world.

Although organizations cannot go to jail, their employees can, and fines can be levied against the organization or any of the responsible agents. To clarify, the organization is legally responsible for the conduct of any of its employees or agents. This is a strong incentive for organizations to do *something*, but as the Ethics in Action box shows, something is often not enough.

Federal Sentencing Guidelines for Organizations (FSGO)

The effectiveness of the FCPA was enhanced with the passage in 1991 of the **Federal Sentencing Guidelines for Organizations (FSGO)** that helps make penalties consistent across organizations due to the misconduct of employees. This law holds organizations liable for the conduct of their employees and agents, even if their actions are contrary to an organization's policies.

Federal Sentencing Guidelines for Organizations (FSGO) helps make penalties consistent across organizations due to the misconduct of employees

The FSGO is intended to both prevent the misconduct and evaluate the effectiveness of these efforts. As such, it was a major cause for companies to establish codes of ethics and ethics training programs (more on these later in the chapter). The reason is that if a company can show that it has a program and made genuine efforts to educate employees and deter misconduct, then fines could be reduced by more than 90 percent.[5]

According to the FSGO, an effective compliance and ethics program contains the elements shown in Table 9.1.[6]

table **9.1**

Elements of an Effective Compliance and Ethics Program Based on the FSGO

Description of Key Elements
1. Appropriate standards and processes to prevent and identify issues
2. Oversight and responsibility by senior leadership (e.g., board of directors or trustees) for the program
3. Effective relevant communications and training related to ethics
4. Monitor and evaluate program compliance including channels for reporting issues and protecting those that do
5. Appropriate and consistent incentives and punishments throughout the organization
6. Ensure appropriate actions on reported issues
7. Demonstrate that the same misconduct does not occur

Another law aimed at increasing accountability for unethical conduct is the Sarbanes–Oxley Act (Sarbox) of 2002.

Sarbanes-Oxley

For most of you reading this book, the scandals associated with Enron, WorldCom, Tyco, Arthur Andersen, and others during that period are history lessons since the unethical behavior and resulting legal actions took place in the 1990s and first part of the 2000s. However, the magnitude of the misconduct and negative consequences were so great that they shaped the conduct of individuals, organizations, and governments ever since. If you're interested in further details, *The Smartest Guys in the Room* is a documentary that provides excellent and provocative insights into the conduct of Enron and Arthur Andersen.

One of the most notable laws passed in answer to these scandals is the Sarbanes-Oxley Act (2002), named after the bill's sponsors, Senators Paul Sarbanes and Michael Oxley. **Sarbanes-Oxley** helps to protect investors from fraudulent financial behavior by requiring stricter reporting, accountability, and penalties for executives, their organizations, and accountants.[7] By itself, this definition doesn't tell you much, but with a bit of additional explanation, you'll see it is nevertheless important.

Sarbanes-Oxley
law to protect investors from fraudulent financial behavior by requiring stricter reporting, accountability, and penalties for executives, their organizations, and accountants

Sarbanes-Oxley was, in part, a reaction to the following phrases and legal defenses used by corporate executives:

I didn't know.
I was unaware.
My organization has tens of thousands of employees, and I cannot possibly know about or be responsible for the actions of every individual.
You'll need to ask our accountants.

All these phrases were used by executives when called out for the unethical conduct of their organizations. As such, the major aim of Sarbanes-Oxley was to increase the accountability of executives, auditors, and accountants. It is intended to prevent passing the buck to others and thus hold these professionals responsible for their respective actions and for those for whom they have responsibility.

Sarbanes-Oxley addresses four areas for reform:

1. Corporate responsibility. Executives cannot (as easily) claim ignorance and avoid consequences of unethical financial conduct. Corporate executives now need to sign off on financial statements, effectively certifying they are accurate and compliant.
2. Criminal punishment. Executives and accountants can be held personally and legally liable for misconduct (e.g., fines and prison).

3. Accounting regulations. Many financial reporting requirements are built into the law, including which records (paper or electronic) need to be kept, for how long, and how to store or save them.
4. Protections for whistleblowers. This law also requires those who witness or have knowledge of violations to report them and, at the same time, provides some measure of protection from retaliation. (Recall what you learned in chapter 5.)

Monsanto, the agribusiness behemoth, paid an $80 million penalty for accounting rule violations related to misstated earnings pertaining to its Roundup product. The SEC, who brought the charges, found that the company did not utilize sufficient internal accounting controls for rebates offered to help combat competition. Further, the firm's accountants either knew or should have known about this deficiency. Beyond the fines paid by the company, three sales executives and three accountants also paid fines for charges against them personally.[8]

The Great Recession or Financial Crisis of 2008 spurred additional legal regulations; the most notable of these is Dodd–Frank, which is explained next.

Dodd–Frank

The Dodd–Frank Act (2010) says little by itself, but the full and actual title is much more revealing. The Dodd–Frank Wall Street Reform and Consumer Protection Act, often referred to simply as **Dodd–Frank**, regulates financial institutions and protects consumers from unethical conduct by lenders, mortgage companies, and other financial institutions.

Dodd–Frank regulates financial institutions and protects consumers from unethical conduct by lenders, mortgage companies, and other financial institutions

Dodd–Frank also is named after two key sponsoring politicians—Senator Chris Dodd and Representative Barney Frank. It is similar to previous laws in that it was a reaction to widespread and devastating unethical conduct; in this instance, the complex financial catastrophe related to mortgage lending and the housing bubble in the early 2000s. When the housing bubble burst in 2008, prices plummeted, mortgages were not paid, and banks and other institutions failed. The financial industry in America nearly froze to a halt, plunging the entire world economy into recession. The collapse of Lehman Brothers (formerly a major Wall Street firm), the bailout of American International Group (an enormous insurer), and the astounding conflicts of interest at the credit rating agencies (S&P, Moody's, and Fitch) were all revealed during the crisis.

The Act is too complex to unpack here. But for our purposes, the essence is to help maintain stability in the financial industry by preventing financial institutions from

- Taking on too much risk and thus requiring the government to bail them out (with taxpayer money).
- Taking advantage of consumers with predatory lending or other detrimental practices and products.[9]

Along with the regulations on banks and lenders, the law created a number of agencies to help advocate for and protect consumers, and still others that oversee the operations and financial health of banks.

Under Dodd–Frank, in some instances, whistleblowers for financial fraud can receive financial rewards.

Now that you have learned about some key federal laws intended to guide and reinforce ethical conduct, we can move on to additional forms of formal control, but instead at the organization level—codes of ethics and codes of conduct.

Codes of Ethics and Conduct

Codes are descriptions and rules regarding what is expected or appropriate, such as dress codes and building codes. Codes related to business conduct and ethics are similar in that they describe expectations for employee behavior and organizational practices, and often, they are accompanied by specific penalties for noncompliance.

Codes of Ethics

codes of ethics general or high level descriptions of expected behaviors and practices that reflect an organization's values

Codes of ethics are general or high level descriptions of expected behaviors and practices that reflect an organization's values. Often, such codes are written using values and value-type language, and as a result, some people find it helpful to think of codes of ethics as value statements. Whatever the case, when done effectively, codes of ethics can guide employee conduct and decision making in many dimensions of their jobs. Codes of ethics, like values, are helpful in that they describe the "spirit" in which people are expected to behave.

For instance, the National Association of Social Workers has an ethics code that reads like a value statement:

- Service
- Social justice
- Dignity and worth of the person
- Importance of human relationships
- Integrity
- Competence[11]

Given the nature of social work, it makes perfect sense that the organization representing and governing the industry would want behaviors and practices to align with this code.

Codes of Conduct

codes of conduct commonly legal-inspired descriptions of expected behaviors and practices related to specific situations and aspects of an organization's business

Codes of conduct are commonly legal-inspired descriptions of expected behaviors and practices related to specific situations and aspects of an organization's business. Dow Jones', a business and financial news company, code is lengthy and has sections devoted to

- Confidential information
- Business relationships and activities
- Compliance with laws and regulations
- Employment
- Environmental concerns
- Compliance with the code[12]

This is essentially a handbook or rule book for a particular organization. The Ethics in Action box describes an abbreviated version of Facebook's code of conduct.

Ethics in Action

Code of Conduct at Facebook

Codes of conduct often read like dense, mind-numbing legal documents that are dozens of pages long. In fact, most are long enough to have a table of contents. To make the point, Facebook's code of conduct even has a preamble or introduction.

> "Employees of Facebook, Inc., or any of its affiliates or subsidiaries ("Facebook"), and others performing work for Facebook or on its behalf, collectively referred to in this code as "Facebook Personnel," are expected to act lawfully, honestly, ethically, and in the best interests of the company while performing duties on behalf of Facebook. This code provides some guidelines for business conduct required of Facebook Personnel. Persons who are unsure whether their conduct or the conduct of other Facebook Personnel complies with this code should contact their manager, another Facebook manager,

Human Resources, or the Legal Department. This code applies to all Facebook Personnel, including members of the Board of Directors (in connection with their work for Facebook), officers, and employees of Facebook, Inc. and its corporate affiliates, as well as contingent workers (e.g., agency workers, contractors, and consultants) and others working on Facebook's behalf. This code is subject to change and may be amended, supplemented, or superseded by one or more separate policies."[13]

It is interesting and insightful to note how the final paragraph aligns or reconciles Facebook's code with local or national laws.

"If any part of this code conflicts with local laws or regulations, only the sections of this code permitted by applicable laws and regulations will apply. Any policies that are specifically applicable to your jurisdiction will take precedence to the extent they conflict with this code."[14]

For Discussion:

1. Which values are evident in the preamble to Facebook's code?
2. Which stakeholders are explicitly noted?
3. Assume you're an employee at Facebook. How might this code help you in your day-to-day job?
4. What shortcomings or problems can you see, as it pertains to the code and employees? What about other stakeholders?

To summarize, codes of ethics and conduct fill many functions and provide numerous benefits. Some of these are outlined in Table 9.2.

table 9.2

Functions and Benefits of Codes of Ethics and Conduct

1. Guide employees in ethical dilemmas (no clear best solution)
2. Reinforce organizational values and culture
3. Create two-way communication on ethical issues between the organization and its stakeholders
4. Ensure consistency of actions by outlining the rights and responsibilities of individuals in various roles
5. Maintain compliance with laws and regulations, including responsibilities for senior executives
6. Build public trust and enhance business reputations
7. Prevent and limit lawsuits
8. Enhance employee morale and recruiting efforts
9. Foster positive relationships with the community
10. Encourage and reward the best and most ethical actors, especially when legal guidelines are insufficient

Source: Josephson Institute on Ethics, "Ten Benefits of Having an Ethics Code," *josephsononbusinessethics.com*, http://josephsononbusinessethics.com/2010/11/ten-benefits-of-having-an-ethics-code/.

Common Codes at Universities

Every university has a student code of conduct, many of which include expectations related to alcohol, drugs, assault, harassment, and the associated processes for disciplinary actions and appeals. If this sounds "legal," then this is likely due to the fact that codes are often written by people with legal knowledge and backgrounds (attorneys and HR).

University honor codes are usually separate documents focusing on academics, and they often include lists and definitions of misconduct and the related disciplinary processes. For instance,

- Cheating
- Falsification
- Plagiarism
- Complicity (helping others violate the code)

To make this more personal, and perhaps clearer too, your personal code of conduct could include how you will treat classmates, professors, friends, and strangers on the street. You would then need to describe common situations or interactions with each of these people, along with how you expect to actually treat them—specific behaviors. Use your personal values and aspirations (e.g., to be a good person) as the foundation and then describe common situations and specific behaviors in these situations.

For Discussion

1. Have you ever looked at the Student Code of Conduct of your school?
2. Do you personally know if it is being used at your school? If yes, then how?
3. If you neither have seen the code nor know of a specific instance it was used, then why do you think this is?
4. If you were the president of your school, what would you do to make a code effective for students?
5. How would you ensure all students are directly aware of its contents and purposes?

The next step is to learn how to develop actual codes and then how to embed them in behaviors and practices via ethics training.

Creating a Relevant and Effective Code for Ethical Conduct

In the previous section, you learned the difference between codes of ethics and codes of conduct, the content commonly contained in each, and their functions and benefits. A valuable way to build on and apply this knowledge is to learn how to develop such codes for a particular job and organization. The process described next, and illustrated in Table 9.3, is the one used successfully by numerous students and clients for many years and across many industries. It is simple and practical, which means you should be able to use it almost anywhere you work.

table **9.3**

Creating a Relevant Code of Ethical Conduct

Most Common Unethical Conduct	Specific Examples	Causes	Expected Actions (Preventative or Reactive)
1.			
2.			
3.			
4.			

Creating a Code for Your Job

When reading the example codes in the previous section, it is quite possible that your eyes rolled back in your head and you teetered on the edge of unconsciousness. Of course, this was *not* due to the author's writing, but instead because codes of ethics often read like value statements, nice, but just words on a page. Codes of conduct are often thirty-page documents of do's, don'ts, reporting procedures, and disciplinary processes. All of this is important but not especially interesting. One of the reasons they aren't very interesting is they aren't real to most employees, meaning they either include content that is irrelevant to their particular jobs, or the elements are so obvious that they are not useful (e.g., don't lie, don't cheat, and don't steal).

Therefore, it is critically important to make codes relevant to each individual's job instead of being dense, legal-like, or otherwise meaningless. Here's how.

Creating and Communicating a Compelling Objective

"Don't break the law" or do it "because I said" are not compelling or particularly meaningful directions for employees. One way to help make the objective compelling is to involve the people actually doing the job today, instead of delegating it to someone in Human Resources, the legal or compliance department, or people who did the job years ago. Besides the fact that things change, people (you) are generally more committed to initiatives or activities to which they contribute. One way to look at this is that their name is on it, they have skin in the game, and if they helped create the code, then they are more likely to follow it.

Therefore, a manager asks the employee the following questions:

1. What are the greatest costs of unethical conduct in your job?
2. Who is affected (which stakeholders) and how?
3. How does crossing the line, or even approaching it by engaging in questionable behavior, diminish your performance in the short and long term.
4. What are the benefits of ethical conduct to you? The other stakeholders noted in #2?
5. How will our organization benefit?

Then, the manager and employee together formulate the objective or desired outcomes of the code. This is captured in a statement using the following template:

"This code of conduct is intended to

A. Objective: comprised of what you revealed in the process above
B. Benefits me in the following ways: 1, 2, and 3

C. Benefits other stakeholders: stakeholder 1 and how, stakeholder 2 and how, and stakeholder 3 and how, etc.
D. Reinforces organizational values: value 1, value 2, value 3, etc."

Common Ethical Challenges, Their Causes, and Solutions

A compelling objective gives you personally meaningful reasons to pursue ethical conduct . . . in other words, motivation. Using table 9.3 as a template, the next step is to identify the most common ethical challenges—dilemmas and the most common forms of unethical conduct—in your particular job.

Common Challenges. You do your job, you know what the temptations are, the situations in which people cut corners or cross the line. Therefore, you should be involved in identifying what the temptations are. However, if you are new to your position and company, then those with experience should also be involved. This is simple. Make a list. If the list is long, then shorten it to the five to ten most common or most consequential forms of unethical conduct.

Causes. Reflect on each ethical challenge noted in the previous step and determine the common causes. Much like the 3-dimensional problem solving for ethics (3D PSE), you are encouraged to consider a range of potential causes such as those that reside with you, pressures from people, incentives, cultural norms, and others. Map these causes to their corresponding challenges.

Expected Behaviors. Construct "if-then" statements taking what you did in the previous steps. If this ethical challenge or situation occurs, then you will do X or Y. As an illustration, X could be declining a bribe, and Y could be reporting the occurrence to your manager, ethics hotline, or another appropriate channel within your organization. It also can be helpful to describe the consequences of noncompliance, but this is up to your manager.

The intent here is to clarify the expected behaviors for the most common challenges you, and others like you, experience in a particular job. That way, when they occur, you are prepared and know what to do, not to do, and whom to notify.

Put It All Together—Including Consequences and Value Alignment

Your manager, or you, then needs to compile the information related to objectives, common challenges, causes, and expectations from all the people doing a particular job. The findings need to be discussed, refined, and agreed upon.

Before finalizing, it is helpful to discuss the consequences of compliance and noncompliance—carrots and sticks—rewards and punishment. Then, this information is finalized, put in writing, shared with and signed by all who participated.

For the manager and employees, one final and important step is to ensure that all the elements of the code align with the values of the organization. If this is done effectively, the result is a code of conduct–code of ethics hybrid of sorts. The benefits to this last values check, if you recall, are that it is best for individuals and organizations when espoused values align with enacted values. The code you just created is a formal control norm, one that powerfully reflects and reinforces the organization's culture and values.

Apply Your Knowledge—Code of Ethical Conduct for Students

Before moving on to the final section, let's apply what you learned. Table 9.2 provides a framework for creating a code of ethical conduct for students in your class. Begin in column 1 by listing the most common forms of unethical conduct for students, then work your way through filling in the other columns and mapping or linking them together.

Let's run through an example to illustrate. A common form or category of unethical conduct by a college student is cheating. However, simply listing cheating as a form of unethical conduct is entirely too general. Cheating comes in many varieties, and thus, it is especially important to specify the type of cheating.

Unethical Conduct	Using a contract paper writer for an assignment.
Specific Example	Hire X company to write Y paper for your English course.

Causes

Personal. Poor performance at the mid-term, need a good grade on the assignment to achieve a B in the course, and you don't like the course.

Contextual

- Professor is a tough grader.
- Course grades are curved (forced distribution), which means your performance is related to the performance of other students, and many others are far more motivated than you.
- Other students in your class are doing the same thing.
- Students rarely get caught using these services, and when they do, penalties are not severe (e.g., allowed to redo the assignment or simply take a zero on the particular assignment).

Actions (map onto causes). Consider each of the causes identified and generate a potential solution or course of action that could help reduce, eliminate, or otherwise change the cause.

Given that this section of the book focuses on the organizational level and business ethics, in the next section, we explore how to create an effective ethics program for an entire organization.

Creating an Effective Ethics Program

The most well-conceived codes with the noblest of intentions are nothing unless or until they are actually put into practice, and this means that ultimate success is largely dependent on codes being embedded in an organization's culture. To this end, we will explain the elements of a **high-quality ethics program** that embeds codes and other ethical norms into an organization's culture and ensures accountability.[15]

high-quality ethics program
embeds codes and other ethical norms into an organization's culture and ensures accountability

For nearly one hundred years, the ethics & compliance initiative (ECI) has established a community of ethics professionals devoted to identifying, sharing, and implementing best practices related to ethics. One particularly useful and ambitious initiative resulted in a framework or means for assessing the quality of an organization's ethics and compliance. It is useful for profit or nonprofit organizations, large or small, and across industries. The five-part framework illustrated in Figure 9.1 is an adaptation and is intended to be used as a means for developing an effective ethics program, one that embeds codes into practice and holds people accountable.[16] The same framework can then be used to evaluate the success of the program.

figure 9.1

5-Part High-Quality Ethics Program

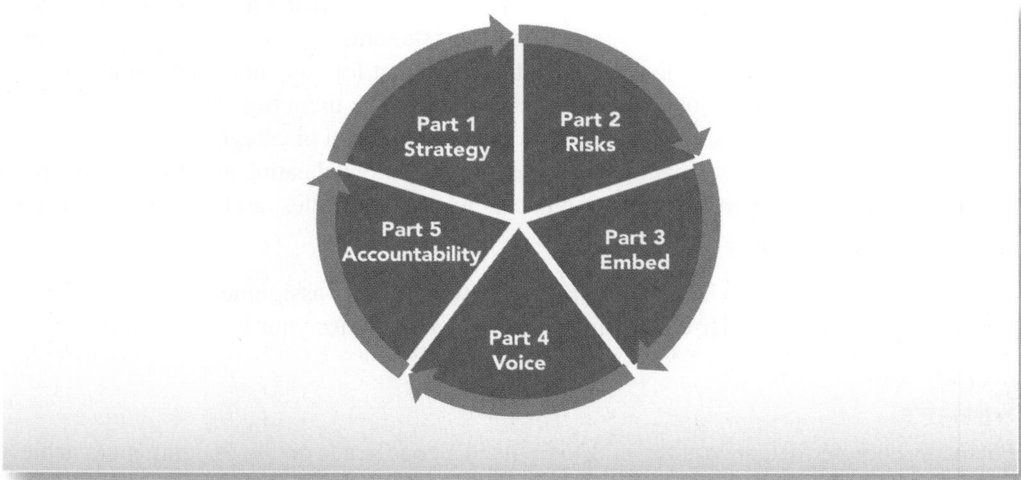

Source: Adapted from Ethics Compliance Initiative, "High-Quality Ethics and Compliance Program—Measurement Framework," *ethics.org*, April 2016, https://www.ethics.org/resources/high-quality-ec-programs-hqp-standards/.

Part 1: Make Ethics Part of Strategy

Many organizations have formal strategic planning processes, but many don't, and for those that do, there are countless ways in which they do such planning. Most contain three key elements:

1. Vision and mission statements that outline what an organization stands for and paints a picture of what it wants to become.
2. Goals designed to realize the mission and vision—how it will be brought to life through its products and services and for which customers.
3. Action planning on how to achieve the goals, and thus realize the mission and vision.

Again, the process is not our focus here. Process is more appropriate for a strategic management course. For our purposes, what is important is that ethics are explicit in every part of the strategic planning process—vision, goals, and action planning.

One strong signal of whether an organization makes business ethics a true priority is who is involved in the process. For instance, if an organization has a compliance officer, or a director of ethics, or if these responsibilities are in an employee's job title, then this at least signals that the organization may take ethics seriously.

fizkes/Shutterstock

Although a job title is nice and can be meaningful, it is also important that such a person or persons be involved with the high-level executives during the actual planning process. They need to have a seat at the table. To clarify the point, it is helpful to make a comparison to strategic human resource management.

For years, many companies have claimed that employees are their greatest asset. If indeed employees are so valuable, then it would make sense that the human resource and talent issues would be included in all elements of an organization's strategic planning. One strong signal whether this is the case or not is to learn who is involved in strategic planning. Does someone from HR have a seat at the table, along with the chief executive officer, chief financial officer, chief marketing officer, and other C-level executives who historically participate? If the answer is "no," then it is highly unlikely that the company is actually serious or strategic about people.

The same goes for ethics. If an organization espouses the value of ethics, then it must enact the value of ethics in its strategic planning. In other words, it needs to walk the talk, from the boardroom to the front lines, from state to state, and country to country.

Part 2: Identify Most Common and Serious Risks

Similar to the process for developing relevant codes of conduct and ethics, an organization needs to identify the most common and potentially consequential ethics risks. Regardless of the size or complexity of an organization, leaders in all areas must determine the ethical challenges they and their people are likely to confront, determine the causes, and establish expected actions.

These can be "rolled up" to the organization level and then used to create a more comprehensive list. This is a ground-up approach and is likely to be more relevant and foster greater employee support than the more common top-down approach, wherein someone "in power" creates the code and dictates it to the organization.

Part 3: Embed in the Organization's Culture

First, you and your employers will be well served to understand and apply the ethical organizational culture elements learned in chapter 8 and the complementary knowledge and tools pertaining to ethical leadership in chapter 7. In these chapters, you learned that ethical cultures include, reflect, and reinforce ethics in their values, norms, and artifacts. For their part, leaders must model and communicate high ethical standards. They do this via multiple channels such as actions, emails, meetings, documents, and strategic plans. Espoused ethical standards must be enacted. The Ethics in Action box provides a widely applicable, easy, and effective means for doing just this.

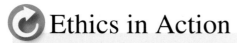

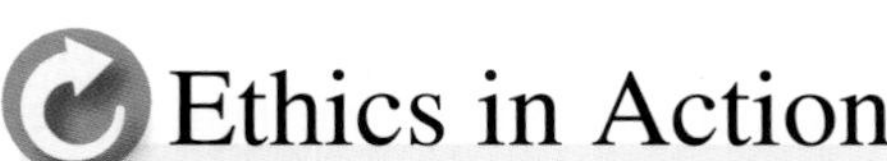

"Value" Every Meeting

What is the value of every meeting? Employees widely complain that most meetings have little value. However, this is a play on words. Some value-driven organizations use every meeting to reflect on and embed values. Here's how you might consider doing this where you work.

At the beginning of every meeting, regardless of its purpose or agenda, start with at least two or three attendees sharing an example of how they "lived" (enacted) one of the organization's values when doing their job in the past few days. You want to establish this as a norm in the organization, which means everyone expects every meeting to start this way. This also means they would have given it some thought prior to the meeting and will thus be at least somewhat prepared to share.

One way to facilitate this is for the leader of the meeting to kick it off by sharing his or her own example. For instance, "Four days ago, I was contacted by a key client who was terribly upset. Not only was the volume and tone of his voice high, but his choice of words was a bit salty. I was inclined to respond in a similar manner, but

Continued

in keeping with our value of respecting all with whom we do business and treating people with empathy, I instead remained calm. I told the client I understood his frustration, that I would be frustrated too, and then set a time to meet and formulate a resolution."

The leader then can ask others in the meeting to share an example of their own, preferably a different value. To ensure everyone participates and all values are illustrated over time, it may also be a good idea to "call on" members and/or specify the value to be addressed.

The embedding process can be taken a step further by asking meeting attendees, before they leave the meeting, to identify a particular value they will live in the next two to three days and how.

This process is for values, but the same process or approach can be adapted to ethical challenges too.

For Discussion:

1. What do you think are the advantages or benefits of this approach?
2. What do you think are the potential drawbacks?
3. How could this potentially be improved?
4. What would be your reaction if you took a job in a company with this type of norm?

Part 4: Require and Enable Voices

psychological safety environments in which employees feel comfortable taking (interpersonal) risks without concerns of being punished for doing so

Leaders are well served to establish workplaces with **psychological safety**, which are environments in which employees feel comfortable taking (interpersonal) risks without concerns of being punished for doing so.[17] You can see by the definition how important psychologically safe workplaces are to cultivating ethical cultures. Employees need to speak up about their experiences and what they witness.

The ideal ethical culture is the one in which all employees, regardless of rank or location, are invested in ethical matters such that they have a voice and can take action. Leaders once again are invaluable. You too can encourage others by joining or supporting them in their efforts.

It also is helpful if you're mindful of not "punishing" them in even subtle ways, such as not talking about the Ethical Elephant in the room or no longer inviting them to lunch or after-work events. This also requires that all employees feel respected, especially when they do the difficult thing such as speaking truth to power.

Ethics hotlines, town hall meetings, online chats, and surveys are the means by which employees can be given voice. However, it is not enough to simply hear them (i.e., collect complaints), but what is collected must be shared and acted up. This brings us to the final part of a high-quality ethic program—accountability.

Part 5: Accountability

The importance of the other parts is demonstrated by leaders sharing what they hear and then engaging employees on how best to address the issues. These actions need to become processes and organizational norms, so too do communications of violations and victories related to ethical conduct.

Accountability needs to be consistent and independent of particular leaders and areas of an organization. Leaders come and go, products and services change, but ethical challenges persist. Therefore, organizations need to create processes that are clear, fair, and predictable, so employees feel more confident and safe using them. An ethics officer and ethics committee can be extremely helpful, as having them signals some level of importance, while at the same time assigning responsibilities to individuals and groups. It also gives employees a clear place to take their issues and concerns.

More generally, leaders must be held accountable for not only their own conduct but also ensuring compliance and commitment to the other four parts of the process. This includes disclosures to appropriate agencies and other applicable regulatory bodies. Although rare in practice, it is important for organizations to build in oversight of their most senior leaders as well, meaning boards of directors or trustees. They must be accountable for their own conduct and that of the organization. You already learned a means for doing this in chapter 8—managing performance for ethics. Ethics, and the five parts of the program, need to be explicit parts of performance expectations, performance measures (verification), and reinforcement (carrots and sticks).

Finally, and very importantly, to realize the full potential of an ethics program, great care must be given to preventing it from becoming a simple check-the-box exercise that managers and other employees complete like a homework assignment. Central to this is the attitude with which leaders communicate about, promote, and act with regard to ethical issues and the program more generally.

In this chapter, you learned some of the foundational elements related to guiding and enforcing ethical conduct at the organizational and national level, as well as how particular formal cultural norms can be used for individual employees and employers. In the next chapter, we will build on this and show you how a growing number of organizations have embedded ethics and social responsibility into their cultures and the often tremendously positive resulting impact. They do well by doing good.

Chapter Summary

1. Laws, regulations, and rules are all formal means by which ethical expectations are signaled and reinforced. They set a minimum standard for ethical conduct.
2. Ethical leaders and organizational cultures are needed to maximize the intended effects of laws, regulations, and rules.
3. Many of the laws and regulations, FCPA, FGSO, Sarbanes-Oxley Act, Dodd–Frank Act, were created in response to business scandals that caused extreme and negative consequences for millions of people.
4. Codes of ethics and codes of conduct describe the expected behaviors of employees.
5. Creating a code of conduct involves identifying common ethical challenges, examples of those challenges, causes, and expected actions.
6. High-quality ethics programs require making ethics a part of strategy, assessing risks, embedding practices in the organization's culture, enabling voice, and ensuring accountability.

Key Terms

codes of conduct 178
codes of ethics 178
Dodd–Frank 177
Federal Sentencing Guidelines (FSGO) 175
Foreign Corrupt Practices Act (FCPA) 174
high-quality ethics program 183
laws 174
psychological safety 186
regulations 174
rules 174
Sarbanes-Oxley 176

CASE STUDY: Better or Worse? You Be the Judge

Title IX is a federal civil rights law enacted in 1972 to guard against sex-based discrimination in education programs or activities that receive federal funding. It also protects against retaliation for those who file complaints or those who testify.[18] Despite the views of some, the intent of Title IX is not to give leverage to women and does not involve quotas. Rather, the goal is to ensure that schools provide equal benefits to both sexes for resources related to scholarships, financial aid, housing, insurance, harassment protections, athletics, and other programs.[19]

What Is Sexual Discrimination? The Answer Evolves

As written in Title IX, "No person in the United States shall, on the basis of sex, be excluded from participation in, be denied the benefits of, or be subjected to discrimination under any education program or activity receiving Federal financial assistance." Sexual harassment and assault were not part of the law until the 1980s when it was then recognized as a form of sexual discrimination. It continued to evolve and was amended in 2011 to motivate universities to more rigorously address sexual misconduct. These changes required schools to do much more, such as

- End harassment.
- Eliminate a hostile work environment if it exists.
- Prevent harassment from happening again.
- Lower standards of evidence.
- No hearings.
- "Single investigator model" in which a single person has the authority to investigate and determine guilt or innocence.
- Sexual harassment includes jokes, gestures, comments, spreading rumors, and creating emails and/or Websites of a sexual nature.
- Penalties for a university's failure to effectively address not just incidents but the larger culture via training and other programs.[20]

Many of these changes were motivated by research showing that one in five women is sexually assaulted during college and that these staggering statistics were due to a flawed college culture across the country. Universities now had broad responsibilities for doing more than addressing particular cases and had to change policies, practices, and behaviors within the institution.[21]

More Major Changes

Until August 2020, all college personnel (e.g., faculty, staff, administrators, coaches, etc.) were required to immediately report any knowledge of any form of potential sexual misconduct or discrimination to the university's Title IX office. However, things have now changed again, notably:

1. University employees are no longer required to report allegations to the Title IX office.
2. Universities can choose the burden of proof they use.
3. Off campus and other facilities not affiliated with the college are not included. Incidents at fraternities, for instance, do need to be investigated because they are sponsored by the school.
4. Live hearings are now required and must allow for cross-examination, not by the students but by advisors.

Continued

The Devil Is in the Details

Sexual harassment is now defined as "any unwelcomed conduct that is so severe, pervasive, and objectively offensive that it effectively bars the victim's access to educational opportunity."[22] Although this definition is more confined than the previous one, it does explicitly include domestic violence, stalking, and dating violence.[23]

The burden of proof aspect is potentially consequential. Previously, colleges needed to meet a "preponderance of evidence" or "more likely than not" standard of proof to rule someone guilty. Legal experts sometimes describe this as "50% plus a feather" (a relatively low bar to clear), meaning the evidence needs to just ever so slightly favor the plaintiff to support a guilty charge. The new standard requires "clear and convincing" evidence, which is a tougher standard and higher bar to clear.

Live hearings are also a dramatic change. Under the previous single-investigator model, most cases were simply conducted on paper and with interviews, if the investigator chose, who then wrote a final report with a decision and punishments if warranted. Now, every matter must go through a process involving three people in the Title IX office, each with different responsibilities in the process.

Motives for the Most Recent Changes

The stated motive for the changes was to simultaneously support victims and ensure fair and due process for the accused. Not surprisingly, however, there are conflicting views regarding the ultimate effect of the changes. Some are concerned that reporting will be more burdensome and thus discourage victims from coming forward. For instance, now that there will be formal hearings with advisors, students may feel they need to have attorneys, which the college will need to pay for.[24] There also are fears that hearings will retraumatize the victims.[25]

On the other side, supporters of the changes feel they are long overdue, as they perceive existing regulations often railroaded the accused students into unfair and damaging predicaments.[26] They also cite universities that have already implemented cross-examination in their processes and did not experience a reduction in complaints filed.[27]

Still other potential implications have been noted. For example, now if a student in an off-campus apartment is touched in an unwanted sexual way, just once, then this would not qualify as an offense. Or, if a professor made sexual comments to student(s), then this would qualify only if they were at a specific student, repeated, or prevented students from going to class.[28]

As some experts point out, the new requirements are only minimum standards to clear the Title IX compliance hurdle. Nothing prevents any particular university from requiring employees (e.g., faculty, students, coaches, and administrators) to report all allegations. Moreover, although the changes explicitly exclude non-university sponsored off-campus facilities, including study-abroad programs, universities are still free to include such policies in student codes of conduct.[29]

For Discussion:

1. Who are the main stakeholders in the case?
2. What effect do you expect these changes to have for victims? Why?
3. If you were a university president, then what would you?
4. Thinking of college students across the country, what effect do you think these changes will have?

Apply Three-Dimensional Problem-Solving for Ethics (3D PSE)

You can apply the 3D PSE from multiple perspectives—victims, alleged offenders, female students, male students, university administrators, other university employees, employees in Title IX offices at universities, or others. Just be sure to specify whose perspective. Let's analyze the case as if you were the president of a university.

figure **9.2**

Three-Dimensional Problem-Solving for Ethics (3D PSE)

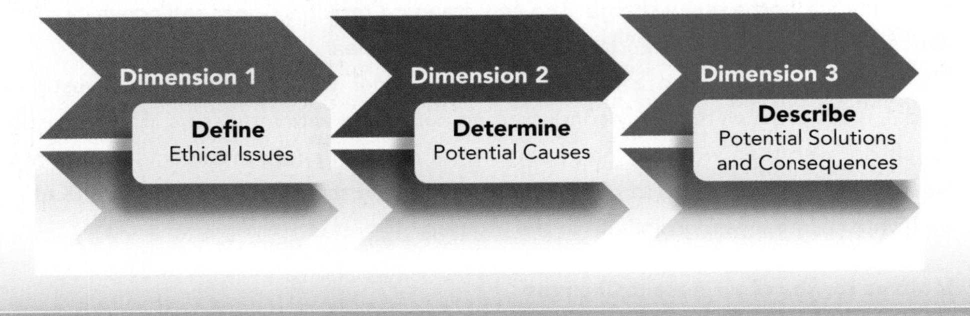

Dimension 1: *Define* the Ethical Challenge

What is the gap in the case? What does the president have, and what does the president want? (Remember, use only details included within the case for your analysis.)

a. From the president's view, describe the current situation versus what is desired.
b. Why is the current situation a problem? What difficulties or undesirable behaviors and outcomes happen as a result of the problem you defined? From the president's perspective, why would he or she care about the problem you defined in Dimension 1?
c. Define the problem in one or at most two sentences, and structure it in terms of what is current versus what is desired.
d. Who are the key stakeholders who affect or are affected by the problem you defined?

Dimension 2: *Determine* the Causes

a. **Individuals.** Given the problem you defined in Dimension 1, describe how many individuals caused the problem as you defined it in Dimension 1. Individuals may not be causes, but you should consider whether there are any or not. If yes, then describe how they contributed to the problem.
b. **Contextual.** What behaviors, policies, and practices caused the problem defined in Dimension 1? These elements may be within your university, or they may reside with other organizations or stakeholder groups.

Dimension 3: *Describe* Your Potential Solutions and the Intended and Unintended Consequences for Stakeholders

For each cause you identified in Dimension 2, answer the following question:

a. From the president's perspective, and then other stakeholders, ***what*** do you recommend he or she do, and ***how*** would you make it happen?

b. **Why would you do it the way proposed?** Explain your motives, along with considering if it reflects a particular ethical decision-making perspective (e.g., utilitarian or universal)?

If your responses to these questions are unsatisfactory, then go back to Dimension 1 and repeat the process. If, however, you are comfortable and confident in your problem-solving efforts thus far, then ensure you achieve the desired outcomes and avoid any unintended consequences.

c. Describe the ***desired and likely effects in the short and long term*** for the key stakeholders involved in the problem and causes (Dimensions 1 and 2)?
d. What ***potential unintended consequences*** may occur with your proposed solution for each of the relevant stakeholders?
e. If any, what are the **implications for *other* stakeholders** (e.g., individuals, organizations, and communities) besides those noted in Dimensions 1 and 2?
f. Will your solution work in an ethical manner? Make a final assessment of whether your chosen solution will reduce or eliminate the causes determined in Dimension 2, and whether it will then remedy the ethical problem defined in Dimension 1. If not, then repeat and refine the dimensions.

Chapter Opener Photo Source: kunisan/Shutterstock

chapter 10

Doing Well By Doing Good

Learning Objectives

AFTER READING THIS CHAPTER, YOU SHOULD BE ABLE TO

LO1 Explain what it means for a business to adopt an environmental, social, and governance (ESG) approach to business.

LO2 Summarize conscious capitalism (CC) and explain how to build a conscious organization.

LO3 Outline and apply the Caux Principles.

LO4 Describe what B-Corps are and why an organization would choose to be one.

WHERE DO **YOU** STAND?

I Paid My Debt, but Will You Pay Me?

Numerous organizations create values that resonate with a wide array of stakeholders. Some percentage of these organizations also create vision statements that are equally inspirational as well as aspirational. For instance, in the 1980s and 1990s, Microsoft's vision was a "computer on every desk in every home running Microsoft software." They achieved this vision.

The vision of another ambitious company was "to become the world's leading energy company—creating innovative and efficient energy solutions for growing economies and a better environment worldwide."

This same company had the following values:

> *Respect*: We treat others as we would like to be treated. We do not tolerate abusive or disrespectful treatment. Ruthlessness, callousness, and arrogance don't belong here.
>
> *Integrity*: We work with customers and prospects openly, honestly, and sincerely. When we say we will do something, we will do it; when we say we cannot or will not do something, then we won't do it.
>
> *Communication*: We have an obligation to communicate. Here, we take the time to talk with one another . . . and to listen. We believe that information is meant to move and that information moves people.
>
> *Excellence*: We are satisfied with nothing less than the very best in everything we do. We will continue to raise the bar for everyone. Here, the great fun for all of us will be to discover just how good we can really be.

1. On the surface, do these values align with your own? Answer (yes/no) and explain.
2. Does this vision seem aspirational, something that might inspire you? Answer (yes/no) and explain.

The company that created this list of values and pursued this vision was Enron.

Introduction

As Enron epitomized, many companies create their lists of words and grandiose statements, most often with truly good intentions. However, the challenge is living the values and realizing the visions. Historically and still, businesses have a reputation of simply striving to make money and for some at any cost as long as they do so abiding by the law. But today, businesses are expected to do far more, they must do well and do good.

This chapter highlights how embracing positive business practices is both good and profitable. To this end, you'll learn how businesses that emphasize environmental, social, and governance (ESG) issues have become more profitable, including for investors. You will also learn how a growing number of organizations and their leaders have adopted conscious capitalism (CC), which is a contemporary means for doing business that embodies many of the business ethics concepts you've learned, such as social responsibility and a broad stakeholder perspective. Better still, you will learn how to implement some of the key elements of CC, such as a compelling purpose and mission. Still other companies have embraced a set of principles intended to provide a common standard for international business. Finally, you'll learn how companies can legally commit to make social and environmental benefits as a central element of their strategies and operations.

More generally, the content of this chapter is both a review of the individual and organizational content you've learned thus far and a bridge to the final section of the book, which focuses on business ethics at the global level. You also are encouraged to make note of concepts and examples of how they are practiced by the organizations included in this chapter. You could potentially target one or more of them as a potential employer or, at the very least, look for other companies with similar values and norms when searching for jobs throughout your career.

Environmental, Social, and Governance (ESG) Approach to Business

Many people believe that the primary focus of business is to earn a profit—the more, the better. This means that when deciding between activities and investments, many employees will choose those that earn the greatest profit—in other words, the most revenue and the least cost. This has often left even the most well-intentioned, enlightened decision makers in challenging positions when confronted with alternatives that seemingly trade profits for "doing good," such as actively reducing their organization's environmental impact or advocating for social change. Put differently, doing good was for charities, and such investments were luxuries that businesses simply could not or should not afford.

Thankfully, however, attitudes are changing, and piles of experience and data now show that these decisions are no longer "either–or," but instead, organizations across industries and around the globe can do well *and* do good.

environmental, social, and governance (ESG) integrating these three nonfinancial factors into an organization's strategy and operations produces superior performance, including financial, compared to organizations that don't

ESG as a Path to Success

A now well-entrenched trend in investing is to evaluate companies on nonfinancial factors related to **environmental, social, and governance (ESG)**, as integrating these three factors into an organization's strategy and operations produces superior performance, including financial, compared to organizations that don't.[1]

When discussing ESG investing,

Environment means reducing inputs and waste along with utilizing cleaner or renewable sources of energy.

Social pertains to using a broad stakeholder approach in organizational decision making, thus considering the impact on and ability to impact people both inside the organization (e.g., fairness and inclusion) and outside (e.g., surrounding communities and social issues in society).

Governance relates to the policies, practices, and procedures used to manage an organization. When these elements are transparent and fair, in addition to being legal, an organization can be said to focus on governance.[2]

Origins of ESG. The term ESG originated in 2005 and grew out of efforts to show that socially responsible business is not a luxury but instead profitable. Advocates of social responsibility had long argued its benefits, but the challenge was to convince investors that using ESG metrics in their decisions would be profitable.

ESG investing differs from **socially responsible investing (SRI),** which avoids investing in companies whose products, services, or practices are considered by some to be immoral or unethical, such as alcohol, tobacco, and fossil fuels.[3] In other words, ESG focuses on accentuating the positive and SRI focuses on avoiding the negative. Let's explore the benefits, examples, and the growing support from prominent business leaders, all with an eye on the implications for business ethics.

socially responsible investing (SRI) avoids investing in companies whose products, services, or practices are considered by some to be immoral or unethical, such as alcohol, tobacco, and fossil fuels

Benefits of an ESG Focus. Support for ESG-oriented business and investing criteria is broad and growing. The fundamental argument for the benefits of ESG is that integrating these elements makes good business sense, as it makes markets, not just individual companies, more sustainable and produces positive outcomes for a wide array of stakeholders. In so doing, such companies also make money. From 2017 to 2020, the S&P 500 Index, a broad measure of the US stock market, increased 32.73 percent, while the S&P 500 ESG Index increased 33.25 percent.[4] The S&P 500 ESG index excludes companies in environmentally dirty or socially stigmatized industries, such as tobacco and guns, and includes those with evidence of environmentally sound and/or health-oriented industries, such as green energy and healthcare.[5] This supported rigorous research covering 2009–2019 that shows no risk–reward trade-offs when including ESG and investment criteria.[6]

Another reason for the growing interest is generational. Millennials are now the largest proportion of the workforce, and their generation values ESG issues more than the previous generations. Because they are the largest, they also invest a large proportion of the money in financial markets. Simply put, they vote with their dollars, which has increased the appeal and success of ESG investing and operations. However, it is both unfair and inaccurate to think that other generations are uninterested, as the trend for sustainable practices is increasing in every age-group.[7]

How Does ESG Create Benefits?. You may be wondering how exactly does an ESG focus lead to superior outcomes? McKinsey Consulting Company helped to provide an answer and identified five links between ESG and value creation (see Table 10.1).

Microsoft is an excellent example. It is especially strong in its focus on environmental factors, such as reducing its carbon footprint, recycling, and renewable energy.[8] The company has been carbon neutral since 2012, meaning that the total greenhouse gases removed from the atmosphere equals the total produced in the process of doing business, and it has a goal of being carbon negative by 2030. The company's efforts have paid off, as investors who use ESG criteria have additional reasons to include Microsoft in its pool of qualified companies. This fact, along with the recognition the company has received, boosted both its reputation and investment returns.[9]

table **10.1**

Environmental, Social, and Governance (ESG) and Value Creation

Type of Value Creation	Description of Benefits
Increases sales	Consumers are attracted to companies with ESG values and practices. Greater support from the government and the community members for products and services (e.g., buy local).
Reduces costs	Reduce production costs such as packaging, materials, energy, and water.
Mitigates regulatory and legal challenges	Greater support from government and regulators such as fewer regulations, lower taxes, and greater subsidies.
Improves productivity and reputation	Boost employee motivation. Attract talent (and customers) through greater social credibility.
Increases investments and performance	Make more sustainable investment choices. Increase investor interest, returns, and loyalty.

Source: Adapted from W. Henisz, T. Koller, and R. Nuttall, "Five Ways that ESG Creates Value," *McKinsey Quarterly*, November 14, 2019, https://www.mckinsey.com/business-functions/strategy-and-corporate-finance/our-insights/five-ways-that-esg-creates-value.

Global ESG investing has grown 68 percent since 2014 and tenfold since 2004. This clearly indicates that executives and investors all over the world believe that an ESG focus is a path to success.[10] The following Ethics in Action box provides an exceptional example of what it means to be an ESG-oriented investment firm.

Ethics in Action

It's Just Money

JUST Capital was created in 2013 by leaders across industries, such as Paul Tudor Jones II, Deepak Chopra, Arianna Huffington, Paul Scialla, and Alan Fleischmann, all of whom were committed to the belief that the world needs more companies that truly believe in and practice fair pay and equal treatment for all workers. Moreover, such organizations need a genuine concern for and investment in good jobs, flourishing communities, and a healthy planet. They measure companies on these and other items people care about, which enables them to rank companies accordingly.

The founders' beliefs are captured in JUST Capital's mission statement:

Build an economy that works for all Americans by helping companies improve how they serve all their stakeholders—workers, customers, communities, the environment, and shareholders. We believe that business and markets can and must be a greater force for good, and that by shifting the resources of the $19 trillion private sectors, we can address systemic issues at scale, including income inequality and lack of opportunity. Guided by the priorities of the public, our *research, rankings, indexes, and data-driven tools help measure and improve corporate performance in the stakeholder economy.*

The intent of JUST Capital leaders is to model these behaviors in how the organization is run and for the recognition of those listed in the rankings to motivate other individuals and organizations to do the same.

For Discussion:

1. What is your response to the comment: "There is just a bunch of billionaires doing good to make themselves feel better. They have so much money that addressing sustainability doesn't really cost them anything personally."
2. Assume you are a billionaire money manager who supports JUST Capital and what it stands for. Now, assume you are trying to convince other money managers to support the cause. What would you say and/or do?
3. Now assume the tables are turned, and another wealthy money manager is trying to persuade you to join the cause. Describe two reasons why you would not support their efforts.

Purpose Beyond Profit

In January 2020, Larry Fink proclaimed that financial firms need to make environmental sustainability a key criterion in their investment decisions. Mr. Fink certainly was not the first person to take this position, but it was the first time that the CEO of the world's largest asset manager, BlackRock, made this statement. Fink didn't just say this in an interview, as a casual conversation, or as an email to employees. He made it a policy of the firm going forward, and he sent this same message to the CEOs of the companies in which BlackRock invests.[11]

Asserting Power to Influence Competitors and Clients. Given his position and the firm's size, this view has the potential to fundamentally change investment practices and thus other industries around the world.[12] Put differently, if the biggest investor decides sustainability is appropriate, then it will be difficult for other investors and the companies they invest in not to follow.

To elaborate, large investors make large investments, which raise the prices of those investments, and other investors are well served to follow as the value of their own investments increase. Moreover, investments are seen as votes that the market values what companies are doing, which means BlackRock will essentially be rewarding companies that pursue sustainability in their strategies and operations. Fink took this a step further still by also saying BlackRock would begin selling its investments in companies that represent "high sustainability risk," such as those in the coal industry.[13]

If this weren't enough, Fink said his firm would begin voting against management teams that do not make environmental progress consistent with the Paris Climate Accord (discussed more in chapter 13).

Momentum Is Building. Neither Fink nor BlackRock is revolutionary in their views. Members of the US Congress and others have protested about the firm's lack of action and poor record on climate issues. Other powerful members of the investment community have also spoken out against BlackRock while pursuing climate-conscious investing.

For instance, Christopher Hohn, a billionaire hedge fund manager in the UK, previously criticized BlackRock and the entire finance industry for not aggressively taking action to improve sustainability. Hohn went so far as to say "dirty" businesses, such as coal, should be punished. Hohn is a climate activist and has donated money to related causes for many years, but more recently, he has been more assertive. In particular, he has targeted banks, regulators, and other institutions involved in the finance and approval of coal-fired power plants around the world. He has taken his fight directly to the companies by not supporting directors who do not act, thus potentially voting them off the board of directors.[14]

Finally, it is possible to make the argument simply in terms of dollars and cents. As of the beginning of 2020, the S&P 500 Energy Sector gained only 2 percent, while the broader S&P 500 nearly tripled. Besides, Fink says that climate issues and BlackRock's position on them are far and away what he gets asked about most from investors.[15]

In the next section, you'll learn about another approach to doing well by doing good. It's called Conscious Capitalism and is embraced by numerous companies, some of which you undoubtedly know.

Conscious Capitalism and How to Build a Conscious Organization

capitalism
an economic system based on private ownership of the means for production and the profits earned and is built on the principles of private property, capital accumulation, voluntary exchange, and competitive markets

Capitalism is an economic system based on private ownership of the means for production and the profits earned and it is built on the principles of private property, capital accumulation, voluntary exchange, and competitive markets.[16] Some individuals and organizations, despite believing in the potential of capitalism, think that the practice has gone down the wrong path as evidenced by

1. Scandals due to unethical conduct.
2. Neglect of stakeholders, including communities and the environment, and the resulting negative consequences.
3. Myth that business is all about profit maximization.
4. Abuses of power and influence that result in personal advantage at the expense of others.[17]

They have instead subscribed to a different form—conscious capitalism—based on the same characteristics as capitalism but practices differently. The spirit is captured in this credo:

> *"We believe that business is good because it creates value, it is ethical because it is based on voluntary exchange, it is noble because it can elevate our existence, and it is heroic because it lifts people out of poverty and creates prosperity. Free enterprise capitalism is the most powerful system for social cooperation and human progress ever conceived. It is one of the most compelling ideas we humans have ever had. But we can aspire to even more."*[18]

Conscious Capitalism

"**Conscious capitalism (CC)** is a way of thinking about capitalism and business, which better reflects where we are in the human journey, the state of our world today, and the innate potential of business to make a positive impact on the world."[19] It is built on the following four tenets (see Figure 10.1):

1. Higher purpose (beyond profit maximization).
2. Stakeholder interdependence (rather than only shareholder value).
3. Conscious leadership (motivated by purpose and service to multiple stakeholders).
4. Conscious cultures.[20]

conscious capitalism (CC)
a way of thinking about capitalism and business, which better reflects where we are in the human journey, the state of our world today, and the innate potential of business to make a positive impact on the world

CC businesses, and their leaders, believe in doing what is right simply because it is right. They do not require someone to "make the business case" (e.g., cost–benefit analysis) but instead will simply decide and act in an ethical manner. This is why some experts see CC as a more virtuous type of business philosophy not so pragmatic, rationale, or instrumental as others (e.g., profit maximization).

Moreover, practitioners of CC loudly claim it is not corporate social responsibility (CSR; recall discussion from chapter 2). Most simply, CC believes that purposefully adding value to all relevant stakeholders, including communities and the environment, are not just nice to-dos but are essential must-dos. This means that more stakeholders are primary and explicitly built into strategic goals, operations, and performance metrics. Some CC leaders, such as John Mackey, cofounder and former CEO of Whole Foods, further differentiate CC from CSR by arguing that most organizations simply have CSR initiatives "bolted on," whereas CC organizations have business ethics and social responsibility in their DNA, which means they pervade everything they do.[21]

Mackey's claim is bold, and many advocates of CSR would take issue with his characterization. CC is nevertheless gaining momentum in business and seeking to make a positive impact just as those who have subscribed to CSR principles.

Let's unpack the CC tenets to better understand their meaning and impact.

Higher Purpose

Responsible businesses earn a profit to survive and meet the expectations of multiple stakeholders (chapter 2). CC businesses also create profits and, in fact, consistently outperform the S&P 500 by 1.5, 2.5, 3, and 10 times in 5-, 10-, 15-, and 20-year periods, respectively.[22]

figure **10.1**

Tenets of Conscious Capitalism

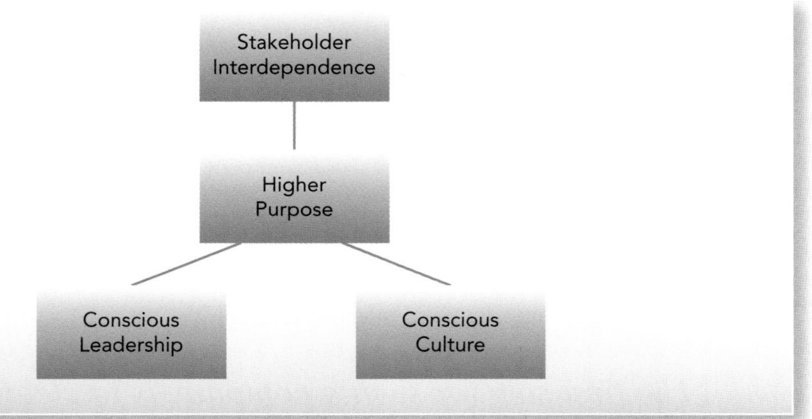

purpose
the reason why an organization exists and gives employees and other stakeholders focus, meaning, and inspiration

However, CC businesses go beyond the bottom line and deeply believe in and pursue an overarching purpose (or mission). **Purpose** describes the reason why an organization exists and gives employees and other stakeholders focus, meaning, and inspiration. In purpose-driven organizations, such as those that practice CC, profits are simply one of the means of realizing the purpose.

CC is practiced by numerous well-known companies, such as Whole Foods, Costco, and The Container Store, who also routinely make the Fortune's 100 Best Companies to Work For lists (see Table 10.2).

table 10.2

Example Companies and Their Purposes

Company	Purpose
Bombas (buy one–give one socks company)	We believe that a more comfortable world is a better world. Everyone, no matter their circumstances, deserves to put on clean clothes that make them feel good. So, we spent years perfecting socks and T-shirts you'll want to live in. Creating apparel you'll never want to take off. For every item you purchase for yourself, we donate an item to someone affected by homelessness.[23]
4ocean (recycler and producer of bracelets)	We're here to clean the ocean and coastlines while working to stop the inflow of plastic by changing the consumption habits.[24]
Motley Fool (financial services)	What difference are we trying to make in the world? "To Help the World Invest—Better." Why each word matters: • To Help: There are many ways to help—some active and some passive (e.g., teaching, leading, listening, collaborating, competing) • The World: We're aiming high. This inspires us to serve as many people as possible and compels us to pursue global services. • Invest: When we talk about investing, we're not limited to stocks. Any resource spent, any future planned for. • Better: Whatever we do, we should do it better than our competitors and better than we've done in the past. Ever higher![25]
Costco (retail)	To continuously provide our members with quality goods and services at the lowest possible prices.[26]
Patagonia (outdoor apparel)	We're in business to save our home planet.[27]
Southwest Airlines (airline)	Connect people to what's important in their lives through friendly, reliable, and low-cost air travel.[28]
Google (social media)	To organize the world's information and make it universally accessible and useful.[29]
Barry-Wehmiller (manufacturing equipment)	Building a better world through business. We're more than just a successful capital equipment and technology solutions firm. We're the kind of company in which you'd like your children to work.[30]

John Mackey, one of the strongest advocates of CC that he deeply embedded at Whole Foods, described the importance of purpose in this way:

> *"The first step for such a company is to clearly define its higher purpose beyond maximizing profits. It*

should then start to design everything it does around creating value for its stakeholders. It should get rid of all metrics that are not connected to value creation for stakeholders. It should then create new metrics that are leading indicators of future performance, measures such as employee passion and customer advocacy."[31]

Given the fact that a compelling purpose is foundational to CC, the Ethics in Action box provides some guidance on how to create one.

Once an organization has created a compelling purpose, the next step is to begin to translate it into how it will be realized via an effective vision.

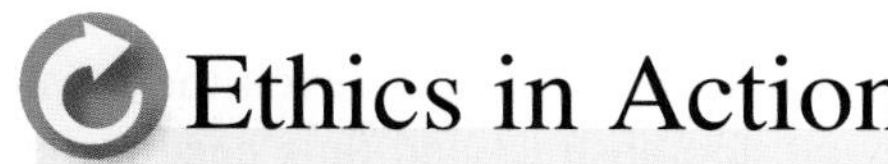

How to Create a Compelling Purpose

There are many ways to create a compelling purpose, but whatever the process it is helpful to reflect, and the following questions can help. For each key stakeholder, ask and answer the following questions:

1. Why does the organization exist?
2. What impact do we want to have and on whom?
3. How will what we do make a positive difference in the world?

As you can see, you need to think big when creating a purpose. It is not about goals and action plans, but instead, it is about impact.

To help further refine your purpose, determine the following:

- Functional benefit: What does our company enable others (people and organizations) to do?
- Emotional benefit: How do people feel about what we provide?
- Ultimate value: What value do our functional and emotional benefits provide to our key stakeholders?

Remember, compelling purpose statements typically do not include a particular product or service, nor are they about being number one or the best in industry. They are about impact like those included in Table 10.2. Once you're reasonably confident with your draft purpose statement, test it with various stakeholders and use their feedback to refine and then retest.

For Discussion:

1. What do you think are the greatest benefits of a compelling organizational purpose? Describe.
2. Which three stakeholders would you include in creating a compelling purpose for your current/past employer or university (if you have not worked)? Explain.
3. What do you think would be the biggest obstacle to creating a compelling purpose?

Ensure Differentiation. Purposes are most powerful not only when they are emotionally compelling but also when they are unique. Jennifer Warshauer, senior manager of enterprise at Clif Bar & Company in California and a long time and skilled expert in CC, explains that purpose statements are most effective when they pass two tests:

1. Uniqueness test. To use this test, ask if your organization's purpose statement could be adopted and effectively pursued by another organization. If the answer is yes, then more work is needed. Perhaps it needs to be more aspirational or the scope needs to be broadened. Whatever the case, part of the power of purpose is that it differentiates one organization from its competitors, as this makes it more attractive to numerous stakeholders—customers, employees (current and future), and investors.
2. Opposite test. Warshauer also recommends stating your purpose in the opposite, for instance, the opposite of "we want to feed the world" is "we want to starve the world." Of course, feeding the world is noble, but the opposite is ridiculous. The point is that if a purpose statement doesn't pass the opposite test, then it is likely too obvious and not actually particularly compelling to other stakeholders.

Visions . . . Aspiration Meets Achievability. Despite their importance, even the most compelling purpose statements are not enough. They are too abstract and thus need to be translated into more concrete details. Some experts even argue that organizational purposes can never be achieved, as they are so aspirational (but not ridiculously so). One way to help do this is with an effective vision, still aspirational but achievable. A **vision** describes a desirable future destination for an organization and answers the following questions:

vision
a desirable future destination for an organization

1. What it will do (e.g., goods and services)?
2. How will we do it?
3. For whom (key customers and possibly geography)?
4. Why should key stakeholders commit to doing business with us (e.g., employees, customers, and investors)?

Accordingly, vision statements are more detailed than purpose statements and add clarity to how the purpose will be realized. When thinking about, writing, and evaluating vision statements, it is helpful to think and speak in terms of images and emotions and not goals, action plans, and achievements. Many students and clients have found it helpful to use the metaphor of their most desirable vacation, perhaps to an exotic location, wherein they immerse in nature's beauty, are pampered like royalty, and live in the moment without a care in the world. If you approach vision statements in this way, you are more likely to use images that capture the emotions of key stakeholders, which in turn can serve to boost their motivation and commitment.

Goals and Action Plans. When an organization has an inspiring purpose and vision, still more work is necessary to bring them to life in actual policies, practices, and behaviors. This is where organizational members (leaders and other employees) need to set goals and create action plans for achieving them. A detailed description of how to do this is beyond the scope of this book, but this is typically the easiest part of the process.

Step 1: Begin with the answers to the four questions related to the vision statements above.

Step 2: Create measurable goals and action plans for each.

Step 3: Execute these plans.

Step 4: Periodically evaluate progress toward the goals.

Step 5: Evaluate the ultimate goal outcomes.

Step 6: Revise and repeat.

Stakeholder Interdependence

As you learned in chapter 1, stakeholders are those who are impacted by or can impact your business. CC businesses think of stakeholders as an interconnected ecosystem, wherein desirable outcomes are sought for all.[32] Again, this is not self-sacrificing altruism, nor is it winner take all. For instance, CC businesses do not pay workers the lowest wages due to few job alternatives for employees in a given market. CC businesses also view competition as positive, a motivation for innovation and excellence, rather than an opponent to destroy. The ecosystem view means that interactions and relationships need to be positive to be sustainable. This broader, positive stakeholder approach is epitomized at The Container Store and illustrated in the Ethics in Action box.

Ethics in Action

I Thrive, You Thrive, We All Thrive

The vision of the Container Store is— *working to build a business where everyone associated with it can thrive together.* Although the company emphatically states it has an employee-first culture, it certainly doesn't stop there. Their web page describes the organization this way:

> *"We know our employee-first mantra defies conventional business wisdom, but at The Container Store, we've found that if you take better care of the employees than anybody else, they really will take better care of the customers than anybody else."*
>
> *"But it doesn't stop with employees. We ask ourselves—"What if everyone associated with a business could thrive?" For us, it's not just a question. It's what we strive to achieve in all that we do for each of our stakeholders—our employees, customers, vendors, the community, and our shareholders. We work to accomplish this by staying true to our employee-first, "yummy" culture, our Foundation Principles, and the tenets of conscious capitalism. The result is a business where happy, well-paid, well-trained employees look forward to coming to work alongside other great people to improve customers' lives by getting them organized; where our vendors' companies can become all they hope and dream for; and where our communities can flourish. And when all of this happens, shareholders benefit from a healthy bottom line. This is when EVERYONE thrives!"*

For Discussion:

1. Besides employees, which stakeholders are evident in this statement?
2. What do you find compelling about The Container Store based on this statement?
3. How do you think the company's approach helps them compete against other retailers?

Means and Ends. In addition to primary and secondary stakeholders, as you learned in chapter 1, CC organizations view stakeholders as both means and ends. For instance, selling consulting services to your clients makes them a means to your profitable ends.[33] However, if you are purpose-driven and have a genuine stakeholder orientation, then your consulting services will provide positive results for your client, such as performance for the employees with whom you worked, and thus the larger organization, and perhaps you positively impacted them by showing what it is like to truly partner with an ethical, responsible, other-oriented professional. This makes your client a "positive ends," not just a means to your profit (end), and it may inspire them not only to provide your firm more business, but it may also cause them to offer you a job in the future and motivate them to conduct themselves in a similar manner.

Stakeholders as Valued Partners. A true stakeholder orientation includes partnering with them to identify and solve their problems. This requires educating yourself beyond your own products or services and gaining insights from their perspective. One critical way of doing this is to identify their needs, in their eyes, not yours. Put differently, you are not simply seeking to identify how your product or service can benefit them, but you are also trying to understand their challenges and determinants of performance more generally. To do this, first identify your key primary stakeholders (those that affect and/or are affected by your business every day; chapter 1). Most organizations have no more than seven, and most jobs have fewer than that. Then, try to put yourself in their position and learn the following.[34]

Answering these questions helps you get a broader and more strategic view of the job of the person with whom you're working, and/or the larger organization.

1. What are their key responsibilities?
2. What are the biggest challenges fulfilling those responsibilities?
3. What are their key goals or objectives for this quarter, the next year, and the next three years?

Again, from each key stakeholder's perspective, determine what they need most from

1. You
2. Your company
3. Your key competitors

Learning these details can help you determine what you do well, what value you and your organization provide, and what your competitor may do better. You have to persist until you've identified three needs for each primary stakeholder. Some CC organizations organize this information in what they call stakeholder maps, which are illustrations of key stakeholders and how each is served by the organization's purpose. Figure 10.2 provides the map similar to The Container Store's featured in the previous Ethics in Action box.

figure **10.2**

Stakeholder Map

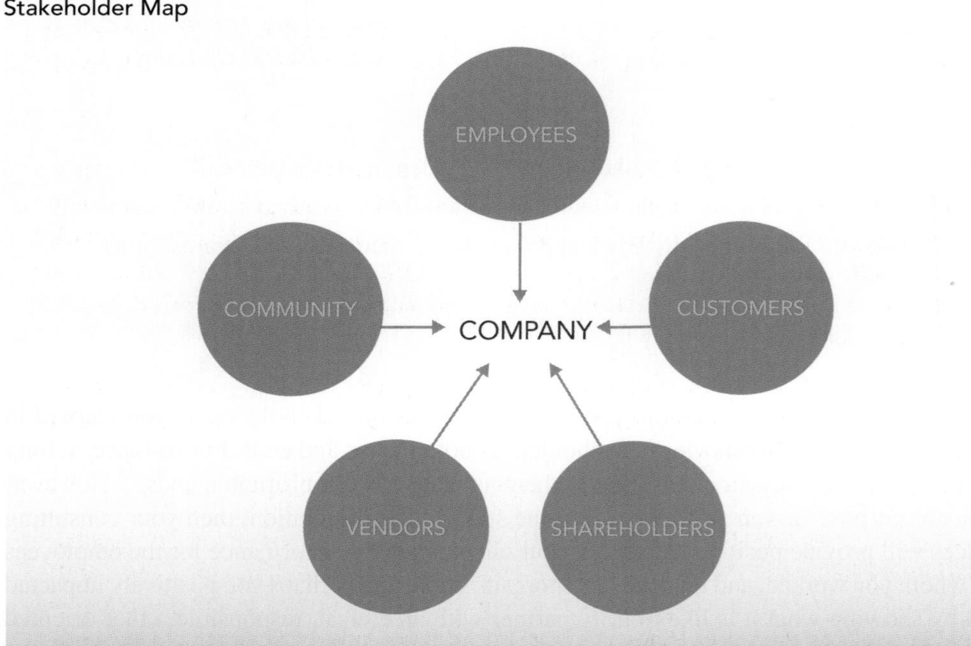

Stakeholder maps do not include the needs and how they will be met, but you can see how this information can be included elsewhere in formulating and implementing strategies (goals and action plans) to serve these stakeholders. More generally, maps and the associated information prepares an organization and its employees to be a true partner with stakeholders, one that adds value to the relationship (e.g., problem solver) rather than largely extracting value from the relationship (e.g., sales).

Conscious Leaders and Conscious Cultures

We discuss these two tenets together as they are intimately connected. Conscious leaders embrace the organization's purpose, which guides their considerations and actions. They also must ensure that the values of a CC organizational culture are translated into norms (policies, practices, and behaviors) throughout the organization. But before marrying them, we will explore some brief separate details first.

Conscious Leaders. Because CC leaders must be both broad and deep in their knowledge and thinking, the role of conscious leaders is especially complex. Like conscious organizations, conscious leaders see others as both means and ends. Take employees, for example. CC leaders see employees as essential means for realizing the organization's purpose and vision, as employees bring these elements to life and create value for other stakeholders. Southwest Airlines has always claimed employees are their most valuable stakeholder. The rationale is that if employees are treated well and their potential is realized, then customers will be pleased, which in turn will grow profits and please shareholders.

James R. Martin/Shutterstock

However, CC leaders also see employees as ends, meaning that they feel a genuine responsibility for their well-being. As such, CC leaders tend to be servant leaders who put the needs of others before their own, invest in the development and satisfaction of employees, and advocate for their interests. By modeling these beliefs in their behaviors, conscious leaders are both the creators and reinforcers of conscious cultures.

Conscious Culture. Similar to the concept of organizational culture, you learned about in chapter 8, CC cultures are built on values. **CC values** can be described in a useful mnemonic—T.A.C.T.I.L.E.[35]

CC values can be described in a useful mnemonic—T.A.C.T.I.L.E. Trust, Accountability, Caring, Transparency, Integrity, Loyalty, Egalitarianism

Trust. Recall from chapter 1 that trust is the belief that another party will consider your interests in their actions. Organizations with CC cultures foster trust vertically and horizontally, meaning that employees trust their supervisors and senior leaders, peers trust peers, and teams trust teams from different areas of the organization. CC cultures also foster trust with external stakeholders—customers, suppliers, shareholders, regulators, and communities.

Accountability. Employees are accountable to each other, including executives to board members, peers, and subordinates. Employees are accountable to customers, which is supported by empowering leadership, which enables them to do what they feel is necessary to meet customer needs and do the right thing.

Caring. Genuine, heartfelt concern for others tends to be returned in kind by others. Caring is a hallmark of CC organizations and is exhibited in policies, practices, and behaviors throughout the organization, such as communications, decision making, and human resource practices related to hiring, developing, promoting, and even discipline.

But as Jennifer Warshauer adds from her experience as a CC leader and developer of conscious cultures,

> *"Caring is different from being nice. It also includes caring enough for radical candor—caring personally and challenging directly . . . it's not simply being nice all the time and hoping everyone likes you."*

Transparency. Openness is another treasured characteristic of CC cultures. For instance, Whole Foods has long made all compensation transparent; every team member can see the compensation of all others including the top management team. They also tend to include a larger proportion of employees in strategic planning.

Integrity. "A conscious culture is marked by strict adherence to truth-telling and fair dealing . . . typically set global standards . . . are guided by what they believe is ethically right, not merely by what is legally required or socially acceptable."[36]

Loyalty. Due to their trusting relationships that also include the other characteristics described, CC organizations and their stakeholders tend to be loyal to each other, which means they are likely to go above and beyond contractual arrangements and actively recommend their respective organizations to others.

Egalitarianism. CC cultures are generally more equal than others. As you'll learn in chapter 11, they have relatively low power distance and thus diminish the differences between senior and junior employees. Executives tend to be frugal and not use private jets or other "benefits" not available to other employees. Salary differences are commonly limited, and historically conscious companies tend to be more transparent about compensation to ensure practices are fair and can be verified by employees.

Organizations and people that possess and live these values are likely to be exceptional in almost every way, including having high ethical standards, high employee satisfaction and engagement, and superior performance. Before moving on, pause for a moment and consider the following For Discussion questions.

For Discussion

1. Would you like to work for an organization that lives T.A.C.T.I.L.E. values? Explain.
2. Would you like to have a manager who you could describe as being TACTILE? Explain.
3. Presumably, you would like to be described by others as T.A.C.T.I.L.E. Describe two things you could do personally to demonstrate these values in your dealings with others.

Another way that organizations can do well by doing good is to follow the Caux Principles, established in 1994 to help promote moral capitalism. This type of economic system considers not just how much it produces but how widely it shares and benefits others including the environment.[37]

The Caux Principles

The **Caux Round Table** (CRT) is a global network of business leaders who are committed to creating a fair, free, and transparent society using a common set of ethical principles.[38] It was founded with the goal of establishing a set of shared values and ethical norms to guide international businesses when navigating cross-cultural challenges (you'll learn more about this in chapter 11).

Caux Round Table (CRT) a global network of business leaders who are committed to creating a fair, free, and transparent society using a common set of ethical principles

The principles listed in Table 10.3 were formulated by executives from Europe, Japan, and the United States, which some experts claim are the most comprehensive set of such guidelines for businesses ever created.[39]

The CRT outlined a set of principles for responsible business and additional sets for government, nongovernment organizations, good citizenship, and wealth. The intent was to create principles that are relevant for organizations and people operating in these different roles and contexts. We focus our attention on those for business.[40]

CRT Principles for Responsible Business

The seven **CRT Principles** for responsible business are based on the belief that neither the law nor the market forces are sufficient for ethical and positive business conduct.[41]

CRT Principles for responsible business are based on the belief that neither the law nor the market forces are sufficient for ethical and positive business conduct

table **10.3**

Caux Round Table Principles for Responsible Business

Principle	Description
Principle 1: Stakeholder orientation	Businesses are responsible to others beyond investors and managers.
Principle 2: Social development	Businesses are responsible for addressing and improving the social issues not just financial performance.
Principle 3: Trust	Businesses are responsible for building trust by going above and beyond the law.
Principle 4: Respect cultural rules and norms	Businesses are responsible for knowing and following cultural rules and norms.
Principle 5: Support responsible globalization	Businesses are responsible for fostering responsible international/global growth.
Principle 6: Respect the environment	Businesses are responsible for protecting the environment.
Principle 7: Be lawful	Businesses are responsible for following legal standards.

Source: Adapted from Caux Round Table for Moral Capitalism Web page, accessed July 13, 2020, https://www.cauxroundtable.org/.

It's More Than Principles . . . Stakeholders Matter Too

The CRT goes beyond simply identifying guiding principles, and also provides **stakeholder management guidelines**, which specify how to responsibly treat key stakeholders. This additional direction can be most helpful, as it can be used as a set of standards to both guide and evaluate ethical conduct. The CRT recommends treating

stakeholder management guidelines specify how to responsibly treat key stakeholders

1. **Customers** with respect and dignity.
2. **Employees** with respect for health, well-being, and appropriate wages.

3. **Shareholders** with genuine and long-term concerns.
4. **Suppliers** with fairness and honesty, including matters related to pricing, licensing, and payment.
5. **Competitors** with fairness, appropriate respect for property and associated rights, and as partners in the development and implementation of socially and environmentally responsible behavior.
6. **Communities** as partners in promoting human rights and sustainable development.[42]

The rationale underlying stakeholder guidance is that no business will succeed in the long term if it does not treat its key stakeholders well. In terms of application, the CRT Principles and outline for stakeholders is intended to serve as the basis of principled leadership, and if done effectively, the principles will be embedded in the organization's cultural values and norms.[43]

Again, members of the CRT believe in and promote capitalism, but they claim that the principles can help organizations realize capitalism's benefits, morally, to the benefit of many others.[44] The principles support the idea that responsible leaders and businesses are stewards or guardians of resources (e.g., human, financial, and environmental), essential partners for mutual advantage, and must respect and protect human dignity.[45]

B-Corporations

Another way that organizations demonstrate their commitment to socially responsible and sustainable practices is by formally certifying as a B-Corporation.

Differences between B-Corporations and Other Companies

B-Corporations (B-Corps)
make a legally binding commitment to explicitly generate public benefits, in addition to financial returns, and consider the impact of their actions on a broad group of stakeholders

First, B-Corporations are for-profit organizations and not charities. **B-Corporations (B-Corps)** make a legally binding commitment to explicitly generate public benefits, in addition to financial returns, and consider the impact of their actions on a broad group of stakeholders. The essence of B-Corps is to consider and add value to a broad range of stakeholders, routinely giving priority to employees and the planet. The first company to be certified B-Corp was King Arthur Flour in 2007,[46] and as of mid-2020, more than 3,400 companies from 150 industries and 71 countries were certified as B-Corps. The leaders of these companies use business—its resources and influence—to do good by solving social and environmental problems.[47]

Patagonia, the outdoor apparel company and long-time B-Corp, captures the essence of public benefit in its mission statement: "We're in the business to save our home planet. We aim to use the resources we have—our business, our investments, our voice, and our imaginations—to do something about it."[48]

Certified B-Corps pledge to follow a "declaration of interdependence" and accept and promote the following beliefs:

- We must be the change we seek in the world.
- All business ought to be conducted as if people and place mattered.
- Through their products, practices, and profits, businesses should aspire to do no harm and benefit all.
- To do so requires that we act with the understanding that we are each dependent upon another and thus responsible for each other and future generations.[49]

New Belgium Brewing Company, based in Fort Collins, Colorado, embraces its B-Corp status. The maker of Fat Tire Amber beer exhibits many notable practices that reflect its values, such as diverting 99.9 percent of its waste from landfills and routinely being rated as one of the best places to work. B-Corps are profit-driven too. New Belgium is the third-largest craft brewery in the United States.[50]

The Benefits of Being a B-Corporation

One reason for being a B-Corp is to increase an organization's competitive edge. By certifying as a B-Corp, an organization is explicitly stating that it values outcomes for more than just shareholders and that employees, communities, and the environment matter. Therefore, this can help differentiate an organization from its competitors and potentially increase its attractiveness to potential employees, customers, and investors.[51]

B-Corps also enjoy other benefits, such as

1. *Marketing*. B-Corp certification can be advertised and become part of a company's brand. Customers, investors, and other stakeholders expect a strong commitment to sustainability and the public good.
2. *Best practices*. B-Corps are a community, one that is open and interested in spreading ideas, experiences, and best practices with others. One organization can benefit from the successes and shared knowledge from others.
3. *Provides a stretch goal*. The certification process is very rigorous and includes a final score. This score then acts as a target to strive for and improve. Like other goals, it helps motivate leaders and employees of the organization, a gauge to measure their progress.
4. *Relieves typical shareholder pressures*. Most public companies experience considerable pressure to cut costs and allocate resources in ways that maximize stock prices. But investors in B-Corps expect a broader stakeholder view and thus are less likely to pressure organizational leaders to increase share prices at all costs.[52]

This sort of thinking turns conventional business wisdom on its head. For instance, Greyston's Bakery has a simple mission that illustrates this: "We don't hire people to bake brownies, we bake brownies to hire people."[53]

However, a common challenge for CRT, B-Corp, and other responsible and sustainable enterprises remains—how to appropriately value these nonfinancial priorities?

How Do We Value "Good"?

We all know that the world of business is quantitative and commonly assessed in financial terms: assets and liabilities, return on equity, market share, quality, and earnings per share. However, for all who believe that doing good is a legitimate, if not a required element of business, challenges remain for measuring this value. The concepts discussed in this chapter do not show up on financial statements that have motivated many, including the CRT, to go for new balance sheet constructs that capture these assets and liabilities.[54]

However, to date, a number of voluntary reporting mechanisms do exist and are quite widely used. For instance,

- Sustainability reports
- Triple bottom line (people, profits, and the planet)
- SDG scorecards
- Social, human, and natural capital protocols

Sustainability reports, for example, are widely used in the pharmaceutical industry. Novartis's ESG report for 2019 is seventy pages long! It includes content related to what the company labels strategic areas:

- Holding ourselves to the highest standards.
- Being part of the solution on pricing and access.
- Addressing global health challenges.
- Being a responsible citizen.[55]

The company also uses a number of performance indicators in each of these areas, and most are not reported in terms of dollars and cents. An example is the percentage of employees trained and certified on Novartis's code of conduct (98 percent), and the number of instances of expense fraud (nine).[56]

Erik Cox Photography/Shutterstock

Clif Bar has its own version that they call the All Aspirations Annual Report in which they measure and account for the performance related to the following "Five Bottom Lines":

1. Business
2. People
3. Planet
4. Brands
5. Community

This report also includes details related to other measures of doing well by doing good, such as the amount of organic ingredients sourced over time, percentage of waste diverted from landfills, and the company is the number one investor in organic food research in the United States. Clif also donates 1 percent of its sales to grassroots nonprofits, and its employees have done more than 150,000 hours of community service since 2001.[57]

Although useful, these are still far short of what is needed. Therefore, genuine opportunities exist for individuals, organizations, and industries that create, share, and embed effective means for measuring and otherwise capturing the value of (nonfinancial) performance linked to doing good.

Hopefully, you now are more convinced that doing good does not require doing less well. The right people, doing the right things, create organizations that can make true and far-reaching positive impacts. Read the end of chapter case, as it will put this claim and your knowledge to the test.

Chapter Summary

1. ESG matters are now the mainstream and common investment criteria. In fact, ESG investing has been one of the fastest growing and best performing areas of investing over the past several years.
2. ESG investing is but one illustration of how a growing number of companies are pursuing purpose beyond profits.
3. CC is an approach to business that is purpose-driven and serves a broader range of stakeholders beyond shareholders and owners. The premise of CC organization and leaders is that capitalism is a powerful tool for improving society.
4. Conscious cultures and leaders espouse and enact T.A.C.T.I.L.E. values—Trust, Accountability, Caring, Transparency, Integrity, Loyalty, and Egalitarianism.
5. Creating, communicating, modeling, and embedding a compelling purpose (mission), vision, and value are powerful tools for leaders of ESG, CC, or other purpose-driven organizations.
6. The CRT and its principles represent the foundation of moral capitalism, which is an attempt by business leaders for business leaders to create a common base for ethical businesses around the world. It also advocates a broad stakeholder approach, including environmental and social concerns.

7. B-Corps are organizations that have formally committed to using their businesses to generate public benefits, in addition to financial returns, and they seek to do this through a broad and interdependent group of stakeholders.

Key Terms

CASE STUDY: So Much Good, but How Much Well Are You Willing to Give?

Pharmaceutical companies are in the business of doing good, as their products improve or even save lives. However, they are not charities and must make a profit, that is, they must also do well to serve their shareholders, owners (for private companies), and raise funds for the development of additional drugs and benefit still more people. This puts pharmaceutical companies and their numerous stakeholders in a challenging position when apparent trade-offs need to be made between doing good (helping others) and doing well (making a profit).

Common and Critical Dilemma

This scenario becomes especially challenging when a company's product is the only option for a particular disease, and if its use dramatically improves serious conditions and/or saves lives. Such decisions are not easy, despite the fact that many drugs do just this; leaders need to choose between helping more people at the expense of potential profits. COVID-19 puts this to the test.

A notable example was Gilead's remdesivir, an existing drug that was found in early research to reduce hospital stays for severely ill COVID patients by four days; the same research showed no reduction in deaths due to its use. This was an early positive outcome in treating the disease and was viewed very positively by everyone. Then, however, the price was announced. Gilead said it would charge patients with private insurance approximately $3,100 for a course of treatment, $2,340 for those with government insurance in the United States and the same for patients in other countries with national health systems.[58]

It may be informative to consider Gilead's mission, vision, focus, and values.[59]

Mission. To advance therapeutics against life-threatening diseases worldwide.

Vision. To discover, develop, and commercialize innovative therapeutics in the areas of unmet medical needs that improve patient care.

Stakeholder focus. Our focus on advancing the care of patients through research and development efforts directly impacts our relationships with physicians, patients and their caregivers, and our employees.

Values: Integrity, inclusion, teamwork, accountability, and excellence.

Continued

Reactions

Reactions to the pricing details were mixed. Critics viewed the price as absurd and complained that Gilead was taking advantage of US citizens. Besides the actual price, they underscored the fact that nearly $100 million in taxpayer money, in the form of government subsidies, was used to develop the drug.[60]

Supporters of Gilead's pricing countered and argued that the pricing is fair, given that there is "no playbook for how to price a new drug during a pandemic."[61] Wall Street analysts claimed the price seemed in line with what they would expect. Still, other supporters pointed to the common practice of pricing drugs based on the cost savings in treatment without the drug, and in the case of someone suffering from COVID, remdesivir could save an estimated treatment cost of $40,000. The benefits are greater still if the drug makes a patient less infectious and enables them to go back to work sooner.[62]

More generally, one expert noted that "Gilead has the power to price remdesivir at will in the US, and no governmental or private insurer could even entertain the idea of walking away from the negotiating table." This means that the company has something that everyone else not only wants but also truly needs.[63] From a purely rational economic perspective, the company could charge whatever the market will pay, which would likely be much higher unless or until other alternatives are identified or developed.

Still, others had additional criticisms, specifically, they took the issue of how the drug was and would be distributed. Gilead initially did not send it where it was most needed, and this caused the Department of Health and Human Services to step in and take over responsibilities for distribution. But their role is scheduled to end in September 2020, and no clear plan has been shared related to how patients' needs will be factored in, and how the company will justify distributing and selling the product outside the United States when current estimates show demand at home will alone outstrip supply.[64]

Price Is a Signal

Price is more than just dollars and cents. Every other company with potential treatments, either existing drugs or those being developed, continues to watch the pricing of remdesivir and stakeholder reactions. Both provide insight regarding what they too can expect in terms of returns and resistance related to their own product. It is important to remember that remdesivir is just the first to show some measure of treatment efficacy, and if research ultimately shows it does not actually save lives, then the price will drop. Nevertheless, other companies will continue to calculate financial possibilities for their own products. The wrong signal could potentially discourage other companies from even trying to find a treatment or cure.

But remdesivir and Gilead are not the whole story. Other reports show that dozens of companies with existing drugs used in intensive care units, and to support critically ill patients, increased their prices shortly after the first COVID-19 case was confirmed in the United States. For instance, some products are used to sedate patients and manage blood clots and blood pressure, while others are commonly used for cancer and help mitigate some COVID-related symptoms. These, and other drugs, have experienced increased demand due to their use in COVID patients. This in turn creates a financial windfall for the companies that sell them.

Continued

For Discussion:

1. Describe your position regarding seeming trade-offs between helping more patients versus making larger profits. Assume you are taking the TV Test and explaining your position during an interview on the national news.
2. If you were the CEO of Gilead, what factors would you consider in making your pricing decisions? Explain.
3. If you were the CEO of Gilead, what factors would you consider in making distribution decisions? Explain.
4. Who would get priority? Justify.
5. Regarding the announced prices ($3,100 and $2,340), describe how these align or conflict with Gilead's mission, vision, focus, and values.
6. Given your answers to questions 1–4, analyze your decisions in terms of how they align or conflict with Gilead's mission, vision, focus, and values.
7. Now assume the role of the following stakeholders and describe your position:
   a. Shareholder
   b. Patient
   c. Employee
   d. Competitor also developing treatments and cures

Apply Three-Dimensional Problem Solving for Ethics (3D PSE)

You can apply the 3D PSE from multiple perspectives, such as that of the CEO of a pharmaceutical company (e.g., Daniel O'Day, CEO of Gilead) who is responsible for making pricing and distribution decisions, an investor, a competitor, a patient, or an employee. Be sure to specify whose perspective you would choose, as your problem-solving is likely to differ considerably depending on your choice. Let's try it with you assuming you are the CEO of Gilead.

figure **10.3**

Three-Dimensional Problem Solving for Ethics (3D PSE)

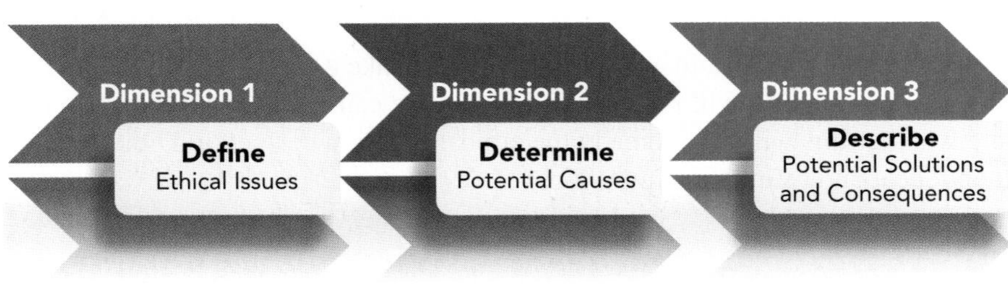

Dimension 1: *Define* the Ethical Challenge

What is the gap in the case? What do you have and what do *you* want?

a. From your view as CEO, what is the current situation with remdesivir, and how do you want it to be?
b. Why is the current situation a problem? What difficulties or undesirable reactions and outcomes have happened as a result of the problem you defined? What might happen because of the problem you defined? Why do you care about the problem you defined in Dimension 1?
c. Define your problem in one or at most two sentences and structure it in terms of what is current versus what is desired.
d. Who are the key stakeholders who affect or are affected by the problem you defined?

Dimension 2: *Determine* the Causes

a. **Individuals.** Given the problem you defined in Dimension 1, are there any characteristics of individuals that may be causes to the problem, such as ethical decision-making approach, work values, and moral principles?
b. **Contextual.** Are there particular norms (practices) that caused the problem, as defined in Dimension 1? These norms (practices) may be for the pharmaceutical industry, healthcare, or government.

Dimension 3: *Describe* Your Potential Solutions and the Intended and Unintended Consequences for Stakeholders

For each cause you identified in Dimension 2, answer the following questions:

a. ***What*** do you recommend and ***how*** would you make it happen?
b. ***Why*** would you do it? Does this reflect a particular ethical decision-making approach (e.g., utilitarian or deontology)? Does it reflect the characteristics of your organization?

If your responses to these questions are unsatisfactory, then go back to Dimension 1 and repeat the process. If, however, you are comfortable and confident in your problem-solving efforts thus far, then ensure you achieve the desired outcomes and avoid any unintended consequences.

c. What is the ***desired and likely effect in the short and long term*** for the key stakeholders involved in the problem and causes (Dimensions 1 and 2)?
d. What ***potential unintended consequences*** may occur with each proposed solution?
e. If any, what are the **implications for *other* stakeholders** (e.g., individuals, organizations, and communities) besides those noted in Dimensions 1 and 2?
f. Will your solution work in an ethical manner? Make a final assessment of whether your chosen solution will reduce or eliminate the causes determined in Dimension 2, and whether this will then remedy the ethical problem defined in Dimension 1. If not, then repeat and refine the dimensions.

Chapter Opener Photo Source: Vadim.Petrov/Shutterstock

PART 4

Global Business Ethics Issues

chapter **11**

A Global Perspective of Business Ethics

Learning Objectives

AFTER READING THIS CHAPTER, YOU SHOULD BE ABLE TO:

LO1 Analyze business ethics challenges when crossing national borders.

LO2 Describe the benefits and elements of a global code of conduct.

LO3 Identify and understand political risks when doing business internationally.

LO3 Articulate means by which ethical conduct is influenced on a global scale.

WHERE DO **YOU** STAND?

Not Good Enough for Me But Good Enough for You?

Global healthcare giant, Johnson and Johnson (J&J), decided to stop selling talc-based baby powder in the United States and Canada but continue to sell these versions in other countries. The decision was a response to nearly 20,000 lawsuits claiming that the product causes ovarian cancer, some of which have already awarded billions of dollars in settlements. The basis of the claims is that the talc is commonly contaminated with asbestos (a carcinogen), as both occur in nature and mix when extracted from the ground, something J&J has allegedly known for decades. J&J produces and sells a cornstarch-based alternative powder in the United States and abroad, and it argues that its actions in the United States are not based on scientific proof but instead due to the bad press associated with claims. J&J has always defended the safety of its products, including appealing legal decisions against it.[1]

This approach by J&J contrasts with what the company did in 1982, when it was learned that numerous bottles of their Tylenol product were tampered with, resulting in the poisoning deaths of seven people. J&J responded without hesitation and immediately recalled all Tylenol products from retailer's shelves. Their decisive action won tremendous goodwill for the company and served as a model for corporate crisis management ever since.[2]

For Discussion:

1. Assume you were the CEO before the decision was made, what would you have done? Explain.
2. Now assume you are Alex Gorsky, CEO of J&J, and a reporter sticks a microphone and camera in your face and asks: "If your product is detrimental for North Americans, isn't it also bad for people everywhere?" How would you respond?
3. Describe which stakeholders are potentially affected, and how, by this decision.
4. Assume you are the director of European Marketing for J&J, what do you tell your customers about the decision?
5. What do you tell your employees about the decision?

Introduction

This chapter is the beginning of Part 4 of the book, wherein we put individual and organizational level ethics in a global or societal context. Each level adds more complexity, which presents both additional business and ethics challenges (and opportunities). Even if you have no interest in taking an international job at this point in your career, whatever job you do take will be with an employer that, to one degree or another, operates in a global business context. The sooner and better you understand the key elements of international business, and the implications for ethics, the more valuable you will be to a range of employers. To help you effectively navigate these complex challenges, we will explore common challenges, cultural differences and their implications, political risk, and a number of ways in which businesses attempt to level the playing field, reduce uncertainty, and increase fairness and trust.

Business Ethics Challenges When Crossing National Borders

national culture
a system of shared values (defining what is important), norms (policies, practices, and behaviors), and artifacts (elements you see, hear, and touch) between citizens or a particular country

A good place to start our discussion in this section of the book is with culture. Like our discussion in chapters 1 and 8 about values and their role in (organizational) culture, national cultures are the same. To clarify, **national culture** is a system of shared values (defining what is important), norms (policies, practices, and behaviors), and artifacts (elements you see, hear, and touch) between citizens or a particular country.[3] National cultures also include deeply entrenched in laws (norms), languages (norms), religions (source of morals, values, norms, and artifacts), ethnic and racial identities (sources of values, norms, and artifacts), and history (can manifest as stories that are artifacts).[4]

Multinational Corporations (MNCs)

multinational corporations (MNCs)
those that have facilities or other assets in at least one country other than its home country

National culture issues apply most often to **multinational corporations (MNCs)**, which are those that have facilities or other assets in at least one country other than their home country.[5] MNCs are typically headquartered in developed countries, and advocates argue that their international operations often create jobs and increase the standard of living in those locations by providing goods, services, and other resources that otherwise would not be available. However, critics say that too often MNCs assert inappropriate political influence over the foreign governments and take advantage of the people and other local resources. In the United States, some MNCs involved in manufacturing have been condemned for offshoring jobs to foreign locations, resulting in reduced wages and jobs in their home countries.[6]

For our purposes, whether a given organization originated and only operates in one country, or its headquarters are in another, all organizations are influenced by the national country in which they operate, regardless of the origin of the company. The Ethics in Action box highlights the international successes and challenges experienced by McDonald's.

Ethics in Action

The Arches Are Golden in Most but Not in All Places

Although McDonald's is an American company based in Chicago, Illinois, it operates 34,000 restaurants in 118 countries and must effectively navigate all of these national cultures.[7] It has been masterful and adapting to cultural differences and innovating its offerings and processes. For instance:

- Fast service and low-priced menus were adopted in the 1960s to meet US workforce changes that included two working parents.
- Franchising to locals in each country it operates helps instill local knowledge and tastes into an otherwise American company.
- Healthy menu items—fruits and salads—helped match changing preferences around the world. Menu items meet local preferences and standards (e.g., the Tama and Tsukimi burgers offered in Japan).
- Serving sizes are smaller outside the United States.
- Chicken products sold in China are made of thighs instead of breasts to meet cultural preferences.
- Veggie burgers are sold in India to cater to the large proportion of vegetarians.[8]

This does not always go well, however, and multiple countries have banned the Golden Arches. Iran banned the company, beginning in 1979 when the country's revolution began along with the now long-lasting and intense political conflict with the United States. Another example was Bermuda in which foreign fast-food restaurants are banned.[9]

But the company has occasionally exploited loopholes only to eventually be shut down. The burger maker also does not operate in Bolivia, not because of legal restrictions, but instead due to a lack of interest and concerns about what it represents. A former Bolivian president once claimed that McDonald's is "not interested in the health of human beings, only in earnings and corporate profits."[10]

For Discussion:

1. Assume you were going to open a McDonald's in Australia, what are the three things you would do to help ensure your success? (You are encouraged to do additional research to inform your answer.)
2. Would these differ if you were going to open one in China? Seattle? (You are encouraged to do additional research to inform your answers.)
3. Explain the importance of national culture when deciding to do business in a country.
4. Assume you own a business. Are there any ethical norms you would not compromise regardless of the business potential? Explain.

Another example is Huawei, a Chinese company based in Shenzhen, Guangdong. It is the world's largest telecommunications supplier and the second largest cell phone manufacturer. Knowing this makes it no surprise to learn that it operates in nearly every country on the planet (170), and this alone suggests it has adapted extremely well to differing cultures.[11]

However, its situation has become more difficult in the recent past due to the US threatening to and then ultimately banning their 5G network equipment. Huawei's phones are scarce in the United States, but the fact that the government has campaigned to have its other products banned on the grounds of national security concerns has been far more damaging. The US government worries about the potential for the Chinese government to use Huawei's equipment to spy on or otherwise intrude into their countries. Huawei's troubles were compounded when the United States convinced the UK to follow suit, and it ordered all Huawei equipment to be removed from its 5G infrastructure in the next several years.[12]

The success of both companies is truly incredible, but both have and continue to have challenges in many places they do business. Two valuable considerations for understanding and managing such differences are national culture dimensions and ethical relativism.

Global Business Values

As with the individual and organizational levels, business values also exist at the country level. Researchers identified business values for working people across twenty-six countries.[13] Like values at other levels, these values are important because they are the fundamental causes of (un)ethical behavior within and especially between countries. The same researchers found that thirty-four values fit into five value categories or dimensions, which are shown and explained in Table 11.1.

Again, as with the individual and organizational levels of business ethics, culture also exists at the country level and is discussed in the following section.

National Culture Framework

The most widely used means for describing and differentiating national cultures were developed by Gert Hofstede, a Dutch social psychologist. His work was motivated by a desire to determine the necessary foundations for society to function effectively. Two dimensions of his framework are especially relevant for our purposes—individualism–collectivism and

table **11.1**

Global Business Values

Underlying Value Dimension	Example Values	Description
Ethical achievement	Responsible, honest, and loyal	Succeed by proper means
Power	Control over others, authority, material wealth, influential, and recognition	Acquire personal control, status, and recognition from others
Other-oriented	Humble, forgiving, accepting of one's situation, self-discipline, privacy, and helpful	Focus on others, follow rules, and maintain harmonious relationships
Globally responsible innovation	Challenge, curiosity, creativity, harmony with nature, and freedom	Desire to innovate while respecting the environment
Universal order	National security, social order, peace, family security, and politeness	Desire for peaceful coexistence with others

Source: Adapted from D. A. Ralston, C. J. Russell, and C. P. Egri, "Business Values Dimensions: A Cross-Culturally Developed Measure of Workforce Values," *International Business Review*, 27 (2018): 1189–99.

power distance. It is important to note these dimensions are relative, meaning that they are useful for comparing countries.

Individualism and Collectivism. **Individualistic cultures** are those in which individuals are expected to make choices and decisions for themselves.[14] Freethinking and independent action are common and accepted. **Collectivistic cultures** are characterized by people knowing and accepting their place within society.[15] Public confrontations are less likely, for instance. The implications of these national culture dimensions for business ethics can be great in both good and bad ways.

individualistic cultures those in which individuals are expected to make choices and decisions for themselves

Greater independence may enable you and other employees to be more innovative and accommodating for a variety of stakeholders. This would presumably be positive, unless or until you cross the line and "do whatever it takes" and serve your own goals or interests. Employees in collectivist cultures would be less likely to assert such autonomy and take the associated risks, as they would tend to value harmony throughout the larger relationship (employees, employer, and customer) and fear their actions may cause any problems. Put more simply, individual achievement and recognition are valued by one culture, while group membership and group accomplishments by the other.[16]

collectivistic cultures characterized by people knowing and accepting their place within society

Table 11.2 illustrates how a number of countries compare in terms of Hofstede's national culture framework.

Power Distance. **Power distance** describes the accepted degree of inequality between superiors and subordinates, and these differences apply in all areas of life (work, family, and social). High power distance is reflected in respect for seniority, authority, age, hierarchy, titles, and status. The United States is a relatively low power distance country compared to France, for instance. Americans are also more likely to address their bosses informally (e.g., by their first names) than would employees in Japan.[17]

power distance the accepted degree of inequality between superiors and subordinates

However, it is important to realize that particular managers and companies can be relatively more or less in terms of power distance. Your first manager in your first job out of college may have expected people to address him or her formally and consult him or her on every decision. This may contrast with your second manager who prefers to go by his or her first name and gives you considerable freedom on how you do your work.

In terms of business ethics, higher power distance cultures are less likely to encourage or tolerate employees speaking out about misconduct of both peers and supervisors. Employees

table 11.2

National Cultures in Terms of Individualism and Power Distance

Country	Individualism	Power Distance
Australia	High	Low
China	Low	High
France	High	High
Germany	High	Low
India	Medium	High
Japan	Medium	Low
Mexico	Medium	High
UK	High	Low
USA	High	Low

Source: Adapted from G. Hofstede, "*Culture's consequences: Comparing values, behaviors and institutions across nations,*" 2nd ed. (Thousand Oaks: Sage, 2001).

are likely to feel that it is their manager's job to know and act on the misconduct of one of their peers, and likewise, it is their manager's superior who is responsible for his or her unethical conduct. Conversely, in low power distance cultures, employees are more likely to hold leaders accountable for their (mis)conduct.[18]

Ethical Relativism

ethical relativism
how expectations and behaviors regarding right and wrong differ and are consequential depending on the cultural context

Whose values and norms should you follow? Should you always follow those that are local, where the business is being done (e.g., the sale, the negotiation, the hiring)? Should you follow those from the company's home country? Your home country? This can be quite complex, challenging, and consequential. As you learned in chapter 2, a relativistic approach to ethical decision making is the one in which you follow the expectations in the immediate context. **Ethical relativism** describes how expectations and behaviors regarding right and wrong differ and are consequential depending on the cultural context.

Recall again the expression, "When in Rome, do as the Romans do" is an example of relativism. At one extreme, pure relativists would argue that all ethical conduct is local, which means that whatever is ethically acceptable in your current country is right. At the other extreme is the ethical imperialist who believes that one set of enduring standards is applicable at all times in all contexts.

You can likely see how both extremes are quite problematic. For instance, execution still occurs in dozens of countries in the world with China, Iran, Saudi Arabia, Iraq, and Pakistan being responsible for the most.[19] However, both the offenses that are punishable by death and how executions are performed differ greatly. Although the United States is among the countries with a death penalty, it is highly unlikely for you to be involved in or responsible for a work colleague's execution. However, stealing, including at work, can have such dramatic consequences in certain places.

Tomas Stehlik/Shutterstock

Similarly, many cultures view gifts quite differently. The United States often views giving gifts at work as a potential conflict of interest. In contrast, some Asian cultures (e.g., China and Japan) view gifts as an important part of social and business etiquette.[20]

Business success at all levels—individual, organizational, country, and the international community—depends on understanding cultural differences and dealing with them effectively. Awareness is the first step in understanding and dealing with such differences. Organizational awareness begins with individual employee awareness, which is the focus of the following Ethics in Action box.

Ethics in Action

Raise *Your* Awareness to Make Your Employer More Aware

The following suggestions can help you increase your personal cultural awareness, which in turn will increase that of your employer, business partners, and coworkers from other countries.[21]

1. *More than ethnicity and race*. Language, food, and skin color all differ, but to be culturally aware, you need to consider more. Learning about dynamics

between employees, supervisors, and customers can tell you volumes about cultural differences and how they might impact business ethics.

2. *Ask questions*. Asking not only provides you with valuable information, but it also shows others you're interested. For business ethics, ask the following questions: What are the most common ethical issues? How are they dealt with?
3. *Plug-in.* Get involved, even if it is just participating informally and sporadically in meals, religious events or practices, holidays, sporting and social events, and business meetings or organizations. You will see and interact with people in different contexts and learn what is "normal."
4. *Nonverbals can be loud.* Body language and the way people interact, besides their words, can tell you many things such as how gender is viewed, senior versus junior, offices (large vs. small and location), and personal items in one's workspace. Do they have many plaques, trophies, certificates, awards, or items related to nonwork interests and people (e.g., sports and family) displayed?
5. *Give to get*. Tell a story to get a story. Share something about yourself and your work experiences that you would like to know about the other. If they don't immediately tell you a story in return, then simply ask, "What about you? Tell me about how this has happened to you, or how this happens where you work."

For Discussion:

1. Consider either your current job (if you have one) or a job you hope to have in the future. Then, also consider your employer has invited an employee from its office in Shanghai, China, to visit for a month. You are responsible for building that person's cultural awareness of the United States. Describe three things that you would do. (Your boss thinks this is very important.)
2. Describe how increasing your personal ethical awareness could help your career, even if you spend all of it working in your home country.

Turning back to the question, "which is correct, following local ethical norms or those of your home country?" What is the correct answer? There isn't one, but there is a way or a process to help guide your actions, those of your coworkers, and the overall organization. It is a global code of conduct.

Global Code of Conduct

Like codes of conduct and ethics you learned about in chapter 9, multinational companies and industries can reap similar benefits from a **global code of conduct**—a set of guidelines for business practice that establish ethical standards for business and employee conduct.[22] This sounds simple enough, but like everything else related to business ethics, the details matter.

global code of conduct
a set of guidelines for business practice that establish ethical standards for business and employee conduct

Motivations for Global Codes

The reasons for the growing interest and use of global codes of conduct are in part a reaction to environmental and human rights activists, who in recent years have become more effective in protesting about how international companies sometimes take advantage of less stringent regulations in other countries. Another reason is related to the Federal Sentencing

Guidelines you learned in Chapter 9, and if you recall, companies that create, implement, and monitor such codes receive more favorable outcomes when bad things do happen (reduced sanctions).

Still other organizations create and use global codes as aspirational goals, that is, ideals to strive for in their attempts to continuously improve and better serve their stakeholders. This

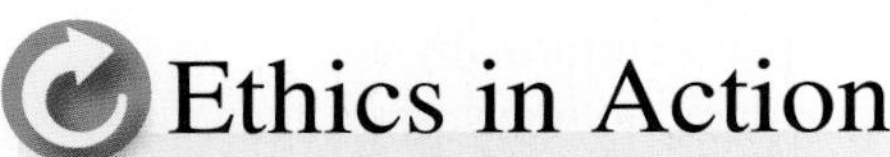

EY Global Code of Conduct

EY is a global professional services (e.g., accounting and consulting) firm employing 280,000 people in 700 offices in 150 countries.[23] It builds its global code using the organization's purpose, values, and ambition.

Purpose: Building a better working world. EY is committed to doing its part in building a better working world. We develop outstanding leaders and teams who create long-term value for all stakeholders, which leads to sustainable growth.

Our values: Who we are. We are people who demonstrate integrity, respect, and teaming; people with energy, enthusiasm, and the courage to lead; and people who build relationships based on doing the right things.

Our ambition. Our ambition was to create long-term value as the world's most trusted, distinctive professional services organization. We create client value, people value, social value, and financial value.

The code helps to guide our behavior, but it is not possible to cover every situation you might encounter. It is intended to help you think about how we live our values in both decision making and our behaviors. We always abide by laws and regulations and our own policies, guidance, and procedures.

If you are unsure of the right course of action, or are faced with a difficult issue, asking yourself the following questions may help you determine the appropriate way to act.[24]

1. Have I consulted appropriately with my colleagues?
2. Are my actions legal and in compliance with the standards of our profession?
3. Am I compromising my integrity or the integrity of EY or EY clients?
4. Am I upholding the values of EY?
5. Am I treating others the way I expect others to treat me?
6. Is my choice of action the most ethical among the possible alternatives? Do I feel good about my choice?
7. If I document my decision, would a reviewer agree with the action I have taken?
8. Would my actions damage the reputation of EY?

If you do not understand the principles contained within the code, or are not sure how to apply them, you should consult with an appropriately qualified colleague to get your questions answered.

For Discussion:

1. Identify four stakeholders this code addresses.
2. Describe three ways this code would help you do your job as a junior consultant at EY.
3. Assume you are interviewing with EY and read the code as part of your preparation. What about the code that would make EY more attractive to you as a potential employer?

Ethics in Action box presents such an example and explains how EY weaves the organization's purpose, values, and stakeholder approach into its code.

Global Codes for Industries

Industries such as banking, mining, and apparel also create and utilize global codes. The reasons parallel those of individual organizations and aim to protect the reputations of the industry members. The rationale is that one bad actor can harm all members of the industry. The other reason industries create codes is to level the playing field for members, meaning that if they all comply, then no member has an unfair advantage of cutting corners and not spending the necessary resources to comply. The banking industry has such a code.

Voluntarily, 105 financial institutions in thirty-eight countries have agreed to follow the **Equator Principles**, which act as guidelines for determining, assessing, and managing the environmental and social risks of projects they finance in countries around the world.[25] Among the goals are to ensure that money is lent responsibly, which means clients need to ensure they will use the money in accordance with agreed-upon ethical, environmental, and social standards, regardless of what the project actually involves (e.g., infrastructure, manufacturing, or agriculture). The ten principles are as follows:

Equator Principles guidelines for determining, assessing, and managing the environmental and social risks of projects they finance in countries around the world

1. Review and categorization
2. Environmental and social assessment
3. Applicable and environmental social standards
4. Environmental and social management system and Equator Principles Action Plan
5. Stakeholder engagement
6. Grievance mechanism
7. Independent review
8. Covenants
9. Independent monitoring and reporting
10. Reporting and transparency[26]

Many of the principles in the list reflect those you've learned about in previous chapters. Also, note the role of independent monitoring and reporting. This has become a fundamental element of business ethics more generally. The idea is that if an organization or industry is going to promote its social responsibility and environmental sustainability to various stakeholders (customers, suppliers, regulators, and employees), then it lends more credibility if they allow independent (outsiders) and qualified monitors to do their own assessment and reporting.

Next, we explore a challenge that confronts most organizations working in multiple countries—political risk.

Political Risk

Business and ethics do not happen in a vacuum. Crossing borders increases uncertainty, which increases risk for businesses and creates ethical challenges. One of the key drivers of uncertainty is **national politics**—the processes related to how people and resources are governed. Numerous aspects of national politics can and do influence business and ethics. Below we address a few.

national politics the processes related to how people and resources are governed

Political Stability and Business Transparency

For business purposes, countries are often described and evaluated in terms of their relative **political stability**, meaning that when change occurs it is orderly, predictable, lawful, and fair, and corruption, terrorism, and conflicts with other countries are rare[27] For instance, The World Bank ranked Monaco as the most stable of 195 countries and Yemen

political stability when change occurs it is orderly, predictable, lawful, and fair, and corruption, terrorism, and conflicts with other countries are rare

cristiano barni/Shutterstock

the least. For comparison, the United States was number sixty-nine, Jamaica was number sixty-eight, and Chile number seventy.[28]

Monaco is one of the smallest countries in the world (less than one square mile) and is ruled by a stable constitutional monarch, currently Prince Albert, whose father was in power for most of the 1900s. It is a tourist haven, given its beauty and location on the Mediterranean, along with gamblers who visit the legendary Monte-Carlo Casino and the Monaco Grand Prix. However, it is the country's banking system with a high priority on client privacy that is foundational to its economy. This characteristic, along with no income tax, has attracted many wealthy residents.[29]

In contrast, Yemen is an extremely poor country ravaged by a civil war waged along religious lines. Corruption, food shortages, and unemployment have been both causes and effects of the war. Different authoritarian leaders have struggled, often violently, for control over a number of years. These conflicts involve other Middle Eastern neighbors who have chosen sides in the war and increased its intensity and duration. The situation is truly dire for citizens, as it is estimated that nearly 80 percent need assistance and protection. The complete chaos deters foreign investment and has destroyed its domestic economy.[30]

business transparency open business and government practices, well-distributed political power, high levels of trustworthiness, and low levels of perceived corruption

Countries are also evaluated in terms of their **business transparency**—those with high levels are characterized by open business and government practices, well-distributed political power, high levels of trustworthiness, and low levels of perceived corruption.[31] The top five most transparent countries in 2020 are

1. Canada
2. Norway
3. Denmark
4. Sweden
5. Switzerland

Four of these countries are in northern Europe, relatively affluent, have high taxes, and are considered quite egalitarian (classless). Some experts underscore the relationship between equality and a lack of corruption, suggesting that as equality increased corruption decreases, and vice versa.

For Discussion

1. Assume you are the founder of a successful business based in the United States, and now you want to expand internationally. What are the challenges in choosing one of the five most transparent countries?
2. Why might you choose to expand into a less rather than a more politically stable country?

Both characteristics can reduce uncertainty for MNCs and other organizations. Next, you'll learn about the role of taxes, currency value, and regulations, all of which can influence business ethics in significant ways.

Taxes and Currency Value

Just like the other financial costs discussed in this chapter (e.g. subsidies and tariffs), taxes can dramatically affect the profitability of a business. On average, corporate taxes around the world have declined dramatically since the 1980s when they were more than 40 percent versus 24 percent now. European countries tend to be the lowest in the developed world, and African countries tend to be the highest. The United States is approximately 25 percent as of 2019, far lower than the 35 percent prior to 2017, and the United Arab Emirates is the highest (55 percent), while the lowest is Barbados (5.5 percent).[32]

For the purpose of business ethics, high taxes discourage investment from outsiders, which means that high taxes make it more difficult for developing countries to attract financial assistance from other countries. The governments of some countries, notably Ireland (12.5 percent) and Hungary (9 percent), have strategically lowered taxes to attract foreign investment, which increases jobs and in turn raises the standard of living for a country's citizens.[33]

Similar strains and advantages can be caused by the value of a country's currency. China, along with many other countries, actively manages the value of its currency (the renminbi) to keep it lower than the US dollar, which in turn makes Chinese products cheaper in the United States and other international markets. However, this is a double-edged sword, meaning that by keeping the value of its currency low, Chinese citizens need to spend more to purchase goods within the country. This scenario caused the United States and other countries to accuse the Chinese of manipulating its currency to unfairly advantage its exports to other countries. The opposite is also true. That is, when a country's currency is strong, its citizens and companies can purchase more in international markets, but its products are also more expensive for customers in those same countries.[34]

Put simply and more generally, if a country keeps the value of its currency cheap compared to those of its major trading partners, then the products it sells are cheaper and more competitive in international markets but more expensive at home. As a result, companies need to carefully consider the value and stability of a country's currency when exploring business opportunities.

Regulations and Compliance

Although the laws, regulations, and their enforcement have obvious differences between countries, their importance cannot be overstated. For instance, China has been the most prized target for foreign expansion plans of many companies. However, the lack of protection for intellectual property has made doing business there quite challenging. It has been necessary for foreign companies across industries to partner with Chinese companies, not

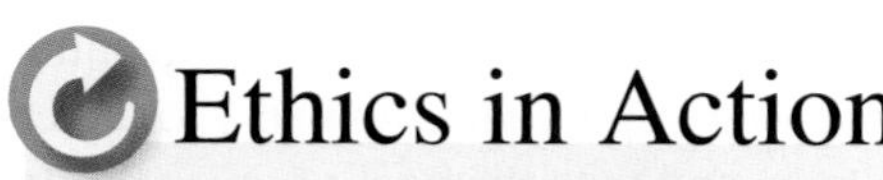

The Plight of Hong Kong[35]

Hong Kong has been a semiautonomous territory of China for decades and was a major source of fuel for China's economic engine in the past; in the 1990s, it contributed nearly 30 percent of its economic output. Hong Kong also became a major financial center for Asia and served as a vital conduit for trade between the East and West. It has historically been socially stable, more democratic, and predictably governed than China, and it possesses a mature and open financial system and one of the world's largest ports.

Continued

Although Hong Kong has been allowed freedom, including a separate legal system, not available to those on the mainland, all was not well. Political unrest reached a boil in 2019 and 2020 in Hong Kong, when millions of citizens protested in the streets wanting greater democratic freedom. The unrest was so intense and prolonged that business ground to a halt, and then COVID-19 made matters worse. But something else potentially made a bigger impact—a change in regulations.

In mid-2020, the Chinese government created and implemented a new national security law to crush dissent and eliminate protests. Citizens can now be arrested and jailed for protesting, or even speaking out, against the Chinese government. This move created tremendous stress for not only Chinese citizens but also companies doing business there, as the new regulations effectively abolished a prior agreement that was to last for fifty years.

More than 1,300 US companies operate in Hong Kong, and the vast majority said they are concerned about the future. Among these concerns is that the changes violate a major trade agreement between Hong Kong and the United States in place since 1992. Now, visas could be revoked, tariffs imposed, property seized, and employees jailed. All of this makes business there far riskier, and many companies are considering vacating offices, bringing employees back home, and closing business. For instance, tech companies, such as Microsoft, Twitter, and Zoom, are particularly concerned that their users' data and intellectual property could be seized under the new regulations.[36]

For Discussion:

1. Assume you are an employee working in Hong Kong for a US company. What would be your two greatest concerns?
2. Assume you are in charge of the Hong Kong office of a foreign bank. What would you do in reaction to the new laws? For instance, what might you do to mitigate employee concerns and customer concerns?

only to gain access to the markets for their products, but also to share their intellectual property and other proprietary information (e.g., manufacturing processes) with these partners. The Ethics in Action box illustrates how China's new national security laws implemented in Hong Kong have dramatically affected business and ethics.

To summarize, political risks are varied, numerous, and potentially highly consequential. Therefore, it is critically important for you, other employees, and your employers to understand and manage them effectively. A common challenge and thus the goal of cross-border business ethics is fairness, that is, how to ensure that the playing field is level for all participants. This is the next topic that we explore.

Leveling the Ethics Playing Field

Cooperation is a fundamental requirement for ethical business conduct at the international or global level, and like individuals, fairness and trust are the essential elements of cooperation between countries. To make the point, how cooperative are you when you feel you're being treated unfairly? How cooperative are you with someone you don't trust? It thus makes sense that key means for facilitating cooperation between countries are also those that ensure fairness and build trust. We explore some of these in the following sections.

Competition Between Countries

When thinking about international trade, many students find it helpful to think of countries like companies in a single industry, for instance, automobiles. Each company in the auto industry wants to compete effectively, which means producing products that are attractive and affordably priced for domestic and foreign customers. Accordingly, each auto company invests its resources (e.g., money and talent) in products it thinks will be competitive (attractive and affordable) today as well as products that will be competitive in the future. For example, many traditional auto companies continue to invest substantial resources into electric and other alternative fuel vehicles that are not that profitable today but are expected to be very profitable in the future.

Subsidies. Countries do the same thing. Each country, particularly those with developed economies and resources to invest, want their products to be competitive with those of other countries, which means both attractive and affordable. Moreover, just like auto companies, countries make investments in industries and their products to increase their competitiveness. Many countries do this, and some of the common financial tools are subsidies and tariffs. **Subsidies** are monetary investments, typically cash grants or tax breaks, made by the government to lower the costs of doing business and increasing competitiveness for particular industries and their associated products.[37]

subsidies
monetary investments, typically cash grants or tax breaks, made by the government to lower the costs of doing business and increasing competitiveness for particular industries and their associated products

The US government has and continues to subsidize many industries. For instance, companies in the energy industry receive cash grants or loans at very favorable rates to develop renewable energy sources and federal land has been leased or sold at low prices for oil production.[41]

lightrain/Shutterstock

The Chinese government also subsidizes many industries, and they have invested heavily in solar power. Their investments in nearly 4,000 centralized projects (those that serve cities, not single homes) across the country have greatly expanded the availability, lowered the costs, and thus increased the usage domestically.[42] Perhaps more impressive, however, is that China is the world leader using more than 50 percent of solar energy produced on the planet. China has dominated solar manufacturing since 2007, supported by approximately $50 billion in loans and subsidies.[43] The Chinese government sees solar energy as a critical source of energy today and as an opportunity in the future, and they have invested their resources accordingly.

Tariffs. **Tariffs** are taxes applied to foreign products to make them more expensive to local customers, which in turn enables domestic competitors to charge higher prices.[44]

tariffs
taxes applied to foreign products to make them more expensive to local customers, which in turn enables domestic competitors to charge higher prices

When viewing countries as companies trying to compete, business ethics issues may not be the first thing that comes to mind. However, if you give it just a bit more thought, you're likely to realize that such competition can be unfair with devastating effects. If the government of a relatively wealthy country, for instance, decides to invest in a particular industry, then it could easily make products from its companies cheaper, if not also better, than those from less-affluent countries.

This means that the rich would get richer and the poor would get poorer. At the extreme, such practices can decimate or even eliminate entire industries in certain countries. One way in which such troubles play out is with **dumping**, which occurs when a country sells products at a price that is unfairly low, such that others cannot compete.[45] To clarify, it is generally acceptable for companies or even countries to sell products at a loss, but the ethical line is crossed when prices are intended to damage or eliminate a competitor.[46]

dumping
when a country sells products at a price that is unfairly low, such that others cannot compete

For instance, Australia has battled with China over steel prices for many years. They argue that China subsidizes its steel industry to such a degree that China can then sell steel to Australia at prices lower than that of its own steel companies. This case is easy for Australians to support, given the country is a primary supplier of iron ore to China, from which it makes the steel it then sells back to them.[47] The Australian government retaliated with tariffs on Chinese imports and products, which the Chinese then retaliated back by hiking tariffs on Australian barley by more than 80 percent.[48]

These types of abuses often intensify and escalate, resulting in trade wars, wherein countries engage in continuing exchanges of financial punishments (subsidies and tariffs). Therefore, remedies are needed to facilitate fair and effective trading between countries, which is exactly the purpose of the WTO.

Ethics in Action

Larger Subsidies Create Cheaper Prices, But What about Competition?

Export subsidies are common in agriculture trade around the globe. Put simply, countries would pay farmers directly or guarantee them prices for their products (e.g., beef, rice, cereal, and pork), effectively lowering the cost of production for each farmer and allowing them to sell their products at a lower price on the global market. Lower prices make the products more competitive with products from other countries.[38]

In the short term, lower prices benefit consumers in poor or developing countries. However, in the longer term, the artificially lowered prices make it difficult, or impossible, for these same countries to sell their products, as their governments cannot afford to subsidize their farmers' products. Producers in disadvantaged countries would cut corners to reduce costs in efforts to compete. For instance, chicken farmers in Africa would "skip" investing in clean processes, hygiene throughout the supply chain, and proper refrigeration to lower product costs and more closely align with prices of imported chickens. This essentially undermined any efforts to develop a domestic chicken industry for these countries.[39]

Agricultural export subsidies were abolished by the World Trade Organization (WTO) in 2015.[40]

For Discussion:

1. Besides subsidized farmers, which stakeholders do you think were harmed by the elimination of agricultural subsidies?
2. Besides domestic farmers (those in poor or developing countries), which stakeholders do you think were benefited?
3. Think of an agricultural product you could justify subsidizing today. Explain.
4. Beyond agriculture, what product you might subsidize in similar ways. Why?

World Trade Organization (WTO)

World Trade Organization (WTO) the only international organization that creates and governs rules of trade to ensure smooth, predictable, and free trade between countries

The **World Trade Organization (WTO)** is the only international organization that creates and governs rules of trade to ensure smooth, predictable, and free trade between countries. It was established in 1995 and comprises more than 160 countries. It is responsible for both creating and enforcing policies, and these actions are guided by a few important principles:[49]

- *Nondiscriminatory.* Member countries agree not to disadvantage products or services offered by other countries or inappropriately favor those from their own. For instance,

China has long been criticized for blocking or impeding foreign competition in many industries, including automobiles and technology, thus giving an unfair advantage to its domestic companies.

- *Minimizing barriers*. Duties and tariffs are effectively taxes on imported products or services, and they can act as significant obstacles to free trade by raising the prices of foreign goods. Many countries also use import quotas to limit competition from foreign competitors.
- *Transparency and predictability*. Returning to the questions regarding the importance of trust and fairness in cooperation, international trade requires predictability. Trading partners need to be able to count on being treated fairly. Furthermore, investors of all sorts dislike uncertainty, and the WTO helps ensure transparency, which lowers uncertainty.
- *Fairness*. History, and still today, is littered with examples of unfair practices, such as those pertaining to export subsidies. The previous Ethics in Action box describes a historical example.
- *Environmental protection*. In addition to the environment, the WTO addresses and supports efforts to protect public health and plant and animal health. It also attempts to ensure that environmental policies are applied equally and fairly to both domestic and foreign companies, which is an attempt to guard against using such policies to unfairly advantage one over another.

The United Nations (UN) plays many roles on the international stage, and one of them is to help ensure sustainable business practices.

United Nations Global Compact (UNGC)

The **United Nations Global Compact (UNGC)** is a call to companies to voluntarily align strategies and operations with universal sustainability principles related to the environment, labor, anti-corruption, and human rights around the world.[51] The UNGC was launched in 1999 and is based on ten principles listed in Table 11.3:

United Nations Global Compact (UNGC) a call to companies to voluntarily align strategies and operations with universal sustainability principles related to the environment, labor, anti-corruption, and human rights around the world

table 11.3

Targets and Principles of the United Nations Global Compact

Human rights
Principle 1: Businesses will support, respect, and protect international human rights
Principle 2: Businesses will ensure that they are not complicit in human rights abuses
Labor
Principle 3: Businesses will uphold the freedom to associate and recognize the right to collective bargaining
Principle 4: Businesses will eliminate all forms of forced labor
Principle 5: Businesses will abolish child labor
Principle 6: Businesses will eliminate employment and occupation discrimination
Environment
Principle 7: Businesses will support environmental protections
Principle 8: Businesses will engage in and promote greater environmental responsibility
Principle 9: Businesses will encourage the development and distribution of environmentally friendly technologies
Anti-corruption
Principle 10: Businesses will work against corruption in all its forms, including extortion and bribery

Source: Adapted from United Nations Global Compact Website, https://www.unglobalcompact.org/what-is-gc/mission/principles.

To assist in communicating and bringing these principles to life, the UNGC created a mission and vision.

Mission and Vision of UNGC. As you learned in chapter 9, an organization's mission describes why it exists, and the vision is what that mission will look like if realized. The UNGC's mission is to mobilize a global movement of sustainable companies and stakeholders to create the world we want.[52] To realize this mission, its vision has two main elements:

1. Do business responsibly by aligning strategies and operations with ten principles related to human rights, labor, environment, and anti-corruption (see Table 11.3).
2. Take actions to advance broad societal goals, such as the UN Sustainable Development Goals (SDGs) via innovation and collaboration.[53]

UN Sustainable Develpment Goals (SDGs)
seventeen diverse initiatives created by the United Nations and intended to unite global stakeholders to end extreme poverty, fight inequality and injustice, and protect the planet

You can see that the UNGC is a global effort to guide and set standards for sustainable and ethical business practices. It has enjoyed broad support with more than 9,500 companies from more than 160 countries committing to participate and pursue its **UN Sustainable Development Goals (SDGs)**, focusing on seventeen diverse initiatives intended to unite global stakeholders to end extreme poverty, fight inequality and injustice, and protect the planet.[54] The initiatives aimed at achieving these goals are illustrated in Figure 11.1.

figure **11.1**

United Nations Global Compact Sustainable Development Goals.

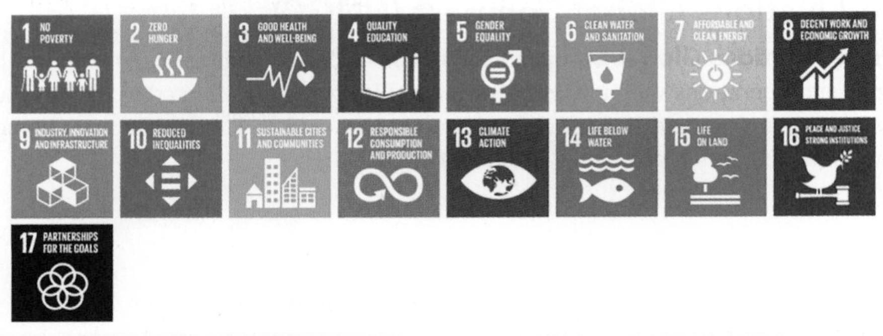

Source: United Nations Global Compact Website, downloaded July 8, 2020: https://www.unglobalcompact.org/sdgs/17-global-goals.

SDG Pioneers. Each year the UNGC identifies SDG pioneers or leaders who have done an exceptional job of translating the SDGs into their local businesses and thereby championing sustainability. In 2019, ten pioneers 35 years old and younger were recognized. For example, Mashook Mujib Chowdhury is a manager of sustainability at the DBL Group in Bangladesh, one of the country's largest textile and clothing companies. He is working to empower women in numerous ways such as helping them improve their personal hygiene and health, develop careers, and send their kids to school. In the process, these efforts address multiple SDGs and foster healthier, happier, and more productive workers for his company. Chowdhury and his company routinely collaborate with nongovernmental organizations and other UNGC member companies to share and implement best practices.[55]

Regan Leahy, who lives in the UK, was also recognized as a pioneer. As assistant manager of the citizenship team at Hogan Lovells, a global law firm, Regan created an online game called "The World We Want" to educate her colleagues about the SDGs, and she has created a similarly focused program for the firm's clients. Through her efforts, she aims to educate and show people how to work toward the SDGs in the contexts of their jobs and businesses.

Her efforts have made an impact. Forty percent of her colleagues who have played the game now say the firm should integrate the SDGs into its strategies and operations.[56]

Now that you have read this chapter, hopefully, you not only understand the complexities of business ethics at the international level, but that you also are more confident in managing these complexities. You will have the opportunity to test and apply your new knowledge in the three-dimensional problem-solving case at the end of the chapter. Your reading and problem solving in this chapter will prepare you well for chapter 12, wherein we'll address some of the key environmental issues confronting businesses and countries around the globe.

Chapter Summary

1. Business ethics become much more complicated when operating in multiple countries due to differences in national cultural values and ethical norms.
2. Power distance and collectivism are two particularly helpful ways to understand and navigate cultural differences.
3. Many organizations create global codes of conduct to help guide practices, behaviors, and decision making when operating in multiple countries. These codes assist in maintaining an organization's values, while at the same time appropriately considering local norms.
4. Political risk, including laws, regulations, and their enforcement are important considerations for business ethics. Besides the potential negative financial consequences, all of these can increase uncertainty, and legal problems for organizations and their employees.
5. Fair competition between companies and countries is often affected and managed using subsidies, tariffs, and the WTO.
6. The UNGC is an attempt to establish a set of common ethical principles between countries and companies related to human rights, labor practices, the environment, and anti-corruption.

Key Terms

business transparency 226
collectivistic cultures 221
dumping 229
ethical relativism 222
Equator Principles 225
global code of conduct 223
individualistic cultures 221
multinational corporations (MNCs) 218
national culture 218
national politics 225
political stability 225
power distance 221
subsidies 229
tariffs 229
UN Global Compact (UNGC) 231
UN Sustainable Development Goals (SDGs) 232
World Trade Organization (WTO) 230

CASE STUDY: You Help Us, You Help You

Cutting costs is a fundamental way to boost profits. Many cost savings are found in supply chains (those involved in the production and delivery of products), and a primary means for cutting supply chain costs is to shift manufacturing to less-expensive producers. For the past twenty years, China has been the most common destination for low-cost production. To put this in perspective, China joined the WTO in 2001, and by 2010, it surpassed the United States as the global manufacturing leader. In 2003, it accounted for more than 4 percent of the global gross domestic product, a general measure of the world economy, and by 2020, it accounted for more than 16 percent—a fourfold increase![57]

Continued

Another opportunity to save costs is to reduce inventory. Before China stepped onto the global stage, companies had been using just-in-time or on-demand inventory systems, which required them to keep a minimal amount of components or completed products on hand (e.g., only fifteen to thirty days' worth),[58] as efficient suppliers could replenish stocks quickly and reliably. Chinese suppliers developed these capabilities too. And when companies around the world shifted manufacturing to China, it meant they have fewer supplies and less inventory in their own countries.

Purposeful and Strategic Growth

This did not happen accidentally. For instance, the US government facilitated these practices and companies eagerly participated, after all, lower costs and higher profits can be intoxicating for business leaders.

For their part, Chinese leaders, notably in government, made it a priority to develop these capabilities and industry dominance in key medical supplies, like personal protective equipment (PPE). Handsome subsidies were, and continue to be provided to companies in these industries. Rules were also imposed, requiring hospitals and others across the country to purchase from local or regional suppliers. Combined, these efforts enabled a number of companies to grow and remain profitable over time. In addition, once the pandemic hit, the Chinese government doubled down and dramatically and immediately expanded production capacity for the same products.[59]

More generally, this scenario represents both tremendous cost savings and increased profits for countless companies in the United States and other countries, while at the same time fueling hyper-growth for many Chinese companies and the economy. It sounds like a win-win, maybe, or at least until the well-known weaknesses were revealed.[60]

Crisis and Calamity

The new coronavirus hit late 2019 and early 2020, which did two things fast. First, it greatly increased the demand for medical supplies in China, and next, it interfered with the production of the same products. The problem multiplied as the virus spread and countries around the globe exhausted their limited inventories, and when these same customers turned to their domestic wholesalers and suppliers to replenish their inventories, they quickly found that they too were out of stock due to a shortage in China. This meant that those in need had to find and create other sources, but this was and remains a daunting task.

US hospitals and other large care providers had even greater difficulties, as they acquire goods as members of group purchasing organizations (GPOs). GPOs, at least in theory, help members negotiate better prices by buying in bulk rather than independently.[61] This cost-saving approach works reasonably well in normal conditions, but the pandemic simply meant their fates were tied together, and individual institutions did not have their own supply chain relationships and thus had few places to turn (i.e., alternatives).

After having surrendered domestic production capacity for personal protective equipment (PPE), including the materials for making and machines for assembling masks

Continued

and respirators, those who needed these products had to do without. The plight of medical workers, first responders, common citizens, and eventually business was intensified by the fact that the US government proved to be an insufficient safety net. The President of the United States could have exercised the Defense Production Act to require American companies to shift their efforts to produce the necessary products, assuming the necessary materials could be acquired. He did, but many argue not to the extent possible or necessary.[62]

Thankfully, however, many large existing companies along with many small ones and motivated entrepreneurs voluntarily sprang into action. However, when COVID-19 cases hit new highs in the summer of 2020, all of these problems were white-hot again—insufficient PPE and other products, insufficient supplier quantities with too many instances of inferior quality, insufficient government support, and still insufficient domestic capacity. Making matters worse for the United States and many other countries, allegations exist that China and other countries that have some domestic capacity are reducing export to build supplies for their own people.[63]

For Discussion:

1. Assume you are the President of the United States. What would you do in the near term to meet domestic needs for PPE?
2. Assume you are the president of a hospital in your hometown, and it continues to be short on supplies of PPE. What would you do?
3. Again, assume you are the President of the United States. Describe what you would do over time to address the shortages in the medical supply industry.
4. More generally, what are your thoughts on how the Chinese built dominance in the medical supply industry?
5. What are your thoughts about how the United States, and other countries, effectively outsourced all of the capabilities for medical supplies?
6. Argue for retaining supplies of a needed product manufactured in your country for its own people.
7. Argue against reserving such products and instead sharing them abroad.
8. What lessons do you take from the scenario described in this case?
9. What are the key business ethics issues between countries illustrated in the case?

Apply Three-Dimensional Problem-Solving for Ethics (3D PSE)

You can apply the 3D PSE from multiple perspectives (see Figure 11.2), such as that of the President of the United States, clinician who needs PPE to stay safe on the job, CEO of a hospital, CEO of a Chinese PPE producer, or CEO or owner of a US company that could devote resources to manufacturing such products. Be sure to specify whose perspective you would choose, as your problem solving is likely to differ considerably depending on your choice. Let's try it with you being the president of a US hospital which is in repeated short supply.

figure 11.2

Three-Dimensional Problem Solving for Ethics.

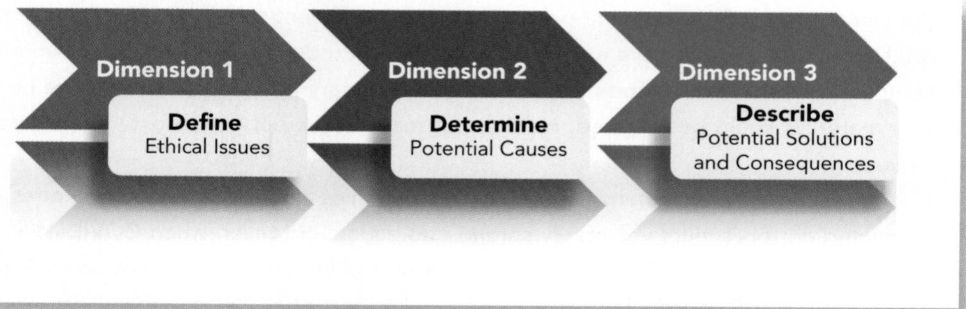

Dimension 1: *Define* the Ethical Challenge

What is the gap in the case? What do you have and what do *you* want?

a. From your view as the hospital president, what is the current situation and how do you want it to be?
b. Why is the current situation a problem? What difficulties or undesirable behaviors and outcomes happen as a result of the problem you defined? Why do you, and hospital executives like you, care about the problem you defined in Dimension 1?
c. Define your problem in one or at most two sentences and structure it in terms of what is current versus what is desired.
d. Who are the key stakeholders who affect or are affected by the problem you defined?

Dimension 2: *Determine* the Causes

a. **Individuals.** Given the problem you defined in Dimension 1, how do the characteristics of individuals (including you, others like you, and government officials) cause the problem, such as ethical decision-making approach, work values, and moral principles?
b. **Contextual.** Are there particular norms (practices) that caused the problem as defined in Dimension 1? Are their industry, country, international trade, or regulatory norms that caused the problem you defined?

Dimension 3: *Describe* Your Potential Solutions and the Intended and Unintended Consequences for Stakeholders

For each cause you identified in Dimension 2, answer the following questions:

a. ***What*** do you recommend as a solution(s), and ***how*** would you make it (them) happen?
b. ***Why*** would you do it the way you proposed? Does this reflect a particular ethical decision-making approach (e.g., utilitarian or deontology)?

If your responses to these questions are unsatisfactory, then go back to Dimension 1 and repeat the process. If, however, you are comfortable and confident in your problem-solving efforts thus far, then ensure you achieve the desired outcomes and avoid any unintended consequences.

c. What is the ***desired and likely effect in the short and long term*** for the key stakeholders involved in the problem and causes (Dimensions 1 and 2)?
d. What ***potential unintended consequences*** may occur with each proposed solution?
e. If any, what are the **implications for *other* stakeholders** (e.g., individuals, organizations, and communities) besides those noted in Dimensions 1 and 2?
f. Will your solution work in an ethical manner? Make a final assessment of whether your chosen solution will reduce or eliminate the causes determined in Dimension 2, and whether this will then remedy the ethical problem defined in Dimension 1. If not, then repeat and refine the dimensions.

Part Opener Photo Source: only_kim/Shutterstock

Chapter Opener Photo Source: Gordon J A Dixon/Shutterstock

chapter 12

Environmental Sustainability Issues at Home and Abroad

Learning Objectives

AFTER READING THIS CHAPTER, YOU SHOULD BE ABLE TO:

LO1 Articulate how externalities can and do influence the environment.

LO2 Identify the key environmental issues confronting business and society today.

LO3 Understand the pros and cons of regulatory solutions to environmental issues.

LO4 Define the characteristics of being environmentally sustainable.

WHERE DO **YOU** STAND?

Plastic Prices Plunge, Potentially a Problem

Plastic is an enormous environmental hazard, one that companies as well as countries and their leaders around the world continue to address. It was a hot topic at the World Economic Forum in Davos, where attendees (e.g., the leaders of Coca-Cola, PepsiCo, and Danone) discussed how they could increase recycling and use of recycled plastics, which in turn would reduce the use of virgin or new plastics. The implications are far-reaching, as plastics are made from oil and fill the oceans and landfills.[1]

For perspective, Coca-Cola alone produces nearly 200,000 plastic bottles per minute, earning it the dubious distinction of the world's most plastics polluting brand. Although the company has goals to use 50 percent recycled plastic by 2030, the company said it will not eliminate single-use plastics, citing that such a move could alienate some customers and negatively impact sales. Coca-Cola also argued that aluminum and glass alternatives are more costly to make in terms of carbon footprint.[2]

Recycling can be an expensive process and has been utilized with varying success in communities, companies, and countries. A major reason for this is economic—single-use plastics are often cheaper in the near term and are thus chosen over recycled options. Fundamental to the recycling challenge at all levels—local communities and countries—is the fact that volume counts, meaning that the recycling business has very small profit margins, which means recyclers need large and predicable volumes of plastic to remain viable. Some European countries approach this problem by insisting that a certain percentage of recycled plastics be used in bottles sold by companies operating on the Continent.

Then COVID hit. Oil prices plummeted, making new, single-use plastic even cheaper still. In approximately one year the prices dropped by 29 percent in the United States, 27 percent in Europe, and 33 percent in Taiwan. This only added to the existing challenges, specifically China's decision to stop accepting (plastic) waste from other countries.

1. Assume you are the CEO of Coca-Cola. What would you do? Use single-use plastics for your bottles or pay 30 percent more for recycled options? Explain your choice, as if you were taking the TV Test.
2. Assume you run your own company, and your only product is packaged in plastic. You are confronted with the same choice. Would it be different or the same? Why?

Introduction

Climate change is a global crisis threatening the future of all people. Throughout history, across the globe, human activity has contributed to this change. However, it is important for us to understand who will do what going forward to change our course toward a more positive and sustainable future. This chapter builds on the concept of sustainability you learned in chapter 2 and explores its implications for environmental sustainability specifically. Many other concepts are foundational here too, notably leadership and social responsibility, as well as the 3D Problem-Solving for Ethics. Your understanding of these complex and critical issues and your ability to address them are, in part, dependent on your grasp of the many concepts covered thus far.

We have addressed environmental sustainability in section 4 of the book as it is truly a societal issue. The action of one individual, or one country, can be undone by the actions of another, as climate issues do not recognize borders. This means that solutions need the cooperation of individuals, organizations, and governments across the globe. Multiple stakeholders are responsible for these problems and also for the solutions; the ethical implications are profound. But before we dive into specific environmental challenges, it is helpful to explore the concept of environmental externalities.

Environmental Externalities—The Environment's Archenemy

Before addressing the business ethics implications of any particular environmental issue, or larger meta-issues like climate change, it is helpful to first understand externalities. Most simply, externalities are benefits and costs not compensated for by other parties. "**Environmental externalities** occur when the environmental impacts of production and consumption activities generate benefits (positive externalities) or costs (negative externalities) not compensated for by other parties."[3]

environmental externalities
the environmental impacts of production and consumption activities generate benefits (positive externalities) or costs (negative externalities) not compensated for by other parties

Our interest is in the external costs, those that are passed on to individuals, communities, and the larger society without impacting the financial results of the producer.[4] For instance, oil companies extract, refine, and sell their product, some of which is ultimately used by motorists as gasoline in their cars. The negative externality is all the pollution that is generated from start to finish in this process—from extracting the oil from the ground to the exhaust from your tailpipe. It is neither calculated nor charged to the oil producer, or to any other party in the chain (e.g., gas stations and drivers). This in turn makes all things that are produced with oil, such as plastics, pharmaceuticals, and fuel, cheaper than they would be if the environmental costs were not externalized. In other words, externalities make all these items more affordable.

Externalities Lower Costs and Increase Affordability

By passing the costs on to numerous stakeholders, oil producers and those that use their products benefit from lower costs. This in turn acts as an incentive for them to produce and consume more oil-based products, which in turn generates more pollution. If oil companies had to pay for these costs (i.e., internalize them), then the cost of oil to the users would be much higher and more accurate, making it less profitable for oil companies and reducing the related pollution.

Many experts have long argued that accounting for such costs is a fundamental element of solving the majority of environmental issues.[5] To clarify, if petroleum producers (e.g., gasoline and plastics), mining companies (e.g., copper and iron ore), and the livestock industry (e.g., cows and chickens) had to internalize the environmental costs of their businesses, then the total prices would increase. You might think, "I already pay enough for all of these goods as it is. I don't want to pay more." That is exactly the point. Such products are cheaper and thus more attractive than they "should" or certainly would be, if such costs were not externalized.

How to Internalize Externalities

Requiring businesses, and in this case those who have a negative environmental impact, to bear the true cost of producing, selling, and using their products and services is fundamental to motivating change. The reasoning is that if the true costs are so great, investors and owners will innovate and find less costly ways of doing the same business by finding cleaner, more efficient, and less environmentally damaging technologies and processes. Alternatively, investors will redirect their resources to altogether different opportunities, those with more affordable cost structures and more promising profitability.[6]

Using power generation as an example, these changes can be motivated using a small number of tools:[7]

1. Taxes. Taxes can be used on pollution generated in the entire process of generating power, such as sourcing of the fuel (e.g., coal or natural gas), transport of that fuel, combustion of the fuel to produce energy, energy transmission to the user (e.g., homes or businesses), and the ultimate use of the power. All of these can be measured, and the tax can be paid at the source or allocated throughout the process to various participants.[8]
2. Emission allowances. Country, regional, or state governments can set emissions limits or caps for the power industry. As part of the program, companies in the industry are issued credits equaling the emissions cap, which they can trade with each other. This allows some companies to exceed the limit, so long as others are below by the same amount. These are *cap and trade programs* and are in wide use across the globe to manage emissions. The state of California has used them extensively.
3. Eliminate subsidies. As you learned previously, subsidies are cash grants or favorable tax treatment from governments to businesses, and they are intended to lower the cost of doing business. Subsidizing polluting businesses, or any with externalities, lowers their costs even more and further distorts the true price of that business. Eliminating them would thus help costs be closer to the true cost (accurate).

These economic tools can serve to internalize the environmental costs of many different types of businesses. In so doing, the true costs will shape the behaviors of many stakeholders, notably investors, managers, and consumers.

In sum, environmental externalities represent serious and complex business ethics issues for governments, businesses, investors, consumers, and others around the world.

For Discussion

1. Describe your view of the ethical implications of environmental externalities? Is it acceptable to "pass them along"? Explain.
2. Does the industry matter? To clarify, do you think the ethical implications for the leaders of companies in petroleum, mining, and livestock (three of the greatest greenhouse emissions producers) are different or the same? Explain.

Keep externalities in mind as you read the remainder of the chapter, beginning with our discussion of some of the key environmental challenges confronting businesses today.

Key Environmental Issues Confronting Business and Society

Environment-related views and actions of individuals, businesses, governments, and other organizations have evolved. Prior to 1970, most denied environmental issues existed, but then things began to change when the first regulations and associated agencies were created in the United States and elsewhere. The emphasis on regulations persisted until the 1990s, when attention was also given to increasing efficiency as a means for reducing consumption and environmental impact. It wasn't until the 2000s when emphasis on sustainability became mainstream, which is now reflected in the fact that the majority of organizations have some sort of explicit environmental policy.[9]

With that as background, we are well aware of the environmental challenges facing the planet and all its inhabitants. For our purposes, we will focus our attention on climate change and energy, water, and air. Of course, these are not the only issues. But if you want to solve complex problems, it helps to break them down. Moreover, these issues are applicable globally today, and thus require cooperation across levels and borders.

Climate Change and Energy

climate change
the long-term change in the average weather patterns around the world

Climate change is the long-term change in the average weather patterns around the world.[10] Climate is regional or global and long term, whereas weather is local and of limited duration. This definition also clearly makes climate change a true global issue. The fact that it is defined as patterns over time should sound familiar, as many of the key concepts in business ethics also concern patterns of behavior over time (e.g., ethical leadership, ethical cultures, individual and corporate responsibility, and sustainability).

Climate change is linked to fossil fuels, which is where humans have harvested nearly all of their energy needs since the last century. This is why we focus on all forms of coal (clean and dirty) and oil (natural gas and other petroleum products), as these are the main fossil fuels that have contributed to the environmental issues we have today. Coal and oil are the major culprits because burning them creates greenhouse gases which trap heat in the atmosphere and warm the planet (see Figure 12.1).

For all of the press and progress regarding alternative energy, the fact remains that humans continue to meet most of their energy needs from fossil fuels, and chief among these is coal. The world still generates approximately 37 percent of its electricity via coal, and the largest countries and economies tend to use the most—China, United States, India, and

figure 12.1

Composition of Greenhouse Gases

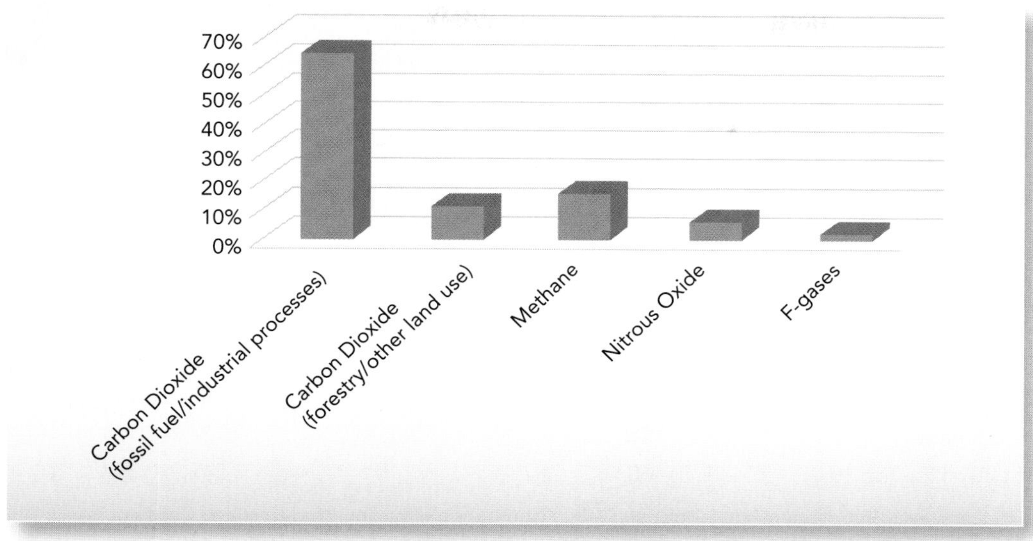

Japan.[11] For comparison, China generates 65 percent of its electricity from coal[12] and the United States 24 percent.[13] After electricity generation, agriculture and industry are the next largest producers of greenhouse gases (see Figure 12.2).

But what happens as developing countries continue to grow? They too primarily use coal, and much of this development is funded by China. And this means the road to the future is dirty, like the past.[14] This also is yet another story of haves and have-nots. More than half of the world's population—nearly 3.5 billion people—use less than 10 percent of the electricity that Americans do. If they want to do better, they need energy, and coal remains a widely available and relatively cheap source.

Oil is the obvious other goliath in terms of energy. The same countries consume most, as noted in Table 12.1, but what is remarkable is the relative amount of consumption. The United States and China each consume many times more than the next countries on the list, and these differences cannot be attributed to population differences either. This scenario

figure 12.2

Greenhouse Gases Emissions by Sector

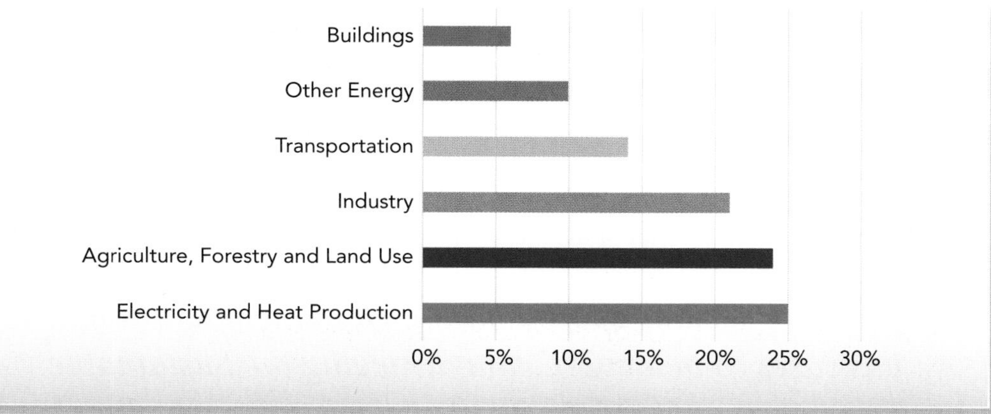

Source: figure 12.1 and 12.2: https://www.epa.gov/ghgemissions/global-greenhouse-gas-emissions-data

table **12.1**

Largest Consumers of Oil by Percentage of World Total

Country	Percentage of World Total Oil Consumption	Population
United States	20	331,002,651
China	14	1,439,323,776
India	4	1,380,004,385
Japan	4	126,476,461
Russia	4	145,934,462
Saudi Arabia	3	34,813,871
Brazil	3	212,559,417
South Korea	3	51,269,185
Germany	2	83,783,942
Canada	2	37,742,154
Total for Top 10	60	3,842,910,304

Source: Energy Information Administration, "What Countries are the Top Producers and Consumers of Oil?", eai.gov: https://www.eia.gov/tools/faqs/faq.php?id=709&t=6. WorldoMeter, "Countries in the World by Population 2020," worldometers.info: https://www.worldometers.info/world-population/population-by-country/.

points to deep-seated cultural differences in values and norms at all levels, but notably business and government.

Thankfully, there is hope. Many companies and countries are on a more productive path. For instance, Peru established a special environmental court to help combat the persistent environmental challenges due to mining, deforestation, illegal wildlife trade, and hazardous waste. Nearly 3,000 cases were brought in the first year it operated. And then there is Norway, perhaps the standard to which all other countries aspire. It generates nearly all of its power from renewable sources, thanks to the availability and usage of hydropower.[15]

Water

Water is life, but despite its fundamental importance, it is routinely polluted and wasted by individuals and industries. These problems are compounded by climate change, which impacts water availability, quality, and quantity. The problem is complex. But higher air temperatures translate into higher water temperatures, and these, in turn, negatively affect aquatic plants and animals, which then impact ecosystems in the sea and on the land. Icecaps melt at the poles and on mountains, and, in turn, sea levels rise and overtake places where hundreds of millions of people live.

Climate change, along with mismanagement, results in less water available for agriculture, which consumes nearly 70 percent of all freshwater used around the world. This complex and consequential scenario is why industry and government are essential to any sustainable water future.[16] Gilbert Houngbo, Chair of United Nations Water Committee, described the scope and severity of the issue very directly when he said:

> *"If we are serious about limiting global temperature increases to below 2°C and achieving the Sustainable Development Goals by 2030, we must act immediately.*

There are solutions for managing water and climate in a more coordinated manner and every sector of society has a role to play. We simply cannot afford to wait."[17]

This is why some experts say, "Water is as important to the world's economy as oil or data."[18] More generally, because it is fundamental to life, some people view water as a basic human right, making water both a moral and ethical issue. For perspective, an estimated 2.2 billion people do not have regular access to safe water for drinking and sanitation, both essential for public health.[19]

This fact was underscored with the COVID-19 pandemic. Handwashing is a first line of defense against the virus, and in regions and countries where water is in short supply, this is a serious problem. Making the problem worse, a World Health Organization report cites that 22 percent of health facilities in the least-developed countries lack sufficient clean water.[20]

Air

Air, like water, is essential for human existence, and it too is intimately linked to climate change and how we energize our lives the world over. It also largely ignores human-imposed borders, such as states, countries, and continents, which is why cooperation is essential.

The World Health Organization (WHO) estimates that air pollution causes nearly seven million premature deaths each year due to its role in lung infections, cancers, and other pulmonary diseases, as well as its effects on people with heart disease. The WHO considers two broad categories of pollution—ambient and household. **Ambient air pollution** is produced by vehicles, power generation, building heating systems, agriculture waste burning, and industry. **Household air pollution** is often the result of smoke related to cooking fires using coal, wood, dung, and kerosene. Although these forms affect those in the developing world more severely, people living in more developed economies also suffer the consequences.[21]

ambient air pollution produced by vehicles, power generation, building heating systems, agriculture waste burning, and industry

household air pollution often the result of smoke related to cooking fires using coal, wood, dung, and kerosene

What is the cause? Most basically, fossil fuel emissions (greenhouse gases) are "cooked" in hot weather and are converted to ozone (smog), which reinforces warming in a feedback loop. As the planet warms, the air worsens, and this problem is intensified by other polluting particles released into the air via forest fires and industry. To clarify, although emissions are reduced, the increased heat converts the remaining emissions to ozone at an even faster rate.[22]

Part of what makes this story so sad is that global warming is undermining the impressive gains many countries have made in reducing air pollution over the past five decades. For perspective, air pollution in the United States is 70 percent lower than it was when the Clean Air Act was passed in 1970 (discussed in the next section). Yet, nearly 50 percent of Americans live in places experts label as unhealthy. Also similar to water, geography matters, as the five places in the United States with the worst air quality are in California.[23]

J Dennis/Shutterstock

Many forces threaten future improvements, notably the government. In the United States, the Clean

table 12.2

Air Pollution Opportunities for Governments and Individuals

Governments
Adopt science-based quality standards. The science is there, use it. Air quality should not be partisan or political.
Enact and enforce legislation to reduce emissions. Like most laws, their success depends on enforcement. Appropriate funding and enforcement must be a priority.
Make air pollution part of public health planning. The threat is real; just ask someone who has experienced a smog attack. If decision makers are not influenced by pollutions statistics, then perhaps health implications will work.
You and Other Individuals
Speak up and speak out to friends, family, employers, and government officials. If you see polluting behaviors, say something. Also, lobby your representatives.
Participate in local efforts to clean the air. Donate your time, money, and presence to existing efforts of others.
Use less electricity. Think devices. Do they all need to be plugged in, overnight, now? Try turning them off when not in use.
Don't burn stuff. Compost, recycle, and use natural gas instead of wood.
Encourage clean transportation. Your school and city government likely have fleets of buses and cars. Encourage the decisions not only to purchase clean transportation but also to retrofit existing vehicles to reduce emissions. Don't sit with your car idling for long periods.[26]

Source: Adapted from American Lung Association, "The State of the Air 2020," stateoftheair.org: http://www.stateoftheair.org/key-findings/.

Air Act is still the cornerstone of air quality progress, but the budget and thus capabilities of the agency are dependent on the whims of politicians. The Trump administration, for instance, has proposed cutting the budget of the Environmental Protection Agency (EPA), who is responsible for enforcement, by nearly a third and loosening some of the restrictions of the Act itself.

The problem is also a story of automobiles, which are heavy polluters. As the world's population continues to grow, and as more people enter the middle class in developing economies, there are more cars on the road.[24]

What are the answers? Cooperation at all levels. Local, state, and national governments, as well as industry and individual citizens, have roles to play. Anyone of these stakeholders can make or break the efforts by others.[25] Table 12.2 illustrates some opportunities for governments and individuals.

Now that you have a sense of some of the major environmental challenges and their causes, we'll explore one of the major ways in which environmental issues have been addressed—government regulation.

The Pros and Cons of Regulatory Solutions to Environmental Issues

It is important to note again that mere compliance with legal standards does not equal ethical conduct. Nevertheless, laws and regulations are an important part of ensuring individuals, organizations, and countries do their part in protecting the environment. Table 12.3 outlines the history of a number of the most notable regulations in the United States.

table **12.3**

Key Environmental Regulations in the United States

Environmental Regulation	Environmental Protection Provided
Clean Air Act (1970)	Establishes national air quality standards and compliance deadlines
Environmental Protection Agency 1970)	Protects human health and the environment
National Environmental Policy Act (1970)	Requires environmental impact studies for all government projects
Federal Water Pollution Control Act (1972)	Prevents, reduces, and eliminates water pollution
Noise Pollution Control Act (1972)	Controls noise emissions of certain manufactured products.
Federal Insecticide, Fungicide, and Rodenticide Act (1972)	Controls sale and use of pesticides
Clean Water Act (1972)	Regulates water pollution from agricultural and industrial facilities
Endangered Species Act (1973)	Protects at-risk species from extinction and their ecosystems
Safe Drinking Water Act (1974)	Protects water above or below ground for drinking use and establishes purity standards
Comprehensive Environmental Response Compensation and Liability Act (1980)	Establishes tax on petroleum and chemical industries, and provides authority to respond to events involving hazardous substances
Oil Pollution Act (1990)	Generates a tax designed to support the EPA's prevention of and response to oil spills
Pollution Protection Act (1990)	Addresses efficiency and cost-saving changes in production, operation, and raw materials use for industry
Energy Policy Act (2005)	Regulates energy efficiency, renewable energy, and includes nuclear energy, fuels, oil, gas, coal, hydrogen, electricity, energy tax incentives, geothermal energy and hydropower, and climate change technology
Energy Independence and Security Act (2007)	Intended to move the USA toward a more sustainable future, including phasing out old technologies (e.g., incandescent light bulbs)

Domestic and International Regulatory Solutions

The EPA is the primary federal agency for environmental issues in the United States, and its mission is to ensure the following:

- Clean air, land, and water
- Environmental risks are assessed using science
- Federal laws are enforced fairly
- Environmental implications are considered in US policies related to—natural resources, human health, economic growth, energy, transportation, agriculture, industry, and international trade
- Accurate environmental information is available to all stakeholders
- Contaminated sites are cleaned by responsible parties
- Chemicals are reviewed for safety.[27]

The responsibilities are obviously quite extensive, and they also provide illustrations of several business ethics concepts.

For Discussion

1. Describe three business ethics concepts clearly included in the EPA's mission.
2. If you were director of the EPA, and thus charged with implementing its mission, what do you think would be your two or three biggest challenges?

treaties and protocols formal, binding written agreements typically between two or more countries or international organizations

ratification when a country both signs its intent to participate, and its national government actually approves it

At the international level, environmental issues are generally governed by **treaties and protocols,** which are formal, binding written agreements typically between two or more countries or international organizations. Despite this definition, not all treaties are binding until ratified. **Ratification** occurs after a country both signs its intent to participate, and its national government actually approves it. Once approved, it is considered ratified and binding, meaning the country accepts the consequences for noncompliance. Treaties have and do play a major role in setting goals and applying some degree of pressure for expected conduct.

The reality is, however, that many countries sign treaties but never ratify them, making compliance purely voluntary and with no consequences. Ratified or not, it still comes back to ethics. The true essence of any treaty, or other regulation for that matter, is the good faith that parties will comply with their respective obligations.

The following are some of the key treaties or protocols related to international environmental sustainability.

Montreal Protocol of 1987 regulates substances that deplete the ozone layer that protects the Earth from solar radiation, known to cause skin cancer and cataracts, reduce agricultural productivity, and damage marine ecosystems

Montreal Protocol. The **Montreal Protocol of 1987** regulates substances that deplete the ozone layer that protects the Earth from solar radiation, known to cause skin cancer and cataracts, reduce agricultural productivity, and damage marine ecosystems.[28] The primary focus is on reducing the damage caused by hydrochlorofluorocarbons (HCFCs) by eliminating their use around the world in refrigeration, air-conditioning, and foams. The Montreal Protocol of 1987 was truly revolutionary in that all 197 members of the United Nations signed and ratified it.

By all accounts, it has been a tremendous success. In the United States alone, it is estimated that by limiting damage, and thus promoting recovery of the ozone layer, substantial health benefits will result in the prevention of:

- 280 million cases of skin cancer
- 1.6 million skin cancer deaths
- 45 million cataracts.[29]

Kyoto Protocol of 1997 major international agreement focused on reducing greenhouse gas emissions

Kyoto Protocol. The **Kyoto Protocol of 1997** is the major international agreement focused on reducing greenhouse gas emissions. Two basic and notable elements are that it sets specific goals, and these goals differ for industrialized versus developing countries. Participating countries were assigned emissions level goals with target dates, at which point a participating country either achieved the targets or missed the targets. Countries that missed their targets then had to compensate, make up for it, by the same amount in the next time period, or they could trade carbon credits with other countries that achieved their own goals. Goals differed for each country, but on average, participating nations were expected to reduce emissions by 5.2 percent by 2012, and if achieved, this would result in an overall reduction of 29 percent for the planet.[30]

As for developed versus developing countries, the Kyoto Protocol acknowledges that the actions of industrialized countries were largely responsible for the state of the planet. Thus, they (thirty-seven countries plus the EU) were asked to limit their emissions, as described above. Whereas, developing countries were expected to invest in and develop cleaner processes for which they would receive carbon credits, which could then be traded with industrialized countries. India and China were exempted altogether.[31]

Ultimately, the Kyoto Protocol fell apart. The United States backed out, arguing it was unfairly penalizing its industries. Combine this with the fact that China was already in hyper-growth mode, the two largest emitters wiped out all of the gains made by the countries that complied.[32]

Paris Climate Agreement. The **Paris Climate Agreement of 2015** aimed to reduce emissions contributing to global warming. It was intended to replace and improve upon the Kyoto Protocol, and it was signed by 197 countries and ratified by 189 by the end of 2019. A critical difference was that both China and the United States were included, the two largest polluters, both of which submitted ambitious goals. One of the major challenges of the agreement was how developed countries would help finance improvements in less-developed countries. Some island nations complained the overall goals were too low, as they feared that even if the goals were achieved, their lands would be flooded by rising seawater from melting ice caps.[33]

Paris Climate Agreement of 2015
aimed to reduce emissions contributing to global warming

The Paris Agreement underscored and attempted to incentivize cooperation, flexibility, and transparency, but sadly no provisions for compliance were made. This meant there are no consequences for noncompliance—all bark and no bite. Also problematic is the threat by President Trump to withdraw the United States in late 2020.[34]

Now that you have knowledge of a few important regulations, it will be helpful to consider the advantages and disadvantages of regulations.

Advantages and Disadvantages of Regulation

Not surprisingly, there are two sides to the story. Some of the common and interrelated criticisms of environmental regulations are as follows:

1. Reduces international competitiveness. Inconsistent regulations give competitors an unfair advantage, as some are required to comply with costly regulations while others are not.
2. Causes increased business costs leading to layoffs and plant closures. Dirty can be "cheap," which is one reason why coal has been used so extensively. Investing in new and other sources and processes costs money.
3. Motivates companies to move offshore. If it can be done cheaper somewhere else, then do the business there.[35]

Simply put, critics claim the costs outweigh the benefits. If the playing field is not level, then companies will move operations to places with lax regulations and lower costs. From a purely economic point of view, this makes perfect sense and is a strong argument. Of course, advocates of environmental regulations have different views:

1. Far less federal money is spent on the environment than is spent on national defense or healthcare. Many advocates explicitly argue that the environment is a key determinant of security and health; therefore, investing in the environment should be considered as important as investing in other sectors.

2. The United States spends about the same percentage of GDP on environmental protection as countries of a similar level of development. The point here is that the playing field is flat and thus fair, given that other countries are competitive while investing the same amount in the environment.
3. Thinking of pollution control and environmental protection as a cost is the wrong mindset. The implication is that these costs do not go away. Instead, they are only pushed into the future when they will be more expensive due to greater degradation of the environment.

For Discussion

1. What is your reaction to the arguments against environmental regulation?
2. What is your reaction to the arguments for environmental regulation?

Bottom line: If environmental protection is valued, then formal controls are not a complete solution. Regulations need to be complemented by broader and deeper ethical considerations, which include ethical leadership with a genuine stakeholder orientation that also emphasizes social responsibility and sustainability. Only then can the full potential or intent of any regulation be realized. We explore this next.

Characteristics of an Environmentally Sustainable Organization

environmental sustainability the ability to meet the needs of the present without compromising the ability of future generations to meet their needs

In chapter 2 we explained that the essence of sustainability is to ensure that actions taken today by you, other individuals, or organizations do not impede or limit the actions and opportunities of others in the future. Also recall that fundamental to the concept of sustainability is time—how actions today influence tomorrow. We use this same thinking to tie together the concepts and issues we've explored in this chapter and make the business case for **environmental sustainability**—the ability to meet the needs of the present without compromising the ability of future generations to meet their needs.[36] We conclude by providing additional guidance and examples on how to realize the benefits.

The Business Case for Environmental Sustainability

Given this book is about business ethics, it is completely appropriate and economically responsible to ask: Why should businesses bother with environmental sustainability? What's in it for them? There are many answers to this question, some of which you learned already, such as the benefits shown in chapter 10 and environmental, social, and governance (ESG) investing. But let's outline a few others that are explicitly "business" and speak to increasing an organization's competitiveness.

1. Brand image. Various studies have shown that the majority of customers consider the positive environmental records of companies with whom they do business.

Positive track records are more than compliance. Customers increasingly look for companies that make environmental sustainability a priority, such as when companies embrace "doing good" and being stewards of the environment in their advertising. A fundamental reason for this is that customers prefer a company whose values align with their own, and for decades people have increased the value they place on the environment.

2. Efficiency. The process of becoming more sustainable commonly involves examining and refining processes to make them more efficient and reducing resources used, such as materials and energy. Efficiencies are gained in countless ways, but among them are simple behaviors with immediate benefits (e.g., turning out the lights and turning off devices), while others require investments in new processes and produce benefits in the long term. The Ethics in Action box related to how Nike raised its game in terms of sustainability provides an excellent example.
3. Regulations. The trend of greater environmental oversight will continue and will likely increase as the negative impacts become more severe and widespread. Therefore, making sustainability a part of an organization's strategy gives it the priority it will require. This should make an organization better prepared to meet (or even exceed) inevitable regulatory requirements. Moreover, being proactive has the potential for organizations to be trendsetters and thus make their practices the industry standard with which competitors need to comply.
4. Talent and investors. Similar to customers, employees also prefer to work for companies whose values align with their own. Younger generations, in particular, have grown up with sustainability being front-page news, a hot topic for debates, and highly valued feature of attractive employers. Environmental scandals, therefore, can influence who applies for jobs at a given company, and they can cause candidates with multiple offers to choose a competitor. Investors also are attracted to such organizations and are increasingly making investment decisions based on ESG factors, as you learned in chapter 10.[37]

Notice also how these elements often complement or reinforce each other. This means that one benefit of an organization's sustainability efforts can be amplified by the others. A bigger bang for your sustainability buck!

For Discussion

1. Can you think of an instance where your choice of a product or service was actually influenced by the environmental track record of a company? Describe.
2. Think of an example—something that actually happened involving a company—that would cause you not to use their product or service. The example did not have to actually influence a decision you made, but it would if you were in the market for their product or service.
3. List three sustainability-related actions by organizations that are especially important to you. In other words, which three sustainability initiatives do you value most?

Who is Good at Sustainability?

Now that you have some sense of the pros and cons, along with how to make the business case for sustainability, it is time to learn which organizations are leading by example. The intention with this final section is not only to inspire you to make environmental sustainability part of your own decision-making regarding products, services, and jobs, but also to provide specific examples of how it is happening today.

Leading by Example. *Barron's* creates an annual list of the most sustainable companies, and as you learned in chapter 10, they show that purpose can indeed be profitable. Sustainability is business for this bunch, no charity.

The top 10 for 2020 are:

1. Agilent Technologies
2. Texas Instruments
3. Voya Financial
4. Tiffany
5. Best Buy
6. HP Inc.
7. Cisco Systems
8. W. W. Grainger
9. Avnet
10. Autodesk

These companies tend to view sustainability as mission-critical, something they incorporate into their organization's strategies, cultures, and throughout their operations. The CEO of Agilent (No. 1), Mike Mullen, regularly talks with shareholders about how the company's efforts and success toward social responsibility boost the bottom line. He says, "We don't calculate NPVs or ROIs (net present values or returns on investment), but our judgment is that doing these things benefits the company." For instance, in response to the new coronavirus, Agilent donated some of its laboratory instruments, software, and other diagnostic products to the Chinese government. The company gets 19 percent of its revenue from China, but McMullen said, "In terms of sustainability, there's a big social component (to) the role you play in your community. This is an opportunity for companies to demonstrate their commitment to the community."[38]

The methodology for determining the rankings is extensive and rigorous. It begins with studying the 1,000 largest public companies in the United States and analyzing data pertaining to five stakeholders: shareholders, employees, customers, community, and the planet. The data include over 230 performance indicators and are collected from numerous sources. These data are organized into twenty-eight distinct topics, ranging from greenhouse gas emissions to workplace safety and diversity, and the distinct topics are then sorted into five key stakeholder categories. Importantly, the elements considered must materially impact financial performance as it relates to peer companies in their industry. The intent is to identify what activities impact financial performance, which would help overcome fading arguments that such efforts are a charity and a luxury that most firms cannot financially afford.[39]

How Do They Do It? Although many of the organizations on the list are incredibly innovative, and they have created a "special sauce" that makes their cultures and approaches to sustainability unique, they tend to share some common elements that you, your employers, and other organizations can adopt.

1. People. They value their employees and make selection, development, performance, and satisfaction a true priority. Turnover at these companies tends to be 25–50 percent lower than their industry peers not on the list. Treating employees well becomes well known and becomes a part of the company's reputation, which in turn attracts additional talented applicants. This also helps ensure and reinforce that employees value environmental stewardship.
2. Costs. Companies on the list tend to realize cost savings in energy, water, waste, and other elements due to their sustainability efforts. Combine these savings with those related to retaining talent, and sustainable companies become skilled if not more enlightened cost controllers.
3. Customers often prefer a stakeholder approach. By treating their employees, communities, and environment well, these companies attract and retain customers better than companies that don't. Realize that advertisers are also (the) major customers for many companies, and few things scare them off as fast as a scandal.
4. A helping hand. An emerging trend among these companies is they are increasingly actively engaging clients, suppliers, and yes, competitors to improve their sustainability.[40] The following Ethics in Action box describes how competitors even collaborated in their environmental efforts.

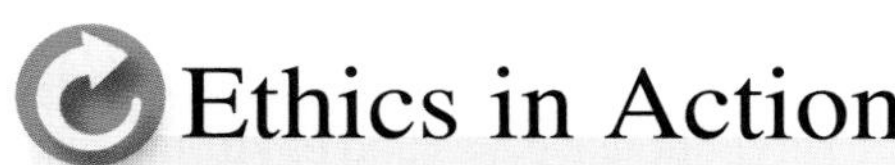

Nike Raised Its Sustainability Game

There was a time when Nike was fiercely criticized for polluting water near its facilities in China, and it was argued that a major reason the facilities were located there was to take advantage of that country's relatively lax environmental regulations.[41] The situation has since improved. Greenpeace, an environmental nongovernmental organization, helped bring awareness to Nike's practices, and it also pressured the company and two of its key competitors (Adidas and Puma) to change. Nike subsequently implemented a "Move to Zero" initiative aimed at zero carbon and zero waste in its operations.[42] These efforts are captured in a quote from Mark Parker, the executive chairman: "If there is no planet, there is no sport."[43]

Current Nike shoes now contain approximately 50 percent recycled manufacturing waste and are made with 100 percent renewable energy.[44] As for water, it now claims zero discharge of hazardous chemicals.[45]

For Discussion:

1. Assume you are deciding between a pair of Nike shoes and another from Adidas. If you were aware these companies had vastly different environmental practices—one a serious polluter and the other not—would it influence your buying decision? Explain your answer/decision.
2. If you are Mark Parker, why would you collaborate with your competitors on sustainability issues? It seems that if there is an advantage, you would want to keep that for Nike and not "share it."

Doing the right thing can also act as insurance when people cross the line of business ethics. For instance, the CEO of Best Buy (No. 5 on the list) was alleged to have had an inappropriate relationship with another executive, which could count against the company. However, the board launched a legitimate investigation into the matter with which the CEO cooperated. This demonstrated effective governance and helped preserve Best Buys' other merits and place on the list. This suggests that sustainable companies with solid ESG do better when things go wrong.[46]

The Role of Renewable Energy and Green Methods

We will conclude the chapter where we started by addressing the role of energy, and how sustainable organizations and countries are changing energy-related sources and practices to impact the planet and other stakeholders.

Recent research has shown that the UK has achieved the greatest reductions in carbon emissions related to electricity production, followed by Denmark. The United States and China are a distant third and fourth, respectively.[47]

From an optimistic point of view, this could be seen as quite positive in that some of the largest economies are making the most progress. However, if the United States and China made the same level of improvements as the UK, then this would result in a nearly 10 percent reduction for the entire planet.[48]

An essential part of the energy solution is to transition to renewables.

Forms of Renewable Energy. Cleaner ways of generating electricity underpin many organizations' and most countries' environmental sustainability efforts, and this is no surprise given electricity generation is the leading contributor to greenhouse gases and environmental degradation. The major forms of modern renewables and the respective proportions of electricity generated by each are shown in Figure 12.3.

The United States, Germany, and France have installed the most wind power, while China, the United States, and India lead in solar power capacity. For perspective, simple rankings are helpful, but they do not tell the complete story. China has clearly made a tremendous commitment to solar power, and they have more than three times the capacity of the United States, which has more than twice the capacity of India.[49]

Are you getting the picture? The United States and China are the biggest contributors and thus have the greatest potential for sustainable leadership and environmental impact.

But a true standout is Germany. This country has installed more sources of renewable energy than any other country, and it seems to be a European thing, as eight out of the

figure **12.3**

Sources and Percentages of Renewable Energy

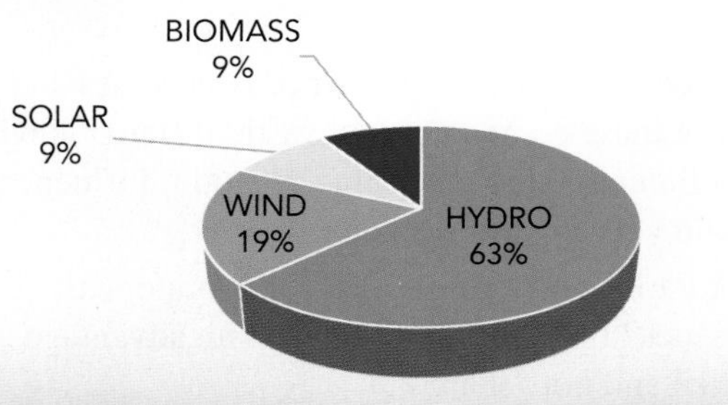

Source: H. Ritchie and M. Roser, Renewable Energy, Our World in Data, 2019: https://ourworldindata.org/renewable-energy#modern-renewables.

top ten countries are in Europe (Canada and Australia are the other two). Remember, for instance, that Norway produces none of its electricity from coal, the dirtiest source of them all, compared to South Africa that uses coal to generate nearly 90 percent of its electricity![50]

sungsu han/Shutterstock

Electric vehicles currently play a small but fast-growing role in using cleaner energy. Globally, in 2017, 1.1 million electric vehicles were purchased, which doubled in two years—2.2 million were sold in 2019.

Green Methods. Renewables are more sustainable sources of energy, but some organizations and countries emphasize what could be termed strategies or perspectives. These are broader approaches rather than sources, such as the following:

Eco-efficiency is doing more with less—using fewer and cleaner inputs to produce outputs (products and services). This includes using less water, energy, and materials, and thus involves the design, distribution, marketing, and use of all consumables.[51] Eco-efficiency is widely available and applied. For instance, when warehouses are converted into offices or condos, it can be eco-efficient to install energy-efficient lights, as well as reuse wood, bricks, and other existing materials.[52]

eco-efficiency doing more with less—using fewer and cleaner inputs to produce outputs (products and services)

Closed-loop production describes processes that reuse material waste created during production for additional or new products. The most common materials are plastic and fabric. Many recycling efforts are described as closed loop. 4ocean, for instance, collects plastic pollution in the ocean and uses it to create its signature bracelets. The shoe company Allbirds has many sustainable practices, including using recycled plastic to make its shoelaces.[53] Sierra Nevada Brewing Company uses the waste from brewing as compost in the soil to grow more barely and hops.[54]

closed-loop production processes that reuse material waste created during production for additional or new products

Cradle-to-grave approaches occur when a company takes responsibility for its products and the materials and energy used from inception, through production, customer use, and return. Many examples exist, and more are provided every day. An old one is beverage companies that collect the bottles or cans in which their beverages are packaged, and then recycle or reuse them. Cell phone and other electronics companies have processes, and even incentives, for customers to return or recycle their old products when they upgrade or buy new ones. This prevents materials, some of them toxic, from going into landfills and reduces their materials costs. HP has long implemented a process by which its spent printer cartridges are put back in the same package and returned to the company for recycling and reuse (both the product and the packaging).

cradle-to-grave approaches when a company takes responsibility for its products and the materials and energy used from inception, through production, customer use, and return

The nature of cradle-to-grave processes makes it a more comprehensive approach to sustainability, as the producer of a product (or service) is responsible for inputs and output throughout the product's life cycle.

Like other chapters, this one was packed with useful knowledge and applications. Hopefully, you see how environmental sustainability requires and integrates many business ethics concepts, such as a stakeholder approach, ethical individuals and leadership, ethical organizational cultures, and conscious organizations. Although environmental sustainability starts and ends with the actions of individuals, it also underscores the importance of cooperation and collaboration between organizations as well as among nations. This means that organizations must play their part. Whether we win or lose our environmental challenges depends on whether we cooperate, and this same argument frames the final chapter. We explore the role of business in social issues and change.

Chapter Summary

1. Externalities distort true costs, and many experts argue such costs must be accounted for in order to address many of the world's most pressing environmental issues.
2. Climate change and energy, water, and air pollution are major environmental challenges across borders.
3. One way to deal with these challenges is with formal regulations, such as treaties and protocols.
4. Ratification is done at the country level and is a critical part of the acceptance and enactment of treaties and protocols.
5. The Montreal and Kyoto Protocols are two of the most important regulations since the late 1980s.
6. The Paris Climate Agreement aimed to reduce greenhouse emissions and was intended as an improvement and replacement to the Kyoto Protocol.
7. Environmental sustainability is fundamental to responsible business activity today and a sustainable society in the future.
8. Environmental sustainability has numerous benefits for businesses, such as brand image, efficient operations, and attracting talent, customers, and investors.

Key Terms

CASE STUDY: Hard Times for You, for Them, but Not for Me

The cruise industry has been devastated by COVID—sick passengers, sick and healthy employees stranded onboard, canceled trips, and lost customer confidence. The cruise industry itself has done its own damage to the environment. All but one of the industry's sixteen cruise lines received grade C or lower, and Carnival Corporation, the world's largest travel company that also owns and operates Princess, Holland America, Costa, and other cruise lines, received an F.[55]

Trouble...

Infractions in the cruise industry are usually related to dumping of polluted discharge from ships into the water. Many of these occur in Alaska, which besides being a popular destination for cruises, has tough standards and robust enforcement. Notable environmental offenses by Carnival include illegally dumping oil into the ocean between 2005 and 2013, which was made even worse by the company's efforts to cover it up. This resulted in a $40 million fine, probation, and oversight by a court-appointed monitor (CAM). Then, in 2018, Carnival Corporation admitted to releasing food waste and plastic into the water, falsifying training records, and inappropriately reporting maintenance and other compliance activities ($20 million fine).[56]

... and More Trouble

Carnival, however, did much more. The same year, 2018, one of its ships was cited for discharging 59,000 pounds of "gray water" (waste from kitchen sinks and appliances, not toilets) into the Great Barrier Reef. Then, there were air pollution fines in 2015, fines for releasing pool water (2011), dumping sewage (2004), and another oily water infraction and cover-up in 2002.

In total, it is estimated that Carnival has paid over $78 million in fines since 2000, and although more than 90 percent of fines were environment-related; still other fines were related to employment infractions, consumer protection, and safety.[57]

Reactions

Carnival created a chief compliance officer position and hired Peter Allen, who then was required to work with a court-appointed monitor (CAM) to help oversee the cruise line's conduct. A company spokesperson said, "Peter is working closely with all our brands, not only on key compliance and performance initiatives, but also on broader efforts around company culture tied to our crew members, ship officers, and the entire workforce." Beyond this the spokesperson said, " . . . Our top priorities are safety, environmental compliance, and protecting the environment."[58] The company also has increased funding for the compliance office from $27 to $47 million dollars and increased its staff from twenty-nine to fifty-five.[59]

The court-appointed monitor conducted an employee survey that revealed other, if not related, issues. Employees reported a lack of trust between employees, managers, and supervisors, along with the belief that employees were blamed for the infractions, rather than determining the underlying causes of the issues. For his part, Arnold Donald, CEO of Carnival Corp since 2013, stated that environmental issues are his top priority along with that of the board.[60]

For Discussion

1. Imagine you're the CEO Carnival Corporation, Arnold Donald, and are put to the TV Test. What would you say if asked to explain the poor environmental record of the company?
2. Which stakeholders are affected by Carnival's conduct and how?
3. Assume you are the court-appointed monitor. What recommendations would you make to help Carnival improve?

Apply Three-Dimensional Problem-Solving for Ethics (3D PSE)

You can apply the Three-Dimensional Problem-Solving for Ethics (3D PSE) from multiple perspectives (see Figure 12.4), such as that of Carnival employees or CEO. But let's try it from the perspective of the court-appointed monitor (CAM). Assume you are

figure 12.4

Three-Dimensional Problem-Solving for Ethics (3D PSE)

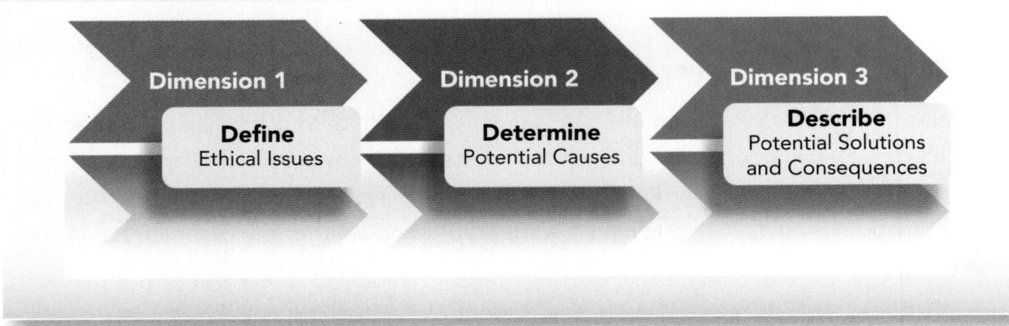

that person and problem-solving for ethics at Carnival. You, of course, can select the perspective of a different stakeholder, just be sure to specify whose perspective you have considered.

Dimension 1: *Define* the Ethical Challenge

What is the gap in the case? What do you have from Carnival, and what do *you* want?

a. From the CAM's view, what is the current situation at Carnival, and how do you think it should be?
b. Why is the current situation a problem? What undesirable behaviors and outcomes happened for Carnival as a result of the problem you defined? Why does Carnival care about the problem you defined in Dimension 1?
c. Define your problem in one or at most two sentences, and structure it in terms of what is current versus what is desired.
d. Who are the key stakeholders, those that affect or those that are affected by the problem you defined? What are the undesirable outcomes for each stakeholder?

Dimension 2: *Determine* the Causes

a. **Individuals.** Given the problem you defined in Dimension 1, what causes can be attributed to individuals, such as the CEO of Carnival or employees? There may be no individual factors at play in the case, but it is a good idea to consider whether there are or not.
b. **Contextual.** What are the potential organizational causes—that is, policies, practices, or other factors—within Carnival? What about the industry, state, or national causes?

Dimension 3: *Describe* Your Potential Solutions and the Intended and Unintended Consequences for Stakeholders

For each cause you identified in Dimension 2, answer the following questions:

a. ***What*** do you recommend, and ***how*** do you recommend it happen?
b. ***Why*** should they do it? Does it reflect a particular ethical decision-making perspective (e.g., utilitarian or universal)?

If your responses to these questions are unsatisfactory, then go back to Dimension 1 and repeat the process. If, however, you are comfortable and confident in your problem-solving efforts thus far, then ensure you achieve the desired outcomes and avoid any unintended consequences.

c. What is the ***desired and likely effect in the short term and long term*** for the key stakeholders involved in the problem and causes (Dimensions 1 and 2)?
d. What ***potential unintended consequences*** may occur with each proposed solution?
e. If any, what are the **implications for *other* stakeholders** (e.g., individuals, organizations, and communities) besides those noted in Dimensions 1 and 2?
f. Will your solution **work in an ethical manner**? Make a final assessment of whether your chosen solution will reduce or eliminate the causes determined in Dimension 2, and whether it will remedy the ethical problem defined in Dimension 1. If not, then repeat and refine the dimensions.

Chapter Opener Photo Source: Volodymyr Burdiak/Shutterstock

chapter 13

The Role of Business In Social Justice And Change

Learning Objectives

AFTER READING THIS CHAPTER, YOU SHOULD BE ABLE TO:

LO1 Describe how changing values influence the contemporary stakeholder approach and business ethics.

LO2 Explain the role of business in creating social justice and change.

LO3 Outline the key elements for reducing income inequality.

LO4 Explain the key elements for reducing health and health care inequality.

LO5 Identify the key elements for reducing racial inequality.

WHERE DO **YOU** STAND?

If Social Inequality Is a Problem, Then Whose Problem Is It?

Social inequality describes the differences in achieved outcomes (e.g., income, education, and health status) and individuals' perceived access to education and health care, which are critical to achieve other valuable outcomes in the future.[1] Social inequality confronts people everywhere, and many view inequalities as global problems that require everyone's attention—individuals, businesses, and governments. Many people with these beliefs feel that inequalities are especially problematic when they are beyond an individual's control, such as their race, gender, and place of birth (low-income neighborhoods or low-income countries). Still, other people believe that life is unfair, but people make their breaks. Exceptional people do exceptional things, despite circumstances, and thus, it is each individual's responsibility to improve their station in life. Therefore, inequalities are challenges that individuals need to overcome and solve on their own.

1. Do you think inequality is a serious problem in the United States? Explain.
2. Do you think inequality is a serious problem in the world? Explain.
3. Do you think wealthy individuals have any responsibility for the poor in their own country? Explain.
4. Do you think wealthy countries have any responsibility for poor countries? Explain.
5. What role, if any, do you think businesses have for addressing inequalities within the countries in which they operate?

Introduction

Throughout this book, you've learned how values, norms, and leadership are critical determinants of business ethics. You also learned that these factors are foundational to sustainability and social responsibility for individuals, organizations, countries, and the larger global society. We conclude the book by applying this knowledge both within and between countries to affect social change and address issues of inequality.

When reading this chapter, look for connections between the concepts and examples you learned in previous chapters along with thinking about your personal role in addressing the challenges highlighted. The purpose of this chapter is to motivate you to identify opportunities. Put differently, your future employers are likely to be engaged in issues you learned in this book (e.g., environmental, social, and governance [ESG]). You may also have a deep-seated desire to make a true impact on social justice, for instance, and thus consider the social justice engagement of companies you consider as employers or business partners. More generally, you are likely to be responsible directly or indirectly for acting on the issues raised in this book. Therefore, as a practical matter, you are well served to take this opportunity to apply your knowledge to guide your job search, performance, and career satisfaction and fulfillment.

social inequality
the differences in achieved outcomes (e.g., income, education, and health status) and individuals' perceived access to education and health care, which are critical to achieve other valuable outcomes in the future

Changing Expectations for Business

"What is the purpose of a business?" If you ask this question to ten random people on the street, the most common answer would be—"to make money." If you then ask a follow-up question—"In addition to money, what else?"—some people would say "that's it, just to make money." However, many would also say things such as provide opportunities for employees and treat them fairly, do right by customers, be conscious of the communities in which they operate, and be good to the environment.

Their responses are quite informative and reveal some useful insights, such as:

1. Organizations need to be *profitable* to survive, that was true and will remain true forevermore.
2. Answers to the follow-up question show that people actually use a *broader stakeholder approach*, meaning they expect companies to do more than simply make money for shareholders.
3. How they qualify their comments about each stakeholder reveal their expectations pertaining to their *ethical treatment*, such as being fair to employees, treating them well and being respectful, and doing right by customers (don't take advantage of them).

Collectively, these points underscore values, which drive expectations for business ethics.

As you have learned in this course, values change more slowly than norms, but they nevertheless change. It is becoming difficult for companies to cater only to shareholders, as people around the world now expect businesses and their leaders to genuinely consider employees, customers, communities, and the environment, not at the expense of shareholders but alongside shareholders.

This change was reflected in how the *Business Roundtable* redefined the purpose of the corporation in 2019. The *Business Roundtable* is a consortium of CEOs from some "of America's leading companies working to promote a thriving US economy and expanded opportunity for all Americans through sound public policy." The new definition specifically states that companies should commit to benefiting all stakeholders including customers, employees, suppliers, communities, and shareholders. This change is notable for many reasons. First, since 1997, when the Roundtable provided its original guidance on corporate governance (the G in ESG), it has explicitly taken a shareholder orientation (recall our discussion from chapter 2). Second, this change was signed and thus was formally supported by the CEOs of 181 companies.[2]

Moreover, companies and their leaders are increasingly expected to be agents of social justice and change. This is the S in ESG that you learned about in chapter 10. In this chapter, we build on this and address the role of businesses, their leaders, and governments in providing social justice.

Business Is All about Profits, Right?

Historically, and still, many people think that the role of business is to increase profits. Businesses need to make money, and performance management systems are currently designed to reward leaders based on earnings per share, stock price, and other financial measures. This fits perfectly with the adage—"what gets measured is what gets done." We, as a society, therefore, get organizations and leaders who have developed skills aimed at managing revenues and costs to deliver the expected financial outcomes. Because this is how it has been for so long, and many would argue still largely that way today, it seems that asking leaders and their companies to do more is wrongheaded or fantasy.[3] Let's test this notion by examining multiple sides of the argument and considering alternatives.

Besides Business, Who Else Is Responsible? Some argue that the above view is misguided. Business leaders go to business school to learn business—how to market products and services, using appropriate accounting controls and financing acumen, while managing people effectively to these ends. Moreover, their profit-maximizing efforts are reinforced by capitalism and free markets. People will vote with their dollars—good will survive and bad will fail. This implies that any personal misconduct by leaders (e.g., bullying or harassment) or organizational misconduct (e.g., exploiting employees and polluting the environment) will eventually be corrected by the market. Good people will be rewarded, and bad people will be out of jobs, or at least positions of authority, and bad organizations will fail to survive.[4]

Furthermore, if business leaders must also be social engineers and take on the responsibility of solving larger issues beyond their departments or companies, then they aren't equipped. This is not what their companies are designed to do. They are designed to make their respective products and services profitable. The organizations are structured this way. Policies and processes are intended to deliver these results.

In contrast, if business leaders are expected to tackle issues of income, health, and racial inequality both inside and outside their organizations, then how would their performance be measured? Economist Greg Mankiw made the point this way:

> *"From a company's share price, a board of directors can glean how well its chief is serving shareholders. That is why boards often hold chief executives accountable by compensating them with stock or stock options. No similar metric is available to judge how effectively a chief executive is serving society as a whole."*[5]

This does not mean that leaders do not care about environmental or social issues, but that these are the responsibility of other organizations, notably government. It is the government's job to fix these issues.

The Government's Role. Governments—through the laws they create and enforce and how they allocate resources (e.g., taxes)—are critically important stakeholders. However, when we talk about government, we are actually talking about people, specifically leadership at the local, state, and national levels. This is why we discuss government here. If you recall from chapter 12, it is not an accident that China produces the majority of the world's medical supplies such as masks and other personal protective equipment (PPE). See the Ethics in Action box for what purposeful government intervention looks like.

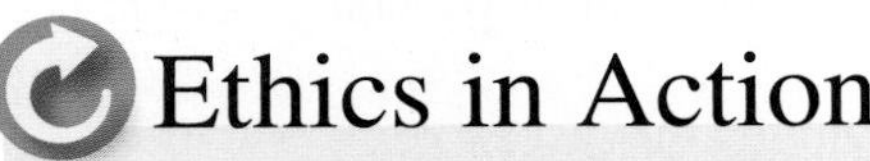

Government Really Means Leadership

China is often criticized, and only occasionally praised, for how its government supports business. One especially timely and notable example is what it has done to create and support the medical equipment industry that now dominates the world in producing masks, gowns, and numerous other forms of PPE and medical devices.

The national government identified these products as both a domestic need and an international opportunity. It made the industry a national strategic priority and provided cheap land and generous loans and subsidies to support its development. The concern in China, as in the United States and other countries, is that demand can be unpredictable or at least uneven—high during flu season and low during the summer. This, in turn, makes investing in increased capacity very risky, if not unwise. The industries and companies would continually cycle through booms and busts. The government also addressed this issue. It required hospitals to purchase from regional and national suppliers, without imports, which helped sustain supply through seasonal fluctuations and over the years.[6]

Talukdar David/Shutterstock

Then, the new coronavirus hit. Supplies were depleted quickly, but China simply turned up the investment and expanded its capacity immensely. For instance, mask production increased twelvefold in February 2020! The material used in masks increased five times, which is fifteen times more than the United States produced even after it increased its own production.[7] All of these numbers add up to preparedness and dominance.

Much of the world depended on and still depends on China for PPE and other medical supplies, and they will for the foreseeable future. Because of China's past investments, they are best positioned to meet their own needs and realize the opportunities of meeting those of the rest of the world going forward. Smart business? Or not?

For Discussion:

1. Some would describe this situation as insightful leadership on the part of the Chinese government. How do you describe it?
2. If "United States" was substituted for "China" in the supply of PPE, would your views change? Why or why not?
3. Argue both for and against requiring companies to purchase from domestic suppliers. Ethical versus unethical.
4. More generally, do you think there is a place for purposeful government action like that illustrated in the case? If yes, give an example. If no, then justify your position.
5. Assume the federal government of the United States was going to develop an industry in a way similar to the Chinese and medical PPE. Describe one industry you would recommend and why.

One economist describes government's responsibilities this way:

1. They need to protect property rights, maintain the rule of law, and guard against corruption.
2. They must ensure that resources are shared fairly (not necessarily equivalently).
3. They must guard against environmental destruction and other externalities (costs borne by parties that did not produce them).[8]

In theory, this is great. If governments at all levels and around the globe consistently and effectively did these three things, the world would be a better place. However, in reality, governments often do not fulfill their obligations.[9] Some people prefer the governments to play a small role and leave issues to be resolved by economics and efficient markets between buyers and sellers.

The Markets Can Solve Inequities

What happens when government and markets fail to meet their responsibilities or function effectively and fairly? Countries throughout the world struggle due to corrupt governments and ineffective markets every day, and the pandemic revealed how consequential such challenges can be. Richard Thaler, a world-renowned economist, described simple and common examples of when supply and demand failed.[10]

Supply and Demand Sets the "Fair" Price. The economics of supply and demand would predict that if demand for PPE increased, then prices would increase to the point in which no buyers were willing to pay. The price would settle at an equilibrium where supply meets demand. However, as Thaler pointed out, and all of us experienced, this generally did not happen, and the reason is fairness. Theoretically, prices should rise along with demand, but most players did not jack up prices due to norms of fairness.

Why does this happen? A norm exists around the world not to take advantage of people when they are down. Any individual or company with supplies could choose to raise their prices, and many entrepreneurs did just this. They stepped in, provided supply to meet demand, and jacked up prices. They were interested in fast money—maximize profits while they could. More evidence for fairness being an entrenched norm was provided by Amazon and eBay, who also intervened, at least in certain instances, to combat vendor's attempts to price gouge and removed them from their platforms.[11]

Fair Is More Successful Than Highest. However, companies that have long-term relationships with people did not do the same, even though they could. Not because they are less entrepreneurial or they don't understand the relationships among supply, demand, and prices, but because they didn't price gouge or take advantage of customers, as they know that after the crisis nobody would do business with them again. They would be labeled as unfair and willing to exploit people with no options during a crisis. As Thaler put it: ". . . large companies are playing the long game, and by behaving 'fairly' they are hoping to retain customer loyalty after the emergency."[12]

mojo cp/Shutterstock

This is exactly what happened. One hospital executive reported paying $6 per mask to an overseas supplier when the domestic supplier who charged thirty-five cents ran out.

It helps to make a comparison to clarify what happened. What if an entrepreneur, trying to capitalize on opportunities created by the pandemic, sold shares of cruise line operator Carnival Corporation and invested all of the money in Zoom's stock? Such a person would be considered a smart trader; nobody would question his or her behavior. The point is that although the opportunity was generated by the same crisis, selling and buying stock did not have implications of fairness, whereas profiting inappropriately on masks and other PPE would have been perceived as unfairly taking advantage of others. In a word, unethical.

Bottom line: Supply and demand and other market mechanisms cannot be the sole solutions to problems facing individuals, organizations, countries, and the world. Simply relying on supply and demand would often result in the rich getting richer, the poor getting poorer, and many being left out. This scenario is common across the planet, and we spend the remainder of the chapter highlighting multiple pressing issues of social justice, the role businesses can play, and what it means to be a socially responsible and ethical organization (and individual). First, we return to our discussion of the role of leaders.

Leadership Is About Opportunity

Because markets and governments fail to function as needed or expected, business and other organizational leaders have the opportunity to step up. When times are tough, such as during periodic economic downturns, many simply hunker down and become increasingly focused on managing the bottom line, typically first, if not mostly, via cost cutting. However, others not only look for but also seize opportunities to grow the top line (revenues) and expand their impact for their stakeholders.

You're likely thinking, "Okay, I know this happens, but why is it that some leaders choose one path while some choose the other?" There are many answers to this question, and you learned one in chapter 10—purpose.

The Power of Purpose. A well-conceived and effectively communicated purpose helps leaders to influence internal and external stakeholders. During good times, leading is relatively easy, resources are abundant, performance goals are being met, and leaders devote energy, time, and other resources to plan for the future. During hard times, such as the Great Recession and the pandemic, leaders are pressured to deliver only to their primary stakeholders. If the organization's purpose is narrowly defined to service shareholders and thus profits above all else, then this is what happens.

However, for leaders whose organizations have a broader purpose, one that includes ESG for instance, they understand that at all times they must service the environment, be socially responsible, and do all things with appropriate management, policies, and practices. For them, this is not different from "good times," as it is who they are and what they do at all times.

More specifically, purpose not only inspires others, but it also helps guide decision making from the top to the bottom of organizations. The following Ethics in Action box highlights how purpose helped a college president more easilty make a very tough decision.

A compelling purpose is a powerful tool for leaders and their organizations. As you've learned in the concepts and examples in this book, many leaders and organizations have created and pursue purposes far broader than profits. They are seeking to impact broader society. Now, many are answering the call for businesses to apply their resources and capabilities to impact social justice and change, which is the focus of the next section and the remainder of the chapter.

Ethics in Action

Purpose Provides Clarity

The continuation of college football during a pandemic required a wide range of decisions and implications to be considered. Coaches and players had to be concerned about preparing and competing safely. But first, presidents needed to decide if their teams were going to play at all.

Big Money

One factor, besides safety, that many college presidents undoubtedly considered was financial. For perspective, revenues at the fifty or so schools that comprise the *power five* conferences topped $4 billion in 2019 (roughly $78 million per school). This Everest-like mountain of money does not include the financial implications for the businesses surrounding the universities and other revenue-generating activities. Tuscaloosa, the home of the University of Alabama, estimates that each home football game generates approximately $20 million dollars for the local economy.[13]

Put the Money Aside

However, all of this was made much simpler, but not easy, for David A. Thomas, the president of Morehouse College in Atlanta, Georgia. When confronted with what to do about the 2020–2021 season, he made the bold move of canceling football. Morehouse was the first scholarship program to do so.[14]

When asked to explain his decision, he said he didn't believe players' health could be guaranteed. Perhaps the fact that the student population at Morehouse is 95 percent Black, and the coronavirus has disproportionately affected Black communities, influenced the decision. Thomas first considered whether he could guarantee that players would be safe. He quickly realized he could not, in part due to the fact that Clemson University in a neighboring state had thirty-seven players on its team test positive, along with the growing rates of infection in his own state.

Melinda Nagy/Shutterstock

Thomas also said, "What I think responsible leadership will do in higher education is ask the question: What business are we in? We are not in the business to provide sports; at least we're not a Morehouse. We're in the business to provide a high-quality education that allows men to prepare themselves for a lifetime of leadership and service and vocational excellence."[15]

It is true that Morehouse's football program does not generate the same amount of revenue for the school as larger universities—Ohio State University leads the nation with $51 million in annual ticket sales.[16] Morehouse doesn't have lucrative TV contracts or even a large stadium (only 9,000 person capacity). But its football program nonetheless has a strong following and rich traditions.

Continued

When questioned further about his decision, President Thomas explained: "I hope that every president asks themselves that question: What business am I in? What am I here for? Now I've got a set of decisions to make, and am I making those decisions consistent with what my institutional purpose is?"[17]

For Discussion

1. Put yourself at that point in time, late June 2020. No conferences or large schools had made decisions yet, and coronavirus cases were spiking in the majority of states. What is your reaction to his decision?
2. How do you think his decision would have differed if Morehouse had a mega football program involving tens of millions of dollars a year like some other universities?
3. Given the stated purpose of Morehouse, what other decisions might this influence, beyond playing football next season?
4. Assume you are president at another school in the same conference as Morehouse (Southern Intercollegiate Athletic Conference), who has not canceled the season for your school. Now assume that after Thomas's decision, you are taking the TV test (explaining your position on the evening news) and are asked to justify why you haven't canceled the football season at your school. What would you say?
5. Provide another, non-COVID related, example of how the stated purpose of Morehouse could assist in decision making.

Business as an Agent for Social Justice and Change

social justice
the view that everyone deserves equal rights, opportunities, and treatment in economic, governmental, and social spheres

Many of the major challenges confronting the world are interrelated, such as energy and climate covered in the previous chapter. In addition, environmental issues are related to social justice. **Social justice** is the view that everyone deserves equal rights, opportunities, and treatment in economic, governmental, and social spheres.[18] The emphasis is on equality, such that a lack of equality (i.e., inequality) results in a lack of justice, and we focus our attention on inequality related to income, health, and race. The complexity of these issues is reflected in the fact that each can serve as both causes and outcomes of inequality, which also means that solutions require a concerted effort by an array of stakeholders. Although individuals and governments have important roles to play, we emphasize the role of businesses and their leaders, as it is argued that businesses have the resources and capabilities that the others do not possess. Businesses, and those that lead them, therefore, have the ability to make enormously impactful change.

Income Inequality

income inequality
the differences in how income is distributed among individuals, groups, populations, social classes, or countries

Income inequality refers to the differences in how income is distributed among individuals, groups, populations, social classes, or countries. Given that income is often a key determinant in the quality of life and access to health care, education, housing, and other critical goods and services, income differences are intimately related to the majority of other social justice issues.[19] The World Economic Forum has identified three primary causes for income inequality, which are as follows:

1. Education
2. Trade
3. Government policies.[20]

Many experts have long argued that income differences continue to widen based on education, as employers across industries and countries continue to pay a premium for those with more and relevant education. International trade has a double-barrel effect, as consumers have a larger selection of products at lower costs, and this increases imports further still, which is made possible by offshoring production and jobs to parts of the world with cheaper labor. Finally, government policies since the 1970s have deregulated industries, reduced unionization, skewed tax benefits, among others, which have increased the gap between high-wage earners and everyone else.[21]

Now that you understand some of the causes, let's turn our discussion to how income inequality is measured.

Measuring Income Inequality. One of the primary ways to measure income inequality is with **household income**—the combined gross income (before taxes) of all members of a household who are fifteen years or older. It is used in a variety of ways to determine the economic health and disparities within a country, region, or group. For instance, household incomes were used to determine the median income in the United States, which as of the last census was $61,372, meaning that half of the working households made more and half made less.[22] Inequality is often assessed by dividing household incomes into five groups or quintiles. In 2018, the averages within each of these groups were as follows:

household income
the combined gross income (before taxes) of all members of a household who are fifteen years or older

Lowest quintile	$13,775
Second quintile	$37,293
Middle quintile	$63,572
Fourth quintile	$101,570
Top quintile	$233,895[23]

Another measure is the **Gini Index** (or coefficient) that measures income distribution, and its value is between 0 (perfectly equal incomes) and 1 (perfectly inequality).[24] A higher Gini Index means that high-income individuals receive a greater share of the total income. Gini Index also measures distribution within, and this means that a wealthy country and a poor country can have similar Gini coefficients if their respective incomes are distributed similarly.[25] For instance, the United States has a Gini Index of .45, which puts it between Peru (.453) and Guyana (.446).[26] However, the United States has the greatest inequality of the G7 countries (UK, Italy, Japan, Canada, Germany, and France).[27]

Gini Index
(or coefficient) measures income distribution, and its value is between 0 (perfectly equal incomes) and 1 (perfectly inequality)

South Africa and Haiti have two of the highest Gini coefficients (.625) and (.608), respectively, while Sweden (.249) and Slovakia (.244) have two of the lowest.[28]

Now that we know how to measure it, what is the state of the world in terms of income inequality?

Income Inequality Is Growing Within and Between Countries. Table 13.1 provides some useful statistics for perspective, and it shows how income inequality has grown substantially both within the United States and around the globe.

table 13.1

Income Inequality in the United States and Around the Globe

Income Inequality in the United States[29]	Global Income Inequality[30]
The eighty-twenty rule applies. The top 20 percent of income earners in the United States have brought in more income than the other 80 percent.	Of the world's population, 71 percent lives in countries where income inequality has grown in the past thirty years.
Income inequality is greater in the United States than in any of the other G7 nations (UK, Italy, Japan, Canada, Germany, and France).	The share of income going to the richest 1 percent increased in 59 percent of countries (the richest are getting an ever-greater share of income gains).
A total of 61 percent of Americans say there is too much inequality, but the differences within particular groups (e.g., income level and political affiliation) can be very large.	The poorest 40 percent of citizens earned less than 25 percent of the income.
The wealth gap—difference between the richest and poorest Americans—doubled between 1989 and 2016.	Inequality within countries is growing at a faster rate than inequality between countries.
The wealthiest have gained the most since the Great Recession	The average income of people living in North America is sixteen times greater than the average of those living in sub-Saharan Africa.

Inequality is accelerating faster within countries than between countries, which is among the notable revelations from Table 13.1. In other words, rich French people are gaining more compared to other citizens of France, than they are compared to rich people in the United States. This is evident in the often intensely polarized political battles happening in countries around the world. Political polarization increases inequalities, as those in power generally seek to serve their own interests more than unite, cooperate, or improve the station of others.

As for income inequality between countries, income inequality has *decreased* in Latin America and some countries in Africa and Asia.[31] This shows that some countries are indeed raising the standard of living of their people when compared to other countries.

Now, however, and as you learned in chapter 12, a consensus has emerged in many countries that all people should have equal access to opportunities and that an individual's opportunities should not depend on factors outside of a person's control, such as gender, race, or geography. This includes income; being born into a family with little money should not preclude you from ever having money yourself.[32]

This presents a dilemma for businesses. On the one hand, from an economics perspective, companies "should" source materials, products, processes, and people efficiently—the best at the lowest cost. On the other hand, some leaders and businesses feel a genuine duty to raise up other people and improve living standards in the process of doing what they do.

Approximately 30 percent of American workers earn less than $10.10 per hour, which puts them below the poverty level, and many of them do not get paid sick time, paid vacations, or sufficient healthcare benefits. If this situation is seemingly so dire for so many, both domestically and abroad, what are the causes? After all, we need to identify the causes if we have any hope of effectively improving the situation.

Primary Causes of Income Inequality. There are many causes of income inequality, and thus other forms of inequality that are linked to income, have many causes. Some of the major ones in the past two or three decades are:

- **Cheap labor and outsourcing.** Companies must be competitive to survive, and managing costs is fundamental to this. Labor is often the greatest cost in many industries, which means all competitors are looking to reduce labor costs. This resulted in many jobs going to China and more recently to India, Vietnam, and Malaysia.[33] Some estimates are that the United States lost 20 percent of its manufacturing jobs since 2000.[34]
- **Education.** Education is a strong predictor of income both in the United States and around the world. Northern European countries have some of the best education systems by any measure, and part of this is due to the availability of a high-quality education to all citizens, while less-developed countries have limited quality and limited access. The United States is in the middle of the pack within the developed world. This is due to the fact that quality and access to education vary greatly .[35]
- **Skills gap.** Employers pay more for valuable skills, and this happens within and between countries. Some countries experience a **brain drain**, the migration of people with valuable skills to another region (or country). Many skilled workers have moved from Romania, Poland, and Italy, to Sweden, Ireland, and Denmark. The former experienced a brain drain and the latter a brain gain. Skills also become obsolete often due to technological advancements or offshoring.[36]
- **Weakening labor influence.** Unionization and the associated collective bargaining have reduced worker influence and thus wages and benefits. This has exacerbated the predicament of lower-skilled, lower-wage workers everywhere, including the United States and Western Europe, which has accelerated the growing gap between incomes.[37]

brain drain
the migration of people with valuable skills to another region (or country)

Countries on the Edge. Poor and developing countries are often quite fragile, meaning that financial and other resources are lacking, which makes them especially vulnerable to crises such as major weather events (e.g., hurricanes, drought, and floods) and the coronavirus pandemic. Much of their basic functioning and growth is supported with money borrowed from other countries and organizations (e.g., International Monetary Fund). However, just like you, when countries borrow money, they must pay it back with interest. For instance, Ethiopia is but one of dozens of countries that spends more on paying back their debt than it does on health care for its citizens. When the pandemic hit, economic output plummeted in Ethiopia, but costs for dealing with the health crisis soared, as it did in all countries. But poor countries already lack resources, which means to provide what is needed to respond to the crisis, the pandemic is only the most recent, they have to spend money they do not have.[38]

Bottom line: Looking at these causes more holistically, you might observe that solving these problems requires both bold leadership within countries and cooperation between countries. Businesses, governments, and individuals all have their roles.

Health and Health Care Inequality

Income inequality is tightly tied to both health and health care inequality. **Health inequality** occurs when one group or population experiences much worse health than another, while **health care inequality** occurs when one group or population experiences meaningful disparities in availability and access to quality care. For the industrialized world, health inequality is typically greater between countries than within countries. Nearly all industrialized countries have national healthcare, meaning that every citizen has some form of coverage. However, the notable exception is the United States. It is one of the wealthiest

health inequality
when one group or population experiences much worse health than another

health care inequality
when one group or population experiences meaningful disparities in availability and access to quality care

countries, but it also has some of the greatest inequalities in health care due to its lack of universal healthcare coverage. For example, the most affluent 1 percent of Americans lives on average fifteen years longer than the poorest 1 percent.[39] Another shocking statistic is 99 percent of maternal mortality (death during childbirth) occurs in the developing countries, and women in Chad have a 1 in 16 chance of dying during childbirth versus women in Sweden who have a 1 in 10,000 chance.[40]

Causes of Heath Care Inequality. In addition to the causes of income inequality, numerous factors drive health and health care inequality both in the United States and around the world. Let's briefly explore a few.

Availability. The fundamental cause of disparities both within and between countries is availability. Experts estimate that, globally, we have a shortage of 15 million health care workers or 20 percent less than what we need.[41] In underdeveloped countries, healthcare systems simply do not exist or those that do exist are so limited (e.g., located only in a few urban centers) that many citizens simply cannot utilize the services. Low-income areas in the United States also suffer availability challenges, as these areas often lack sufficient clinics, clinicians, and transportation.[42]

Access. For developed countries, the differences within are largely matters of access to health care. Quality care exists, but it is more or less difficult to access. Again, this is perhaps most stark in the United States. Quality aside, to access care in the United States, one must have insurance. The old and the poor get government insurance (Medicare for the elderly and Medicaid for the poor), but the vast majority of the population receives, or not, insurance through their employers. Not only has the number of employers providing health insurance declined over time, but the ever-increasing costs have been passed on to employees, making access prohibitively expensive for many.[43]

Poor people are sicker. In all countries, lower-income people and groups are on average sicker. They not only have more chronic diseases such as high blood pressure and diabetes, but many of their illnesses are also not detected and treated early. Lack of prevention and early treatment then leads to additional and more severe outcomes such as strokes, blindness, and amputations.[44]

Rising costs. Combined with the previous causes, rising costs present challenges around the globe. In the United States, cost is a reason some percentage of people across all income levels choose not to purchase health insurance. Deductibles, premiums, and other employee contributions to employer health plans have increased over 255 percent since 2006.[45] Rising costs increase rationing in other places, which means that more costly procedures are performed less frequently everywhere.[46]

Effects and Costs of Health Inequality. Everyone pays something. Sick people pay with poor health, diminished abilities and quality of life, and reduced life expectancy. In the United States, and more modestly elsewhere, sick people are asked to pay if they can. Many cannot, which is why medical expenses are the number one cause of personal bankruptcy in the United States, accounting for 67 percent. It is important to note that many of these people have insurance, but the portion they are required to pay exceeds their financial resources.[47]

Hospital use and thus costs increase because people with the least access and availability go to hospitals because they have nowhere else to get care. Using the diabetes example, if untreated, many people have crises that cause coma and put them in the hospital. US hospital costs increase further still due to the requirement to treat the uninsured, which costs approximately $10 billion per year. This is paid by either insured patients or tax dollars, both of which increase as a result.[48] The costs are multiplied when the lost productivity, lost employment and income taxes, and increases in welfare payments are considered.[49]

It is worth noting that even those on Medicare in the United States are insufficiently protected. It is estimated that the average sixty-five-year-old couple retiring in 2019 will need $285,000 to cover health and medical expenses during retirement. Most people simply cannot cover such costs.[50]

To summarize, in the less-developed world, health inequality is largely driven by availability (it doesn't exist), whereas in developed countries, inequalities are linked to access (exists but can't get it). All of this is exacerbated by the fact that healthcare costs have risen faster than income all over the world.

Next, we address racial inequality.

Racial Inequality in America

Income and health inequalities are tightly intertwined with racial and ethnic inequalities. Before going any further, it is helpful to differentiate race and ethnicity. **Race** involves shared biological traits such as skin color and body shape, and it is inherited across generations. **Ethnicity** is something people acquire, learn, or share with others such as where they live or their culture and religion.[51] The two are often used interchangeably, but they are technically different. They can also overlap; people of many different races are Christians (same ethnicity).

race
shared biological traits such as skin color and body shape, and it is inherited across generations

ethnicity
something people acquire, learn, or share with others such as where they live or their culture and religion

For our purposes, we focus our attention on racial inequality in America. However, it is worth noting that both race and ethnicity are bases for discrimination and inequality throughout the world, and some of the greatest atrocities in human history were and are based on ethnicity, particularly religion, such as the Holocaust and internment camps for Uighurs in China.

Forms and Causes of Racial Inequality in the United States. Inequities exist along racial lines for almost any aspect of life such as income, wealth (value of assets minus debts), health and health care, and education. Using wealth as an example, the median net worth of non-Hispanic whites is approximately $143,000 and for Blacks it is $12,920. This is not a typo; the difference is more than ten times. Making matters worse is that the gap is increasing over time. Net worth for whites is increasing while it is decreasing for nonwhites. A fundamental reason is that 25 percent of Black families have $0 net worth. This is why the number is so low.[52]

The causes are historical and persistent. Slavery, among other horrible oppressions, prevented Black from earning an income and accumulating wealth. Importantly, wealth is accumulated over time, and Black Americans simply have not had generations over which wealth has accumulated for non-enslaved Americans. As such, Black and other minorities have been behind and remain behind (unequal) compared to others.

An inability to accumulate wealth was greatly exacerbated by **Jim Crow laws**, which were a collection of local and state statutes that maintained segregation, some of which were created and implemented immediately following the Civil War and continued until 1968.[53] Some of the legal limitations were as follows:

Jim Crow laws
a collection of local and state statutes that maintained segregation, some of which were created and implemented immediately following the Civil War and continued until 1968

- Black people were forbidden from holding certain jobs.
- Denied the right to vote.
- Attend certain schools (compulsory and higher education).
- Control where people lived.
- Segregation of prostitutes by race.[54]

Jim Crow was a minstrel (song and dance) show with a white actor who painted his face ("blackface") and portrayed Black people as inferior and incapable. Even government programs, such as Social Security, long excluded farm and domestic workers from benefits, which were the vast majority of the jobs held by Black people in the South.[55]

Although a number of laws improved the situation on paper—the Civil Rights Act of 1964, Voting Rights Act of 1965, the Fair Housing Act of 1968—inequalities are still widespread and deeply embedded, including in the workplace.[56]

Racial Inequality at Work. The number of companies in the S&P 500 that have Black CEOs is just five in 2020.[57] So, it is no wonder that more generally, Black men earn approximately 87 cents for every dollar white men do, and this gap illustrates the common wage disparities between races in the American workforce (see Figure 13.1). When gender is also considered, then a double whammy occurs. Black women comprise just more than 6 percent of the workforce, but they hold 10 percent of low-wage jobs (approximately $11/hour or $23,000/year) and only 2.7 percent of high-wage jobs ($48/hour or $110,000/year).[58]

Although these are long-term patterns, change may finally be on the horizon. Two-thirds of Generation Z'ers (twenty-five years and younger) reported that how a company addresses the Black Lives Matter (BLM) movement will influence whether they will buy the company's products or use its services.[59] This suggests that the youngest generation in the market today does more than simply value equality as some abstract ideal, but rather they expect others to express similar values in their actions. Therefore, companies have an opportunity, and strong incentive, to make changes potentially long overdue. For instance, executives of CrossFit and Condé Naste resigned after insensitive and racially inappropriate attitudes came to light. In contrast, Ben & Jerry's was handsomely rewarded.

Anuradha Mittal, chair of the company's board of directors, personally participated in protests related to George Floyd. She was so moved that she thought the company should express its support of the growing movement. Members of the executive team were already doing just this when she reached out. Ultimately, Ben & Jerry's partnered with the National Association for the Advancement of Colored People (NAACP) and Color of Change to make a call to action with recommendations for how to end racial violence and increase accountability and consequences for police. The content, just over 700 words, was powerful, as was the title of the post on its Website and social media accounts:[60] "We Must Dismantle White Supremacy: Silence is NOT an Option."[61]

The reaction was overwhelmingly positive, and hundreds of thousands of people shared it. This example was part of a groundswell of corporate support wherein numerous other companies have taken other actions as highlighted in the next Ethics in Action box.

figure **13.1**

Wage Differences Between Men of Various Races in the US Workforce

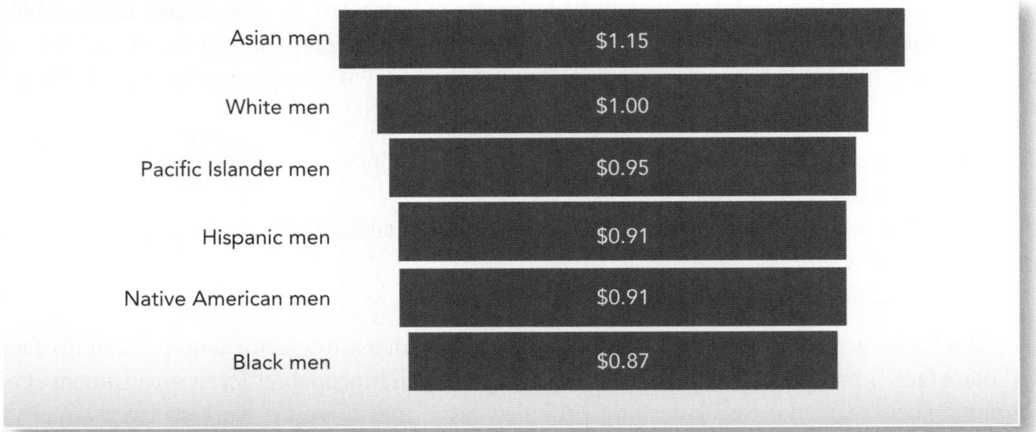

Asian men	$1.15
White men	$1.00
Pacific Islander men	$0.95
Hispanic men	$0.91
Native American men	$0.91
Black men	$0.87

Source: Adapted from S. Miller, "Black Workers Still Earn Less than Their White Counterparts," Society of Human Resource Management, shrm.org, June 11, 2020: https://www.shrm.org/resourcesandtools/hr-topics/compensation/pages/racial-wage-gaps-persistence-poses-challenge.aspx.

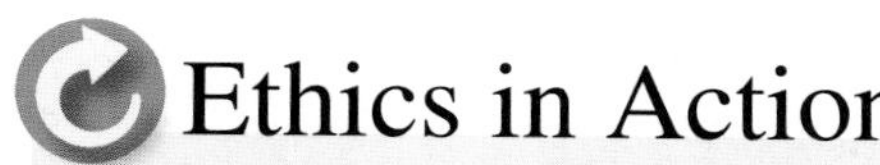

Ethics in Action

A 15 Percent Pledge Is an Excellent Start

In support of the BLM movement, numerous retailers began devoting 15 percent of their shelf space to Black-owned businesses. Among those who committed were

- Sephora
- Rent the Runway
- West Elm.[62]

The rationale is that the designated space increases the likelihood that products from Black-owned companies will make it to market, sell, and thus create additional opportunities for others, and so on. Some have expanded this idea. For instance, West Elm also committed to ensure that 15 percent of its corporate-level employees would be Black.[63]

More generally, a majority of Americans across age and racial boundaries agree with the BLM movement and support changes as shown in Figure 13.2.

Perceptions also differ and matter as shown in Figure 13.3.

It thus appears that businesses and their leaders have multiple reinforcing reasons for actively joining the movement and more generally tackling racial inequality:

1. *It's the right thing to do*. This means racial equality is consistent with espoused values of many organizations, and now, they need to ensure that their policies, practices, and other norms align.
2. *Financial benefits*. Customers and other stakeholders are modifying their behaviors based on those of the company.
3. *Consistent with society's values and expectations*. Perhaps things have really changed, and the seeming shift in values will translate into concerted and effective action and change.

figure **13.2**

Support for Black Lives Matter Movement

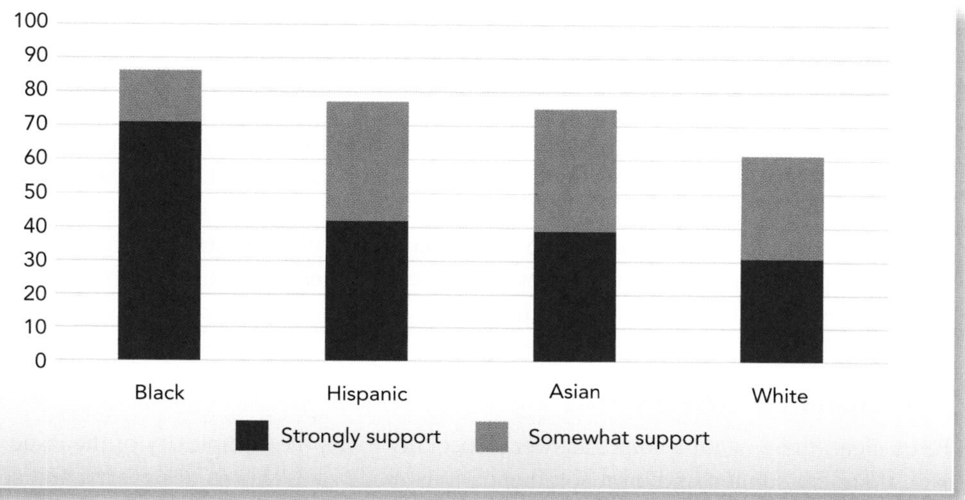

Source: adapted from K. Parker, J. M. Horowitz, and M. Anderson, "Amid Protests, Majorities Across Racial and Ethnic Groups Express Support for the Black Lives Matter Movement," Pew Research Center.

figure 13.3

Perceived Obstacles

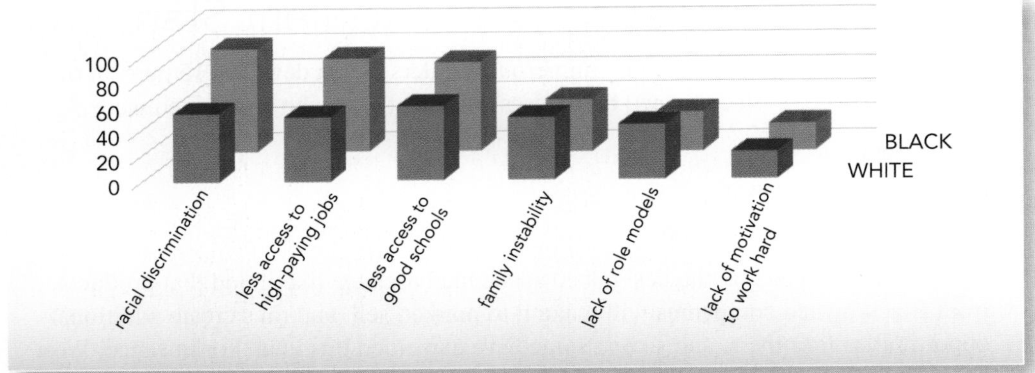

Source: Adapted from K. Parker, J. M. Horowitz, and M. Anderson, "Amid Protests, Majorities Across Racial and Ethnic Groups Express Support for the Black Lives Matter Movement," Pew Research Center, pewsocialtrends.org, June 12, 2020: https://www.pewsocialtrends.org/2020/06/12/amid-protests-majorities-across-racial-and-ethnic-groups-express-support-for-the-black-lives-matter-movement/.

To conclude this section, the underlying motive and goal for social justice are to ensure that the potential of individuals and populations is not limited by or dependent on where they were born. Put most simply, being born poor does not mean one should live and die poor. Advocates of social justice argue that regardless of skin color, parents, or country—all factors beyond one's control—every individual should have access to quality education, appropriate health care, and sufficient opportunities to lead a safe and fulfilling life. In the next sections, we'll explore some recommendations on how to achieve challenging goals in terms of income, health and health care, and race.

Effectively addressing these issues will help meet two fundamental goals of social justice. The first is to ensure that the benefits created by business, and society more generally, are shared widely. The second is to safeguard that the associated costs do not fall disproportionately on those who cannot afford to bear them.[64]

Solving Income Inequality

Essentially, domestic wages need to increase for a large percentage of the working populations in the United States and other countries. Related to the United States, what would you propose? One option floated by politicians, businesspeople, and others is to prevent outsourcing. This can be problematic, in that it essentially tells businesses that they should not operate efficiently, and instead do everything they need with American workers. Even if possible, this course of action would deny people in other countries of often much-needed opportunities.

Alternatively, protectionist trade policies, tariffs, and subsidies could be used. Sure, this is an option, but to identify potential downsides, one only needs to look at the damage caused to both China and the United States due to their escalating trade war over the past few years. Besides, recall what you learned in chapter 12 about subsidies. One common shortcoming is that while making the developed country's producers "stronger," they can price local producers out of the market, which can and has prevented countries from developing their own capabilities and industries.

Solutions for the World

To be clear, there is not a single answer, especially given the complexity of the issue. However, there are some common recommendations made by a chorus of experts, and some of these are outlined in Table 13.2.

table **13.2**

Potential Solutions to Income Inequality at Home and Abroad

Solution	Description
Education[65]	Education is a clear predictor of income and thus a fundamental element of any remedy to income inequality. To make the point, can you imagine any solution that would not include increasing the quality and access to education?
Upskilling[66]	Identify the needed skills for the key industries and then invest in programs to deliver them to two populations: (1) those currently working whose skills are "at risk" of becoming obsolete and (2) high school, college, and vocational programs designed with skill development and continuous learning at their core.
Valuable human capital	It is a bit simplistic to say—"Let workers unionize." Technically, this is protected by law, which means that something more is needed. Unions have both advantages and disadvantages. The past few years have also seen an increase in employee activism, which is the contemporary form of concerted action. What is needed is a different orientation toward employees, not simply as means to ends, but as humans with innate value, worthy and deserving of development. Fundamental to this is a reasonable or living wage rather than the truly minimum wage historically used in the United States.[67]

How to pay for all of this? Any solution for national programs necessarily involves the government, which often includes taxes. The details of such a tax policy are beyond the scope of this chapter and book, but there are two basic sources that can be used separately or in combination.

1. *Close loopholes*. Billions of dollars are lost each year in either unfair or unproductive loopholes in the existing tax code. Closing (some of) these could go a long way to paying for generous and effective programs.
2. *Economic sustainability tax*. A separate tax could be levied on either the wealthiest of Americans or particular economic activity such as a trading transaction tax on Wall Street (e.g., a small tax on each trade).[68]

It also is important to note that the issues and recommended solutions are made more challenging by the fact that the cost of education has dramatically outpaced the rate of inflation more generally as well as wage growth. This means that even if you have the advantages of living in the industrialized world, a key cause and thus solution to income inequality has gotten dramatically more expensive in the 2000s.[69]

Living Wages Versus Minimum Wages

The US minimum wage has been $7.25 since 2009, and if you do the calculations (40 hours/week × 50 weeks = 2,000 hours × $7.25), then this results in $14,500 in gross pay for the year.

Could you pay your tuition if you made this much? Could you also pay your rent and food expenses? What about transportation? Even those with modest lifestyles would find it nearly impossible to cover the most basic expenses.

For perspective, the **poverty level**, which is the annual income used by the government to qualify individuals and families for federal assistance programs, was $12,760 in 2020 for a single adult, $17,240 for a couple, and $26,200 for a family of four.[70] This means the minimum wage is little more than the poverty level in the United States, and most individuals

poverty level
the annual income used by the government to qualify individuals and families for federal assistance programs

would be hard-pressed to support themselves on this wage, and families would find it nearly impossible.

living wage
the income required to meet the basic needs, be independent of financial assistance, and maintain housing and food security

In contrast, the **living wage** is the income required to meet the basic needs, be independent of financial assistance, and maintain housing and food security. Of course, this differs depending on where you live, but for the United States as a whole in 2019 the living wage was estimated to be $16.54 per hour, $34,404 per individual, or $68,808 for a family of four (two working adults and two nonworking children).[71] By the way, this does not allow for any vacation time, unless you are fortunate enough to get paid vacation.

Some basic knowledge and simple calculations illustrate how desperately low many incomes are, which means that small changes are just that small. This big problem seemingly requires big changes.

Some businesses have taken charge of the situation and raised wages, such as Target, Bank of America, Costco, and Facebook.[72] But the target of a $15 minimum wage still leaves many individuals with financially stressful lives.

United Nations' Recommendations for Combatting Income Inequality

The United Nations has combatting inequality as part of its mission and has generated some fundamental recommendations that can be applied throughout the world.

1. **Promote access to opportunities.** Any plan without access to opportunities to improve their station in life by earning fair and sufficient wages will be suboptimal. Education is foundational to jobs and wages. Providing quality education to both children and adults is critical and puts governments at all levels (local and national) around the world at the center of solutions. They need to invest in education infrastructure, pay competitive wages to teachers, and support childcare, which assists in their development while enabling parents to work. Australia, Finland, Japan, and Sweden provide excellent examples in developed countries, while Brazil and China have both dramatically improved education in their countries. For their part, businesses can provide targeted internships and other outreach programs to provide opportunities for young people, and partnering with educational institutions can help ensure curricula that match the skills sought by employers. Businesses also need to pay fair and sufficient wages and in international locations hire and develop locally.[73]
2. **Macroeconomic policies for reducing inequality.** Governments and businesses need to align policies and practices that purposefully address key inequalities. Taxes and other incentives can influence the behaviors of individuals, organizations, and entire industries. Scandinavian and a few Western European countries (Netherlands, France, and Belgium) are well known for their social safety nets, specifically widely available support for health care, childcare, unemployment, and disability. These same countries have promoted education, health, and fair wages. None is a panacea, but rather they provide examples to inspire and guide others to adopt and modify to meet their own needs.[74]
3. **Discrimination.** You might cast the entire income inequality discussion in terms of discrimination, as unequal treatment is the root. This means that businesses and other organizations need to not just pay lip service to matters of equality based on gender, race, ethnicity, age, or other characteristics. They need to act by adopting policies and practices that serve a broad array of appropriate stakeholders simultaneously and fairly. This does not mean it is all the same but rather that one is not served at the expense of others.[75]

Values and norms are fundamental to all of these efforts. If an individual or organization values equality, then it must align its norms to actively deliver equality. This means more than guarding against discrimination, it also requires policies, practices, and leader attitudes and behaviors that actively develop equality.

Although businesses are in the best position to lead, this does not let governments off the hook. Government, through laws and financial tools (e.g., taxes, grants, and loans), is powerful in both motivating and reinforcing the actions of businesses and individuals. For instance, laws lag, but they nevertheless can powerfully influence the impact of business operations on the environment via incentives and penalties.

California, for example, arguably has shaped environmental practices at the country level for the past fifty years. It sets emission standards that dramatically influence automotive designs and products for companies around the world, not just those based in the US. Every manufacturer wants to sell there, which means they meet their standards.[76] Remember our example of the European Union's (EU) digital privacy policy. To do business with citizens of the EU, companies must comply with their data privacy standards. Even if you take issue with some aspects of how China has developed its medical supply industry, there are lessons to learn. As with the other examples, this shows the power of concerted effort to influence the actions of individuals, organizations, industries, and even entire countries. Similar tools can be applied to inequality, such as forgiving debt owed by individuals and countries.

Erasing Debt

Some experts recommend that an extremely impactful way to improve inequality on a global scale is for wealthier countries to forgive the debt owed to them by poorer countries. Just like individuals, countries with money lend it to countries that need it. Many suspended or otherwise paused debt payments in response to the pandemic, but some are suggesting that the debt be erased altogether. This would help relieve the immense financial stress experienced by these countries and, at the same time, enable them to redirect resources internally, which could assist their response to the pandemic and eventually other domestic needs.[77]

Similar recommendations have been made regarding student load debt. Senator Elizabeth Warren and others have presented plans to forgive all or percentage of student loan debt for some qualified percentage of borrowers. These numbers are enormous—approximately \$1.6 trillion owed by nearly 50 million Americans as of early 2020. This would improve the financial standing of tens of millions of Americans, who could then save or otherwise invest or spend their money in ways that improve their own lives, those of their children, and bolster the larger economy.[78]

Potential Remedies for Health

Social justice issues related to health and health care are enormous, to say the least. This means that the recommendations here are necessarily brief. Nevertheless, most of the following recommendations gleaned from experts are applicable both in the United States and abroad.

Reduce Costs

A common challenge for health systems globally is cost. Increases in the cost of health care outpace more general inflation and wage increases in developed countries, and in developing countries, the cost of building the infrastructure to train professionals and deliver care (e.g., clinics and hospitals) is simply too great.

In the United States, health care is a decades-long and often intense (political) debate. What nearly everyone agrees about is that the rate of cost increases is not sustainable. In 1970, the United States spent just more than 6 percent of its gross domestic product on health care and other industrialized countries spent on average 5 percent. Now that gap has exploded—approximately 18 percent versus just under 10 percent.[79] It is helpful to translate this into how much is spent per citizen.[80]

United States	$10,224
Switzerland	$8,009
Germany	$5,728
Sweden	$5,511
Comparable country average	$5,280
Canada	$4,826
Japan	$4,717
Australia	$4,543
United Kingdom	$4,246

Cost reduction and control is one of the main arguments made by those who advocate for a universal health system in the United States. Not only it would provide nearly universal access and all but eliminate bankruptcies due to devastating medical bills, but it also removes many of the costs and inefficiencies found in the current system. The most notable ones are listed below:

1. **Too many payors.** Providers of care (e.g., doctors and hospitals) are paid by insurers, which are too numerous to count. This causes providers to deal with a dizzying array of policies, practices, and payment amounts from all of the various insurers. This is inefficient. Under a universal plan, all care is submitted to and paid for by one insurer—the government. Most providers already are reimbursed by the government—via Medicare and Medicaid—which means they possess the necessary technology, skills, and knowledge today.[81]
2. **Limited cost control.** Supplies, pharmaceuticals, equipment, and the innumerable other items provided by vendors would be negotiated with one customer, instead of the current multitude of facilities, providers, and payors. This would provide the system consolidated and thus greater influence over costs and cost increases.[82]
3. **Insufficient quality of care.** Hospitals, doctors, and other care providers are forced to compete against each other and provide high-quality care at reasonable prices. By answering to one payor, all of the data end up in one place, making comparisons of quality of care outcomes easier, along with prices charged.[83] As it is now, you and your friend can go to the same hospital, receive the same procedure, yet be charged wildly different prices. This is exactly what happened in Texas. Two friends were tested for the coronavirus, and one received a $199 bill and the other $6,408.[84]

Cost, although critically important to make health care accessible and sustainable, is only one fundamental part of what is needed. We must also make it available.

Increase Availability and Access

At the global level, training and deploying qualified health professionals is fundamental to any effective plan. Training veritable armies of needed health workers is a challenge not only in terms of cost but also in terms of geography. To address this, businesses and governments can utilize distance-learning platforms. Just as universities and schools around the world have gone remote, driven by COVID-19, similar technologies can be used for both training and treatment. New health workers can be trained in larger numbers from afar; think of the millions of Americans who are receiving their education online. Health professionals with high-level skills or special knowledge, who are often concentrated in cities, can use technology to diagnose and collaborate with locals on treatment.[85]

Great strides have already been made in the area of mental health, which is underserved in the best health systems and completely absent in many. Silvercloud, an Irish mental health provider, has combined virtual sessions, asynchronous care, and in-person sessions to reach six times as many patients than it did previously. The remote elements make care available to those previously excluded due to geographic limitations, as well as to those who would otherwise not seek mental health care due to the associated stigma.[86]

In the United States, as in all other countries, health care is largely determined by the federal government. This means it is your attempts, and those of your employers, to influence politicians what type of system is best.

Reconciling Racial Inequality

Making progress on other forms of inequality, particularly income, will help improve racial inequality. However, business can and needs to play a significant role.

Businesses and Other Organizations

Waiting on or relying on governments or other organizations to take the lead is unwise, as too often the result is inaction and disappointment. Businesses and other organizations have the skill and resources to act on their own and influence the policies, practices, and behaviors of others. For example, the Southeastern Conference (SEC) of collegiate sports took a stand on the Confederate emblem on the Mississippi State flag that many viewed as support for slavery. The issue emerged and receded over a number of years, but in 2020 it came to the fore, and many individuals and organizations acted. When the Mississippi state government showed reluctance to remove the emblem, the SEC's commissioner stated that it was time for the emblem to go. If it didn't, he would prevent any SEC sports from playing playoff games in the state. This pressure added to that from National Association for Stock Car Auto Racing's (NASCAR) decision to ban the display of Confederate flags at its events, the positions of presidents of several of the state's universities, and opinions of many of the state's citizens. The legislature changed the flag.[87]

Still other organizations are putting their money where their mouths are, meaning they are holding executives accountable for improving race, diversity, and inclusion. The following Ethics in Action box describes how.

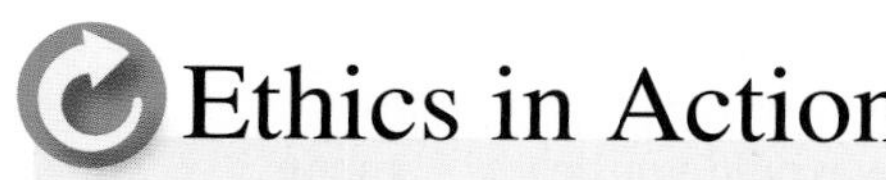

Racial Equality Pays

Like many chief executives and other leaders, Charles Jones, the CEO of an Ohio utility, FirstEnergy, felt that his leadership team was not embracing his resolute desire to hire women and people of color. He took action and linked bonuses to these goals.[88]

Continued

Put Your Own Pay at Risk

Mr. Jones did what other effective leaders do. He put his own pay at risk in the same way he required of his executives—10 percent the first year and 15 percent the next. This not only leads by example, or models the behavior he expects from others, but it also builds trust and commitment from others.

Simple but Not Common

Tying some portion of pay to goals is not new, of course, but actually doing it is remarkably rare. Only 78 of 3,000 companies (less than 3 percent) surveyed actually tied some portion of executive pay to diversity goals. The researchers further added that the very limited details shared by these companies led them to suspect that number is actually lower.[89]

What Are the Outcomes?

The first year of the program resulted in no bonuses, as the company (its executives) did not achieve two of the three related goals. It paid bonuses in the second year for hiring women and others from underrepresented groups for managerial jobs, but employees' responses to survey questions regarding diversity at the company did not meet the expectations.[90]

Mr. Jones is a realist and says that although he has no evidence of actual racism, the fact that employees in the company are 90 percent white proved that it must exist in some percentage.[91]

Progressive When Progressives Aren't

For comparison, many investors, consultants, and employees have pressured countless other companies to adopt such practices. One such company is Google, which strongly rejected such a practice. However, other tech companies have accepted. Satya Nadella, CEO of Microsoft, has approximately 17 percent of his cash bonus linked to diversity goals. Uber has implemented a similar program, but it tracks and rewards such goals over a three-year period, which has not passed yet.[92]

Still, other companies claim that such goals are unnecessary. JPMorgan Chase, the largest US bank, said it has increased the number of Black managers and executive directors by more than 50 percent in four years. A spokesperson of the bank stated that senior leadership does not believe in such short-term goals, "because they're looking to our leaders to develop and implement strategies that provide long-term, sustainable outcomes to drive diversity, equity, inclusion, and ultimately success of our diverse employees."[93]

For Discussion

1. Describe a reason not to tie some portion of compensation to such goals.
2. If you were an executive, and the board decided to tie 15 percent of your compensation to racial equality–type goals, how would you react? Explain.
3. Assume you own a company, why would you implement such a program?
4. Now assume that you are a competitor of FirstEnergy, and your company does not have such goals. Also, assume that you need to explain the reason on the evening news—the TV test—what would you say?

Your Efforts and Those of Other Individuals

The actions spurred by the killing of George Floyd are only the most recent in a long history of the struggle to overcome racial inequality in America. Much can be learned from the past experiences and efforts. A number of people active in the civil rights movement of the 1960s shared some sage advice for those taking up the challenge today.

1. **Pay attention to those who march with you.** This can be literal, actually march, but its meaning is broader. Support can come from people who look like you and those who couldn't be more different. Their support should be acknowledged and fostered. For instance, during the protests of 2020, many police officers knelt and marched alongside the protestors.
2. **(White) People now see it.** The internet and social media have enabled young and old around the globe to actually see violence against Black people and other minorities. News and images of events are shared in real time, which means people today can actually see and learn about what is happening, how race is a factor, which makes it more emotional and more real, even if the majority cannot actually know what it is to be the target. In the past, it was simply word of mouth, yours against someone else's, often the police or other people in power (typically also members of the majority).
3. **Reconcile rather than reject.** Besides nonviolent tactics, seek to have your opposition understand the situation and experience. Nobody will be converted from foe to friend without first understanding your side of the matter. Strive to persuade instead of conquering.
4. **Vote!** If laws and other norms aren't the cause of inequality, they are powerful reinforcers. Therefore, it is necessary to elect leadership that both understands and is motivated to enact change—not political acrobatics but genuine engagement.[94]

Then There Is Government

Recall from earlier in the chapter, government means leadership at the local, state, and national levels. And one of government's more powerful tools are taxes. Plainly and simply, equality requires investment. Just as inequality didn't happen accidentally, neither will a more equal and just future. Therefore, government leaders need to utilize effective **progressive taxes**, which take a larger percentage of income from high-income groups than from low-income groups and are based on the ability to pay.[95] The United States and many other countries have such systems, but the challenge is with effective implementation. Such practices are well intentioned and theoretically appropriate, but the loopholes and complexity undermine their potential. Several economists and politicians have proposed solutions, and most of them include the wealthy paying more, and the dollars collected being invested in ways that improve access and opportunities.

progressive taxes take a larger percentage of income from high-income groups than from low-income groups and are based on the ability to pay

Education Access. The strongest predictor of high income is the education level of one's parents. This means that racial and other forms of inequality ideally improve the access to education for parents and their children. Many developed countries, such as Australia, the Netherlands, France, and Belgium, effectively do and have done this. The government pays for or subsidizes education for citizens, which thus greatly increases access without saddling them with debt. The United States has lagged these and many other countries for many years in both access and quality of education.

Many experts argue that investing in people through education is more effective than either welfare or a universal basic income (i.e., the government pays a fixed amount to each citizen).[96] One way to pay for this is a Child Savings Account focused on education. Those who are able would be allowed to invest tax-free, and government and/or employers could provide matching funds. Some research has shown that such accounts and investments can close the education gaps between whites and Blacks by nearly 80 percent.[97]

Simply reaching out to students—sending them applications or recruiting at their schools—has been shown to dramatically increase the number of students who actually apply and get accepted. This entire process can be facilitated by offering generous scholarships.

Boost Wages. Minimum wages can be legally mandated only by the government, and the fact that it hasn't increased since 2009 provides little hope that they will drive the needed changes. Instead, and as noted previously, companies can take it upon themselves to pay what they feel is a fair wage. Of course, the counterargument is that this increases the cost of doing business, which in turn reduces the number of employees a business can hire, and at the same time, it increases prices to customers. Companies in the United States have already done this, across industries, and none of them appears to be struggling. Nevertheless, a level playing field for all competitors in a given industry is what is needed. Therefore, either the government can set a reasonable minimum wage or companies within industries and geographies can agree to do so on their own. For instance, $15 per hour will pay for much more in Starkville, Mississippi, than it will in San Francisco, California.

Investing in Children Now. A very interesting proposal was made by Professor William Darity at the Samuel DuBois Cook Center on social equity. He outlines baby bonds. As funny as it may sound, the concept itself is not new, only the application to babies. The United States sold war bonds in World War II to help finance military efforts, which are similar to US Treasury Bonds, in that they are issued by the government and pay interest to the investors. Similarly, baby bonds could be issued, and the money received could create a trust to be used to close equity gaps, such as by investing in quality education and health care for the country's children. Investors would, in effect, earn two types of return—financial from the interest earned on the bonds and the improved equity in our society.[98]

Fundamentally, the decisions confronting governments pertain to the allocation of resources. Such allocations reflect priorities, which reflect underlying values. Government leaders at all levels and around the world loudly proclaim they value equality and the advancement of all people, but business ethics issues arise when what they actually do does not clearly and effectively align with these values.

Closing Comments

Although this book and your course likely conclude at this point, my most sincere hope is that your personal efforts for ensuring and improving ethical business conduct have only begun. To realize the promise the future holds for you, other individuals, and the human race depends on the actions of individual citizens and employees, as well as the leaders of companies and governments, both large and small.

The most powerful form of influence you have is your own behavior, which means it all starts with you. Lead by example in all areas of your life, not simply because your employers expect it, but because you expect it from yourself. Your actions can and will influence others, and together, we all can travel a more equitable, sustainable, prosperous, and fulfilling path. Put differently, no single individual, company, or country can save the planet from climate change. It requires concerted effort, and that requires some parties to lead, others to follow, but all to participate. Be sure to do your part.

The intent of this book was not to give you answers but instead to equip you with knowledge and practical tools to navigate the business ethics challenges you will be confronted with throughout your career. Some of these challenges will be extremely difficult and consequential, but it is easier to make the difficult choice when you are confident you are doing it for the right reasons.

Chapter Summary

1. Although values can be difficult to change, they do change, and they in turn change the expectations for stakeholders and business ethics.
2. Business, government, and their leaders are critical for social responsibility and business ethics.
3. Social justice is the view that everyone deserves equal rights, opportunities, treatment income, health, and social spheres. People now expect businesses and their leaders to play an active role in social justice and change.
4. Inequality related to income, health and health care, and race are three critical social justice issues on which businesses are expected to act.
5. Income inequality is tightly linked to most other forms of inequality, which means that addressing it is foundational to improving social justice and the lives of people within and between countries around the world.
6. The causes and costs of inequality are complex and great, but numerous examples exist of how individuals, organizations, and countries are successfully confronting them.

Key Terms

brain drain 271
ethnicity 273
Gini Index 269
health care inequality 271
health inequality 271
household income 269
income inequality 268
Jim Crow laws 273
living wage 278
poverty level 277
progressive taxes 283
race 273
social justice 268
social inequality 262

CASE STUDY: Multiple Bites of the Profit Pie

The pandemic has been very profitable for health insurance companies; their profits doubled from 2019 to 2020. How did this happen? Most basically, it is because despite the fact that many health care providers have been overwhelmed, hospitals stopped doing expensive elective surgeries. This means that insurers did not pay billions of dollars in claims they would in normal times. Large sums have been saved because all other types of providers shut down too (e.g., doctors offices and dentists).[99]

This means that the position of larger insurers, such as CVS, Humana, and UnitedHealth, differs dramatically from nearly every other stakeholder. Individuals have lost their jobs and thus coverage, and their employers have shut down causing revenues to shrink, making it difficult to pay the premiums for the employees that remain.

Ever-Present Possibility

Long before the pandemic, politicians, executives of insurance companies, and the customers (companies and individuals) realized the insurance companies effectively have little or no competition. An individual's employer typically works with only one insurer, and individuals purchasing insurance on their own often have limited options based on where they live (most health insurance does not cross state lines).

Profiteering Protection

To help guard against excessive profits, the Affordable Care Act (ACA) stipulates how health insurers must allocate the money they collect from customers (i.e., insurance premiums). Specifically, 80 cents on every dollar collected from individuals and small companies must be spent on their health care, and 85 cents on every dollar collected from large companies must be spent on health care of their employees. The remaining 15–20 percent can be used on administrative, marketing, and other overhead, as well as profits.

Any money left over must be returned to customers in the form of rebates. Remember, the numbers are giant—the country spends trillions, insurers make billions, and rebates to individuals are in the hundreds. For instance, individuals who purchased health insurance under the ACA in 2019 should on average receive a $420 rebate. Remember, this is before the pandemic.

Not So Fast

However, insurers are not required to pay out rebates every year. The argument is that averaging rebates over three years increases accuracy, which also means that individuals should not expect large rebate checks any time soon, despite the enormity of their profits in the first half of 2019. It also is important to consider that uncertainty confronting insurers is as large as their profits. Costs for treating COVID-19 patients will continue to grow, as more people get sick and health problems linger for those infected in the past. People are returning to clinicians' offices, and hospital procedures have resumed. Of course, there is hope for effective treatments and vaccines, the prices of which cannot be known because they have not been developed yet.

Even More Complexity

If this isn't complicated enough, then it is also important to realize that several of the largest health insurers do far more than simply insurance. For instance, CVS is vertically integrated, which means under its umbrella are Aetna (health insurer), the pharmacies where you shop, and a pharmacy benefit manager (PBM, a business that administers the drug plan component of company health plans). Only profits made by Aetna, the insurance part of CVS, are required to follow the revenue distributions noted above.

Some critics thus argue that total profits could be even higher than those reported by the insurance companies. To elaborate, when owned by the same company, the insurer is not going to "negotiate" very forcefully with the pharmacy or PBM that it also owns, which suggests overall prices in the "system" are higher than that would be if these elements were separate.

However, this criticism is exactly the opposite of the argument made by executives of insurers, PBMs, and pharmacies over the past three decades when they justified their motives for merging into integrated conglomerates. More specifically, they claimed that by putting all of these elements under the umbrella of a single company, they could reduce or eliminate many unnecessary costs and thus reduce prices to companies and individuals. In other words, combined they would be more efficient.

Politicians and others have long debated the advantages and disadvantages, and the pandemic added significantly more fuel.

For Discussion:

1. Assume you are the CEO of CVS (Larry Merlo). Who are your three most important stakeholders? What are your responsibilities for each of them?

2. If you were the CEO of CVS, or another large insurer, and you had to do the TV test to explain your enormous profits during the early months of the pandemic, what would you say?
3. Should the profits of large, integrated healthcare companies be subject to limitations? If yes, then who should set them and how? If no, then explain.
4. The high costs of health insurance are a major reason why Americans are underinsured (very little coverage) or uninsured. Explain what responsibility you think large healthcare companies, like those in the case, have to address this problem.
5. Assume you think healthcare companies have some amount of responsibility, then identify two other stakeholders and describe their responsibilities in addressing health care inequality in America.

Apply Three-Dimensional Problem Solving for Ethics (3D PSE)

You can apply the three-dimensional problem solving for ethics (3D PSE) from multiple stakeholder perspectives, such as the CEO of a large, integrated healthcare company; executive of a large employer who contracts for services from such companies on behalf of employees; an individual who purchases health insurance privately (not through an employer); or a member of Congress who is motivated to change health care in America (in some way or another). However, let's analyze the case from the perspective of the CVS CEO, Larry Merlo. Of course, you can select the perspective of a different stakeholder, just be sure to specify your choice.

figure **13.4**

3D Problem Solving for Ethics (3D PSE)

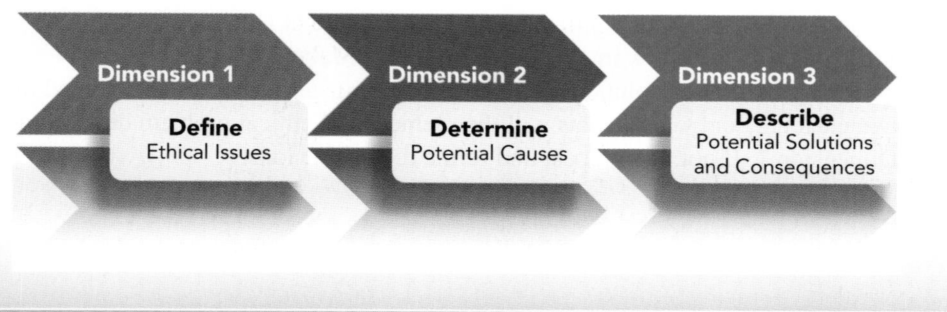

Dimension 1: *Define* the Ethical Challenge

What is the gap in the case? What is the situation confronting Mr. Merlo, and what does he want?

a. From his view, what is the current situation at CVS, and how does he think it should be?

b. Why is the current situation a problem? What undesirable behaviors and outcomes happened for CVS as a result of the problem you defined? Why does Merlo/CVS care about the problem you defined in Dimension 1?
c. Define your problem in one or at most two sentences and structure it in terms of what is current versus what is desired.
d. Who are the key stakeholders who affect or are affected by the problem you defined? What are the undesirable outcomes for each stakeholder?

Dimension 2: *Determine* the Causes

a. **Individuals.** Given the problem you defined in Dimension 1, what causes can be attributed to individuals, whether they are healthcare company executives, executives at employers, employees, members of Congress, or others?
b. **Contextual.** What are the potential organizational causes, that is, policies, practices, or other factors within the carnival? What about potential causes at the industry or national level?

Dimension 3: *Describe* Your Potential Solutions and the Intended and Unintended Consequences for Stakeholders

For each cause identified in Dimension 2, answer the following questions:

a. ***What*** do you recommend as CEO, and ***how*** do you recommend making it happen?
b. ***Why*** should the action be taken? Does it reflect a particular ethical decision-making perspective (e.g., utilitarian or universal)?

If your responses to these questions are unsatisfactory, then go back to Dimension 1 and repeat the process. However, if you are comfortable and confident in your problem-solving efforts thus far, then ensure that you achieve the desired outcomes and avoid any unintended consequences.

c. What is the ***desired and likely effect in the short and long term*** for the key stakeholders involved in the problem and causes (Dimensions 1 and 2)?
d. What ***potential unintended consequences*** may occur with each proposed solution?
e. If any, what are the **implications for *other* stakeholders** (e.g., individuals, organizations, and communities) besides those noted in Dimensions 1 and 2?
f. Will your solution **work in an ethical manner**? Make a final assessment of whether your chosen solution will reduce or eliminate the causes determined in Dimension 2, and whether this will then remedy the ethical problem defined in Dimension 1. If not, then repeat and refine the dimensions.

Chapter opening photo credit: KaliAntye/Shutterstock

CASE **STUDY**

The Cause, Effect, and Impact of amazon

OVERVIEW

Although best known for redefining retail and forever changing the way products are sold and people shop, Amazon also has innovated and applied technology to become one of the largest and most influential artificial intelligence, Web services, and cloud computing companies in the world. But that is not all. The Amazon umbrella is enormous and covers streaming (e.g., movies and music), video content (Amazon Studios), e-books and readers (Kindle and Fire), publishing, and digital assistants (e.g., Alexa and Echo). And if that isn't enough, it also acquired Whole Foods, Zappos, Twitch, and Ring, among many others.

All of this helps explain why Amazon is the most valuable retailer ($1 trillion market capitalization) and second-largest private employer (approximately 1 million employees) in the United States; Walmart is second and first in these same categories. An organization of this size, with operations in nearly 200 countries, is confronted with countless business ethics challenges, making it a great case study to illustrate the breadth, depth, and impact of business ethics. This case can therefore be used in a variety of ways.

1. First, it can be used as a running case to discuss how the concepts from each chapter apply to Amazon.
2. Second, just as the book is organized into parts corresponding to individual, organizational, and societal business ethics issues, the Amazon case can be divided accordingly and used as a review, test, or project for individuals or teams to work on for each unit of the course.
3. Third, it can be used as cumulative assignment or capstone discussion for the course.

Where It Started and Its Path

Amazon was created in 1994 by Jeff Bezos, a young and successful investment banker, who saw an opportunity to sell books during the early days of the internet. At that point in time, the internet was in its infancy, especially online retailing. By the end of the decade, however, Amazon went public, expanded into the UK and Germany, and began selling music, videos, consumer electronics, software, and numerous other items.

In 2002 Amazon Web Services (AWS) was created. Originally, AWS provided internet use statistics to marketers and other companies. By 2010 AWS had expanded tremendously to include shared computing power, data storage, and other services, which are pillars of the company today. It has since become a technical and operational foundation of all-things internet, as a substantial proportion of what individuals, companies, and governments do on the web is done via one or more of Amazon and AWS's services.

Along with its contemporary tech giants—Apple, Facebook, Google, and Microsoft—Amazon has become a juggernaut, whose economic, cultural, and environmental impact cannot be overstated. Amazon has had critics since the turn of the century, beginning with those who accused it of single-handedly eliminating independent bookstores, and then all but one of the largest bookstore chains (Barnes & Noble still operates). Critics now come from all directions, which is little surprise, given that it controls nearly fifty percent of all e-commerce in the U.S. (Walmart and eBay account for less than 10 percent each).[1] In 2010 it had approximately $34 billion in annual net revenues, which grew nearly nine times in ten years to $280 billion in 2019.[2]

Joy and Pain

Millions upon millions of retail customers love Amazon—low prices, enormous selection, fast delivery, and effective service. Long-term investors also are delighted by the stratospheric stock price returns since its initial public offering, and some number of these are the hundreds of thousands if not millions of people the company has employed over the years. However, along with Amazon's growth and success has come an increasing number of detractors. Bezos, for instance, continues to frustrate some Wall Street analysts and investors by resisting pressure to focus more on quarterly and annual profits (short-term performance) and return cash to investors in the form of dividends. Bezos instead has always and continues to be willing to invest heavily in unprofitable products, services, and markets, sometimes for years, if he believes they will support long-term goals. Amazon dissenters also go far beyond money and Wall Street. In the past few years, employees have been some of the most notable critics and have spoken out and actively protested against a raft of issues. Among these are the company's inaction related to environmental issues, and the intended use of some of its products.

Impact on the Environment

Over 300 employees signed a statement deriding the company's lack of progress on reducing its carbon footprint. They did so despite Amazon's policy forbidding employees from commenting publicly on policies without prior approval. Some employees created a group called Amazon Employees for Climate Justice, which has been pressuring the company to make its goals more ambitious, including moving its carbon-neutral goal to 2030 from 2050, terminate contracts with companies that directly or indirectly support oil and gas production, and end support for all politicians and lobbyists who do not support climate change. These employee complaints join those of consumer and environmental activists who also challenge the company to improve the impact of its packaging and assert its influence on sellers and buyers to do their part in improving sustainability efforts.[3]

Who Do We Work For?

Among the concerns are that numerous products and services could facilitate surveillance and racism, such as the facial recognition product developed for the government and law enforcement. Similar complaints have been made regarding AWS as the host for the Immigration and Customs Enforcement (ICE) efforts, particularly those related to workplace raids, detention, and deportation.[4]

Buyers and Sellers have Issues Too

Amazon has also been accused of censorship. The company has a vague policy stating that it "reserves the right to determine whether content provides an acceptable experience," which is what it uses to remove certain books, such as multiples titles related to different forms of hate: books by former Ku Klux Klan leader David Duke, others related to the American Nazi party, and still others that are anti-Semitic. The company is thus attempting to balance free-speech and offensive content, a dilemma also confronting social media companies (e.g., Twitter, Facebook, and YouTube).

Amazon has suffered backlash from two important stakeholders. Some readers, for instance, believe they have the right to access and read anything they like, while others clamor to remove content that is objectionable to them. Compounding the issue further still are millions of third-party sellers, publishers, and authors, who create and publish the content who feel the company is infringing on their rights and/or livelihoods. And for perspective, Amazon's control is immense, as they currently account for nearly sixty-six percent of the sales for new, used, and digital books in the US[5], which equated to over 4000 items per minute in 2019.[6]

Continued challenges and failures have caused numerous companies to stop selling their products on Amazon. For instance, Ikea, Nike, and Birkenstock have all pulled their products in recent years, citing unfair and brand damaging practices related to pricing and insufficient policing of counterfeits.[7]

It's All About Data

It should be no surprise that a company built on using customer data to predict and motivate sales also uses it to track employee productivity. Amazon was founded on the principle of fast and cheap, which means that warehouse employees, in particular, need to sort, pack, track, and move very efficiently. Reports reveal that hundreds of employees at individual facilities are fired every year for not meeting productivity targets. Multiplied by the more than seventy fulfillment centers (warehouses) in North America, that equates to thousands of employees a year.[8]

Performance Management—Metrics and Consequences

Performance management is a rigorous, and for some, a harrowing experience at Amazon. One element is called the Pivot Program, wherein underperforming employees are given a choice—take a severance package, including an agreement not to sue the company, or an employee can choose to engage in an intense performance improvement plan.[9]

Critics claim this is just another way the company pressures employees, which some have even said is used inappropriately (illegally) to remove employees for non-performance reasons. Still others allege that Pivot is a way to reduce legal liability in employee terminations, given the stipulations of the severance agreements. Supporters of the program counter that it as a fair and transparent means for giving employees opportunities for improvement and career choices.[10]

One common metric used in the company's fulfillment centers is *time off task* (TOT), which is time not scanning and thus not moving items through the delivery process. The bottom five percent of performers on TOT are put on a training plan to improve performance, which is one step towards termination. Goals have always been challenging, which is supported by company statements that they are not performing to standards until or unless they are achieved by 75 percent of employees.[11]

On one side of this argument is that the system is a machine that only sees numbers, not people, while the other side says the company is simply utilizing what it does best, which is to use data to operate more efficiently and meet customer expectations.[12]

Employee performance monitoring may not stop here, however. The company has developed and patented wristbands that measure each employee's every movement, The bands will even provide a nudge or vibration if an employee has been inactive too long. When questioned about the potential for abuse and privacy invasion, the company responded and said it already uses similar devices, which are intended purely to build efficiency into tasks (increase speed).[13]

Compensation

Although the company is widely regarded as an innovator and even a disruptor, little press is given to how Amazon has innovated its compensation practices. These practices do not suit everyone, but the company has stuck with them for many years. Some key features are:

- Below market salaries, but above market total compensation. This is achieved via stock and non-cash bonuses.
- The company is often viewed as stingy with cash, except for signing bonuses, and instead prefers to incentivize and reward employees with the company's stock, which over time has appreciated considerably.
- The vesting periods—the time required for an employee to cash out stock rewards–is often five years or more. Many companies require employees to hold company stock for four years for it to be fully vested, sold, and thus converted to cash.
- These same practices are applied throughout the organization—top to bottom.[14]

The underlying motives for Amazon's compensation practices are to get employees to think long term and act like owners, as well as to enable the company to invest the cash it produces back into the company. Additional evidence is found in how it compensates executives. For instance, stock awards can be very large, over $20 million in a given year for individual executives. Bezos, however, takes only an $80,000 per year salary but owns more than ten percent of the company's stock, which makes him the richest person on the planet.[15]

How Does Bezo's Leadership Affect The Company?

Remember, all of the previous discussion is created or at least influenced by Amazon leaders, most often beginning and ending with Bezos. As is common with founders, Bezos' personality and persona are embedded in Amazon. He is data-driven and rational, as are the processes of the company. He embraces innovation and risk-taking, and he expects the same from the employees and the larger organization. The company also continually innovates in both small and major ways, such as incremental refinements to processes, as well as blue-sky thinking that led to the Kindle, Amazon Prime, and Amazon Web Services.[16]

The Best and The Worst

Bezos' performance and leadership style have been both heralded and criticized. In the early days of the company, *Time* magazine selected him as Person of the Year in 1999,[17] and then in 2014 *Harvard Business Review* ranked him as the top-performing living CEO.[18] The former for his transformation of the book business and e-commerce, and the latter for the phenomenal performance of the company's stock price over time. This long-term performance is consistent with Bezos' self-proclaimed focus on customer satisfaction and growth. In the pursuit of this he has routinely ignored analyst and investor calls for dividends, greater transparency, and keener focus on profits. Short-term financial performance (e.g., earnings per share and profit) has consistently been traded for investments in new technologies and markets, along with improvements within the company.[19] Importantly, however, Bezos' rankings have shown volatility similar to the company's stock.

By 2019, Jeff Bezos didn't even make the rankings of best-performing CEOs. A major reason for this fall was how performance was measured. In contrast to previous years, the stock price of a CEO's company was no longer enough, Harvard Business Review began also considering environmental, social, and governance (ESG) metrics. As one reporter explained, "ESG comprised 20% of the total CEO score in years past, it became more important in 2019. ESG now comprises 30% of the total CEO score, which proved fatal for Bezos." The increased weighting of factors such as working conditions, employment policies, and antitrust issues hurt Amazon and Bezos.[20]

Conflicting views are evident in Bezos' own description, which is codified in one of Amazon's 14 Leadership Principles—be right a lot. When asked what this means, he said: "Good leaders are right a lot... People who are right a lot, they listen a lot, and people who are right a lot, change their mind a lot."[21]

Decision Making

Decisiveness was on full display in 2015, when a scathing article was released describing Amazon's culture as toxic and uncaring. Among Bezos' reactions was to immediately implement an empathy initiative, wherein employees would grade each other—100 representing the "nicest" employee to 0 as "pure evil"—and the bottom 10 percent would be terminated in short order. He followed this up with the following justification: "We can't be the greatest retailer in the world unless we are also the kindest... So, my message to all Amazonians is loud and clear: be kind or taste my wrath. Love, Jeff."[22]

Decisiveness is a hallmark of his leadership, such as the decision to boost Amazon's minimum wage to at least $15. When asked about the motive for the change, the CEO said "We listened to our critics, thought hard about what we wanted to do, and decided we want to lead." Implementation of the new wage didn't take a year, like it would have in many companies. It went into effect within a month, lightning-fast for a company with hundreds of thousands of employees.[23]

As for Bezo's leadership style, the transformational elements are widely-acknowledged. However, many also describe him as abusive and demeaning, and some also accuse him of relentlessly pressuring sellers and competitors to yield to Amazon's interests and might. Bezos justifies his actions with his unyielding pursuit of "low prices, vast selection, and fast, reliable delivery."

He has long had a singular focus on customer service and satisfaction, and he can show similar determination to pursue ideas that are unpopular with other leaders within the company. For instance, many opposed the idea of free shipping and the Amazon Prime program, when Bezos first presented it in 2004. Many of the dissenters complained it would further erode already puny margins, which incidentally, Amazon routinely lost money for many years.[24]

Although long-questioned about his perceived lack of philanthropy, given his extreme wealth, Bezos has in recent years invested or donated money to a number of causes. The Bezos Academy was started in late 2020, and it provides free preschool and for low-income children. The Academy is part of a larger Bezos Day One Fund which he launched in 2018 with $2 billion, which focuses on funding non-profits that help homeless families, and on creating a network of tier-one preschools in low-income communities.[25]

The Culture That Is Amazon

The many elements described in this case thus far are either causes or results of Amazon's culture. Most fundamentally, Jeff Bezos' personal characteristics and actions have always and continue to shape the values, norms, and thus the culture of the company. These elements, in turn, are primary drivers of how it treats and reacts to various stakeholders—employees, customers, regulators, and sellers. Much of this begins with the founding and enduring vision—"to be Earth's most customer-centric company; to build a place where people can come to find and discover anything they might want to buy online."[26]

Values and Guiding Principles

To help bring the Amazon vision to life, the company uses four guiding principles:

1. Customer obsession rather than competitor focus
2. Passion for invention
3. Commitment to operational excellence
4. Long-term thinking

As noted above, the values are reflected in many of the company's policies, practices, and employee behaviors. The incessant drive for greater efficiency in processes, lower prices, and customer satisfaction is reinforced by performance metrics, hiring, and decision making. This is consistent with Bezos' desire to maintain a "start-up culture," even at the company's immense size and reach. He explained in Amazon's 2017 annual report the importance of maintaining a sense of urgency and a willingness to experiment, make quick decisions, and adopt trends early.[27]

Underlying all of these cultural elements, Bezos describes, is a determination to establish a culture that fosters high standards in all that the employees and company do. High standards not only translate into better products and better service for customers, but they also attract high caliber talent. He continues and adds,

> *"... a culture of high standards is protective of all the 'invisible' but crucial work that goes on in every company. I'm talking about the work that no one sees. The work that gets done when no one is watching... Once you've tasted high standards, there's no going back."*[28]

We use our Leadership Principles every day, whether we are discussing ideas for new projects or deciding on the best approach to solving a problem. It is just one of the things that makes Amazon unique.

table **14.1**

Amazon's Leadership Principles

Leadership Principles	Descriptions
1 **Customer Obsession**	Leaders start with the customer and work backwards. They work vigorously to earn and keep customer trust. Although leaders pay attention to competitors, they obsess over customers.
2 **Ownership**	Leaders are owners. They think long term and don't sacrifice long-term value for short-term results. They act on behalf of the entire company, beyond just their own team. They never say, "that's not my job."
3 **Invent and Simplify**	Leaders expect and require innovation and invention from their teams and always find ways to simplify. They are externally aware, look for new ideas from everywhere, and are not limited by "not invented here." As we do new things, we accept that we may be misunderstood for long periods of time.
4 **Are Right, A Lot**	Leaders are right a lot. They have strong judgment and good instincts. They seek diverse perspectives and work to disconfirm their beliefs.
5 **Learn and Be Curious**	Leaders are never done learning and always seek to improve themselves. They are curious about new possibilities and act to explore them.
6 **Hire and Develop the Best**	Leaders raise the performance bar with every hire and promotion. They recognize exceptional talent, and willingly move them throughout the organization. Leaders develop leaders and take seriously their role in coaching others. We work on behalf of our people to invent mechanisms for development like Career Choice.
7 **Insist on the Highest Standards**	Leaders have relentlessly high standards — many people may think these standards are unreasonably high. Leaders are continually raising the bar and drive their teams to deliver high quality products, services, and processes. Leaders ensure that defects do not get sent down the line and that problems are fixed so they stay fixed.
8 **Think Big**	Thinking small is a self-fulfilling prophecy. Leaders create and communicate a bold direction that inspires results. They think differently and look around corners for ways to serve customers.
9 **Bias for Action**	Speed matters in business. Many decisions and actions are reversible and do not need extensive study. We value calculated risk taking.
10 **Frugality**	Accomplish more with less. Constraints breed resourcefulness, self-sufficiency, and invention. There are no extra points for growing headcount, budget size, or fixed expense.
11 **Earn Trust**	Leaders listen attentively, speak candidly, and treat others respectfully. They are vocally self-critical, even when doing so is awkward or embarrassing. Leaders do not believe their or their team's body odor smells of perfume. They benchmark themselves and their teams against the best.
12 **Dive Deep**	Leaders operate at all levels, stay connected to the details, audit frequently, and are skeptical when metrics and anecdote differ. No task is beneath them.
13 **Have Backbone; Disagree and Commit**	Leaders are obligated to respectfully challenge decisions when they disagree, even when doing so is uncomfortable or exhausting. Leaders have conviction and are tenacious. They do not compromise for the sake of social cohesion. Once a decision is determined, they commit wholly.
14 **Deliver Results**	Leaders focus on the key inputs for their business and deliver them with the right quality and in a timely fashion. Despite setbacks, they rise to the occasion and never settle.

Source: Amazon company Website, downloaded October 10, 2020: https://www.amazon.jobs/en/principles.

It Takes Talent, Loads and Loads of Talent

Critical to Amazon's culture and success are its people. How the company hires is an important first step. A foundation to successful hiring is the *Bar Raiser Program*. The goal of the program is to hire, "people who will innovate on behalf of customers." Bar Raisers are interviewers outside of the area in which a candidate will be hired, and they are included to ensure the hiring process is both objective and the candidate aligns with the 14 leadership principles.[29]

Bar Raisers also are expected to hire candidates who are better than fifty percent of the employees currently in a particular job, thus bar raiser, and who have genuine future potential within the company. Bar Raisers are, therefore, an integral part of the interviewing process and undergo extensive training, which enables them to assist recruiters, hiring managers, and others involved in the process to identify, evaluate, and make offers to the most appropriate candidates for the responsibilities of the target job.[30]

As for the interview process itself, it can be quite rigorous and lengthy. However, because of the company's tremendous size, and the number of seasonal hires, the process can be quite different depending on the role. Amazon, however, tries to make it efficient for both candidates and the company, and to this end it provides considerable tutorials and guidance online to help remove uncertainty and facilitate the process. For instance, some positions require cover letters, while others do not. Guidance is also provided regarding common questions, phone interviews, in-person interviews, and technical interviews. The company also explicitly recommends that candidates consider and be prepared to discuss failures they have experienced in their working lives. The rationale is that Amazon values risk-taking, which inevitably generates failures. Failures, however, are simply experiences along the path to successful innovations.[31]

Finally, the company also informs candidates that many positions require writing skills—it is a writing culture. Amazon prides itself on no PowerPoint or other presentations using slides. Instead, employees are expected to write and often read written explanations of programs, ideas, and progress at the beginning of meetings. These memos are common and may be several pages long.[32]

Make a "Career Choice" at Amazon

Amazon also invests in employees' education. Hourly employees who have worked for the company for a year are eligible to participate in the Career Choice program, which will pre-pay 95 percent of tuition, fees, and books for those who want to further their education. Certificates and Associate degree programs qualify, and different from many companies, the topics of study do not need to align with the employee's job within Amazon (e.g., nursing, mechanic, and lab technician). However, the curriculum does need to be in an area specified as "in high demand" by the U. S. Bureau of Labor Statistics. The company further supports these efforts, in some instances, by providing onsite facilities for instruction.[33]

What About Diversity and Inclusion?

Amazon states that diversity and inclusion are central to its customer-centric culture. This means that hiring diverse employees, and utilizing their talents in everything the company does, enables the company to better serve customers, selling partners, employees, and other stakeholders. To support these efforts, the company tracks the representation of women and underrepresented minorities throughout its global operations. As of the end of 2019, for instance, 43 percent of all employees were women, and women accounted for 28 percent of management positions globally. Figure A.1 illustrates the racial/ethnic composition of Amazon's U.S. workforce.

Employee Experiences Are Diverse Too

Amazon was among the companies that voluntarily boosted its minimum wage to $15 per hourfor part-time, full-time, temporary, and seasonal workers. It also lists the minimum wage paid for various jobs in the descriptions on its website. The company's retirement plans have generous fifty percent employer contributions, and employees have a variety of family and parental leave options.[34]

figure **14.1**

Racial and Ethnic Composition of Amazon United States' Workforce (2019)

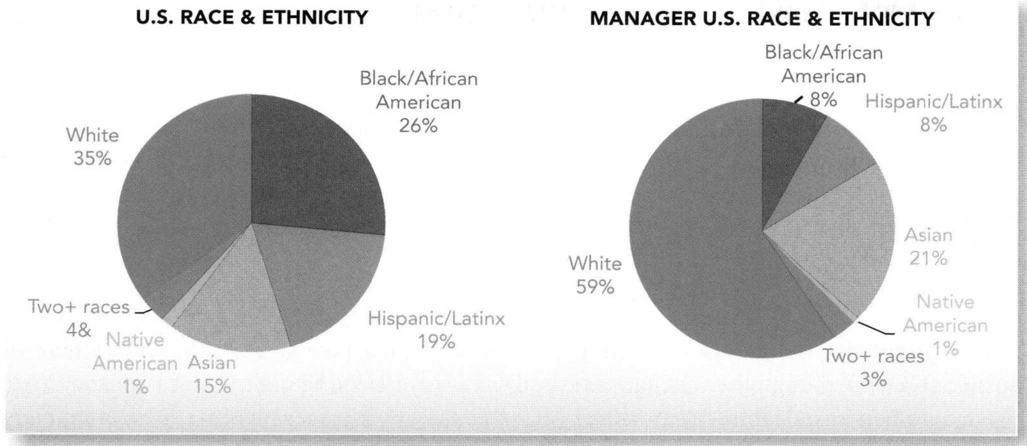

Source: Amazon company Website, downloaded October 10, 2020: https://www.aboutamazon.com/working-at-amazon/diversity-and-inclusion/our-workforce-data.

Although Amazon has employed millions of people over the years, and provided a fulfilling and lucrative career for many, not all have been happy. Complaints from warehouse workers are common, especially during peak times—holidays and Prime Day—when they work longer, harder shifts. In addition, workers often cite that breaks are too few and too short. Some facilities are so large that it can take fifteen minutes to walk from the job location to the break room. Reports filed with the Occupational Safety and Health Administration (OSHA), show injuries at Amazon facilities can be three times higher than the national average for warehouse workers. These complaints are compounded by what some call unrealistic performance expectations, such as packing 700 items per hour, regardless of equipment breakdowns or other delays. One worker who quit because of the conditions said, "I couldn't handle it. I'm a human being, not a robot."[35]

COVID-19 exacerbated many of the issues. For instance, Amazon fired four employees who spoke out against the company's handling of virus and ensuring the safety of its warehouse employees. The company responded to criticisms and explained that the employees were terminated for violating safety procedures, such as not physically distancing and intimidation, not for speaking out about working conditions and health and safety (whistleblowing). This was unpersuasive for some, notably, some members of Congress who requested additional information on the matter from the company.[36]

Employee issues persist related to unionization. From its early days, Amazon has actively discouraged unionization in both the U.S. and the UK. Such efforts are illegal in both countries, yet efforts by employees continue, as do their claims that the company has inappropriately discouraged or even punished such efforts. Amazon allegedly terminated over 800 employees in the UK linked to a union drive, and it also allegedly hired a consulting firm to help thwart such activities. It also is alleged that the company even measures the likelihood of which Whole Foods stores, one of its acquisitions, will unionize.[37]

Some complaints and issues with Amazon have resulted in legal action, and these are explored next.

Legal Challenges

Of course, a company the size of Amazon will have its share of legal issues, and sometimes it ends up on the right side of the law and others not.

Government Concerns and Actions

Over the years, Amazon has attracted considerable attention from legislators at all levels (federal, state, and local) and numerous federal agencies. The Federal Trade Commission (FTC), for instance, routinely handles complaints against the company and levies fines for various forms of misconduct. A particularly unflattering one involved the company allegedly promoting purchases from children without parental consent. More generally, regulators in both the U.S. and Europe continue to express concerns about seemingly monopolistic power and associated anti-competitive practices. Although nothing has come to fruition yet, experts speculate that Amazon could be broken-up into smaller companies,[38] like AT&T in the 1980's, or at least significant restrictions placed on what it can do, how, and where.

Anti-competitive behaviors. These possibilities directly involve the U.S, Department of Justice (DOJ). Among other allegations, the DOJ is investigating claims that Amazon drops products when it finds third-party sellers offer them at lower prices on other sites, effectively limiting competition. Germany and the UK have already banned such practices. Still, other investigations focus on algorithms that favor the company's own products, rather than primarily serving customer interests.[39]

Death and taxes? Maybe neither. According to the old cliché there are two things in life no person can avoid—death and taxes. Amazon is unlikely to ever die, although for a long time it did avoid paying taxes. First is the issue of sales tax. For many years, the company collected little if any sales tax, which competitors and other critics complained unfairly lowered the cost to consumers and increased an already substantial price advantage to Amazon over brick and mortar retailers. This was legal until 2017, when laws changed requiring the company to charge and collect sales taxes in states that require it. However, many third-party sellers that use the platform still do not collect sales taxes.[40]

And then there are corporate income taxes. Despite is continued stratospheric growth, in both 2018 and 2019 the company paid no corporate income tax. Although some critics claim that the lack of taxes paid is illegal, the company claims it simply uses existing tax laws and associated loopholes, such as tax credits for research and development and allowable deductions for stock-based compensation.[41]

The issue of taxes also gained front-page attention in the recent past when it effectively ran a lottery in which cities and states bid for the location of a second headquarters—HQ2. New Jersey offered approximately $7 billion in tax breaks, with the hopes that the jobs and associated boost to housing and business would more than offset the breaks given to the company. The HQ2 project is simply an expansion of hundreds of millions of dollars in tax incentives the company has received from various state and local governments to entice the company to build warehouses and data centers within their boundaries.[42]

Compliant and cooperative. Despite all the negative press related to legal and regulatory issues, Amazon also makes efforts to comply with the law. In the summer of 2020, for instance, it banned the sale of seeds and plants on its platform after thousands of U.S. customers complained about receiving unsolicited seeds from places postmarked in China. These actions aligned with the U.S. Department of Agriculture's ban on products that are dangerous or need to be quarantined. Amazon was not the first company to act, but it did follow the lead of all 50 states that banned the same products from China. As with other problematic sellers, Amazon has taken action to identify and ban them.[43]

Code Amazon

Amazon, like many other companies, has an explicit code of conduct for its employees. But because of its immense size and diverse businesses, it also has codes for particular areas of the business, including those related to users of Amazon Web Services (AWS) and buyers and sellers on its retail platform. The expectations in their Code of Business Conduct and Ethics are organized into twelve categories:

1. Compliance with Laws, Rules, and Regulations
2. Conflicts of Interest
3. Insider Trading Policy
4. Discrimination and Harassment
5. Health and Safety
6. Price Fixing
7. Bribery; Payments to Government Personnel
8. Recordkeeping, Reporting, and Financial Integrity
9. Questions; Reporting Violations
10. Periodic Certification
11. Board of Directors
12. Waivers[44]

The categories in the company's code are similar to those found in many public companies, and most of them align with various laws and regulations in the various states and countries in which Amazon operates. Bribery, for example, applies both within and outside the United States, and is governed by a host of laws, notably for Foreign Corrupt Practices Act in the United States and similar statutes in other countries.

Amazon Web Service's (AWS) has a code of conduct for its community and applies to live, virtual, and across various platforms (e.g., blogs and social media). The AWS code outlines the expected behaviors and consequences for violators. The blogs, online forums, and social media section describes one aspect of expected behavior as:

> *"You will not engage in any form of harassing, offensive, discriminatory, or threatening speech or behavior, including (but not limited to) relating to race, gender, gender identity and expression, national origin, religion, disability, marital status, age, sexual orientation, military or veteran status, or other protected category."*[45]

Violators are disqualified from participating in future live and virtual events.[46] Such sanctions are potentially devastating, as AWS is the largest provider of web services (cloud computing infrastructure) in the world with nearly forty percent market share, double its closest competitor, Microsoft's Azure.[47]

Putting Its Best Foot Forward

Environment, social, and governance (ESG) is now mainstream. Not only has it garnered the attention of Wall Street, but also the majority of Fortune 500 companies now have formal ESG goals. The movement, as well as the goals, are largely derived from the Sustainable

Development Goals of United Nations Global Compact. Central among these goals are reducing an organization's waste and carbon footprint, supporting the well-being of the larger society, beyond one's own customers, employees, and shareholders, and ensuring accountability and ethical conduct throughout the organization.[48]

However, Amazon's enormity puts it in a precarious position. It is simultaneously a cause and solution to many ESG challenges.

Environmental Impact

Because of the sheer scale of its businesses, not the least of which is delivering products to homes and businesses around the world, Amazon pollutes the environment. Some of the most notable are those related to product packaging, greenhouse emissions from data centers, warehouses, and deliveries, as well as toxic materials used in countless products it sells. Studies estimate that the growth in e-commerce in general, will increase delivery vehicles on the roads by more than 36 percent, which in turn will increase traffic congestion and emissions.[49]

The company has been less than transparent when compared to other large tech companies, but the figures that are available showed that in 2018 it generated more emissions than two of its largest vendors combined—FedEx and United Parcel Service (UPS).[50]

The Amazon Prime membership program has been wildly successful since its inception in 2005. With over 150 million members, it generates billions of dollars in revenue for the company, in part, because it provides free and fast shipping to customers. Opponents claim that despite the convenience and attractiveness to customers, it has amplified consumerism by lowering the costs, which in turn increases the number of orders, decreases efficiencies in delivery, and boosts packaging and environmental costs. Prime members, and other customers, increasingly order common household products (e.g., detergent and razors), and this trend accelerated due to COVID. Moreover, faster delivery times make consolidating orders more difficult, reducing many environmental benefits that may have been possible.[51]

Amazon has responded. The company purchased 100,000 electric vehicles, improved packaging programs that reduced weight by twenty-seven percent and over 800 tons in just over ten years. It has also committed to zero-carbon by 2040 and plans to run on one-hundred percent renewable energy by 2030. To be fair, it is important to note that customers have a shared responsibility in these issues. Amazon offers customers of the option of consolidating orders by delaying delivery dates, which in turn provides opportunities to reduce packaging and the number of deliveries.[52]

Some experts defend Amazon saying although it is difficult to measure the company's environmental impact, it is likely less than before when most goods were purchased by individuals driving their own cars to stores.[53] Although many critics still complain about a lack of transparency (e.g., measurement and reporting) by Amazon regarding its actual impact on the environment.

Social Impact

As Amazon's penetration of markets around the world intensifies, so too do its issues surrounding the fair treatment of employees, competitors, and communities. Its treatment of employees has resulted in ever-growing unrest and activism, such as strikes by employees in Germany, Poland, Spain, and Italy over low wages and difficult working conditions. One reason for strikes, already noted above, is that the company has almost completely avoided unionization of employees, although it disputes this claim. Unions often provide employees collective bargaining and other means of influence on their employers, and they can help guard against or mitigate the claims related to scheduling, hours, and performance goals.

Some of its harshest critics say that the company is engaged in a "race to the bottom" on labor practices, all in pursuit of lower prices, faster delivery, and greater satisfaction for customers.[54]

To be fair, as the company grows, it increases jobs and income opportunities for hundreds of thousands of employees. The benefits of each new fulfillment center ripple through the local economy, improving real estate, retail, and countless other aspects of the economy. However, the company also was condemned for its handling of COVID-19 in many of its facilities. Employees, their families, and health officials all clamored for greater transparency regarding the number of employees infected, as well as greater efforts to protect those who continued to work.

Governance and Government

Bezos serves and both CEO and Chairman of the board, which some experts consider suboptimal as each role have enormous responsibilities, making it difficult for one person to do both. Besides the practical challenges, since Bezos is also the founder, combining the roles concentrates too much power in one person.

Governance concerns are multiplied by the complexity of Amazon's businesses. For instance, various stakeholders are now asking the company to assess whether and to what extent its products and services are being used to exploit people and violate human rights. As noted earlier, some concerns focus on the potential for exploitation and violation of human rights, as the company's artificial intelligence, vast data, and other technologies and services can be used for surveillance activities by police, governments, and other organizations. The company has yielded to certain pressures and halted further development of its facial recognition product.[55]

Besides avoiding taxes, as noted earlier, Amazon has greatly increased its attempts to influence lawmakers by increasing lobbying expenditures nearly f percent since 2012. Furthermore, the United States government is an ever-growing customer, whether it is using AWS or purchasing products The U.S. government spends approximately $50 billion per year on consumer goods (e.g., coffee, paper, chairs, electronics).[56]

Global Reach and Global Impact

Amazon has markets in thirteen countries outside of the United States.[57] The largest are Germany, UK, and Japan. Although sales in these countries combined do not equal sales in the United States, foreign countries are some of the company's greatest growth opportunities.[58] India is a particular focus, given it has 1.3 billion people and wide acceptance of e-commerce, but government concerns may ultimately limit this opportunity.[59] Like other countries, the Indian government is under pressure from domestic businesses who fear that Amazons entry will be their demise.

It Isn't Easy

Beginning with China, Amazon was determined to do business there and started in 2004. But government restrictions on foreign retailers caused the company to exit in 2019. Multiple European regulators are actively investigating the impact of Amazon and what to do about it. Their most basic concern is competition. Governments in all countries, like the United States, are concerned that Amazon will eliminate or at least handicap domestic competition. Put differently, they fear Amazon's mix of low prices, enormous selection, and fast delivery will overwhelm the local companies. This concern has been the basis for some antitrust investigations. A specific concern among regulators is that because Amazon is both a seller of products and the manager of the platform on which competitors sell their products, it has and uses unfair advantage. These are not idle threats, as the European Union regulator already fined Google $5 billion and required it to change its advertising practices.[60]

Competition presents another type of challenge for Amazon's global expansion. But this version is the competition from other online retailers. Just as China has its own (Alibaba and JD.com), so too do Latin America and India. More generally, cumbersome bureaucracy and unreliable infrastructure could prove disastrous for a company that counts on efficiency in all it does. However, more recent efforts to enter Australia, Turkey, and Israel will be telling. But it does have another resource that few competitors can match—money! Its enormous success enables it to endure unprofitable efforts for years, thus enabling it to outlast and prevail when others cannot.[61]

But There is Love and Hope

LinkedIn ranks the most desirable companies to work for in countries around the world. And in 2019, Amazon was number one in the U.S., United Kingdom, Australia, India, Japan, China, Canada, Germany, and Mexico. This suggests that not only does Amazon provide an enormous number of jobs—more than 330 people are hired every day—but that many employees like working for the company. It has received similarly impressive rankings from *Fortune's* World's Most Admired Companies.[62]

Taken altogether, Amazon has generated positive experiences and benefits for literally hundreds of millions of people around the globe since the mid-1990s, and it is on track to expand its impact to millions of others well into the future. As this case has also described, the company's impact is not only substantial in scope and scale, but it also generates undesirable outcomes for individuals, organizations, industries, and the environment. Although governments in the United States and across the planet will undoubtedly assert more influence on the company, its operations, and its impact, other stakeholders will play significant roles of their own. Pressure from employees, for instance, is likely to expand and increase, but ultimately it will be Jeff Bezos and other leaders who will determine whether Amazon will prove to be a steward to the people and the planet while generating increasing profits.

Chapter opening photo credit: Jonathan Weiss / Shutterstock.com

Notes

Chapter 1

1.1. M. Ellwood, "Coronavirus Air Travel: These Numbers Show the Massive Impact of the Pandemic," *Conde Nast Traveler*, April 13, 2020, https://www.cntraveler.com/story/coronavirus-air-travel-these-numbers-show-the-massive-impact-of-the-pandemic.

1.2. A. Picchi, "Airlines Should Return Cash to Travelers—Not Just Offer Vouchers, Lawmakers Say," *CBSNews.com*, May 13, 2020, https://www.cbsnews.com/news/airlines-cash-vouchers-refund/.

1.3. Adapted from B. Gert and J. Gert, "The Definition of Morality," in *The Stanford Encyclopedia of Philosophy*, ed. Edward N. Zalta, Fall 2017 ed., https://plato.stanford.edu/archives/fall2017/entries/morality-definition.

1.4. Adapted from P. M. Lencioni, "Make Your Values Mean Something," *Harvard Business Review*, July 2002, https://hbr.org/2002/07/make-your-values-mean-something.

1.5. Adapted from K. Kelly and P. R. Murphy, "Reducing Accounting Aggressiveness with General Ethical Norms and Decision Structure," *Journal of Business Ethics* (2019), https://link.springer.com/content/pdf/10.1007/s10551-019-04290-w.pdf.

1.6. Adapted from J. Moriarty, "Business Ethics," in *The Stanford Encyclopedia of Philosophy*, ed. Edward N. Zalta, Fall 2017 ed., https://plato.stanford.edu/archives/fall2017/entries/ethics-business/.

1.7. S. Krawcheck, "When to Risk Your Career for Ethical Reasons," *FastCompany.com*, January 18, 2017, https://www.fastcompany.com/3067239/when-to-risk-your-career-for-ethical-reasons.

1.8. B. Knox, "Employee Volunteer Programs Are Associated with Firm-Level Benefits and CEO Incentives: Data on the Ethical Dilemma of Corporate Social Responsibility Activities," *Journal of Business Ethics* 162 (2020): 449–72.

1.9. T. Popomaronis, "Billionaire Warren Buffett Has a 'Simple' Test for Making Tough Decisions—Here's How It Works," *CNBC.com*, May 11, 2019, https://www.cnbc.com/2019/05/10/billionaire-warren-buffett-use-this-simple-test-when-making-tough-decisions.html.

1.10. K. Amadeo and S. Anderson, "2008 Financial Crisis: Causes, Costs, and Whether It Could Happen Again," *thebalance.com*, May 7, 2020, https://www.thebalance.com/2008-financial-crisis-3305679#cost-of-the-crisis.

1.11. M. Auerback, "The Failure to Punish White-Collar Crime after the 2008 Financial Crisis Helped Produce President Donald Trump," *Commondreams.org*, August 29, 2018, https://www.commondreams.org/views/2018/08/29/failure-punish-white-collar-crime-after-2008-financial-crisis-helped-produce.

1.12. J. Eaglesham, "Missing: Stats on Crisis Convictions," *The Wall Street Journal,* May 13, 2012, https://www.wsj.com/articles/SB10001424052702303505504577401911741048088.

1.13. "Bernanke: More Execs Should Have Gone to Jail," *CNBC.com,* October 4, 2015, http://www.cnbc.com/2015/10/04/bernanke-more-bank-execs-should-have-been-jailed-for-financial-crisis.html.

1.14. R. Freudenreich, F. Ludeke-Freund, and S. Schaltegger, "A Stakeholder Theory Perspective on Business Models: Value Creation for Sustainability," *Journal of Business Ethics* (February 8, 2019), https://link.springer.com/content/pdf/10.1007/s10551-019-04112-z.pdf.

1.15. N. Zhong, S. Wang, and R. Yang, "Does Corporate Governance Enhance Common Interests of Shareholders and Primary Stakeholders?" *Journal of Business Ethics* 141 (2017): 411–31.

1.16. *Ibid.*

1.17. P. Barnes, "Lawsuit against Facebook Uses Public Accommodation Law to Challenge Advertising," *Forbes.com*, November 1, 2019, https://www.forbes.com/sites/patriciagbarnes/2019/11/01/lawsuit-against-facebook-uses-public-accommodation-law-to-challenge-advertising/#5efa0c733d29.

1.18. T. Hsu and E. Lutz, "More Than 1,000 Companies Boycotted Facebook. Did It Work?" *The New York Times*, August 1, 2020, https://www.nytimes.com/2020/08/01/business/media/facebook-boycott.html.

1.19. N. Zhong, S. Wang, and R. Yang, "Does Corporate Governance Enhance Common Interests of Shareholders and Primary Stakeholders?" *Journal of Business Ethics* 141 (2017): 411–31.

1.20. Legal Information Institute, "Bribery," *Cornell Law School*, accessed August 17, 2020, https://www.law.cornell.edu/wex/bribery.

1.21. Ziavash, "20 Countries Where Bribery in Business is Common Practice," *Worldatlas.com*, April 25, 2017, https://www.worldatlas.com/articles/20-countries-where-bribery-in-business-is-common-practice.html.

1.22. M. Kouchaki and I. H. Smith, "Building an Ethical Career," *Harvard Business Review*, January–February 2020, accessed May 12, 2020, https://hbr.org/2020/01/building-an-ethical-career.

1.23. B. L. Connelly, T. R. Crook, J. G. Combs, D. J. Ketchen, and H. Aguinas, "Competence- and Integrity-Based Trust in Interorganizational Relationships: Which Matters More?" *Journal of Management* 44 (2018): 919–45.

1.24. *Ibid.*

1.25. *Ibid.*

1.26. Created from Edelman Trust Barometer 2020, accessed May 10, 2020, https://www.edelman.com/sites/g/files/aatuss191/files/2020-01/2020%20Edelman%20Trust%20Barometer%20Executive%20Summary_Single%20Spread%20without%20Crops.pdf.

1.27. R. Morales-Sanchez, M. Orta-Perez, and M. A. Rodriguez-Serrano, "The Benefits of Auditor's Sustained Ethical Behavior: Increased Trust and Reduced Costs," *Journal of Business Ethics* (2019), https://link.springer.com/content/pdf/10.1007/s10551-019-04298-2.pdf.

1.28. Edelman Trust Barometer 2020, accessed May 10, 2020, https://www.edelman.com/sites/g/files/aatuss191/files/2020-01/2020%20Edelman%20Trust%20Barometer%20Executive%20Summary_Single%20Spread%20without%20Crops.pdf..

1.29. Edelman Trust Barometer Spring Update: Trust and the Covid-19 Pandemic, May 5, 2020, accessed May 15, 2020, https://www.edelman.com/research/trust-2020-spring-update.

1.30. *Ibid.*

1.31. *Ibid.*

1.32. Adapted from M. Kouchaki and I. H. Smith, "Building an Ethical Career," *Harvard Business Review*, January–February 2020, accessed May 12, 2020, https://hbr.org/2020/01/building-an-ethical-career.

1.33. M. Schwantes, "The Job Interview Will Soon Be Dead. Here's What the Top Companies Are Replacing It With," *Inc. Magazine*, March 6, 2017, accessed May 15, 2020, https://www.inc.com/marcel-schwantes/science-81-percent-of-people-lie-in-job-interviews-heres-what-top-companies-are-.html.

1.34. Adapted from D. Dezube, "How to Interview to Uncover Candidate's Ethical Standards," *Monster.com*, accessed May 13, 2020, https://hiring.monster.com/employer-resources/recruiting-strategies/interviewing-candidates/interview-questions-to-ask-candidates/.

1.35. J. Westland, "How Gap Analysis Can Improve Your Project Management," *Projectmanager.com*, January 8, 2019, https://www.projectmanager.com/blog/gap-analysis-project-management.

1.36. M. Corkery, D. Yaffe-Bellany, and D. Kravitz, "As Meatpacking Plants Reopen, Data about Worker Illness Remains Elusive," *NYTimes.com*, May 25, 2020, https://www.nytimes.com/2020/05/25/business/coronavirus-meatpacking-plants-cases.html.

1.37. *Ibid.*

1.38. *Ibid.*

1.39. *Ibid.*

1.40. T. Telford and K. Kindy, "As They Rush to Maintain U.S. Meat Supply, Big Processors Saw Plants Become COVID-19 Hot Spots, Worker Illnesses Spike," *Washingtonpost.com*, April 25, 2020, https://www.washingtonpost.com/business/2020/04/25/meat-workers-safety-jbs-smithfield-tyson/.

Chapter 2

2.1. E. MacLaren, "What Are 'Study Drugs'?," *American Addiction Centers*, July 5, 2019, https://drugabuse.com/adderall/history-and-statistics-of-study-drugs/.

2.2. *Ibid.*

2.3. T. Brumbaugh, "From Chill Pills to Study Pills," *TCU360.com*, August 17, 2019, https://www.tcu360.com/2019/08/from-chill-pills-to-study-pills/.

2.4. I. Baumane-Vitolina, I. Cals, and E. Sumilo, "Is Ethics Rational? Teleological, Deontological, and Virtue Ethics Theories Reconciled in the Context of Traditional Economic Decision Making," *Economics of Finance* 39 (2016): 108–14.

2.5. A. West, "Multinational Tax Avoidance: Virtue Ethics and the Role of Accountants," *Journal of Business Ethics* 153 (2018): 1143–156.

2.6. CBC Radio, "Seattle CEO Who Pays Workers at Least $70, US Says It's Paying Off in Spades," posted March 2, 2020; accessed May 17, 2020, https://www.cbc.ca/radio/asithappens/as-it-happens-monday-edition-1.5482390/seattle-ceo-who-pays-workers-at-least-70k-us-says-it-s-paying-off-in-spades-1.5482394.

2.7. *Ibid.*

2.8. Adapted from T. Kollen, "Acting Out of Compassion, Egoism, and Malice: A Schopenhauerian View on the Moral Worth of CSR and Diversity Management Practices," *Journal of Business Ethics* 138 (2016): 215–29; and R. Audi, "Objectivity Without Egoism: Toward a Balance in Business Ethics," *Academy of Management Learning & Education* 8 (2009): 263–74.

2.9. J. Overall, "Unethical Behavior in Organizations: Empirical Findings that Challenge CSR and Egoism Theory," *Business Ethics: A European Review* 25 (2016): 113–27.

2.10. K. B. DeTienne, C. F. Ellerston, M C. Ingerson, and W. R. Dudley, "Moral Development in Business Ethics: An Examination and Critique," *Journal of Business Ethics* (November 18, 2019).

2.11. I. Baumane-Vitolina, I. Cals, and E. Sumilo, "Is Ethics Rational? Teleological, Deontological, and Virtue Ethics Theories Reconciled in the Context of Traditional Economic Decision Making," *Economics of Finance* 39 (2016): 108–14.

2.12. A. West, "Multinational Tax Avoidance: Virtue Ethics and the Role of Accountants," *Journal of Business Ethics* 153 (2018): 1143–156.
2.13. G. Demuijnck, "Universal Values and Virtues in Management Versus Cross-Cultural Moral Relativism: An Educational Strategy to Clear the Ground for Business Ethics," *Journal of Business Ethics* 128 (2015): 817–35.
2.14. Adapted from R. C. Solomon, "Corporate Roles, Personal Virtues: An Aristotelean Approach to Business Ethics," *Business Ethics Quarterly* 2 (1992): 317–39.
2.15. RAC company Website, accessed August 26, 2020, https://www.berry.net/company/mission-and-values/.
2.16. *Ibid.*
2.17. M. Velasquez, et al., "Ethical Relativism," *Markkula Center for Applied Ethics*, August 1, 1992, https://www.scu.edu/ethics/ethics-resources/ethical-decision-making/ethical-relativism/.
2.18. T. Segal, "The Enron Scandal: The Fall of a Wall Street Darling," *Investopedia*, May 4, 2020, https://www.investopedia.com/updates/enron-scandal-summary/.
2.19. "Nepotism," Inc. Magazine, inc.com, accessed August 15, 2020, https://www.inc.com/encyclopedia/nepotism.html.
2.20. M. Chittock, "All in the Family: The Good, the Bad and Ugly of Keeping Jobs Warm for a Relative," *BBC, bbc.com*, October 6, 2015, https://www.bbc.com/worklife/article/20151006-where-a-job-is-never-regarded-as-100-yours.
2.21. G. Iacurci, "How Much Unemployment Will I Get? That Depends on Your State," *CNBC.com*, April 9, 2020, https://www.cnbc.com/2020/04/09/how-much-unemployment-will-i-get-that-depends-on-your-state.html.
2.22. S. Fiorillo, "What Is the Average Income in the U.S.?," *TheStreet.com*, February 11, 2020, file:///D:/Dropbox/!Ethics%20Book/2%20Chapter%20Ethics/Pros%20and%20cons%20of%20activist%20investors--McKinsey%202019.pdf https://www.thestreet.com/personal-finance/average-income-in-us-14852178.
2.23. Gatesfoundation Website, https://www.gatesfoundation.org/.
2.24. Adapted from M. DeCourcey, "Looking Ahead: Top CSR Trends in 2020," *US Chamber of Commerce*, January 10, 2020, https://www.uschamberfoundation.org/blog/post/looking-ahead-top-csr-trends-2020.
2.25. J. Runyon, "9 Charities Worth Donating To," *Lifehack.org*, accessed May 17, 2020, https://www.lifehack.org/articles/money/9-charities-worth-donating.html.
2.26. TOMS company Website, https://www.toms.com/blakes-bio.
2.27. K. Caprino, "Bombas: How this Mission-Driven Organization Remains Profitable and Impactful, Even in Times of Crisis," *Forbes.com*, March 30, 2020, https://www.forbes.com/sites/kathycaprino/2020/03/30/bombas-how-this-mission-driven-organization-remains-profitable-and-impactful-even-in-crisis-times/#5f332af2b5a6.
2.28. D. Herbest, "People's 50 Companies that Care: See our 2019 List of Employers Who Win by Giving Back," *People.com*, July 24, 2019, https://people.com/human-interest/people-50-companies-that-care-2019/?slide=7167277.
2.29. S. Brown, J. Cyriac, and S. Oberhollenzer, "The Pros and Cons of Activist Investors," McKinsey & Company, May 2019, accessed May 19, 2020. https://www.mckinsey.com/~/media/McKinsey/Business%20Functions/Strategy%20and%20Corporate%20Finance/Our%20Insights/The%20pros%20and%20cons%20of%20activist%20investors/The-pros-and-cons-of-activist-investors-VF.pdf?shouldIndex=false.
2.30. W. Feuer, "Apple Now Has $207.06 Billion in Cash On Hand, Up Slightly from Last Quarter," *CNBC.com*, January 28, 2020, accessed May 19, 2020, https://www.cnbc.com/2020/01/28/apple-q1-2019-cash-hoard-heres-how-much-cash-apple-has-on-hand.html.
2.31. Carl Icahn, Wikipedia; accessed May 17, 2020, https://en.wikipedia.org/wiki/Carl_Icahn.
2.32. T. Franck, "Bill Ackman Warned 'Hell Is Coming' Because of the Virus: He Then Pocketed $2B in Bets Against Markets," *CNBC.com*, March 25, 2020, accessed May 19, 2020, https://www.cnbc.com/2020/03/25/bill-ackman-exits-market-hedges-uses-2-billion-he-made-to-buy-more-stocks-including-hilton.html.
2.33. S. Grob Plante, "Shopping Has Become a Political Act. Here's How It Happened," *Vox.com*, October 7, 2019, https://www.vox.com/the-goods/2019/10/7/20894134/consumer-activism-conscious-consumerism-explained.
2.34. J. Wingard, "Employee Activism Is the New Normal. So What Is Amazon Leadership Freaking Out?," *Forbes.com*, January 10, 2020, https://www.forbes.com/sites/jasonwingard/2020/01/10/employee-activism-is-the-new-normal-so-why-is-amazon-leadership-freaking-out/#2c8aab0a27f1.
2.35. S. Grob Plante, "Shopping Has Become a Political Act. Here's How It Happened," *Vox.com*, October 7, 2019, https://www.vox.com/the-goods/2019/10/7/20894134/consumer-activism-conscious-consumerism-explained.
2.36. *Ibid.*
2.37. J. Wingard, "Employee Activism is the New Normal. So, What is Amazon Leadership Freaking Out?," *Forbes.com*, January 10, 2020, https://www.forbes.com/sites/jasonwingard/2020/01/10/employee-activism-is-the-new-normal-so-why-is-amazon-leadership-freaking-out/#2c8aab0a27f1.
2.38. Free Enterprise Project, "Levi's Criticized for Putting Politics Ahead of Pants," *Nationalcenter.org*, July 10, 2019, https://nationalcenter.org/ncppr/2019/07/10/levis-criticized-for-putting-politics-ahead-of-pants/.
2.39. P. Goyal, Z. Rahman, and A. A. Kazmi, "Corporate Sustainability Performance and Firm Performance Research," *Management Decisions* 2 (2013): 361–79.

2.40. D. Quinjones, "Just How Huge Are Mexico's Auto Exports to the US? How Fast Have They Grown?," *Wolfstreet.com*, February 15, 2019, https://wolfstreet.com/2019/02/15/auto-exports-from-mexico-to-the-us-surge-nearly-10/.
2.41. Adapted from A. Cain, "An Inside Look on how Home Improvement Giants Lowe's and Home Depot are Battening Down the Hatches for Hurricane Dorian," *Business Insider*, August 31, 2019, https://www.businessinsider.com/home-depot-lowes-hurricane-dorian-2019-8.
2.42. P. Fain, "Philosophy Degrees and Sales Jobs," *Inside Higher Ed*, August 2, 2019, https://www.insidehighered.com/news/2019/08/02/new-data-track-graduates-six-popular-majors-through-their-first-three-jobs.
2.43. H. Zhang, "Dick's Sporting Goods Will Stop Selling Guns at 440 More Stores," *CNN.com*, March 10, 2020, https://www.cnn.com/2020/03/10/business/dicks-sporting-goods-remove-guns-from-440-stores/index.html.
2.44. V. Caval, "Why Dick's Sporting Goods Decided to Stop Selling Guns: CEO," *finance.yahoo.com*, October 8, 2019, https://finance.yahoo.com/news/why-dicks-sporting-goods-decided-to-stop-selling-guns-ceo-231006766.html.
2.45. *Ibid.*
2.46. *Ibid.*
2.47. T. Hsu, "Dick's Sporting Goods Shifts from Guns Evan as Sales Suffer," *The New York Times*, March 12, 2019, https://www.nytimes.com/2019/03/12/business/dicks-sporting-goods-stock-gun-control.html?action=click&module=RelatedLinks&pgtype=Article.
2.48. *Ibid.*
2.49. C. Jones and J. Bote, "Some Employees Call on Walmart to Stop Selling Guns in Wake of Mass Shootings," *USAToday.com*, August 7, 2019, https://www.usatoday.com/story/money/2019/08/07/walmart-workers-call-walkout-stop-guns-wake-mass-shootings/1941705001/.
2.50. ATF Website, https://www.atf.gov/resource-center/data-statistics.
2.51. H. Zhang, "Dick's Sporting Goods Will Stop Selling Guns at 440 More Stores," *CNN.com*, March 10, 2020, https://www.cnn.com/2020/03/10/business/dicks-sporting-goods-remove-guns-from-440-stores/index.html.

Chapter 3

3.1. A. North, C. Grady, L. McGann, and A. Romano, "262 Celebrities, Politicians, CEOs, and Others Who Have Been Accused of Sexual Misconduct Since April 2017," *Vox, vox.com*, January 9, 2019, https://www.vox.com/a/sexual-harassment-assault-allegations-list/frankie-shaw.
3.2. Adapted from H. Latan, C. J. C. Jabbour, and A. B. L. de Sousa Jabbour, "Ethical Awareness, Ethical Judgment and Whistleblowing: A Moderated Mediation Analysis," *Journal of Business Ethics* 155 (2019): 289–304.
3.3. *Ibid.*
3.4. Adapted from L. Kutsch, "Can We Rely on Our Intuition," *Scientific American*, scientificamerican.com, August 15, 2019, https://www.scientificamerican.com/article/can-we-rely-on-our-intuition/.
3.5. *Ibid.*
3.6. Adapted from E. Rousselet, B. Brial, R. Cadario, and A. Beji-Becheur, "Moral Intensity, Issue Characteristics, and Ethical Issue Recognition," *Journal of Business Ethics* 163 (2020): 347–63.
3.7. Adapted from T. T. Moores, H. J. Smith, and M. Limayem, "Putting the Pieces Back Together: Moral Intensity and Its Impact on the Four-Component Model," *Business and Society Review* 2 (2018): 243–68.
3.8. Adapted from T. M. Jones, "Ethical Decision Making by Individuals in Organizations: An Issue-Contingent Model," *Academy of Management Review* 2 (1991): 366–95.
3.9. *Ibid.*
3.10. Adapted from S. A. Morris and R. A. McDonald, "The Role of Moral Intensity in Moral Judgments: An Empirical Investigation," *Journal of Business Ethics* 14 (1995): 715–26.
3.11. E. Levenson, L. del Valle, and S. Moghe, "Harvey Weinstein Sentenced to 23 Years in Prison After Addressing His Accusers in Court," *CNN*, cnn.com, March 11, 2020, https://www.cnn.com/2020/03/11/us/harvey-weinstein-sentence/index.html#:~:text=Harvey%20Weinstein%20was%20sentenced%20Wednesday%20in%20a%20New,and%20encouraged%20women%20to%20speak%20out%20against%20.
3.12. Adapted from T. M. Jones, "Ethical Decision Making by Individuals in Organizations: An Issue-Contingent Model," *Academy of Management Review* 2 (1991): 366–95.
3.13. *Ibid.*
3.14. *Ibid.*
3.15. *Ibid.*
3.16. *Ibid.*
3.17. *Ibid.*
3.18. S. A. Morris and R. A. McDonald, "The Role of Moral Intensity in Moral Judgments: An Empirical Investigation," *Journal of Business Ethics* 14 (1995): 715–26.
3.19. A. Newman, H. Le, A. North-Samardzic, and M. Cohen, "Moral Disengagement at Work: A Review and Research Agenda," *Journal of Business Ethics,* May 9, 2019: 1–36.
3.20. *Ibid.*
3.21. R. Fida, C. Tramontano, M. Paciello, V. Ghezzi, and C. Barbaranelli, "Understanding the Interplay among Regulatory Self-Efficacy, Moral Disengagement, and Academic Cheating Behavior during Vocational

Education: A Three-Wave Study," *Journal of Business Ethics* 153 (2018): 725–40.

3.22. M. L. Farnese, C. Tramontano, R. Fida, and M. Paciello, "Cheating Behaviors in Academic Context: Does Academic Moral Disengagement Matter?," *Procedia—Social and Behavioral Sciences* 29 (2011): 356–65.

3.23. O. Sezer, R. Gino, and M. H. Bazerman, "Ethical Blind Spots: Explaining Unintentional Unethical Behavior," *Current Opinions in Psychology* 6 (2015): 77–81.

3.24. M. H. Bazerman and A. Tenbrunsel, "Ethical Breakdowns," *Harvard Business Review*, April 2011: 1–9.

3.25. *Ibid.*

3.26. *Ibid.*

3.27. A. Betz, "What it Means that Teachers Are Mandated Reporters," *Education Corner*, educationcorner.com, accessed July 17, 2020, https://www.educationcorner.com/teachers-mandated-reporters.html.

3.28. M. H. Bazerman and A. Tenbrunsel, "Ethical Breakdowns," *Harvard Business Review*, April 2011: 1–9.

3.29. J. Forkin, "'Pharma Bro' Martin Shkreli Moved from Federal Prison After Claim He Was Running Drug Company with Banned Cellphone," *cnbc.com*, April 24, 2019, https://www.cnbc.com/2019/04/24/pharma-bro-martin-shkreli-moved-from-prison-after-rule-breaking.html.

3.30. T. Burrus, "Protecting Gun Manufacturers from Frivolous Lawsuits," *CATO Institute, cato.org*, September 11, 2019, https://www.cato.org/blog/protecting-gun-manufacturers-frivolous-lawsuits ; and Giffords Law Center, "Gun Industry Immunity, lawcenter.giffords.org, accessed July 17, 2020, https://lawcenter.giffords.org/gun-laws/policy-areas/other-laws-policies/gun-industry-immunity/.

3.31. J. Stempel, "U.S. Judge Tosses Former SAC Capital Trader's Insider Trading Guilty Plea," *Reuters*, reuters.com, June 21, 2019, https://www.reuters.com/article/us-sac-insidertrading-lee/u-s-judge-tosses-former-sac-capital-traders-insider-trading-guilty-plea-idUSKCN1TM2IU.

3.32. Inspired by M. H. Bazerman and A. Tenbrunsel, "Ethical Breakdowns," *Harvard Business Review*, April 2011: 1–9.

3.33. *Ibid.*

3.34. *Ibid.*

3.35. B. Goldstein, "Seattle Seahawks Beware: New Head Coach Pete Carroll Reeks of Scandal," *bleacherreport.com*, accessed July 17, 2020, https://bleacherreport.com/articles/407209-why-you-should-be-scared-of-pete-carroll.

3.36. K. Gemmell, "A Timeline of USC Turmoil, Scandals, and Coaching Upheaval," *espn.com*, October 13, 2015, https://www.espn.com/blog/ncfnation/post/_/id/117845/a-timeline-of-usc-turmoil-scandals-and-coaching-upheaval.

3.37. A. Reimer, "Pete Carroll, Not Bill Belichick, Should Be Considered the NFL's Foremost Cheater," *Forbes*, forbes.com, September 22, 2016, https://www.forbes.com/sites/alexreimer/2016/09/22/pete-carroll-not-bill-belichick-should-be-considered-the-nfls-foremost-cheater/#a48873d579f1; and K. Gemmell, "A Timeline of USC Turmoil, Scandals, and Coaching Upheaval," *espn.com*, October 13, 2015, https://www.espn.com/blog/ncfnation/post/_/id/117845/a-timeline-of-usc-turmoil-scandals-and-coaching-upheaval.

3.38. "Bankruptcy Data Releases 2018 Corporate Bankruptcy Review," *Business Insider*, businessinsider.com, January 13, 2019, https://markets.businessinsider.com/news/stocks/bankruptcydata-releases-2018-corporate-bankruptcy-review-1027863585#.

3.39. P. Eavis, "These Companies Gave Their CEOs Millions, Just before Bankruptcy," *The New York Times*, nytimes.com, June 23, 2020, https://www.nytimes.com/2020/06/23/business/ceo-bonsues-before-bankruptcy-coronavirus.html.

3.40. M. Spector and J. DiNapoli, "On Eve of Bankruptcy, US Firms Shower Execs with Bonuses," *reuters.com*, July 17, 2020, https://www.reuters.com/article/us-health-coronavirus-bankruptcy-bonuses/on-eve-of-bankruptcy-us-firms-shower-execs-with-bonuses-idUSKCN24I1EE.

3.41. W. Shoulberg, "Big-Buck Bonuses for Big-Time Execs in Bad Bankruptcy Times," *Forbes*, forbes.com, June 9, 2020, https://www.forbes.com/sites/warrenshoulberg/2020/06/09/pre-bankruptcy-retention-bonusesat-hertz-penney-libbey-others-are-rampant/#51062d793758.

3.42. P. Eavis, "These Companies Gave Their CEOs Millions, Just before Bankruptcy," *The New York Times*, nytimes.com, June 23, 2020, https://www.nytimes.com/2020/06/23/business/ceo-bonsues-before-bankruptcy-coronavirus.html.

3.43. W. Shoulberg, "Big-Buck Bonuses for Big-Time Execs in Bad Bankruptcy Times," *Forbes*, forbes.com, June 9, 2020, https://www.forbes.com/sites/warrenshoulberg/2020/06/09/pre-bankruptcy-retention-bonusesat-hertz-penney-libbey-others-are-rampant/#51062d793758.

3.44. L. Shen, "The 20 Biggest Companies that have Filed for Bankruptcy because of the Coronavirus Pandemic," *Fortune*, fortune.com, June 29, 2020, https://fortune.com/2020/06/29/companies-filing-bankruptcy-2020-during-coronavirus-pandemic-covid-19-economy-industries/,

3.45. M. Spector and J. DiNapoli, "On Eve of Bankruptcy, US Firms Shower Execs with Bonuses," *reuters.com*, July 17, 2020, https://www.reuters.com/article/us-health-coronavirus-bankruptcy-bonuses/on-eve-of-bankruptcy-us-firms-shower-execs-with-bonuses-idUSKCN24I1EE.

Chapter 4

4.1 Adapted from L. Frias, "Mark Zuckerberg Said Facebook Employees Who Move Out of Silicon Valley May Face Pay Cuts," *Businessinsider.com*, May 21, 2020, https://www.businessinsider.com/zuckerberg-facebook-salary-employees-moving-out-of-silicon-valley-2020-5.

4.2 J. J. Lee et al., "Lay Theories of Effortful Honesty: Does the Honesty-Effort Association Justify Making a Dishonest Decision?" *Journal of Applied Psychology* 104 (2019): 659–77.

4.3 T. Beck et al., "Can Honesty Oaths, Peer Interaction, or Monitoring Mitigate Lying?" *Journal of Business Ethics* 163 (2020): 467–84.

4.4 P. W. Paese, A. M. Schreiber, and A. W. Taylor, "Caught Telling the Truth: Effects of Honesty and Communication Media in Disruptive Negotiations," *Group Decision and Negotiation* 12 (2003): 537–66.

4.5 Adapted from S. M. Heathfield, "What Is Integrity?" *The Balance Careers*, June 22, 2020, https://www.thebalancecareers.com/what-is-integrity-really-1917676.

4.6 Inspired by S. Heathfield, "What Is Integrity—Really?" *thebalancecareers.com*, October 31, 2019, https://www.thebalancecareers.com/what-is-integrity-really-1917676.

4.7 *Ibid.*

4.8 C. Lattimer, "5 Essential Behaviors You Need to Maintain Your Integrity as a Leader," *Inc.com*, February 4, 2016, https://www.inc.com/lindsay-blakely/protests-houston-night-light-pediatrics.html.

4.9 Phrase in quote—"integrity under fire"—taken from R. C. Solomon, *Ethics and Excellence: Cooperation and Integrity in Business* (New York: Oxford University Press, 1992), 192.

4.10 D. R. Comer and M. Schwartz, "Highlighting Moral Courage in the Business Ethics Course," *Journal of Business Ethics*, 2017, 146: 703–23.

4.11 Adapted from "5 Ways to Build Moral Courage in the Workplace," *managefearlessly.com*, April 10, 2012, http://managefearlessly.com/blog/5-ways-build-moral-courage-workplace.

4.12 C. Curtis, "A Reminder of What Colin Kaepernick Actually Said, and a Timeline of His Actions," *USAToday.com*, June 4, 2020, https://ftw.usatoday.com/2020/06/colin-kaepernick-anthem-protest-timeline-message/.

4.13 K. Bellware, "Wells Fargo CEO Blames Multimilion-Dollar Fraud on the Lowest Level Employees," HuffPost, September 14, 2016: https://www.huffpost.com/entry/john-stumpf-wells-fargo_n_57d87d54e4b0fbd4b7bc4c85.

4.14 G. Belli, "Why You Should Never Lie on a Resume: 7 Stories of People Who Got Caught," *payscale.com*, January 18, 2019, https://www.payscale.com/career-news/2019/01/why-you-should-never-lie-on-a-resume-7-stories-of-people-who-got-caught.

4.15 V. Bolden-Barrett, "More Than a Third of People Admit to Lying on Resumes," *hrdrive.com*, January 17, 2020, https://www.hrdive.com/news/more-than-a-third-of-people-admit-to-lying-on-resumes/570565/.

4.16 "17 Successful Executives Who Have Lied on Their Resumes," *businessinsider.com*, June 19, 2020, https://www.businessinsider.in/strategy/17-successful-executives-who-have-lied-on-their-resumes/slidelist/48087109.cms.

4.17 K. Heller, "James Patterson Mostly Doesn't Write His Books. And His New Readers Mostly Don't Read, Yet," *washingtonpost.com*, June 6, 2016, https://www.washingtonpost.com/lifestyle/style/james-patterson-doesnt-write-his-books-and-his-newest-readers-dont-read/2016/06/06/88e7d3c0-28c2-11e6-ae4a-3cdd5fe74204_story.html.

4.18 *Ibid.*

4.19 Forbes 2020 Celebrity 100 Earnings, "#15 James Patterson," June 4, 2020, https://www.forbes.com/profile/james-patterson/#2609327f1ea6.

4.20 "Famous Ghostwritten Books and Their Ghostwriters," *dereklewis.com*, https://dereklewis.com/famous-ghostwritten-books-and-their-ghostwriters/ accessed June 23, 2020.

4.21 J. Robbins, "The Ethics of Authorship: Is Ghostwriting Plagiarism?" *insidehighered.com*, February 23, 2015, https://www.insidehighered.com/blogs/sounding-board/ethics-authorship-ghostwriting-plagiarism.

4.22 "What Is Plagiarism?" *plagiarism.org*, May 18, 2017, https://www.plagiarism.org/article/what-is-plagiarism.

Chapter 5

5.1. A. Satariano, "How My Boss Monitors Me While I Work from Home," *The New York Times,* nytimes.com, May 6, 2020, https://www.nytimes.com/2020/05/06/technology/employee-monitoring-work-from-home-virus.html?smid=em-share.

5.2. *Ibid.*

5.3. *Ibid.*

5.4. D. Whincup, "Do Me a Favour—Internships and the Bribery Act," *Employment Law Worldview*, July 26, 2016, https://www.employmentlawworldview.com/do-me-a-favour-internships-and-the-bribery-act/.

5.5. Adapted from C. L. Hart, "What Is a Lie?," *psychologytoday.com*, May 16, 2019, https://www.psychologytoday.com/us/blog/the-nature-deception/201905/what-is-lie.

5.6. U. Boda, "Doctors Losing Medical Licenses," *emedevents.com*, September 12, 2018, https://www.emedevents.com/MedblogPosts/medblogpage/doctors-losing-medical-licenses.

5.7. United States Department of Justice, "Dallas Doctor Sentenced on Health Care Fraud Conviction," *justice.gov*, August 9, 2017, https://www.justice.gov/usaondtx/pr/dallas-doctor-sentenced-health-care-fraud-conviction.

5.8. S. Sah, "Conflict of Interest Disclosure as a Reminder of Professional Norms," *Organizational Behavior and Human Decision Processes* 154 (2019): 62–79.

5.9. Adapted from S. M. Heathfield, "Conflicts of Interest in the Workplace," *thebalancecareers.com*, November 25, 2019, https://www.thebalancecareers.com/conflict-of-interest-1918090.

5.10. J. Kelly, "McDonald's Sues Former CEO Steve Easterbrook Alleging Multiple Sexual Relationships with Workers," *Forbes*, forbes.com, August 11, 2020, https://www.forbes.com/sites/jackkelly/2020/08/11/mcdonalds-sues-former-ceo-steve-easterbrook-alleging-multiple-sexual-relationships-with-workers/#5904b94c5cac.

5.11. A. Robaton, "Most Americans Are Hourly Workers," *cbsnews.com*, February 17, 2017, https://www.cbsnews.com/news/most-americans-are-hourly-workers/.

5.12. T. Barrabi, "NCAA March Madness to Cost Employers $13.3B in Lost Productivity, Firm Says," *foxbusiness.com*, March 21, 2019, https://www.foxbusiness.com/markets/ncaa-march-madness-to-cost-employers-13-3b-in-lost-productivity-firm-says.

5.13. Adapted from H. McGurgan, "How Do Employees Steal Time While at Work?", *smallbusiness.chron.com*, accessed June 20, 2020, https://smallbusiness.chron.com/employees-steal-time-work-38624.html.

5.14. C. Thiel, A. E. MacDougall, and Z. Bagdasarov, "Big (Benevolent) Brother: Overcoming the Drawbacks of Employee Monitoring through Ethical Administration," *Organizational Dynamics* 48 (2019): 19–28.

5.15. "Managing Workplace Monitoring," *shrm.org*, March 13, 2019, https://www.shrm.org/resourcesandtools/tools-and-samples/toolkits/pages/workplaceprivacy.aspx.

5.16. Justice Information Sharing, "Electronic Communications Privacy Act of 1986," accessed June 23, 2020, https://it.ojp.gov/PrivacyLiberty/authorities/statutes/1285.

5.17. Adapted from "Managing Workplace Monitoring," 2019.

5.18. *Ibid.*

5.19. *Ibid.*

5.20. *Ibid.*

5.21. *Ibid.*

5.22. *Ibid.*

5.23. *Ibid.*

5.24. *Ibid.*

5.25. Adapted from J. Rosenfeld et al., "COVID-19: Screening Employee Temperatures: What Employers Need to Know," *WilmerHale.com*, April 3, 2020, https://www.wilmerhale.com/en/insights/client-alerts/20200403-screening-employee-temperatures-what-employers-need-to-know.

5.26. *Ibid.*

5.27. *Ibid.*

5.28. Inspired by L. Nagle-Piazza, "5 Workplace Privacy Rules California Employers Must Follow," *shrm.org*, July 25, 2018, https://www.shrm.org/resourcesandtools/legal-and-compliance/state-and-local-updates/pages/california-employee-privacy-rights.aspx.

5.29. S. O'Brien, "Employers Check Your Social Media Before Hiring. Many Then Find Reasons Not to Offer You a Job," *cnbc.com*, August 10, 2018, https://www.cnbc.com/2018/08/10/digital-dirt-may-nix-that-job-you-were-counting-on-getting.html.

5.30. M. Barthel, "Employers Are Still Avoiding Former Inmates," *theatlantic.com*, November 5, 2019, https://www.theatlantic.com/politics/archive/2019/11/are-states-complying-ban-box-laws/601240/.

5.31. C. Stacy and M. Cohen, "Ban the Box and Racial Discrimination," *urban.org*, February 2017, https://www.urban.org/sites/default/files/publication/88366/ban_the_box_and_racial_discrimination_4.pdf.

5.32. A. Liptak, "Civil Rights Law Protects Gay and Transgender Workers, Supreme Court Rules," June 16, 2020, https://www.nytimes.com/2020/06/15/us/gay-transgender-workers-supreme-court.html.

5.33. Adapted from "What Is Whistleblowing," *HRZone.com*, accessed June 20, 2020, https://www.hrzone.com/hr-glossary/what-is-whistleblowing.

5.34. G. Wearden, "GlaxoSmithKline Whistleblower Awarded $96m Payout," *The Guardian*, October 27, 2010, https://www.theguardian.com/business/2010/oct/27/glaxosmithkline-whistleblower-awarded-96m-payout.

5.35. E. Kelton, "The SEC Whistleblower Program: Make or Break Time," *Forbes.com*, February 26, 2020, https://www.forbes.com/sites/erikakelton/2020/02/26/the-sec-whistleblower-program-make-or-break-time/#4536d7a85139.

5.36. T. Agovino, "Whistleblowers: An Early Detection System," *shrm.org*, February 1, 2020, https://www.shrm.org/hr-today/news/all-things-work/pages/whistleblowers-an-early-detection-system.aspx.

5.37. *Ibid.*

5.38. Government Accountability Project, accessed June 20, 2020, https://whistleblower.org/timeline-us-whistleblowers/.

5.39. M. Ilyushina, "Edward Snowden Requests a Three-Year Extension of Russian Residency," *cnn.com*, April 16, 2020, https://www.cnn.com/2020/04/16/europe/edward-snowden-russian-residency-intl/index.html.

5.40. "The Isolation Is Just Momentous When You've Spoken Truth to Power," *whistleblowersblog.org*, November 8, 2017, https://www.whistleblowersblog.org/2017/11/articles/features/the-isolation-is-just-momentous-when-youve-spoken-truth-to-power/.

5.41. Adapted from R. Khan, "Whistleblower: Warrior, Saboteur, or Snitch?" *Forbes*, July 5, 2018, https://www.forbes.com/sites/roomykhan/2018/07/05/whistleblower-warrior-saboteur-or-snitch/#39a75a856362.

5.42. "National Donate Life Month—April 2019 Donation and Transplantation Statistics," *donatelife.net*, accessed June 20, 2020, https://www.donatelife.net/wp-content/uploads/2016/06/2019-NDLM-Donation-and-Transplantation-Statistics-FINAL-Jan2019.pdf.
5.43. J. Jarvie, "Ethical Dilemmas in the Age of Coronavirus: Whose Lives Should We Save?" *latimes.com*, March 19, 2020, https://www.latimes.com/world-nation/story/2020-03-19/ethical-dilemmas-in-the-age-of-coronavirus-whose-lives-should-we-save.
5.44. *Ibid.*
5.45. *Ibid.*
5.46. *Ibid.*

Chapter 6

6.1. D. Wakabayashi, "Google Employees Are Free to Speak Up. Except on Antitrust," *The New York Times*, October 13, 2020: https://www.nytimes.com/2020/10/13/technology/google-employees-antitrust.html?smid=em-share.
6.2. U.S. Department of Labor Website, https://www.dol.gov/agencies/oasam/centers-offices/civil-rights-center/internal/policies/workplace-harassment/2012.
6.3. "What Is the Difference between Harassment and Discrimination?," *Swartz and Swidler Webpage*, https://swartz-legal.com/difference-harassment-discrimination/.
6.4. M. Jameel, L. Shapiro, and J. Yerardi, "More than 1 Million Employment Discrimination Complaints have been Filed with the Government since 2010. Here's What Happened to Them," *The Washington Post*, washingtonpost.com, February 28, 2019, https://www.washingtonpost.com/graphics/2019/business/discrimination-complaint-outcomes/.
6.5. F. Polli, "Using AI to Eliminate Bias from Hiring," *Harvard Business Review*, hbr.com, October 29, 2019, https://hbr.org/2019/10/using-ai-to-eliminate-bias-from-hiring.
6.6. Z. Rohrich, "Why These Companies are Rethinking the Use of AI in Hiring," *PBS*, pbs.org, November 26, 2019, https://www.pbs.org/newshour/world/agents-for-change/why-these-companies-are-rethinking-the-use-of-ai-in-hiring.
6.7. *Ibid.*
6.8. "Implicit Bias," Perception Institute, perception.org, accessed July 21, 2020, https://perception.org/research/implicit-bias/.
6.9. Adapted from F. Polli, "Using AI to Eliminate Bias from Hiring," *Harvard Business Review*, hbr.com, October 29, 2019, https://hbr.org/2019/10/using-ai-to-eliminate-bias-from-hiring.
6.10. *Ibid.*
6.11. J. Dastin, "Amazon Scraps Secret AI Recruiting Tool That Showed Bias Against Women," *Reuters*, reuters.com, October 9, 2019, https://www.reuters.com/article/us-amazon-com-jobs-automation-insight/amazon-scraps-secret-ai-recruiting-tool-that-showed-bias-against-women-idUSKCN1MK08G.
6.12. Adapted from Z. Rohrich, "Why These Companies are Rethinking the Use of AI in Hiring," *PBS*, pbs.org, November 26, 2019, https://www.pbs.org/newshour/world/agents-for-change/why-these-companies-are-rethinking-the-use-of-ai-in-hiring.
6.13. *Ibid.*
6.14. Adapted from F. Polli, "Using AI to Eliminate Bias from Hiring," *Harvard Business Review*, hbr.com, October 29, 2019, https://hbr.org/2019/10/using-ai-to-eliminate-bias-from-hiring.
6.15. Society of Human Resource Management, "Screening and Evaluating Candidates," shrm.org, accessed July 21, 2020, https://www.shrm.org/resourcesandtools/tools-and-samples/toolkits/pages/screeningandevaluatingcandidates.aspx.
6.16. *Ibid.*
6.17. Bureau of Labor Statistics, "NLS FAQs," January 16, 2020, https://www.bls.gov/nls/questions-and-answers.htm.
6.18. Adapted from A. Doyle, "What Can Employers Say About Former Employees?," *thebalancecareers*, November 26, 2019, https://www.thebalancecareers.com/what-can-employers-say-about-former-employees-2059608.
6.19. *Ibid.*
6.20. *Ibid.*
6.21. *Ibid.*
6.22. A. Doyle, "How to Handle a Bad Reference," *thebalancecareers.com*, August 13, 2019, https://www.thebalancecareers.com/how-to-handle-bad-references-from-employers-2062977.
6.23. S. O'Brien, "Employers Check Your Social Media Before Hiring. Many Then Find Reasons Not to Offer You a Job." *CNBC*, cnbc.com, August 10, 2018, https://www.cnbc.com/2018/08/10/digital-dirt-may-nix-that-job-you-were-counting-on-getting.html?__source=sharebar|email&par=sharebar.
6.24. L. Nagele-Piazza, "What Employee Speech Is Protected in the Workplace?," *Society of Human Resource Management*, shrm.com, July 23, 2018, https://www.shrm.org/resourcesandtools/legal-and-compliance/employment-law/pages/employee-free-speech-in-the-workplace.aspx.
6.25. *Ibid.*
6.26. K. Conger, "Senators Want to Know if Amazon Retaliated Against Whistle-Blowers," *The New York Times*, nytimes.com, May 7, 2020, https://www.nytimes.com/2020/05/07/technology/amazon-coronavirus-whistleblowers.html?smid=em-share.
6.27. T. Spiggle, "Your Free Speech Rights (Mostly) Don't Apply at Work," *Forbes*, forbes.com, September 28, 2018, https://www.forbes.com/sites/tomspiggle/2018/09/28/free-speech-work-rights/#1e6495e638c8.
6.28. Adapted from S. Fonnesbeck, "Free Speech in the Workplace," *HR Daily Advisor*, hrdailyadvisor.

com, June 10, 2019, https://hrdailyadvisor.blr.com/2019/06/10/free-speech-in-the-workplace/.

6.29. I. A. Hamilton, "Elon Musk Says He's Taking a Break from Twitter," *Business Insider*, businessinsider.com, June 2, 2020, https://www.businessinsider.com/elon-musk-taking-a-break-twitter-2020-6.

6.30. *Ibid.*

6.31. *Ibid.*

6.32. E. Stewart, "Truly, What Is Up with Elon Musk?," *Vox*, vox.com, May 1, 2020, https://www.vox.com/recode/2020/5/1/21244346/elon-musk-tesla-twitter-stock-price-coronavirus-grimes.

6.33. Adapted from S. Fonnesbeck, "Free Speech in the Workplace," *HR Daily Advisor*, hrdailyadvisor.com, June 10, 2019, https://hrdailyadvisor.blr.com/2019/06/10/free-speech-in-the-workplace/.

6.34. *Ibid.*

6.35. T. Beer, "Starbucks Flips: Employees Can Now Wear Black Lives Matter Attire," *Forbes*, forbes.com, June 12, 2020, https://www.forbes.com/sites/tommybeer/2020/06/12/starbucks-reverses-course-will-allow-employees-to-wear-black-lives-matter-attire/#1e7ec87f7c33.

6.36. S. A. Holt, "Have You Read Your Social Media Policy Lately? Much Has Changed," *HR Daily Advisor*, hrdailyadvisor.com, March 5, 2019, https://hrdailyadvisor.blr.com/2019/03/05/have-you-read-your-social-media-policy-lately-much-has-changed/.

6.37. *Ibid.*

6.38. C. Dusterhoff, J. B. Cunningham, and J. N. MacGregor, "The Effects of Performance Rating, Leader-Member Exchange, Perceived Utility, and Organizational Justice on Performance Appraisal Satisfaction: Applying a Moral Judgment Model," *Journal of Business Ethics* 119 (2014): 265–73.

6.39. "Reinventing the Wheel: How Companies Like GE, Adobe, and Deloitte Get Rid of the Performance Reviews with One on Ones," *Lighthouse*, accessed August 25, 2020, https://getlighthouse.com/blog/get-rid-of-the-performance-review/.

6.40. K. Evans-Reber, "Here's What Can Happen When Companies Get Rid of Performance Reviews," *Forbes*, forbes.com, February 19, 2020, https://www.forbes.com/sites/forbeshumanresourcescouncil/2020/02/19/heres-what-can-happen-when-companies-get-rid-of-performance-reviews/#46a340215451.

6.41. C. Dusterhoff, J. B. Cunningham, and J. N. MacGregor, "The Effects of Performance Rating, Leader-Member Exchange, Perceived Utility, and Organizational Justice on Performance Appraisal Satisfaction: Applying a Moral Judgment Model," *Journal of Business Ethics* 119 (2014): 265–73.

6.42. Adapted from G. Jacobs, F. D. Belschak, and D. N. Den Hartog, "(Un)Ethical Behavior and Performance Appraisal: The Role of Affect, Support, and Organizational Justice," *Journal of Business Ethics* 121 (2014): 63–76.

6.43. Adapted from C. Dusterhoff, J. B. Cunningham, and J. N. MacGregor, "The Effects of Performance Rating, Leader-Member Exchange, Perceived Utility, and Organizational Justice on Performance Appraisal Satisfaction: Applying a Moral Judgment Model," *Journal of Business Ethics* 119 (2014): 265–73.

6.44. Adapted from G. Jacobs, F. D. Belschak, and D. N. Den Hartog, "(Un)Ethical Behavior and Performance Appraisal: The Role of Affect, Support, and Organizational Justice," *Journal of Business Ethics* 121 (2014): 63–76.

6.45. Adapted from L. Mackenzie, J. Wehner, and S. Correll, "Viewpoint: Why Most Performance Evaluations Are Biased and How to Fix Them," *Society of Human Resource Management*, shrm.org, January 16, 2019, https://www.shrm.org/resourcesandtools/hr-topics/employee-relations/pages/viewpoint-why-most-performance-evaluations-are-biased-and-how-to-fix-them.aspx.

6.46. Adapted from J. Pinsker, "The Pointlessness of the Workplace Drug Test," *The Atlantic*, theatlantic.com, June 4, 2015, https://www.theatlantic.com/business/archive/2015/06/drug-testing-effectiveness/394850/.

6.47. L. Nagele-Piazza, "Workplace Drug Testing: The Pros and Cons," *Society of Human Resource Management*, shrm.org, January 21, 2020, https://www.shrm.org/resourcesandtools/legal-and-compliance/state-and-local-updates/pages/the-pros-and-cons-of-workplace-drug-testing.aspx.

6.48. Adapted from J. Pinsker, "The Pointlessness of the Workplace Drug Test," *The Atlantic*, theatlantic.com, June 4, 2015, https://www.theatlantic.com/business/archive/2015/06/drug-testing-effectiveness/394850/.

6.49. L. DePillis, "Companies Drug Test a Lot Less Than They Used to—Because it Doesn't Really Work," *The Washington Post*, washingtonpost.com, March 10, 2015, https://www.washingtonpost.com/news/wonk/wp/2015/03/10/companies-drug-test-a-lot-less-than-they-used-to-because-it-doesnt-really-work/.

6.50. Z. Hrynowski, "What Percentage of Americans Smoke Marijuana?," *Gallup*, gallupnews.com, January 31, 2020, https://news.gallup.com/poll/284135/percentage-americans-smoke-marijuana.aspx.

6.51. J. M. Jones, "U.S. Support for Legal Marijuana Steady in Past Year," *Gallup*, gallup.com, October 23, 2019, https://news.gallup.com/poll/267698/support-legal-marijuana-steady-past-year.aspx.

6.52. C. A. Cano and K. J. Russo, "Drug and Alcohol Testing Law Advisor," *Jackson Lewis*, drugtestadvisor.com, December 6, 2019, https://www.drugtestlawadvisor.com/2019/12/drug-and-alcohol-testing-policy-check-up-are-you-ready-for-2020/.

Chapter 7

7.1. A. Twin and K. Khartit, "Non-Disclosure Agreement (NDA)," *Investopedia*, Investopedia.com, July 28, 2020, https://www.investopedia.com/terms/n/nda.asp.
7.2. Adapted from A. Martin, "How NDAs Help Some Victims Come Forward against Abuse," *Time*, time.com, November 28, 2017, https://time.com/5039246/sexual-harassment-nda/.
7.3. *Ibid.*
7.4. *Ibid.*
7.5. *Ibid.*
7.6. K. Wagner, "Google's CEO Has No Problem Releasing Employees from Nondisclosure Agreements So Women Can Speak Out," *Vox*, vox.com, January 19, 2018, https://www.vox.com/2018/1/19/16911564/google-sundar-pichai-susan-wojcicki-nda-sexual-harassment-kara-swisher.
7.7 House, R., Javidan, M., Hanges, P., & Dorfman, P. (2002). "Understanding cultures and implicit leadership theories across the globe: An introduction to project GLOBE," *Journal of World Business* 37(1), 3–10.
7.8. Adapted from M. E. Brown and L. K. Trevino, "Ethical Leadership: A Review and Future Directions," *The Leadership Quarterly* 17, no. 6 (2006): 595–616.
7.9. Adapted from L. K. Trevino, L. P. Harman, and M. Brown, "Moral Person and Moral Manager: How Executive Develop a Reputation for Ethical Leadership," *California Management Review* 42 (2000): 128–42.
7.10. *Ibid.*
7.11. J. Arnholz, "Cyclist Who Famously Flipped off Trump Motorcade Wins Election in Virginia," *ABCNews.go.com*, November 6, 2019, https://abcnews.go.com/Politics/cyclist-famously-flipped-off-trump-motorcade-wins-election/story?id=66791339.
7.12. M. Keeley, "White Woman Who Called Cops on Black Man, Placed on Leave at Work, Issues Apology," *Newsweek.com*, May 26, 2020, https://www.newsweek.com/white-woman-who-called-cops-black-man-placed-leave-work-issues-apology-1506408.
7.13. D. Bieler, "Michael Vick '30 for 30' Seeks to Add Context to his Dogfighting Saga," *The Washington Post*, January 30, 2020, https://www.washingtonpost.com/sports/2020/01/30/michael-vick-30-30-seeks-add-context-his-dogfighting-saga/.
7.14. E. Newcomer, "In Video, Uber CEO Argues with Driver over Falling Fares," *Bloomberg.com*, February 28, 2017, https://www.bloomberg.com/news/articles/2017-02-28/in-video-uber-ceo-argues-with-driver-over-falling-fares.
7.15. J. Elman, "Where Is Former Baltimore Ravens Star Ray Rice Now?" *Sportscasting.com*, March 27, 2020, https://www.sportscasting.com/where-is-former-baltimore-ravens-star-ray-rice-now/.
7.16. N. Ochsner, "NC Blue Cross CEO Resigns Following DWI Arrest, Interim CEO Named," *WBTV.com*, September 25, 2019, https://www.wbtv.com/2019/09/26/nc-blue-cross-ceo-resigns-following-dwi-arrest-interim-ceo-named/.
7.17. B. Hollingsworth, "'Porngate' Scandal Rocks Pennsylvania State Government," *CNSNews.com*, February 19, 2016, https://www.cnsnews.com/news/article/barbara-hollingsworth/porn-scandal-rocks-pennsylvania-state-government.
7.18. Adapted from R. C. Solomon, "Corporate Roles, Personal Virtues: An Aristotelian Approach to Business Ethics," *Business Ethics Quarterly* 2 (1992): 317–39.
7.19. K. Cameron, "Responsible Leadership as Virtuous Leadership," *Journal of Business Ethics* 98 (2011): 25–35.
7.20. G. Wang and R. D. Hackett, "Conceptualization and Measurement of Virtuous Leadership: Doing Well by Doing Good," *Journal of Business Ethics* 137 (2016): 321–45.
7.21. K. Cameron, "Responsible Leadership as Virtuous Leadership," *Journal of Business Ethics* 98 (2011): 28.
7.22. Adapted from K. Cameron, "Responsible Leadership as Virtuous Leadership," *Journal of Business Ethics* 98 (2011): 25–35.
7.23. *Ibid.*
7.24. A. Harrison, J. Summers, and B. Mennecke, "The Effects of the Dark Triad of Unethical Behavior," *Journal of Business Ethics* 153, no. 1 (2018): 53–77.
7.25. Adapted from Mayo Clinic, "Narcissistic Personality Disorder," *Mayoclinic.org*, https://www.mayoclinic.org/diseases-conditions/narcissistic-personality-disorder/symptoms-causes/syc-20366662.
7.26. Adapted from E. Grijalva, P. Harms, D. Newman, B. Gaddis, and R. Fraley, "Narcissism and Leadership: A Meta-Analytical Review of Linear and Non-Linear Relationships," *Personnel Psychology* 68, no. 1 (2015): 1–47.
7.27. "The 20 Richest American Billionaires," *Forbes.com*, April 7, 2020, https://www.forbes.com/sites/hayleycuccinello/2020/04/07/the-20-richest-american-billionaires-2020/#4515c2a31aeb.
7.28. M. Maccoby, "Narcissistic Leaders: The Incredible Pros, the Inevitable Cons," *Harvard Business Review*, January 2004, https://hbr.org/2004/01/narcissistic-leaders-the-incredible-pros-the-inevitable-cons.
7.29. Adapted from E. Grijalva, P. Harms, D. Newman, B. Gaddis, and R. Fraley, "Narcissism and Leadership: A Meta-Analytical Review of Linear and Non-Linear Relationships," *Personnel Psychology* 68, no. 1 (2015): 1–47.
7.30. Adapted from D. Lancer, "Understanding the Mind of a Narcissist," *Psychology Today*, April 10, 2018, https://www.psychologytoday.com/us/blog/toxic-relationships/201804/understanding-the-mind-narcissist.
7.31. *Ibid.*
7.32. *Ibid.*
7.33. A. Harrison, J. Summers, and B. Mennecke, "The Effects of the Dark Triad of Unethical Behavior,"

Journal of Business Ethics 153, no. 1 (2018): 53–77.

7.34. *BBC Magazine*, "10 of Popular Culture's Best Machiavellian Characters," BBC.com, May 23, 2013, https://www.bbc.com/news/magazine-22537324.

7.35. Adapted from D. Hartley, "Meet the Machiavellians: These Master Manipulators Are Natural Con Artists and Dangerous Companions," *Psychology Today*, September 8, 2015, https://www.psychologytoday.com/us/blog/machiavellians-gulling-the-rubes/201509/meet-the-machiavellians.

7.36. E. Skorstad, "Stop Dark Triad Overlords Destroying Your Business," *thehrdirector.com*, November 17, 2017, https://www.thehrdirector.com/features/cultural-change/stop-dark-triad-overlords-destroying-your-business/.

7.37. A. Harrison, J. Summers, and B. Mennecke, "The Effects of the Dark Triad of Unethical Behavior," *Journal of Business Ethics* 153, no. 1 (2018): 53–77.

7.38. Adapted from K. M. Robinson, "Sociopath vs. Psychopath: What's the Difference?" *WebMD.com*, https://www.webmd.com/mental-health/features/sociopath-psychopath-difference#1.

7.39. Adapted from *Psychology Today*, Psychopathy, accessed May 25, 2020, https://www.psychologytoday.com/us/basics/psychopathy.

7.40. J. McCullough, "The Psychopathic CEO," *Forbes.com*, December 9, 2019, https://www.forbes.com/sites/jackmccullough/2019/12/09/the-psychopathic-ceo/#4ccde3ac791e; G. Marks, "21 Percent of CEOs Are Psychopaths. Only 21 Percent?" *Washingtonpost.com*, September 16, 2016, https://www.washingtonpost.com/news/on-small-business/wp/2016/09/16/gene-marks-21-percent-of-ceos-are-psychopaths-only-21-percent/.

7.41. T. Kostigen, "The 10 Most Unethical People in Business," *MarketWatch.com*, January 15, 2009, https://www.marketwatch.com/story/the-10-most-unethical-people-in-business; J. K. Wall, "WellPoint CFO's Affairs Exposed by Lawsuit," *IBJ.com*, June 11, 2007, https://www.ibj.com/articles/12950-wellpoint-cfo-s-affairs-exposed-by-lawsuit.

7.42. T. Chamorro-Premuzic, "1 in 5 Business Leaders May Have Psychopathic Tendencies—Here's Why, According to a Psychology Professor," *CNBC.com*, April 9, 2019, https://www.cnbc.com/2019/04/08/the-science-behind-why-so-many-successful-millionaires-are-psychopaths-and-why-it-doesnt-have-to-be-a-bad-thing.html.

7.43. T. Chamorro-Premuzic, "Why Bad Guys Win at Work," *Harvard Business Review*, November 2, 2015, https://hbr.org/2015/11/why-bad-guys-win-at-work.

7.44. M. Fugate, "Ethical v. Legal Liability," *TEDxSMU*, April 23, 2015, https://www.youtube.com/watch?v=veXPk4Zeqtk.

7.45. L. Li, "Rule by Law and Governance by Law," *Building on the Rule of Law in China,* no. 1 (2017): 145–215.

7.46. M. Fugate, "Ethical v. Legal Liability," *TEDxSMU*, April 23, 2015, https://www.youtube.com/watch?v=veXPk4Zeqtk

7.47. "Measuring the Return on Character," *Harvard Business Review*, April 2015, https://hbr.org/2015/04/measuring-the-return-on-character.

7.48. *Ibid.*

7.49. *Ibid.*

7.50. B. van Camp, "The Importance of Character in Leadership," *LinkedIn.com*, January 3, 2017, https://www.linkedin.com/pulse/importance-character-leadership-brenda-van-camp/.

7.51. "Measuring the Return on Character," *Harvard Business Review*, April 2015, https://hbr.org/2015/04/measuring-the-return-on-character.

7.52. M. M. Crossan, A. Byrne, G. H. Seijts, M. Reno, L. Monzani, and J. Gandz, "Toward a Framework of Leader Character in Organizations," *Journal of Managerial Studies* 54 (2017): 986–1017.

7.53. Adapted from C. Roach, M. Newbert, and F. Joy, "The CEO's New Role: Chief Empathy Officer," *Edelman.com*, March 31, 2020, https://www.edelman.com/covid-19/perspectives/ceos-new-role-chief-empathy-officer.

7.54. J. Bennett, "Leaders Are Crying on the Job. Maybe That's a Good Thing," *The New York Times*, May 3, 2020, https://www.nytimes.com/2020/05/03/us/politics/crying-politicians-leadership.html?smid=em-share.

7.55. M. Fugate, "Ethical v. Legal Liability," *TEDxSMU*, April 23, 2015, https://www.youtube.com/watch?v=veXPk4Zeqtk

7.56. L. Zhang, S. Ren, X. Chen, D. Li, and D. Yin, "CEO Hubris and Firm Pollutions: State and Market Contingencies in a Transitional Economy," *Journal of Business Ethics* 161, no. 5 (2020): 459–78.

7.57. A. Hayes, "Bernie Madoff," *Investopedia*, May 8, 2020, https://www.investopedia.com/terms/b/bernard-madoff.asp.

7.58. M. Fugate, "Ethical v. Legal Liability," *TEDxSMU*, April 23, 2015, https://www.youtube.com/watch?v=veXPk4Zeqtk

7.59. J. Carreyrou, *Bad Blood: Secrets and Lies in a Silicon Valley Startup* (New York: Alfred A. Kopf, 2018);C. Breen, "Elizabeth Holmes and Theranos Are Back in the News. Here's What You Need to Know About the Story. Holmes Said Theranos Would Revolutionize Health Care. That Never Happened," *thelily.com*, March 20, 2019, https://www.thelily.com/elizabeth-holmes-and-theranos-are-back-in-the-news-heres-what-you-need-to-know-about-the-story/.

7.60. A. Hartmans and P. Leskin, "The Rise and Fall of Elizabeth Holmes, the Theranos Founder Awaiting Trial on Federal Charges of 'Massive Fraud,'" *BusinessInsider.com*, April 13, 2020, https://www.businessinsider.com/theranos-founder-ceo-elizabeth-holmes-life-story-bio-2018-4.

7.61. *Ibid.*

7.62. *Ibid.*
7.63. C. Breen, "Elizabeth Holmes and Theranos Are Back in the News. Here's What You Need to Know About the Story. Holmes Said Theranos Would Revolutionize Health Care. That Never Happened," *thelily.com*, March 20, 2019, https://www.thelily.com/elizabeth-holmes-and-theranos-are-back-in-the-news-heres-what-you-need-to-know-about-the-story/.
7.64. J. Carreyrou, *Bad Blood: Secrets and Lies in a Silicon Valley Startup* (New York: Alfred A. Kopf, 2018).
7.65. *Ibid.*

Chapter 8

8.1. J. A. Chatman and S. E. Cha, "Leading by Leveraging Culture," *California Management Review* (Summer 2003): 20–34.
8.2. Y. Berson, S. Oreg, and T. Dvir, "CEO Values, Organizational Culture and Firm Outcomes," *Journal of Organizational Behavior* 29, no 5. (2008): 615–33.
8.3. M. Schwantes, "Research Has Revealed the Top 5 Behaviors that Fortune 500 Companies Like Apple, Amazon, and Microsoft Live By," *Inc.com*, August 8, 2019, https://www.inc.com/leigh-buchanan/sweet-spot-skirts-wellhaven-pet-health-face-masks.html.
8.4. The Honest Company Website, downloaded September 23, 2020: https://inside.6q.io/the-honest-company-and-their-corporate-culture/.
8.5. Warby Parker Website, downloaded September 23, 2020: https://www.warbyparker.com/culture.
8.6. Accenture Website, downloaded September 23, 2020: https://www.accenture.com/us-en/about/corporate-citizenship/core-values.
8.7. L. Dormehl, "Today in Apple History: Apple Lays Out Its Core Company Values, Cult of Mac, September 23, 2020: https://www.cultofmac.com/446380/today-apple-history-apple-lays-core-company-values/
8.8 M. Schwantes, "Research Has Revealed the Top 5 Behaviors that Fortune 500 Companies Like Apple, Amazon, and Microsoft Live By," *Inc.com*, August 8, 2019, https://www.inc.com/leigh-buchanan/sweet-spot-skirts-wellhaven-pet-health-face-masks.html.
8.9. B. Mirza, "Toxic Workplace Cultures Hurt Workers and Company Profits," *SHRM.com*, September 25, 2019, https://www.shrm.org/ResourcesAndTools/hr-topics/employee-relations/Pages/Toxic-Workplace-Culture-Report.aspx.
8.10 Adapted from M. Houshmand, J. O'Reilly, S. Robinson, and A. Wolff, "Escaping Bullying: The Simultaneous Impact of Individual and Unit-Level Bullying on Turnover Intentions," *Human Relations* 65 (2012): 901–918.
8.11. T. Vahle-Hinz, A. Baethge, and R. Van Dick, "Beyond One Work Day? A Daily Diary Study On Causal and Reverse Effects Between Experienced Workplace Incivility and Behaving Rude Towards Others," *European Journal of Work and Organizational Psychology* 28 (2019): 272–85; A. Murrell, "Stopping the Downward Spiral of Workplace Incivility," *Forbes.com*, July 16, 2018, https://www.forbes.com/sites/audreymurrell/2018/07/16/stopping-the-downward-spiral-of-workplace-incivility/#4967a87954ef.
8.12. Adapted from G. Namie, "2017 WBI U.S. Workplace Bullying Survey," *Workplacebullying.org*, June 2017, https://www.workplacebullying.org/wbiresearch__trashed/wbi-2017-survey/.
8.13. *Ibid.*
8.14. *Ibid.*
8.15. G. Namie, "2017 WBI U.S. Workplace Bullying Survey," *Workplacebullying.org*, June 2017, https://www.workplacebullying.org/multi/pdf/2017/E&W-Reactions.pdf.
8.16. "What Is the Difference between Harassment and Discrimination?," *Swartz and Swidler*, https://swartz-legal.com/difference-harassment-discrimination/.
8.17. U.S. Department of Labor Website, https://www.dol.gov/agencies/oasam/centers-offices/civil-rights-center/internal/policies/workplace-harassment/2012.
8.18. J. C. Taylor, "#MeToo: Where Was HR?," *HR Magazine*, February 2018, 4, https://www.shrm.org/hr-today/news/hr-magazine/0218/pages/metoo-where-was-hr.aspx.
8.19. EEOC, "Harassment," *EEOC.gov*, April 9, 2019, https://www.eeoc.gov/laws/types/harassment.cfm.
8.20. Adapted from A. Segal, "*5 Ways to* Strengthen Your Harassment Complaint Process," *HR Magazine*, April 2018, 64–65; J. A. Segal, "Upgrade Your Anti-Harassment Policy," *HR Magazine*, March 2018, 64–65, https://www.shrm.org/hr-today/news/hr-magazine/0418/pages/5-ways-to-strengthen-your-anti-harassment-complaint-process.aspx.
8.21. T. Vahle-Hinz, A. Baethge, and R. Van Dick, "Beyond One Work Day? A Daily Diary Study On Causal and Reverse Effects Between Experienced Workplace Incivility and Behaving Rude Towards Others," *European Journal of Work and Organizational Psychology* 28 (2019): 272–85; A. Murrell, "Stopping the Downward Spiral of Workplace Incivility," *Forbes.com*, July 16, 2018, https://www.forbes.com/sites/audreymurrell/2018/07/16/stopping-the-downward-spiral-of-workplace-incivility/#4967a87954ef.
8.22. E. Krell, "How to Conduct an Ethics Audit," *Society of Human Resource Management*, SHRM.org, April 1, 2010, https://www.shrm.org/hr-today/news/hr-magazine/pages/0410agenda_social.aspx#:~:text=An%20ethics%20audit%20is%20a,is%20to%20make%20these%20comparisons.
8.23. Adapted from M. Schwantes, "Research Has Revealed the Top 5 Behaviors that Fortune 500 Companies Like Apple, Amazon, and Microsoft Live By," *Inc.com*, August 8, 2019, https://www.inc.com/leigh-buchanan/sweet-spot-skirts-wellhaven-pet-health-face-masks.html.
8.24. Created from R. J. Anderson and M. Axisa, "Astro's Sign-Stealing Scandal: What to Know About MLB's Penalties Against Houston," *CBSSports.com*, January

18, 2020, https://www.cbssports.com/mlb/news/astros-sign-stealing-scandal-what-to-know-about-mlbs-penalties-against-houston/; W. Leitch, "The Astros Cheating Scandal has Only Gotten Nuttier," *NYMag.com*, February 18, 2020, https://nymag.com/intelligencer/2020/02/houston-astros-cheating-scandal.html; and M. McCann, "A Union Divided: Astros Cheating Scandal Rocks MLB Players Association," *SI.com*, February 19, 2020, https://www.si.com/mlb/2020/02/18/houston-astros-cheating-scandal-mlbpa.

Chapter 9

9.1. C. Coble, "What's the Difference between Laws and Regulations?" *FindLaw.com*, October 23, 2015, https://blogs.findlaw.com/law_and_life/2015/10/whats-the-difference-between-laws-and-regulations.html.
9.2. S. Surbhi, "Differences between Rules and Regulations," *Keydifferences.com*, July 26, 2018, https://keydifferences.com/difference-between-rules-and-regulations.html.
9.3. Adapted from Securities and Exchange Commission, "Spotlight on Foreign Corrupt Practices Act," *sec.gov*, https://www.sec.gov/spotlight/foreign-corrupt-practices-act.shtml.
9.4. W. Wysong et al., "The Asia Pacific Top Ten FCPA Enforcement Actions of 2019," February 3, 2020, https://www.steptoe.com/en/news-publications/the-asia-pacific-top-ten-fcpa-enforcement-actions-of-2019.html.
9.5. K. Read, "The Federal Sentencing Guidelines for Organizations (FSGO): Compliance and Ethics Program Ideas and Innovation," *convercent.com*, June 18, 2018, https://www.convercent.com/blog/the-federal-sentencing-guidelines-for-organizations-fsgo-compliance-and-ethics-program-ideas-innovation.
9.6. C. Miller, "The Tail Wagging the Dog: Institutional Corruption and the Federal Sentencing Guidelines for Organizations (FSGO)," *ethics.harvard.edu*, August 20, 2013, https://ethics.harvard.edu/blog/tail-wagging-dog.
9.7. W. Kenton and J. Berry-Johnson, "Sarbanes-Oxley (SOX) Act of 2002," *investopedia.com*, February 4, 2020, https://www.investopedia.com/terms/s/sarbanesoxleyact.asp.
9.8. U.S. Securities and Exchange Commission, February 9, 2016, https://www.sec.gov/news/pressrelease/2016-25.html.
9.9. History, "Dodd-Frank Act," *history.com*, August 21, 2018, https://www.history.com/topics/21st-century/dodd-frank-act.
9.10. M. Koba, "Dodd-Frank Act: CNBC Explains," *cnbc.com*, May 11, 2012, https://www.cnbc.com/id/47075854.
9.11. National Association of Social Workers Website, "Read the Code of Ethics," https://www.socialworkers.org/About/Ethics/Code-of-Ethics/Code-of-Ethics-English.
9.12. "Simple Code of Conduct Examples," *yourdictionary.com*, https://examples.yourdictionary.com/simple-code-of-conduct-examples.html.
9.13. Facebook Webpage, "Investor Relations," https://investor.fb.com/corporate-governance/code-of-conduct/default.aspx.
9.14. *Ibid.*
9.15. Adapted from Ethics Compliance Initiative, "High-Quality Ethics and Compliance Program—Measurement Framework," *ethics.org*, April 2016, https://www.ethics.org/resources/high-quality-ec-programs-hqp-standards/.
9.16. *Ibid.*
9.17. A. Edmondson and Z. Lei, "Psychological Safety: The History, Renaissance, and Future of an Interpersonal Construct," *Academy of Management Annals* 1 (2014): 23–43.
9.18. "What Is Title IX?" *titleix.harvard.edu*, accessed June 25, 2020, https://titleix.harvard.edu/what-title-ix.
9.19. Adapted from U.S. Department of Education, "Title IX and Sex Discrimination," *ed.gov*, April 2015, https://www2.ed.gov/about/offices/list/ocr/docs/tix_dis.html.
9.20. R. S. Melnick, "Analyzing the Department of Education's Final Title IX Rules on Sexual Misconduct," *brookings.edu*, June 11, 2020, https://www.brookings.edu/research/analyzing-the-department-of-educations-final-title-ix-rules-on-sexual-misconduct/.
9.21. *Ibid.*
9.22. *Ibid.*
9.23. S. Brown, "What Colleges Need to Know about the New Title IX Rules," *chronicle.com*, May 6, 2020, https://www.chronicle.com/article/What-Colleges-Need-to-Know/248717.
9.24. *Ibid.*
9.25. G. Anderson, "U.S. Publishes New Regulations on Campus Sexual Assault," *insiderhigher.com*, May 7, 2020, https://www.insidehighered.com/news/2020/05/07/education-department-releases-final-title-ix-regulations.
9.26. Adapted from S. Brown, "What Colleges Need to Know About the New Title IX Rules," *chronicle.com*, May 6, 2020, https://www.chronicle.com/article/What-Colleges-Need-to-Know/248717.
9.27. *Ibid.*
9.28. *Ibid.*
9.29. R. S. Melnick, "Analyzing the Department of Education's Final Title IX Rules on Sexual Misconduct," *brookings.edu*, June 11, 2020, https://www.brookings.edu/research/analyzing-the-department-of-educations-final-title-ix-rules-on-sexual-misconduct/.

Chapter 10

10.1. W. Henisz, T. Koller, and R. Nuttall, "Five Ways that ESG Creates Value," *McKinsey Quarterly*, November

14, 2019, https://www.mckinsey.com/business-functions/strategy-and-corporate-finance/our-insights/five-ways-that-esg-creates-value.

10.2. *Ibid.*

10.3. G. Kell, "The Remarkable Rise of ESG," *Forbes.com*, July 11, 2018, https://www.forbes.com/sites/georgkell/2018/07/11/the-remarkable-rise-of-esg/#102dd37a1695.

10.4. N. George, "ESG Mean More Growth & Income . . . Seriously," *profitableinvesting.com*, June 25, 2020, https://profitableinvesting.investorplace.com/income-investors-digest/2020/06/25/esg-means-more-growth-income-seriously/.

10.5. "The S&P 500 ESG Index Integrating Environmental, Social, and Governance Values into the Core," *S&P Global*, spglobal.com, April 11, 2019, https://www.spglobal.com/en/research-insights/articles/the-sp-500-esg-index-integrating-environmental-social-and-governance-values-into-the-core.

10.6. M. Sargis and P. Wang, "How Does Investing in ESG Companies Affect Returns?" *Morningstar.com*, February 19, 2020, https://www.morningstar.com/insights/2020/02/19/esg-companies.

10.7. Adapted from J. Enomoto, "8 of the Best Stocks to Buy for ESG Investors," *investorplace.com*, February 25, 2020, https://investorplace.com/2020/02/8-of-the-best-stocks-to-buy-for-esg-investors/.

10.8. *Ibid.*

10.9. J. Detrixhe, "Microsoft Stock Is the Biggest Winner from Environmental and Socially Responsible Investing," *Quartz*, February 18, 2020, https://qz.com/1803716/microsoft-is-the-biggest-recipient-of-esg-rsi-stock-fund-investment/.

10.10. W. Henisz, T. Koller, and R. Nuttall, "Five Ways that ESG Creates Value," *McKinsey Quarterly*, November 14, 2019, https://www.mckinsey.com/business-functions/strategy-and-corporate-finance/our-insights/five-ways-that-esg-creates-value.

10.11. A. Ross Sorkin, "BlackRock CEO Larry Fink: Climate Crisis Will Reshape Finance," *nytimes.com*, February 24, 2020, https://www.nytimes.com/2020/01/14/business/dealbook/larry-fink-blackrock-climate-change.html.

10.12. *Ibid.*

10.13. *Ibid.*

10.14. M. Green, "A British Billionaire Is Trying to 'Starve' Coal Plants and Save the Environment by Begging Banks to Cut Off Their Financing," *businessinsider.com*, March 3, 2020, https://www.businessinsider.com/british-hedge-fund-billionaire-hohn-launches-campaign-to-starve-coal-plants-of-finance-2020-3.

10.15. A. Ross Sorkin, "BlackRock CEO Larry Fink: Climate Crisis Will Reshape Finance," *nytimes.com*, February 24, 2020, https://www.nytimes.com/2020/01/14/business/dealbook/larry-fink-blackrock-climate-change.html.

10.16. Adapted from S. Jahan and A. S. Mahmud, "What Is Capitalism?" *imf.org*, June 2015, https://www.imf.org/external/pubs/ft/fandd/2015/06/basics.htm.

10.17. Adapted from J. Mackey and R. Sisodia, *Conscious Capitalism* (Boston, MA: Harvard Business Review Press, 2014), 15–21.

10.18. Conscious Capitalism Web page, accessed July 12, 2020, https://www.consciouscapitalism.org/credo.

10.19. *Ibid.*

10.20. J. Mackey and R. Sisodia, *Conscious Capitalism* (Boston, MA: Harvard Business Review Press, 2014), 15–21.

10.21. *Ibid.*

10.22. R. Sisodia, T. Henry, and T. Eckschmidt, *Conscious Capitalism Field Guide* (Boston, MA: Harvard Business Review Press, 2018).

10.23. Bombas Web page, accessed July 12, 2020, https://bombas.com/pages/about-us.

10.24. 4Ocean Web page, accessed July 12, 2020, https://www.4ocean.com/pages/about.

10.25. Motley Fool Web page, accessed July 12, 2020, https://www.fool.com/investing/general/2012/06/19/mission-statement-window-to-a-companys-soul.aspx.

10.26. *Ibid.*

10.27. Patagonia Web page, accessed August 29, 2020, https://www.patagonia.com/activism/.

10.28. Southwest Web page, accessed August 29, 2020, http://investors.southwest.com/our-company/purpose-vision-and-the-southwest-way.

10.29. Motley Fool Web page, accessed July 12, 2020, https://www.fool.com/investing/general/2012/06/19/mission-statement-window-to-a-companys-soul.aspx.

10.30. Barry Wehmiller Website, accessed August 29, 2020, https://www.barrywehmiller.com/.

10.31. J. Fox, "What Is It that Only I Can Do?" *Harvard Business Review*, January-February 2011, 3–7.

10.32. J. Mackey and R. Sisodia, *Conscious Capitalism* (Boston, MA: Harvard Business Review Press, 2014), 15–21.

10.33. R. Sisodia, T. Henry, and T. Eckschmidt, *Conscious Capitalism Field Guide* (Boston, MA: Harvard Business Review Press, 2018).

10.34. *Ibid.*

10.35. Adapted from Mackey J. and R. Sisodia, *Conscious Capitalism* (Boston, MA: Harvard Business Review Press, 2014), 15–21; R. Sisodia, T. Henry, and T. Eckschmidt, *Conscious Capitalism Field Guide* (Boston, MA: Harvard Business Review Press, 2018).

10.36. J. Mackey and R. Sisodia, *Conscious Capitalism* (Boston, MA: Harvard Business Review Press, 2014), 219–220.

10.37. Adapted from A. Fitzsimons, "Moral Capitalism," *theharvardindependent.com*, February 13, 2019, https://www.harvardindependent.com/2019/02/moral-capitalism/.

10.38. Caux Round Table for Moral Capitalism Web page, accessed July 13, 2020, https://www.cauxroundtable.org/.

10.39. *Ibid.*
10.40. *Ibid.*
10.41. *Ibid.*
10.42. *Ibid.*
10.43. *Ibid.*
10.44. *Ibid.*
10.45. A. B. Carroll, "Caux Round Table Principles for Responsible Business," in *The Encyclopedia of Corporate Social Responsibility*, ed. S. O. Idowu (Springer, 2012) Springer, Berlin.
10.46. "How and Why to Become a B-Corp," *circleup.com*, April 20, 2017, https://circleup.com/blog/2017/04/20/how-and-why-to-become-a-b-corporation/.
10.47. Certified B-Corporation Website, accessed July 12, 2020, https://bcorporation.net/certification/legal-requirements.
10.48. *Ibid.*
10.49. Certified B-Corporation Website, accessed July 12, 2020, https://bcorporation.net/about-b-corps.
10.50. *Ibid.*
10.51. S. Kim, M. J. Karlesky, C. G. Myers, and T. Schifeling, "Why Companies Are Becoming B-Corporations," *Harvard Business Review*, June 17, 2016, https://hbr.org/2016/06/why-companies-are-becoming-b-corporations.
10.52. Adapted from C. Kohn, "5 Benefits to Becoming a Certified B-Corp," *unreasonablegroup.com*, August 4, 2015, https://unreasonablegroup.com/articles/5-benefits-to-becoming-a-b-corp/.
10.53. "How and Why to Become a B-Corp," *circleup.com*, April 20, 2017, https://circleup.com/blog/2017/04/20/how-and-why-to-become-a-b-corporation/.
10.54. Caux Round Table for Moral Capitalism 2019 Year in Review, *Pegasus*, February 2020, https://www.cauxroundtable.org/wp-content/uploads/2020/02/Pegasus-February-2020.pdf.
10.55. Novartis Website, accessed July 14, 2020, https://www.novartis.com/sites/www.novartis.com/files/novartis-in-society-report-2019.pdf.
10.56. *Ibid.*
10.57. Clif Bar Company Website, accessed August 29, 2020, https://issuu.com/clifbar/docs/2019_clif_bar_all_aspirations_report?fr=sOWNmYjIzNDI1Ng.
10.58. G. Kolata, "Remdesivir, the First Coronavirus Drug, Gets a Price Tag," *nytimes.com*, June 29, 2020, https://www.nytimes.com/2020/06/29/health/coronavirus-remdesivir-gilead.html.
10.59. Gilead Web page, accessed July 14, 2020, https://www.gilead.com/purpose/mission-and-core-values.
10.60. S. Lupkin, "Remdesivir Priced at More than $3100 for a Course of Treatment," *npr.org*, June 29, 2020, https://www.npr.org/sections/health-shots/2020/06/29/884648842/remdesivir-priced-at-more-than-3-100-for-a-course-of-treatment.
10.61. G. Kolata, "Remdesivir, the First Coronavirus Drug, Gets a Price Tag," *nytimes.com*, June 29, 2020, https://www.nytimes.com/2020/06/29/health/coronavirus-remdesivir-gilead.html.
10.62. S. Lupkin, "Remdesivir Priced at More than $3100 for a Course of Treatment," *npr.org*, June 29, 2020, https://www.npr.org/sections/health-shots/2020/06/29/884648842/remdesivir-priced-at-more-than-3-100-for-a-course-of-treatment.
10.63. *Ibid.*
10.64. *Ibid.*
10.65. D. Bunis, "Companies Raise Prices on COVID-19 Drugs, Others in Middle of Pandemic," *AARP.org*, June 30, 2020, https://www.aarp.org/politics-society/advocacy/info-2020/covid-drug-prices-increase.html.

Chapter 11

11.1. T. Hsu and R. C. Rabin, "Johnson & Johnson to End Talc-Based Baby Powder Sales in North America," *The New York Times*, May 20, 2020, https://www.nytimes.com/2020/05/19/business/johnson-baby-powder-sales-stopped.html?smid=em-share.
11.2. C. Haberman, "How an Unsolved Mystery Changed the Way We Take Pills," *The New York Times*, September 16, 2018, https://www.nytimes.com/2018/09/16/us/tylenol-acetaminophen-deaths.html.
11.3. N. R. Prince, J. B. Prince, and R. Kabst, "National Culture and Incentives: Are Incentive Practices Always Good?" *Journal of World Business* 55 (2020), https://web.a.ebscohost.com/ehost/detail/detail?vid=14&sid=94d18e49-460f-4dc7-8509-0c8886482485%40sessionmgr4007&bdata=JmxvZ2luLmFzcCUzZmN1c3RpZCUzZG1hZ24xMzA3JnNpdGU9ZWhvc3QtbGl2ZQ%3d%3-d#AN=142765891&db=bth.
11.4. P. Pavao and M. Natario, "A Tale of Different Realities: Innovation Capacity in the European Union Regions," in *The Role of Knowledge Transfer and Open Innovation*, ed. H. Almeida and B. Sequeira (IGI Global, 2019), https://www.igi-global.com/chapter/a-tale-of-different-realities/211487.
11.5. J. Chen and G. Scott, "Multinational Corporation," *Investopedia.com*, February 25, 2020, https://www.investopedia.com/terms/m/multinationalcorporation.asp.
11.6. *Ibid.*
11.7. McDonald's Website, "Your Right to Know," accessed June 28, 2020, https://www.mcdonalds.com/gb/en-gb/help/faq/18525-what-countries-does-mcdonalds-operate-in.html.
11.8. B. Racoma, "How McDonald's Adapts around the World," *daytranslations.com*, January 4, 2019, https://www.daytranslations.com/blog/how-mcdonalds-adapts-around-the-world.
11.9. M. Jones, "9 Countries That Have Banned McDonalds," *rd.com*, January 3, 2020, https://www.rd.com/list/countries-banned-mcdonalds/.
11.10. *Ibid.*
11.11. Huawei Website, "Huawei Facts," accessed June 28, 2020, https://www.huawei.com/us/facts.

11.12. S. Keane, "Huawei Ban Timeline: UK Bans Chinese Company from its 5G Network," *cnet.com*, July 15, 2020, https://www.cnet.com/news/huawei-ban-full-timeline-us-restrictions-china-trump-executive-order-uk-ban/.
11.13. D. A. Ralston, C. J. Russell, and C. P. Egri, "Business Values Dimensions: A Cross-Culturally Developed Measure of Workforce Values," *International Business Review* 27 (2018): 1189–99.
11.14. Geert Hofstede, "The 6-D Model of National Culture," accessed June 28, 2020, https://geerthofstede.com/culture-geert-hofstede-gert-jan-hofstede/6d-model-of-national-culture/.
11.15. *Ibid.*
11.16. Adapted from Geert Hofstede, *Culture's Consequences: Comparing Values, Behaviors and Institutions across Nations*, 2nd ed. (Thousand Oaks: Sage, 2001), 169–70.
11.17. *Ibid.*
11.18. A. Mar, "10 Examples of Power Distance," *Simplicable.com*, accessed June 29, 2020, https://simplicable.com/new/power-distance.
11.19. BBC News, "Death Penalty: How Many Countries Still Have It?" *bbc.com*, October 14, 2018, https://www.bbc.com/news/world-45835584.
11.20. 1-World Global Gifts, "International Gift Giving Etiquette," Japan and China, accessed July 15, 2020, http://www.1worldglobalgifts.com/japangiftgivingetiquette.htm.
11.21. Adapted from R. Kapil, "Five Ways to Be More Culturally Aware," *mentalhealthfirstaid*, July 22, 2019, https://www.mentalhealthfirstaid.org/2019/07/five-ways-to-be-more-culturally-aware/.
11.22. A. Carroll, "Global Codes of Conduct," in *The Sage Encyclopedia of Business Ethics and Society*, ed. R. W. Kolb (Thousand Oaks: Sage, 2018), 1601–606.
11.23. EY Website, accessed June 28, 2020, https://assets.ey.com/content/dam/ey-sites/ey-com/en_gl/home-index/ey-global-code-of-conduct-english.pdf.
11.24. EY Website, accessed June 28, 2020, https://www.ey.com/en_gl/locations.
11.25. Equator Principles Website, accessed June 28, 2020, https://equator-principles.com/.
11.26. *Ibid.*
11.27. Adapted from A. Hussain, "Can Political Instability Hurt Economic Growth?" *worldbank.org*, June 1, 2014, https://blogs.worldbank.org/endpovertyinsouthasia/can-political-stability-hurt-economic-growth; "Political Stability Country Rankings," *theglobaleconomy.com*, accessed July 9, 2020, https://www.theglobaleconomy.com/rankings/wb_political_stability/.
11.28. "Political Stability Country Rankings," *theglobaleconomy.com*, accessed July 9, 2020, https://www.theglobaleconomy.com/rankings/wb_political_stability/.
11.29. "Monaco Country Profile," *bbc.com*, May 18, 2018, https://www.bbc.com/news/world-europe-17615784.
11.30. "Yemen Crisis: Why Is There a War?" *bbc.com*, June 19, 2020, https://www.bbc.com/news/world-middle-east-29319423.
11.31. U.S. News 2020 Best Countries Rankings, "Most Transparent Countries," *usnews.com*, accessed July 9, 2020, https://www.usnews.com/news/best-countries/best-transparency.
11.32. E. Asen, "Corporate Tax Rates around the World," *taxfoundation.org*, December 10, 2019, https://taxfoundation.org/publications/corporate-tax-rates-around-the-world/.
11.33. *Ibid.*
11.34. A. Swanson, "The U.S. Labeled China a Currency Manipulator. Here's What It Means." *nytimes.com*, August 6, 2019, https://www.nytimes.com/2019/08/06/business/economy/china-currency-manipulator.html.
11.35. Adapted from M. Sigalos, "How China's National Security Law Could Change Hong Kong Forever," *cnbc.com*, July 1, 2020, https://www.cnbc.com/2020/07/01/chinas-national-security-law-hong-kong-global-financial-center.html.
11.36. R. Heilweil, "TikTok Pulls Out of Hong Kong as Tech Companies Push Back against New Security Law," *vox.com*, July 7, 2020, https://www.vox.com/recode/2020/7/6/21315060/google-facebook-twitter-hong-kong-china-user-data-request.
11.37. Adapted from M. Hall, "Governments' Influence on Markets," *Investopedia.com*, June 11, 2018, https://www.investopedia.com/articles/economics/11/how-governments-influence-markets.asp#subsidies-and-tariffs.
11.38. H. Strubenhoff, "The WTO's Decision to End Agricultural Export Subsidies Is Good News for Farmers and Consumers," *brookings.edu*, February 8, 2016, https://www.brookings.edu/blog/future-development/2016/02/08/the-wtos-decision-to-end-agricultural-export-subsidies-is-good-news-for-farmers-and-consumers/.
11.39. *Ibid.*
11.40. H. Strubenhoff, "The WTO's Decision to End Agricultural Export Subsidies Is Good News for Farmers and Consumers," *brookings.edu*, February 8, 2016, https://www.brookings.edu/blog/future-development/2016/02/08/the-wtos-decision-to-end-agricultural-export-subsidies-is-good-news-for-farmers-and-consumers/.
11.41. M. Davis, "Government Subsidies for Business," *Investopedia.com*, June 25, 2019, https://www.investopedia.com/articles/basics/11/introduction-to-government-subsidies.asp#types-of-energy-subsidies.
11.42. M. Xu and S. Singh, "UPDATE 1—China Sets 2019 Subsidies for Large-Scale Solar Power Projects at $248 Million," *reuters.com*, July 11, 2019, https://www.reuters.com/article/china-solar-subsidy/update-1-china-sets-2019-subsidies-for-large-scale-solar-power-projects-at-248-mln-idUSL4N24C1XN.
11.43. J. Baker, "Solar Leader China Is Slashing Its Subsidies on Solar Power—What You Need to Know," *forbes.*

com, June 18, 2018, https://www.forbes.com/sites/jillbaker/2018/06/18/solar-leader-china-is-slashing-its-subsidies-on-solar-power-what-you-need-to-know/#1cc067e82f9a.

11.44. Adapted from M. Hall, "Governments' Influence on Markets," *Investopedia.com*, June 11, 2018, https://www.investopedia.com/articles/economics/11/how-governments-influence-markets.asp#subsidies-and-tariffs.

11.45. World Trade Organization Website, accessed July 17, 2020, https://www.wto.org/english/thewto_e/whatis_e/tif_e/agrm8_e.htm.

11.46. The Conversation, "China Used Anti-Dumping Rules Against Us Because What Goes around Comes around," *theconversation.com*, May 19, 2020, https://theconversation.com/china-used-anti-dumping-rules-against-us-because-what-goes-around-comes-around-138541.

11.47. *Ibid.*

11.48. *Ibid.*

11.49. World Trade Organization Website, accessed July 7, 2020, https://www.wto.org/english/thewto_e/thewto_e.htm.

11.50. *Ibid.*

11.51. United Nations Global Compact Website, accessed July 8, 2020, https://www.unglobalcompact.org/about.

11.52. United Nations Global Compact Website, accessed July 8, 2020, https://www.unglobalcompact.org/what-is-gc/mission.

11.53. *Ibid.*

11.54. United Nations Global Compact Website, accessed July 8, 2020, https://www.unglobalcompact.org/sdgs/17-global-goals.

11.55. United Nations Global Compact Website, accessed July 8, 2020, https://www.unglobalcompact.org/sdgs/sdgpioneers/2019/chowdhury.

11.56. United Nations Global Compact Website, accessed July 8, 2020, https://www.unglobalcompact.org/sdgs/sdgpioneers/2019/leahy.

11.57. L. O'Leary, "The Modern Supply Chain Is Snapping," *The Atlantic*, theatlantic.com, March 19, 2020, https://www.theatlantic.com/ideas/archive/2020/03/supply-chains-and-coronavirus/608329/.

11.58. *Ibid.*

11.59. K. Bradsher, "China Dominates Medical Supplies, in This Outbreak and the Next," *The New York Times*, nytimes.com, July 5, 2020, https://www.nytimes.com/2020/07/05/business/china-medical-supplies.html.

11.60. N. Irwin, "It's the End of the World Economy as We Know It," *The New York Times*, nytimes.com, April 16, 2020, https://www.nytimes.com/2020/04/16/upshot/world-economy-restructuring-coronavirus.html?smid=em-share.

11.61. L. O'Leary, "The Modern Supply Chain Is Snapping," *The Atlantic*, theatlantic.com, March 19, 2020, https://www.theatlantic.com/ideas/archive/2020/03/supply-chains-and-coronavirus/608329/.

11.62. A. Siripurapu, "What Is the Defense Production Act?" *Council on Foreign Relations*, cfr.org, April 29, 2020, https://www.cfr.org/in-brief/what-defense-production-act.

11.63. K. Bradsher and L. Alderman, "The World Needs Masks. China Makes Them, but Has Been Hoarding Them," *The New York Times*, nytimes.com, April 2, 2020, https://www.nytimes.com/2020/03/13/business/masks-china-coronavirus.html?action=click&module=RelatedLinks&pgtype=Article.

Chapter 12

12.1. Adapted from E. Chasan, "The Oil Crash Created a Recycled Plastic Trap," *bloombergquint.com*, May 6, 2020, https://www.bloombergquint.com/business/oil-crash-means-single-use-plastic-is-back-as-recycling-struggles.

12.2. D. Thomas, "Davos 2020: People Still Want Plastic Bottles, Says Coca-Cola," *BBC*, bbc.com, January 21, 2020, https://www.bbc.com/news/business-51197463.

12.3. F. Eidelwein et al., "Internationalization of Environmental Externalities: Development of a Method for Elaborating the Statement of Economic and Environmental Results," *Journal of Cleaner Production* 170 (2018): 1316–327.

12.4. *Ibid.*

12.5. Adapted from Y. Braouezec and R. Joliet, "Time to Invest in Corporate Social Responsibility and the Value of CSR Operations: The Case of Environmental Externalities," *Managerial and Decision Economics* 40 (May 1, 2019): 539–49.

12.6. *Ibid.*

12.7. Adapted from D. Garcia-Gusano, I. R. Istrate, and D. Iribarren, "Life-Cycle Consequences of Internalizing Socio-Environmental Externalities of Power Generation," *Science of the Total Environment* 612 (2018): 386–91.

12.8. *Ibid.*

12.9. R. Meyer, "How the U.S. Protects the Environment, From Nixon to Trump," *The Atlantic*, theatlantic.com, March 29, 2017, https://www.theatlantic.com/science/archive/2017/03/how-the-epa-and-us-environmental-law-works-a-civics-guide-pruitt-trump/521001/.

12.10. NASA, "Overview: Weather, Global Warming, and Climate Change," *climate.nasa.gov*, https://climate.nasa.gov/resources/global-warming-vs-climate-change/.

12.11. International Energy Agency—Clean Coal Center, "Top Coal-Fired Power Generating Countries," March 12, 2019, https://www.iea-coal.org/top-coal-fired-power-generating-countries/.

12.12. J. Clemente, "Coal Isn't Dead. China Proves It," *Forbes.com*, January 23, 2019, https://www.forbes.com/sites/judeclemente/2019/01/23/coal-is-not-dead-china-proves-it/#42cc29a665fa.

12.13. US Energy Information Administration, https://www.eia.gov/tools/faqs/faq.php?id=427&t=3.

12.14. J. Clemente, "Coal Isn't Dead. China Proves It," *Forbes.com*, January 23, 2019, https://www.forbes.com/sites/judeclemente/2019/01/23/coal-is-not-dead-china-proves-it/#42cc29a665fa.

12.15. L. Kolb and S. Stebbins, "Countries Doing the Most (and Least) to Protect the Environment," *USAToday*, July 14, 2019, https://www.usatoday.com/story/money/2019/07/14/climate-change-countries-doing-most-least-to-protect-environment/39534413/.

12.16. United Nations, "World Water Development Report 2020—'Water and Climate Change,'" *unwater.org*, March 21, 2020, https://www.unwater.org/world-water-development-report-2020-water-and-climate-change/.

12.17. *Ibid.*

12.18. T. Hundertmark, K. Lueck, and B. Packer, "Water: A Human and Business Priority," *McKinsey Quarterly*, May 2020, https://www.mckinsey.com/business-functions/sustainability/our-insights/water-a-human-and-business-priority.

12.19. United Nations, "World Water Development Report 2020—'Water and Climate Change,'" *unwater.org*, March 21, 2020, https://www.unwater.org/world-water-development-report-2020-water-and-climate-change/.

12.20. The Conversation, "Coronavirus: What Might More Hand Washing Mean in Countries with Water Shortages?," *theconversation.com*, March 30, 2020, https://theconversation.com/coronavirus-what-might-more-hand-washing-mean-in-countries-with-water-shortages-134625.

12.21. World Health Organization, "Air Pollution," *who.int*, https://www.who.int/health-topics/air-pollution#tab=tab_3.

12.22. R. Hersher, "Climate Change Undercuts Air Pollution Improvements," *NPR.org*, April 21, 2020, https://www.npr.org/2020/04/21/838641963/climate-change-undercuts-air-pollution-improvements.

12.23. *Ibid.*

12.24. Adapted from American Lung Association, "The State of the Air 2020," *stateoftheair.org*, http://www.stateoftheair.org/key-findings/.

12.25. *Ibid.*

12.26. *Ibid.*

12.27. United States Environmental Protection Agency, "Our Mission and What We Do," *epa.gov*, https://www.epa.gov/aboutepa/our-mission-and-what-we-do.

12.28. US Department of State, "The Montreal Protocol and Substances that Deplete the Ozone Layer," *state.gov*, February 11, 2019, https://www.state.gov/key-topics-office-of-environmental-quality-and-transboundary-issues/the-montreal-protocol-on-substances-that-deplete-the-ozone-layer/.

12.29. *Ibid.*

12.30. C. Tardi, "The Kyoto Protocol," *investopedia.com*, September 26, 2019, https://www.investopedia.com/terms/k/kyoto.asp.

12.31. *Ibid.*

12.32. *Ibid.*

12.33. Encyclopedia Britannica, "Paris Agreement," *Britannica.com*, https://www.britannica.com/topic/Paris-Agreement-2015.

12.34. *Ibid.*

12.35. Adapted from F. Arnold, "Environmental Protection: Is it Bad for the Economy? A Non-technical Summary of the Literature," *epa.org*, July 10, 1999, https://www.epa.gov/environmental-economics/environmental-protection-it-bad-economy-non-technical-summary-literature.

12.36. M. Evans, "What Is Environmental Sustainability?," *thebalancesmb.com*, August 11, 2019, https://www.thebalancesmb.com/what-is-sustainability-3157876.

12.37. Adapted from M. Rogers, "6 Benefits of Becoming a Sustainable Business," *environmentalleader.com*, March 29, 2016, https://www.environmentalleader.com/2016/03/6-benefits-of-becoming-a-sustainable-business/.

12.38. L. P. Norton, "These are the 100 Most Sustainable Companies in American," *Barrons.com*, February 7, 2020: https://www.barrons.com/articles/the-100-most-sustainable-companies-51581095228.

12.39. *Ibid.*

12.40. *Ibid.*

12.41. A. Brettman, "Nike, Adidas, Puma Agree with Greenpeace to Clean Water in Worldwide Production by 2020," *Oregonlive.com*, January 10, 2020, https://www.oregonlive.com/playbooks-profits/2011/11/nike_adidas_puma_agree_with_gr.html.

12.42. *Nike.com*, accessed May 20, 2020, https://www.nike.com/sustainability.

12.43. *Ibid.*

12.44. *Ibid.*

12.45. A. Brettman, "Nike, Adidas, Puma Agree with Greenpeace to Clean Water in Worldwide Production by 2020," *Oregonlive.com*, January 10, 2020, https://www.oregonlive.com/playbooks-profits/2011/11/nike_adidas_puma_agree_with_gr.html.

12.46. Adapted from L. P. Norton, "These are the 100 Most Sustainable Companies in American," *Barrons.com*, February 7, 2020, https://www.barrons.com/articles/the-100-most-sustainable-companies-51581095228.

12.47. B. Assirati, "The Countries are Leading the Charge to Clean Energy," *World Economic Forum*, wforum.org, February 6, 2019, https://www.weforum.org/agenda/2019/02/these-countries-are-leading-the-charge-to-clean-energy/.

12.48. *Ibid.*

12.49. H. Ritchie and M. Roser, "Renewable Energy, Our World in Data, 2019," https://ourworldindata.org/renewable-energy#modern-renewables.

12.50. B. Assirati, "The Countries Are Leading the Charge to Clean Energy," *World Economic Forum*, wforum.org, February 6, 2019, https://www.weforum.org/agenda/2019/02/these-countries-are-leading-the-charge-to-clean-energy/.

12.51. L. Cucek and Z. Kravanja, "Overview of Environmental Footprints," *Assessing and Measuring Environmental Impact and Sustainability*, 2015, https://www.sciencedirect.com/topics/engineering/eco-efficiency.
12.52. H. Srinivas, "Eco-Efficiency," *gdrc.org*, https://www.gdrc.org/sustdev/concepts/04-e-effi.html.
12.53. T. Wallace, "Closed Loop Production: Sustainability across the Supply Chain," *thefutureofcommerce.com*, https://www.the-future-of-commerce.com/2020/01/23/closed-loop-production/.
12.54. K. Hunt, "What's a Closed Loop System?," *Green Matters*, August 15, 2018, https://www.greenmatters.com/business/2018/08/15/Z16xhYS/closed-loop-system-sustainability-production.
12.55. M. Matousek and A. Cain, "10 Times Carnival has Come under Fire for Skirting Environmental Regulations," *Businessinsider.com*, March 30, 2020, https://www.businessinsider.com/carnivals-history-of-environmental-violations-cruise-industry-2020-3.
12.56. *Ibid.*
12.57. Good Jobs First, "Violation Tracker for Carnival Corp, 2020," https://violationtracker.goodjobsfirst.org/parent/carnival-corp.
12.58. M. Matousek and A. Cain, "10 Times Carnival Has Come under Fire for Skirting Environmental Regulations," *Businessinsider.com*, March 30, 2020, https://www.businessinsider.com/carnivals-history-of-environmental-violations-cruise-industry-2020-3.
12.59. T. Doven, "Federal Judge Frustrated over Carnival's Continued Pollution While on Probation," *Miamiherald.com*, January 8, 2020, https://www.miamiherald.com/news/business/tourism-cruises/article239089503.html.
12.60. *Ibid.*

Chapter 13

13.1. C. Binelli, M. Loveless, and S. Whitefield, "What Is Social Inequality and Why Does It Matter? Evidence from Central and Eastern Europe," *World Development* 70 (2015): 239–48.
13.2. Business Roundtable, "Business Roundtable Redefines the Purpose of a Corporation to Promote 'An Economy that Serves All Americans,'" August 19, 2019, https://www.businessroundtable.org/business-roundtable-redefines-the-purpose-of-a-corporation-to-promote-an-economy-that-serves-all-americans.
13.3. A. Murray and D. Meyer, "Society's Problems Need Our Best Business Minds," *Fortune*, fortune.com, July 27, 2020, https://fortune.com/2020/07/27/societal-problems-need-our-best-business-minds-ceo-daily/.
13.4. Adapted from N. G. Mankiw, "C.E.O.'s Are Qualified to Make Profits, Not Lead Society," *The New York Times*, nytimes.com, July 24, 2020, https://www.nytimes.com/2020/07/24/business/ceos-profits-shareholders.html.
13.5. *Ibid.*
13.6. Adapted from K. Bradsher, "China Dominates Medical Supplies, in This Outbreak and the Next," *The New York Times*, nytimes.com, July 5, 2020, https://www.nytimes.com/2020/07/05/business/china-medical-supplies.html.
13.7. *Ibid.*
13.8. N. G. Mankiw, "C.E.O.'s Are Qualified to Make Profits, Not Lead Society," *The New York Times*, nytimes.com, July 24, 2020, https://www.nytimes.com/2020/07/24/business/ceos-profits-shareholders.html.
13.9. Adapted from A. Murray and D. Meyer, "Society's Problems Need Our Best Business Minds," *Fortune*, fortune.com, July 27, 2020, https://fortune.com/2020/07/27/societal-problems-need-our-best-business-minds-ceo-daily/.
13.10. Adapted from R. Thaler, "The Law of Supply and Demand Isn't Fair," *The New York Times*, nytimes.com, May 20, 2020, https://www.nytimes.com/2020/05/20/business/supply-and-demand-isnt-fair.html?smid=em-share.
13.11. *Ibid.*
13.12. *Ibid.*
13.13. S. Berkowitz, "Major Public College Football Programs Could Lose Billions in Revenue If No Season Is Played," *USAToday*, usatoday.com, April 15, 2020, https://www.usatoday.com/story/sports/ncaaf/2020/04/14/college-football-major-programs-could-see-billions-revenue-go-away/2989466001/.
13.14. B. Witz, "Should We Play? Two College Football Teams Have Very Different Answers," *The New York Times*, nytimes.com, July 1, 2020, https://www.nytimes.com/2020/07/01/sports/ncaafootball/coronavirus-college-football-hbcus-clemson.html?smid=em-share.
13.15. *Ibid.*
13.16. S. Berkowitz, "Major Public College Football Programs Could Lose Billions in Revenue If No Season Is Played," *USAToday*, usatoday.com, April 15, 2020, https://www.usatoday.com/story/sports/ncaaf/2020/04/14/college-football-major-programs-could-see-billions-revenue-go-away/2989466001/.
13.17. B. Witz, "Should We Play? Two College Football Teams Have Very Different Answers," *The New York Times*, nytimes.com, July 1, 2020, https://www.nytimes.com/2020/07/01/sports/ncaafootball/coronavirus-college-football-hbcus-clemson.html?smid=em-share.
13.18. Adapted from "What Is Social Justice?" *The San Diego Foundation*, sdfoundation.org, March 24, 2016, https://www.sdfoundation.org/news-events/sdf-news/what-is-social-justice/.
13.19. K. Amadeo and M. J. Boyle, "Income Inequality in America," *The Balance*, thebalance.com, June 15, 2020, https://www.thebalance.com/income-inequality-in-america-3306190#:~:text=Updated%20June%2015%2C%202020%20Income%20inequality%20is%20

a,investment%20earnings%2C%20rent%2C%20and%20sales%20of%20real%20estate.

13.20. O. Baranoff, "What's Caused the Rise in Income Inequality in the US?" *World Economic Forum*, May 5, 2015, https://www.weforum.org/agenda/2015/05/whats-caused-the-rise-in-income-inequality-in-the-us/.

13.21. *Ibid.*

13.22. J. Kagan and T. J. Catalano, "Household Income," *Investopedia*, Investopedia.com, July 5, 2020, https://www.investopedia.com/terms/h/household_income.asp.

13.23. "Household Income Quintiles," *Tax Policy Center*, taxpolicycenter.org, March 24, 2020, https://www.taxpolicycenter.org/statistics/household-income-quintiles.

13.24. K. Amadeo and M. J. Boyle, "Income Inequality in America," *The Balance*, thebalance.com, June 15, 2020, https://www.thebalance.com/income-inequality-in-america-3306190#:~:text=Updated%20June%2015%2C%202020%20Income%20inequality%20is%20a,investment%20earnings%2C%20rent%2C%20and%20sales%20of%20real%20estate.

13.25. J. Chappelow and P. Westfall, "Gini Index," *Investopedia*, investopedia.com, February 3, 2020, https://www.investopedia.com/terms/g/gini-index.asp.

13.26. World Population Review, "Gini Coefficient by Country 2020," worldpopulationreview.com, accessed August 3, 2020, https://worldpopulationreview.com/country-rankings/gini-coefficient-by-country.

13.27. J. M. Horowitz, R. Igielnik, and R. Kochhar, "Trends in Wealth and Income Inequality," *Pew Research Center*, pewsocialtrends.org, January 9, 2020, https://www.pewsocialtrends.org/2020/01/09/trends-in-income-and-wealth-inequality/.

13.28. World Population Review, "Gini Coefficient by Country 2020," worldpopulationreview.com, accessed August 3, 2020, https://worldpopulationreview.com/country-rankings/gini-coefficient-by-country.

13.29. Created from K. Schaeffer, "6 Facts about Economic Inequality in the U.S.," *Pew Research*, pewresearch.org, February 7, 2020, https://www.pewresearch.org/fact-tank/2020/02/07/6-facts-about-economic-inequality-in-the-u-s/.

13.30. Created from United Nations World Inequality Report 2020, accessed July 25, 2020, https://www.un.org/development/desa/dspd/wp-content/uploads/sites/22/2020/01/World-Social-Report-2020-FullReport.pdf.

13.31. *Ibid.*

13.32. *Ibid.*

13.33. S. Radu, "Countries Seen to Have the Lowest Manufacturing Costs," *US News & World Report*, usnews.com, February 14, 2019, https://www.usnews.com/news/best-countries/slideshows/countries-seen-to-have-the-lowest-manufacturing-costs.

13.34. K. Amadeo and M. J. Boyle, "Income Inequality in America," *The Balance*, thebalance.com, June 15, 2020, https://www.thebalance.com/income-inequality-in-america-3306190#:~:text=Updated%20June%2015%2C%202020%20Income%20inequality%20is%20a,investment%20earnings%2C%20rent%2C%20and%20sales%20of%20real%20estate.

13.35. *Ibid.*

13.36. S. Srivastava, "Brain Drain v. Brain Gain," *Assembly of European Regions*, aer.eu, February 19, 2020, https://aer.eu/brain-drain/.

13.37. D. Fine et al., "Inequality: A Persisting Challenge and its Implications," *McKinsey Global Institute*, mckinsey.com, June 2019, https://www.mckinsey.com/~/media/McKinsey/Industries/Public%20and%20Social%20Sector/Our%20Insights/Inequality%20A%20persisting%20challenge%20and%20its%20implications/Inequality-A-persisting-challenge-and-its-implications.pdf.

13.38. A. Ahmed, "Why the Global Debt of Poor Nations Must be Canceled," *The New York Times*, nytimes.com, April 30, 2020, https://www.nytimes.com/2020/04/30/opinion/coronavirus-debt-africa.html.

13.39. K. Amadeo, "Health Care Inequality in America," *The Balance*, thebalance.com, June 22, 2020, https://www.thebalance.com/health-care-inequality-facts-types-effect-solution-4174842.

13.40. World Health Organization, "10 Facts on Health Inequalities and Their Causes," *WHO*, who.int, April 2017, https://www.who.int/features/factfiles/health_inequities/en/.

13.41. K. Safavi, "Tackling Inequalities in Health Care Worldwide," *US News & World Report*, usnews.com, June 28, 2019, https://www.usnews.com/news/best-states/articles/2019-06-28/commentary-tackling-inequalities-in-healthcare-worldwide.

13.42. Adapted from K. Amadeo, "Health Care Inequality in America," *The Balance*, thebalance.com, June 22, 2020, https://www.thebalance.com/health-care-inequality-facts-types-effect-solution-4174842.

13.43. *Ibid.*

13.44. *Ibid.*

13.45. *Ibid.*

13.46. *Ibid.*

13.47. M. P. Cussen, "Top 5 Reasons Why People Go Bankrupt," *Investopedia*, Investopedia.com, February 24, 2020, https://www.investopedia.com/financial-edge/0310/top-5-reasons-people-go-bankrupt.aspx.

13.48. Adapted from K. Amadeo, "Health Care Inequality in America," *The Balance*, thebalance.com, June 22, 2020, https://www.thebalance.com/health-care-inequality-facts-types-effect-solution-4174842.

13.49. Adapted from World Health Organization, "10 Facts on Health Inequalities and Their Causes," *WHO*, who.int, April 2017, https://www.who.int/features/factfiles/health_inequities/en/.

13.50. E. O'Brien, "Here's the Shocking Amount a Couple Retiring Today Will Spend on Health Care," *Money*, money.com, April 2, 2019, https://money.com/health-care-in-retirement-average-costs/.

13.51. E. Bryce, "What's the Difference between Race and Ethnicity?" *Live Science*, livescinence.com, February 8, 2020, https://www.livescience.com/difference-between-race-ethnicity.html.
13.52. K. Amadeo, "Racial Wealth Gap in the United States," *The Balance*, thebalance.com, June 10, 2020, https://www.thebalance.com/racial-wealth-gap-in-united-states-4169678.
13.53. "Jim Crow Laws," *History*, history.com, June 23, 2020, https://www.history.com/topics/early-20th-century-us/jim-crow-laws.
13.54. *Ibid.*
13.55. K. Amadeo, "Racial Wealth Gap in the United States," *The Balance*, thebalance.com, June 10, 2020, https://www.thebalance.com/racial-wealth-gap-in-united-states-4169678.
13.56. *Ibid.*
13.57. K. Bhasin, G. L. Porter, and J. Green, "Corporations Face a Reckoning on Race: What You Need to Know," *Bloomberg BusinessWeek*, Bloomberg.com, July 22, 2020, https://www.bloomberg.com/news/storythreads/2020-07-22/corporations-face-a-reckoning-on-race.
13.58. S. Miller, "Black Workers Still Earn Less Than Their White Counterparts," *Society of Human Resource Management*, shrm.org, June 11, 2020, https://www.shrm.org/resourcesandtools/hr-topics/compensation/pages/racial-wage-gaps-persistence-poses-challenge.aspx.
13.59. K. Bhasin, G. L. Porter, and J. Green, "Corporations Face a Reckoning on Race: What You Need to Know," *Bloomberg BusinessWeek*, Bloomberg.com, July 22, 2020, https://www.bloomberg.com/news/storythreads/2020-07-22/corporations-face-a-reckoning-on-race.
13.60. J. Holman and T. Buckley, "How Ben & Jerry's Perfected the Delicate Recipe for Corporate Activism," *Bloomberg BusinessWeek*, bloomberg.com, July 22, 2020, https://www.bloomberg.com/news/features/2020-07-22/how-ben-jerry-s-applied-its-corporate-activism-recipe-to-blm?srnd=storythread.
13.61. K. Bhasin, G. L. Porter, and J. Green, "Corporations Face a Reckoning on Race: What You Need to Know," *Bloomberg BusinessWeek*, Bloomberg.com, July 22, 2020, https://www.bloomberg.com/news/storythreads/2020-07-22/corporations-face-a-reckoning-on-race.
13.62. *Ibid.*
13.63. J. Holman, "West Elm Joins 15% Pledge to Boost Black-Owned Brands on Shelves," *Bloomberg BusinessWeek*, July 10, 2020, https://www.bloomberg.com/news/articles/2020-07-10/west-elm-joins-15-pledge-to-boost-black-owned-brands-on-shelves?srnd=storythread.
13.64. United Nations World Inequality Report 2020, accessed July 25, 2020, https://www.un.org/development/desa/dspd/wp-content/uploads/sites/22/2020/01/World-Social-Report-2020-FullReport.pdf.
13.65. Adapted from K. Amadeo and M. J. Boyle, "Income Inequality in America," *The Balance*, thebalance.com, June 15, 2020, https://www.thebalance.com/income-inequality-in-america-3306190#:~:text=Updated%20June%2015%2C%20 2020%20Income%20inequality%20is%20 a,investment%20earnings%2C%20rent%2C%20and%20sales%20of%20real%20estate.
13.66. *Ibid.*
13.67. *Ibid.*
13.68. *Ibid.*
13.69. Adapted from D. Fine et al., "Inequality: A Persisting Challenge and Its Implications," *McKinsey Global Institute*, mckinsey.com, June 2019, https://www.mckinsey.com/~/media/McKinsey/Industries/Public%20and%20Social%20Sector/Our%20Insights/Inequality%20A%20persisting%20challenge%20 and%20its%20implications/Inequality-A-persisting-challenge-and-its-implications.pdf.
13.70. U.S. Department of Health and Human Services, "Poverty Guidelines for 2020," January 8, 2020, https://aspe.hhs.gov/poverty-guidelines.
13.71. C. A. Nadeau, "New Living Wage Data for Now Available on the Tool," *Living Wage Calculator*, livingwage.mit.edu, March 3, 2020, https://livingwage.mit.edu/articles/61-new-living-wage-data-for-now-available-on-the-tool.
13.72. C. Connley, "Amazon, Facebook and 8 Other Companies that Have Committed to Raising Their Minimum Wage," *CNBC*, cnbc.com, May 25, 2019, https://www.cnbc.com/2019/05/24/glassdoor-10-companies-that-have-committed-to-raising-minimum-wage.html.
13.73. Adapted from United Nations World Inequality Report 2020, accessed July 25, 2020, https://www.un.org/development/desa/dspd/wp-content/uploads/sites/22/2020/01/World-Social-Report-2020-FullReport.pdf.
13.74. *Ibid.*
13.75. *Ibid.*
13.76. Adapted from S. Ricketts, R. Cliffton., L. Oduyeru, and B. Holland, "States are Laying a Roadmap for Climate Leadership," *Center for American Progress*, americanprogress.org, April 30, 2020, https://www.americanprogress.org/issues/green/reports/2020/04/30/484163/states-laying-road-map-climate-leadership/.
13.77. A. Ahmed, "Why the Global Debt of Poor Nations Must Be Canceled," *The New York Times*, nytimes.com, April 30, 2020, https://www.nytimes.com/2020/04/30/opinion/coronavirus-debt-africa.html.
13.78. Z. Friedman, "Elizabeth Warren: I'll Forgive Student Loans On Day 1 as President," *Forbes*, forbes.com, January 14, 2020, https://www.forbes.com/sites/zackfriedman/2020/01/14/elizabeth-warren-student-loan-de-bt-forgiveness/#3cb1b0af7604.

13.79. B. Sawyer and C. Cox, "How Does Health Spending in the US Compare to Other Countries?" *Peterson-KFF Health System Tracker*, healthsystemtracker.org, December 7, 2018, https://www.healthsystemtracker.org/chart-collection/health-spending-u-s-compare-countries/#item-average-wealthy-countries-spend-half-much-per-person-health-u-s-spends.
13.80. *Ibid.*
13.81. Adapted from K. Amadeo, "Why Do We Need to Reform U.S. Health Care?" *The Balance*, thebalance.com, June 6, 2020, https://www.thebalance.com/why-reform-health-care-3305749.
13.82. *Ibid.*
13.83. *Ibid.*
13.84. S. Kliff, "Two Friends in Texas Were Tested for Coronavirus. One Bill Was $199. The Other? $6408," *The New York Times*, nytimes.com, July 15, 2020, https://www.nytimes.com/2020/06/29/upshot/coronavirus-tests-unpredictable-prices.html.
13.85. Adapted from K. Safavi, "Tackling Inequalities in Health Care Worldwide," *US News & World Report*, usnews.com, June 28, 2019, https://www.usnews.com/news/best-states/articles/2019-06-28/commentary-tackling-inequalities-in-healthcare-worldwide.
13.86. *Ibid.*
13.87. A. Blinder, "SEC Warns Mississippi over Confederate Emblem on State Flag," *The New York Times*, nytimes.com, June 18, 2020, https://www.nytimes.com/2020/06/18/sports/sec-mississippi-state-flag.html?smid=em-share.
13.88. P. Eavis, "Want More Diversity? Some Experts Say Reward CEOs for It," *The New York Times*, nytimes.com, July 14, 2020, https://www.nytimes.com/2020/07/14/business/economy/corporate-diversity-pay-compensation.html?smid=em-share.
13.89. *Ibid.*
13.90. *Ibid.*
13.91. *Ibid.*
13.92. *Ibid.*
13.93. *Ibid.*
13.94. Inspired by and adapted from E. Barry, "7 Lessons (and Warnings) From Those Who Marched with Dr. King," *The New York Times*, nytimes.com, June 19, 2020, https://www.nytimes.com/2020/06/17/us/george-floyd-protests.html?smid=em-share.
13.95. Internal Revenue Service, "Understanding Taxes," accessed August 3, 2020, https://apps.irs.gov/app/understandingTaxes/student/whys_thm03_les03.jsp.
13.96. Adapted from K. Amadeo, "Racial Wealth Gap in the United States," *The Balance*, thebalance.com, June 10, 2020, https://www.thebalance.com/racial-wealth-gap-in-united-states-4169678.
13.97. *Ibid.*
13.98. *Ibid.*
13.99. Adapted from R. Abelson, "Major US Health Insurers Report Big Profits, Benefiting from the Pandemic," *The New York Times*, nytimes.com, August 5, 2020, https://www.nytimes.com/2020/08/05/health/covid-insurance-profits.html?campaign_id=2&emc=edit_th_20200806&instance_id=21008&nl=todaysheadlines®i_id=49995115&segment_id=35370&user_id=d534e3e0d563ef1d5b6d265161127da7.

Case Study

14.1. A. Palmer, "More Brands are Leaving Amazon, but the Strategy Could Backfire," CNBC.com, January 10, 2020: https://www.cnbc.com/2020/01/10/more-brands-are-leaving-amazon-but-the-strategy-could-backfire.html.
14.2. C. Dunne, "15 Amazon Statistics You Need to Know in 2020," RepricerExpress, downloaded September 13, 2020: https://www.repricerexpress.com/amazon-statistics/.
14.3. M. K. Pratt, "Amazon's Environmental Impact Delivers Climate Change Concerns," SearchAWS, February 4, 2020: https://searchaws.techtarget.com/feature/Amazons-environmental-impact-delivers-climate-change-concerns.
14.4. S. Beslik, "How Sustainable is Amazon? An ESG Analysis of the Retail Giant," Medium.com, May 31, 2020: https://medium.com/@sasjabeslik/how-sustainable-is-amazon-an-esg-analysis-of-the-retail-giant-e8b07cc8a8eb.
14.5. D. Streitfeld, "In Amazon's Bookstore, No Second Chances for the Third Reich," *The New York Times*, February 9, 2020: https://www.nytimes.com/2020/02/09/technology/amazon-bookstore-nazis.html?nl=todaysheadlines&emc=edit_th_200210&campaign_id=2&instance_id=15850&segment_id=21129&user_id=d534e3e0d563ef1d5b6d265161127da7®i_id=499951150210.
14.6. https://www.oberlo.com/blog/amazon-statistics.
14.7. A. Palmer, "More Brands are Leaving Amazon, but the Strategy Could Backfire," CNBC.com, January 10, 2020: https://www.cnbc.com/2020/01/10/more-brands-are-leaving-amazon-but-the-strategy-could-backfire.html.
14.8. C. Lecher, "How Amazon Automatically Tracks and Fires Warehouse Workers for 'Productivity,'" The Verge, April 25, 2019: https://www.theverge.com/2019/4/25/18516004/amazon-warehouse-fulfillment-centers-productivity-firing-terminations.
14.9. C. Coombs, "How Amazon Stacks the Deck Against Workers Fighting to Keep Their Jobs, The Daily Beast, August 8, 2019: https://www.thedailybeast.com/how-amazons-performance-reviews-are-stacked-against-workers.
14.10. C. Coombs, "How Amazon Stacks the Deck Against Workers Fighting to Keep Their Jobs, The Daily Beast, August 8, 2019: https://www.thedailybeast.com/how-amazons-performance-reviews-are-stacked-against-workers.
14.11. C. Lecher, "How Amazon Automatically Tracks and Fires Warehouse Workers for 'Productivity,'"

The Verge, April 25, 2019: https://www.theverge.com/2019/4/25/18516004/amazon-warehouse-fulfillment-centers-productivity-firing-terminations.

14.12. C. Lecher, "How Amazon Automatically Tracks and Fires Warehouse Workers for 'Productivity,'" The Verge, April 25, 2019: https://www.theverge.com/2019/4/25/18516004/amazon-warehouse-fulfillment-centers-productivity-firing-terminations.

14.13. C. Yeginsu, "If Workers Slack Off, the Wristband Will Know," *The New York Times*, February 1, 2018: https://www.nytimes.com/2018/02/01/technology/amazon-wristband-tracking-privacy.html

14.14. R. Ferracone, "Dare to be Different—The Case of Amazon.com," *Forbes*, April 23, 2019: https://www.forbes.com/sites/robinferracone/2019/04/23/dare-to-be-different-the-case-of-amazon-com/#45ccaa3ccb99.

14.15. Adapted from R. Ferracone, "Dare to be Different—The Case of Amazon.com," *Forbes*, April 23, 2019: https://www.forbes.com/sites/robinferracone/2019/04/23/dare-to-be-different-the-case-of-amazon-com/#45ccaa3ccb99

14.16. D. McGinn, "The Numbers in Jeff Bezos' Head," *Harvard Business Review,* November 2014: https://hbr.org/2014/11/the-best-performing-ceos-in-the-world?cm_sp=Article-_-Links-_-Comment#section_bezos.

14.17. Time Magazine, December 27, 1999: http://content.time.com/time/covers/0,16641,19991227,00.html.

14.18. D. McGinn, "The Numbers in Jeff Bezos' Head," *Harvard Business Review,* November 2014: https://hbr.org/2014/11/the-best-performing-ceos-in-the-world?cm_sp=Article-_-Links-_-Comment#section_bezos.

14.19. D. McGinn, "The Numbers in Jeff Bezos' Head," *Harvard Business Review,* November 2014: https://hbr.org/2014/11/the-best-performing-ceos-in-the-world?cm_sp=Article-_-Links-_-Comment#section_bezos.

14.20. R. Aydin, "The 35 Best CEOs in the World, According to Harvard Business Review," Business Insider, October 26, 2019: https://www.businessinsider.com/best-ceos-in-world-harvard-business-review-excludes-jeff-bezos-2019-10.

14.21. T. Locke, "Jeff Bezos: This is the One Amazon Leadership Principle that 'Surprises People' the Most," CNBC.com, October 11, 2019: https://www.cnbc.com/2019/10/11/jeff-bezos-amazon-leadership-principle-that-surprises-people.html.

14.22. A. Borowitz, "Amazon Chief Says Employees Lacking in Empathy Will Be Instantly Purged," *The New Yorker*, August 17, 2015: https://www.newyorker.com/humor/borowitz-report/amazon-chief-says-employees-lacking-empathy-will-be-instantly-purged.

14.23. J. Bariso, "It Took Jeff Bezos Exactly 5 Words to Teach a Major Lesson on Emotional Intelligence," *Inc. Magazine*, October 3, 2018: https://www.inc.com/justin-bariso/emotional-intelligence-amazon-minimum-wage-15-dollars-jeff-bezos-ceo-major-lesson.html.

14.24. D. McGinn, "The Numbers in Jeff Bezos' Head," *Harvard Business Review,* November 2014: https://hbr.org/2014/11/the-best-performing-ceos-in-the-world?cm_sp=Article-_-Links-_-Comment#section_bezos.

14.25. A. Au-Yeung, "Jeff Bezos Announces the First Bezos Academy, A Free Preschool for Students from Low-Income Families," *Forbes*, September 22, 2020: https://www.forbes.com/sites/angelauyeung/2020/09/22/jeff-bezos-announces-the-first-bezos-academy-a-free-preschool-for-students-from-low-income-families/#6425500e7ff7.

14.26. Amazon company Website, downloaded September 16, 2020: https://www.amazon.jobs/en/working/working-amazon.

14.27. S. Thompson, "Why Jeff Bezos Puts Relentless Focus on Amazon's Company Culture," *Inc.*, June 25, 2018: https://www.inc.com/sonia-thompson/how-jeff-bezos-cultivates-a-culture-of-high-standards-at-amazon.html.

14.28. S. Thompson, "Why Jeff Bezos Puts Relentless Focus on Amazon's Company Culture," *Inc.*, June 25, 2018: https://www.inc.com/sonia-thompson/how-jeff-bezos-cultivates-a-culture-of-high-standards-at-amazon.html.

14.29. Amazon company Website, downloaded October 10, 2020: https://www.amazon.jobs/en/principles.

14.30. Amazon company Website, downloaded October 10, 2020: https://www.amazon.jobs/en/principles.

14.31. Amazon company Website, downloaded October 10, 2020: https://blog.aboutamazon.com/working-at-amazon/whats-it-like-to-interview-at-amazon.

14.32. Amazon company Website, downloaded October 10, 2020: https://blog.aboutamazon.com/working-at-amazon/whats-it-like-to-interview-at-amazon.

14.33. Amazon company Website, downloaded October 10, 2020: https://www.aboutamazon.com/working-at-amazon/career-choice.

14.34. Amazon company Website, downloaded October 10, 2020: https://www.aboutamazon.com/amazon-fulfillment/working-here/compensation-and-benefits.

14.35. M. Sainato, "'I'm Not a Robot': Amazon Workers Condemn Unsafe, Grueling Conditions at Warehouse," *The Guardian*, February 5, 2020: https://www.theguardian.com/technology/2020/feb/05/amazon-workers-protest-unsafe-grueling-conditions-warehouse/.

14.36. K. Conger, "Senators Want to Know if Amazon Retaliated Against Whistleblowers," *The New York Times*, nytimes.com, May 7, 2020: https://www.nytimes.com/2020/05/07/technology/amazon-coronavirus-whistleblowers.html?smid=em-share.

14.37. J. Peters, "Whole Foods in Reportedly Using a Heat Map to Track Stores at Risk of Unionization," The Verge, April 20, 2020: https://www.theverge.com/2020/4/20/21228324/amazon-whole-foods-unionization-heat-map-union.

14.38. B. Unglesbee, "Is Amazon on Aa Collision Course with the Government?", Retail Dive, September 30, 2019: https://www.retaildive.com/news/is-amazon-on-a-collision-course-with-the-government/563622/.
14.39. B. Unglesbee, "Is Amazon on Aa Collision Course with the Government?", Retail Dive, September 30, 2019: https://www.retaildive.com/news/is-amazon-on-a-collision-course-with-the-government/563622/.
14.40. A. Pagano and S. Kovach, "Amazon Will Pay $0 in Federal Taxes this Year—Here's How the $793 Billion Company Gets Away with It," Business Insider, February 14, 2019: https://www.businessinsider.com/amazon-not-paying-taxes-trump-bezos-2018-4.
14.41. A. Pagano and S. Kovach, "Amazon Will Pay $0 in Federal Taxes this Year—Here's How the $793 Billion Company Gets Away with It," Business Insider, February 14, 2019: https://www.businessinsider.com/amazon-not-paying-taxes-trump-bezos-2018-4.
14.42. A. Pagano and S. Kovach, "Amazon Will Pay $0 in Federal Taxes this Year—Here's How the $793 Billion Company Gets Away with It," Business Insider, February 14, 2019: https://www.businessinsider.com/amazon-not-paying-taxes-trump-bezos-2018-4.
14.43. A. Waller, "Amazon Bans Sale of Foreign Seeds in the U.S.," *The New York Times*, September 7, 2020: https://www.nytimes.com/2020/09/07/us/amazon-seeds.html.
14.44. Amazon company Website, downloaded October 10, 2020: https://ir.aboutamazon.com/corporate-governance/documents-and-charters/code-of-business-conduct-and-ethics/default.aspx.
14.45. Amazon company Website, downloaded October 10, 2020: https://aws.amazon.com/codesofconduct/.
14.46. Amazon company Website, downloaded October 10, 2020: https://aws.amazon.com/codesofconduct/.
14.47. R. K. Sharma, "What is Amazon Web Services and Why Should You Consider It?," Net Solutions, January 23, 2020: https://www.netsolutions.com/insights/what-is-amazon-cloud-its-advantages-and-why-should-you-consider-it/.
14.48. R. Razdan, "Rethinking ESG Targets for Companies Like Amazon, Apple, and Analog Devices," *Forbes*, July 1, 2020: https://www.forbes.com/sites/rahulrazdan/2020/07/01/rethinking-esg-targets-for-companies-like-amazon-apple-and-analog-devices/#508bddc61343.
14.49. M. K. Pratt, "Amazon's Environmental Impact Delivers Climate Change Concerns," SearchAWS, February 4, 2020: https://searchaws.techtarget.com/feature/Amazons-environmental-impact-delivers-climate-change-concerns.
14.50. S. Beslik, "How Sustainable is Amazon? An ESG Analysis of the Retail Giant," Medium.com, May 31, 2020: https://medium.com/@sasjabeslik/how-sustainable-is-amazon-an-esg-analysis-of-the-retail-giant-e8b07cc8a8eb.
14.51. T. Nguyen, "Amazon's 1-Day Shipping in Convenient—and Terrible for the Environment," Vox.com, October 16, 2019: https://www.vox.com/the-goods/2019/10/16/20917467/amazon-one-day-shipping-bad-for-environment.
14.52. M. K. Pratt, "Amazon's Environmental Impact Delivers Climate Change Concerns," SearchAWS, February 4, 2020: https://searchaws.techtarget.com/feature/Amazons-environmental-impact-delivers-climate-change-concerns.
14.53. T. Nguyen, "Amazon's 1-Day Shipping in Convenient—and Terrible for the Environment," Vox.com, October 16, 2019: https://www.vox.com/the-goods/2019/10/16/20917467/amazon-one-day-shipping-bad-for-environment.
14.54. S. Beslik, "How Sustainable is Amazon? An ESG Analysis of the Retail Giant," Medium.com, May 31, 2020: https://medium.com/@sasjabeslik/how-sustainable-is-amazon-an-esg-analysis-of-the-retail-giant-e8b07cc8a8eb.
14.55. S. Beslik, "How Sustainable is Amazon? An ESG Analysis of the Retail Giant," Medium.com, May 31, 2020: https://medium.com/@sasjabeslik/how-sustainable-is-amazon-an-esg-analysis-of-the-retail-giant-e8b07cc8a8eb.
14.56. S. Beslik, "How Sustainable is Amazon? An ESG Analysis of the Retail Giant," Medium.com, May 31, 2020: https://medium.com/@sasjabeslik/how-sustainable-is-amazon-an-esg-analysis-of-the-retail-giant-e8b07cc8a8eb.
14.57. Linn Works, downloaded October 10, 2020: https://blog.linnworks.com/amazon-global-international-sites.
14.58. B. Droesch, "Amazon's Worldwide Sales Will Rise 20.2% This Year as Reliance on E-Commerce Grows," Business Insider, July 9, 2020: https://www.businessinsider.com/amazon-global-ecommerce-sales-will-reach-416-billion-in-2020-2020-7.
14.59. R. Siegel and J. Slater, "International Pushback Disrupts Amazon's Momentum to Expand Its Empire Worldwide," *The Washington Post*, May 10, 2019: https://www.washingtonpost.com/business/economy/international-pushback-disrupts-amazons-momentum-to-expand-its-empire-worldwide/2019/05/10/76bd5d26-6507-11e9-82ba-fcfeff232e8f_story.html.
14.60. R. Siegel and J. Slater, "International Pushback Disrupts Amazon's Momentum to Expand Its Empire Worldwide," *The Washington Post*, May 10, 2019: https://www.washingtonpost.com/business/economy/international-pushback-disrupts-amazons-momentum-to-expand-its-empire-worldwide/2019/05/10/76bd5d26-6507-11e9-82ba-fcfeff232e8f_story.html.
14.61. R. Abramson, "Amazon's International Challenges Push the Company Towards Smaller Markets," CTech, January 5, 2019: https://www.calcalistech.com/ctech/articles/0,7340,L-3761347,00.html.
14.62. Amazon company Website, downloaded October 10, 2020: https://blog.aboutamazon.com/working-at-amazon/amazon-recognized-as-a-linkedin-top-company-in-nine-countries.

Index

A

B

C

D

E

F

G

H

I

Q

R

S

T

U

V

W

Z